SPOKEN HAUSA

J RONAYNE COWAN
RUSSELL G. SCHUH

D1501425

Spoken Language Services, Inc.

Library of Congress Cataloging in Publication Data

Cowan, J Ronayne, and Schuh, Russell G., joint authors
   Spoken Hausa
   1. Hausa language--Grammar.
I. Title
PL8232.C6   493'.72'821   75-26629
ISBN 0-87950-401-3

Spoken Language Services, Inc.
P.O. Box 783
Ithaca, New York 14851

TABLE OF CONTENTS

FOREWORD

This book, in various pre-publication versions, has been used in Hausa classes at several American universities since 1969. We believe that there is ample material presented with such flexibility that any class which completes the book will know a considerable amount of Hausa, regardless of the pedagogical persuasions of teachers and students.

The book was originally intended as a first-year university course. Professor Schuh, after almost four years of teaching from this book, has found that it would be virtually impossible to cover all twenty-five units in one academic year. It is recommended therefore that the book also be used as the basis for an intermediate course, supplemented by readings and additional grammatical exercises.

There is no comprehensive glossary included in the book. Therefore students should be continually making their own reference vocabulary based on the vocabulary of each unit and additional vocabulary learned in class. The instructor might also order one or more of the available dictionaries as supplementary texts (see references below).

A number of people have helped in one way or another at various stages in the development of this book. Several of the dialogues were originally created by A. Abdulmalik Mani while he and Professor Cowan were producing Hausa teaching materials at the Staff Development Center in Kaduna, Nigeria. During the writing of the first version of this book, Salisu Abubakar provided some original material as well as technical advice. It is also M. Salisu's voice which is heard on the accompanying tapes. They were recorded at Stanford University by Professor Will Leben, with the help of Mr. Peter Easton. More recently, Dauda M. Bagari has made some suggestions which have been incorporated into this version of the book.

Finally, the authors express their appreciation to Carey Beth Hockett who copy-edited and made camera-ready typescript for this book.

J Ronayne Cowan

Russell G. Schuh

1

SELECTED REFERENCE ON THE HAUSA LANGUAGE

Dictionaries

Abraham, R.C. Dictionary of the Hausa Language, 2nd edition. University of London Press, 1962.
[Hausa-English: The most readily available large dictionary of Hausa. A very good reference book by any standard, but overly technical at the beginning level.]

Bargery, G.P. A Hausa-English Dictionary and English-Hausa Vocabulary. Oxford University Press, 1934.
[Hausa-English and English-Hausa: The most complete dictionary of Hausa, but unfortunately out of print. Though Abraham's dictionary improves on Bargery in tone marking and has more exemplification, Bargery has many more entries and often his definitions are clearer.]

Newman, Paul, et al. Sabon K̃amus na Hausa zuwa Turanci. Oxford University Press, in press.
[Hausa-English: Developed expecially with Hausa-speaking secondary school students in mind, but incorporating all the most recent knowledge of Hausa structure plus many words only recently introduced into the language. It will replace Abraham and Bargery as the standard reference for all but the most technical Hausa language research.]

Skinner, Neil. Hausa-English Pocket Dictionary. Longmans of Nigeria, 1959.
[Hausa-English: Does not compete with the above dictionaries technically, especially in the marking of tone and vowel length, but it is an inexpensive and convenient little book for finding the meaning of everyday words in Hausa.]

Skinner, Neil. K̃amus na Turanci da Hausa. Northern Nigerian Publishing Company, Ltd., 1965.
[English-Hausa: Has a large number of entries, including Hausa renderings of many English idiomatic phrases. For the non-Hausa speaker, it must be used in conjunction with one of the good Hausa-English dictionaries since tone and vowel length are not marked and the definitions are very brief.]

Grammars

Abraham, R.C. The Language of the Hausa People. University of London Press, 1959.
[Reference grammar: The most complete reference grammar. Though poorly organized, it contains a huge number of facts. Too technical for the beginning student.]

Kraft, Charles H. and Anthony Kirk-Greene. Teach Yourself Hausa. The English Universities Press, Ltd., 1973.
[Pedagogical grammar: Competently written grammar in the Teach Yourself series format.]

Grammars *(continued)*

Maxwell, J. Lowry and Eleanor M. Forshey. <u>Yau da Gobe: A Hausa Grammar for Beginners</u>. Sudan Interior Mission, Jos, Nigeria, 1963.

[Pedagogical grammar: The best "traditional" pedagogical grammar of Hausa. Still a valuable book, though it falls short of more modern works in not marking tone and vowel length.]

Readers*

Abraham, R.C. <u>Hausa Literature and the Hausa Sound System</u>. University of London Press, Ltd., 1959.

[Contains selections in Hausa from a variety of sources, all marked for tone and vowel length and with translations. The second section gives many details on the pronunciation of Hausa.]

Kirk-Greene, A.H.M. and Yahaya Aliyu. <u>A Modern Hausa Reader</u>. David McCay Company, New York, 1967.

[Contains speeches, articles from newspapers, and other examples of Hausa used in a modern context. Tone and vowel length are not marked.]

Kraft, Charles H. <u>A Hausa Reader</u>. University of California Press, 1973.

[Contains material covering a wide variety of topics drawn from many sources. Especially valuable are the readings on cultural subjects. Tone and vowel length are marked.]

Skinner, Neil. <u>Hausa Readings: Selections from Edgar's Tatsuniyoyi</u>. The University of Wisconsin Press, 1968.

[Folktales, mostly in dialects other than "Standard" Hausa of Kano. Tone and vowel length are not marked. Some tales are presented in <u>ajami</u> script.]

There is a fair amount of material published in Hausa, including a weekly newspaper, <u>Gaskiya Ta Fi Kwabo</u>, published by Northern Nigerian Newspapers, Kaduna, Nigeria. Most of the Hausa literature (folktales, novels, poems, plays, etc.) is published by the Northern Nigeria Publishing Company, Ltd., P.O. Box 412, Zaria, Nigeria. This material was virtually all written for native speakers of Hausa and thus even the most "elementary" books are too complicated for beginning learners of Hausa.

Besides literature published in Hausa, the language has been the subject of a considerable amount of scholarly research and many technical articles are to be found in the various journals dealing with African languages such as <u>African Language Studies</u>, <u>Afirka und Übersee</u>, <u>Journal of African Languages</u>, and <u>Studies in African Linguistics</u>. Probably the most important single article in Hausa remains F.W. Parsons, 'The Verbal System in Hausa', <u>Afirka und Übersee</u>, 44:1-36 (1960).

*While these readers are meant for learners of Hausa and thus contain grammatical and explanatory notes, the material in all of them is too complex for students with less than a half year or more of Hausa.

INSTRUCTIONS TO THE TEACHER

I. Introduction

   This course incorporates what we feel to be the most efficient pedagogical devices existing in the field of foreign and second language teaching
today. Although basically patterned after the aural-oral method, the course
contains at least two features which have not always been stressed in this
approach: increased emphasis on oral comprehension, and provision for loosely
controlled conversation at the first year level.
   The goal of the course is to develop a high degree of facility in
speaking Hausa. By this we mean that the student should be able to speak
Hausa as fast as he speaks English (that is, without frequent and extended
pauses), with few grammatical errors, and with good pronunciation. Upon
completion of the course the student will have the wherewithal to express
in Hausa any thought that he can express in English, the only limitation
here being that of vocabulary. He will, of course, not be a fluent speaker
of Hausa at this stage, but the solid foundation that he will have gained
will greatly assist him in achieving higher levels of proficiency in speaking,
reading, and writing.

II. Instructional Techniques

   A. Oral Drill

   The most effective method of developing new language habits requires
the student to spend time practicing the new language aloud. Rote memorization and frequent repetition of utterances in the foreign language are
the cornerstones of this method. Since both of these activities, particularly
the latter, can be extremely fatiguing, it follows that an effective language
teacher will recognize this and plan his instruction so as to minimize
fatigue and boredom in the classroom. The following instructional techniques
and suggestions on how to apply them to these materials are offered with this
goal in mind.

   B. Repetition

   Both choral and individual repetition of utterances should be done
naturally and with vigor. One serious error that may be committed by a
teacher or informant is allowing students to repeat utterances as a mono-
tonous chant. Such chanting reinforces incorrect speech habits by causing
students to internalize unnatural intonation patterns, and almost always
puts the students to sleep.
   A second serious error that should be avoided is permitting uneven
reproduction of utterances in choral repetition, i.e., in chorus some
students tend to repeat more quickly, some more slowly, the result being
an unintelligible jumble. Such uneven repetition is discouraging and
destroys the students' interest in these activities. The use of backward
buildup, described in section C, enables the teacher to avoid this pitfall.
   Repetition should be varied. The procedure we advocate is to begin
with choral repetition, then turn more to individual repetition. The
teacher or informant should strive to provide a good model for the student.
By this we mean that he should model the sentences at normal conversational
speed. If the student hesitates or stumbles the teacher should use backward
buildup to help him form the sentence. Rather than allow long pauses to
occur while the student is attempting to pronounce a given segment of an
utterance, the teacher should repeat that segment and the ensuing words and
have the student repeat after him. The following hypothetical example shows
a teacher introducing a sentence from Dialogue A of Unit XIV.

5

Teacher:		Ā'á̱, bàn gan sù ba.
Class:		Ā'a̱, bàn gan sù ba.
Teacher:		Ā'a̱, bàn gan sù ba.
Class:		Ā'a̱, bàn gan sù ba.
Teacher: (pointing to one student)		Ā'a̱, bàn gan sù ba.
Student:		Ā'a̱, bàn gā sù ba.
Teacher:		gan sù ba.
Student:		gan sù ba.
Teacher:		Ā'a̱, bàn gan sù ba.
Student:		Ā'a̱, bàn gan sù ba.
Teacher: (pointing to another student)		Ā'a̱, bàn gan sù ba.
Student: (says sentence with incorrect tones)		Ā'a̱, bàn gàn sū ba.
Teacher: (stressing the tones)		bàn gan sù ba.
Student: (pronounces the tones incorrectly again)		
Teacher:		No, you're not getting the tones right. Listen and repeat this sequence:
		dàh, dah, dàh, dah (low-high-low-high).
Student:		dàh, dah, dàh, dah
Teacher:		Dà kyâu. Again: bàn gan sù ba.
Student:		bàn gan sù ba.
Teacher:		Gàbā ɗaya: Ā'a̱, bàn gan sù ba.
Class:		Ā'a̱, bàn gan sù ba.
Teacher: (pointing to the next student)		

   Correction should always take the form of helping the student produce
a more accurate repetition. The teacher should encourage the student to
make an effort to repeat a sentence, but supply a model of the phrase he
is having difficulty with the instant it appears that the student is not
going to be able to complete the sentence without some assistance. The goal
is not to test the student's memory or his learning capacity, but to get him
to reproduce the utterance several times as perfectly as possible.
   Finally, repetition activities should never be allowed to drag. If
the activity moves briskly the students will not lose interest nor will
their concentration slacken. Twenty minutes of repetition is the absolute
maximum that any class can stand before some sort of break, that is, a change
of activity becomes necessary. To exceed this limit will result in considerable frustration and absolutely no learning on the part of the students.

6

C. Backward Buildup

This technique should be used whenever students falter in reproducing an utterance. The teacher begins by saying the last word or words of the sentence, and the student repeats these. Gradually the teacher expands the utterance by adding additional segments until the whole sentence has been built up from the end. The following example,

bà zā kà yi ƙòƙarī kà gamā̀ zuwā̀ ƙarfè̀ biyu ba?

of Unit XII.   is taken from Dialogue A

Teacher:	Tô, sàkè fàɗā! Ƙarfè̀ biyu ba?
Class:	Ƙarfè̀ biyu ba?
Teacher:	Zuwā̀ ƙarfè̀ biyu ba?
Class:	Zuwā̀ ƙarfè̀ biyu ba?
Teacher:	Kà gamā̀ zuwā̀ ƙarfè̀ biyu ba?
Class:	Kà gamā̀ zuwā̀ ƙarfè̀ biyu ba?
Teacher:	Yi ƙòƙarī kà gamā̀ zuwā̀ ƙarfè̀ biyu ba?
Class:	Yi ƙòƙaiī ... (some of the students begin to stumble and leave some words out at this point) ... zuwā̀ ƙarfè̀ biyu ba?
Teacher:	Gàbā̄ ɗaya. Kà gamā̀ zuwā̀ ƙarfe̋ biyu ba?
Class:	Kà gamā̀ zuwā̀ ƙarfè̀ biyu ba?
Teacher:	Yi ƙòƙarī kà gamā̀ zuwā̀ ƙarfè̀ biyu ba?
Class:	Yi ƙòƙarī kà gamā̀ zuwā̀ ƙartè̀ biyu ba?
Teacher:	Bà zā kà yi ƙòƙarī kà gamā̀ zuwā̀ ƙarfè̀ biyu ba?
Class:	Bà zā kà yi ƙòƙarī kà gamā̀ zuwā̀ ƙarfè̀ biyu ba?
Teacher:	Dà kyâu! Màlàm Smith. Bà zā kà yi ƙòƙarī kà gamā̀ zuwā̀ ƙarfè̀ biyu ba?
Mr. Smith:	Bà zā kà yi ƙòƙarī kà gamā̀ zuwā̀ ƙarfè̀ biyu ba?

The backward buildup technique should not be confined to very long sentences, rather it should be used whenever the class has difficulty in repeating a sentence.

D. Useful Phrases

In the course of the first few days of instruction the students should learn certain phrases which they will hear and use daily in class. Some of these are commands that the teacher will use during instruction. The following are suggested:

Sàkè fàɗā	'Repeat'
Sàkè fàɗā à̀ hankàlī	'Speak slowly'
Gàbā̄ ɗaya	'All together' (This can be used to initiate choral drill)
Bàn ji ba	'I don't/didn't understand' (This has the sense of 'Sorry, I didn't hear what you said.' It will be useful in earlier stages of the course when the students are still having difficulty with the sounds of Hausa.)

7

Bàn gānè ba   'I don't/didn't understand' (This has the sense of
'I don't comprehend.' This phrase might better be
delayed until the latter part of the course, for
example, until the units which have comprehension
practices, when the students will have occasion to
use it.)

The teacher should not attempt to explain the grammar of these expressions;
the students should simply memorize them for use in class. They should be
introduced on the first day and used consistently thereafter.

III. Methodology Applied to Various Sections of the Materials

In II. we outlined the method to be used with these materials. In
this section we will suggest how certain instructional techniques should
be applied to each of the component parts of the course.

A. Pronunciation Drills

Most of the pronunciation drills are in Units I - III. However, there
is some selected review and intonation practice in Units IV - VIII. We
feel that pronunciation is a continual problem, and a conscientious teacher
will still be correcting mistakes in tone and vowel length when the students
are on Unit XXIV. We thus oppose a long period (for example several weeks)
devoted to nothing but pronunciation practice. At the same time, it is
obvious that students must make their greatest effort at mastering the Hausa
sound system at the very beginning of the course, and for this reason the
pronunciation drills have been concentrated in the earlier units.

We have tried to obviate the feeling of frustration and boredom that
students frequently experience at not being able to "get at the language"
because they are required to spend lots of time working on pronunciation.
Thus, the first three units also contain extensive work on greetings which,
as is pointed out in 1.0, are an essential part of any conversation.

It is recommended that the teacher never exceed a period of 12 minutes
when working on any of the following kinds of pronunciation drills: Repetition
Drills, Reproduction Drills, or Contrast Drills. Discrimination Drills are
less fatiguing and require more time. Again the best procedure is to begin
with choral repetition, going through the entire drill, and then move to
individual repetition. The teacher is urged to vary the pronunciation work
in Units I - III by interspersing practice on the dialogues which practice
the greetings. The following sample lesson plan for Unit II illustrates how
a 50 minute period may take in both activities.

LESSON PLAN: UNIT II
(50 Minutes)

Time	Activity
10 minutes	Practice Dialogue A. The teacher pronounces each sentence three times and the students repeat. Students are allowed to look at the vocabulary as teacher clarifies any questions on meaning (no more than one minute is expended in this vocabulary check). Teacher has half of the class take the part of Sà'a/Sà'Tdù and the other half take the part of Maryamà/Mammàn. Teacher repeats and each half responds with its part. Teacher moves to individual practice with the first two exchanges (the first four sentences).
12 minutes	Repetition Drill for /ƙ/ and /ts/. Teacher gives short articulatory description of sound and reproduces for the benefit of the class. The class repeats words after the informant, first in chorus, then individually. If time

8

remains, move in to /'/.

10 minutes	Return to Dialogue A. Choral repetition is followed by pairs of students acting out the first two exchanges without looking at their books. More choral and individual repetition of the rest of the dialogue is followed by acting out the last three exchanges, and some students will now be encouraged to take parts and act out the entire dialogue.
10 minutes	Practice /ē/ and /ai/ under II. Vowels and Diphthongs for 6 minutes. Try to get through the Contrast Drill for /ē/ vs. /ai/ before the 10 minute period has elapsed. If extra time remains, do the Descrimination Drill (/ē/ vs. /ai/).
8 minutes	Begin practicing Dialogue B, using the same procedure that was employed for Dialogue A.
Homework Assignment:	The students will be required to memorize Dialogue A. They will act it out on the following day without looking at their books.

B. Dialogues

The purpose of the dialogues is to provide the students with an opportunity to internalize Hausa speech patterns by engaging in a realistic conversation that could take place in a Hausa-speaking country. Unless the students memorize the dialogues so that they can take the parts of the speakers and reproduce them quickly and accurately, the dialogues will not have served their purpose. Rote memorization of the dialogues should be facilitated by intensive oral practice in the classroom and in the language laboratory. The following procedure is suggested for teaching the dialogues.

Day 1

1. The informant reads through the dialogue sentence by sentence while the students listen.
2. The informant or teacher models each sentence and the students repeat in chorus. The goal here is to get one satisfactory repetition of each sentence. The students may look at their books during this practice and follow the English translations. However, the teacher should suppress any interruptions or requests for a more precise translation of the Hausa or the grammar involved.
3. The teacher answers questions about the translations of the Hausa sentences and indicates new grammar points that are being exemplified in the dialogue. Lengthy discussions of syntax should be avoided at this point, since the students will more fully understand the grammar of the Hausa after they have read the grammar section. What is important is that students are not completely confused about any of the English translations. (The student will be aided by the more literal translations of sentences which appear in parentheses.)
4. The teacher should now begin practicing the first dialogue, using choral repetition and individual repetition as indicated in B. The longer dialogues, those consisting of from nine to twelve sentences, should be broken into smaller sections, that is, two or three exchanges (four to six sentences), drilled, and then acted out. When the students seem to have mastered these, the teacher should move on to the remaining sentences and drill them. These two (or three) sections can be put together to form the entire dialogue.

9

Every effort should be made to get the students eyes away from the printed page. It is strongly recommended that the students be required to close their books when drilling the dialogues for mastery. They will resist this at first, but before long they will see that this policy pays off by increased actuation of the material.

As homework the students will be required to memorize the dialogue (or a portion of the dialogue) which has been practiced in class. On the following day, pairs of students will act out the dialogue without looking at their texts.

C. Grammar

The grammar has been included purely as a reference resource, and was not intended to form a part of the classroom activities. The teacher should have the students read through the grammar sections (outside of class) which treat the systactic structures contained in the material covered in class that day. Occasionally the students may have some questions about the grammar they have read as homework. These should be answered briefly the next day. The teacher is strongly urged to: a) not spend any extended period of time in class dicoursing on Hausa grammar, b) tactfully put off any questions which students may ask on grammar that will be covered in future units. (Such questions might conceivably arise either as a result of a student's having read ahead or having noticed one of the rare instances where a grammatical structure that is not discussed in the grammar section of a particular unit has had to be included in a dialogue sentence for the sake of presenting colloquial, idiomatic Hausa.)

D. Comprehension Practices

The Comprehension Practices are designed to develop oral comprehension. A three-step procedure is suggested.

1. The informant or teacher reads through the passage while the students listen. During this reading the informant pauses a few seconds to translate any new words or expressions. The students may look at their books during this reading.
2. The informant reads through the passage a second time. This time the students listen with their books closed.
3. The informant asks the students the questions at the end of the passage. They answer them without looking at their books. If the comprehension passage is long, it is best to break up the second reading into short sections, and ask the questions that apply to these.

E. Grammatical Drills

The Grammatical Drills provide extensive practice on the syntactic structures which form the teaching points of a given unit. The following procedures should be observed when drilling.

1. The drilling should be fast and vigorous. The teacher should first explain how the drill works, and illustrate the procedure by modeling the example sentence with the help of the informant or one of the students. The teacher then starts the drill by pointing to one of the students and supplying the cue sentence.
2. In cuing the students, the teacher should move around in the class in a fixed order. At this stage the object of the drill is not to test the students but to get them to form a grammatically correct sentence. Every effort short of supplying the student with the correct answer should be made to encourage them to construct a correct sentence. As a general rule the students should perform the drill without looking at their books

10

the first time, but if the cues are long or the drill is complex, books may be used. (In most cases where these conditions exist, instructions on how to perform the drill suggest that the students look at their books.)
3. After the students have worked through the drill once, the instructor should lead them through it again. This time the students should not look at their books, and the instructor may now deviate from his fixed order of cuing.
4. If the students are still having trouble forming the sentences, the instructor should lead them through the drill a third time and then move on to another drill even though he may still be dissatisfied with the students' performance. Their imperfect performance can be corrected by returning to review the drill later. The total time for drilling a block of grammatical drills should never exceed 20 minutes.

F. Guided Conversations

Previous work on dialogues, comprehension practices, and drills culminates in the guided conversations. Here the tight restrictions that characterized the former activities are released, and the students are given a chance to utilize the material they have studied to develop some freedom of expression through improvization.

The text contains rather specific guidelines as to which subjects relate to the material the students have covered and how these might be developed into free conversations. Sample conversations and pertinent vocabulary items have been included along with suggestions of what to talk about.

The goal of the guided conversations is twofold: 1) to develop fluency in what has been learned in any particular unit and 2) to remind the students that Hausa is a vehicle for expressing ideas freely just like their own language.

The role of the teacher or informant in this activity is that of an encourager, critic, and resource-person. He should attempt to break down student inhibitions by encouraging them to speak, either by asking questions whenever the conversations lag or by suggesting other subjects the students can talk about. We suggest that the teacher suppress the urge to correct all but the most serious grammatical errors until the end of the conversation, since the students may become inhibited if they are interrupted too frequently.

The teacher should not expect a great deal at first. In the earlier units guided conversations that last thirty seconds should be considered satisfactory. Later on the students should be able to converse freely for about a minute. The teacher should keep in mind that the goal of this activity is not to develop originality or individuality of expression but rather to encourage the students to use what they have learned in a largely uncontrolled conversation. For this reason, the introduction of lots of new vocabulary and idioms should be avoided.

The conversation suggestions may also be used for written assignments. In those units where the guided conversations are "artificial" situations (that is, not about things or events which are actually taking place in the classroom), students could be required to write dialogues based on the conversation suggestions. Then, for conversation in class one student may explain the events that take place in the dialogue he has written after which the situation is acted out as a conversation between two or more students. The dialogues the students have written should not simply be read in class, however, since this would defeat the purpose of the guided conversation section.

PHONOLOGY

I. Introduction

The description of the Hausa sound system which follows has been written with the language learner in mind. It therefore contains only information that may assist the student in attaining a high standard of pronunciation. We sincerely hope that teachers will stress pronunciation throughout the course, in particular the correct pronunciation of tone and vowel length, since these are the greatest hurdles for speakers of English and other Indo-European languages. The phonology presented in this section is intended as añ aid to achieving good pronunciation of Hausa, something which can only be acquired through concentrated imitation of tapes or a native informant.

When a pair of slanted lines, / /, encloses a letter, this means that the letter represents a sound rather than the orthographic representation of the sound. Whenever the orthographic representation differs from the symbol for the sound, this will be indicated in the description of the sound.

II. Vowels and Diphthongs

Hausa has five long and five short vowels. In this book the same alphabetical letter will be used for long and short vowels, since this is the practice in Hausa orthography. We will, however, indicate long vowels by a bar over the vowel; thus a would indicate Hausa short /a/, whereas ā indicates that the vowel is long.

Hints on the pronunciation of Hausa vowels are offered below. The cross section diagrams of the tongue positions are not to be considered as absolute; they are presented only to assist the student in understanding what is meant by height and position (forward or back) of the tongue in the mouth.

A. /i/(short) and /ī/(long) are produced with the tongue in the front of the mouth close to the roof of the mouth as shown in Figure 1. The lips are unrounded. Hausa /i/ is very similar to the /i/ in English sit; /ī/ is similar to the French fini.

B. /e/(short) and /ē/(long) are produced with the tongue in the front of the mouth slightly lower than for /i/ and /ī/, and the mouth is just a little more open. Again, the lips are unrounded for both these vowels. Hausa /e/ is similar to the vowel in English bet. Hausa /ē/ is somewhat lower in the mouth than the vowel in French pré. Figure 2 shows the approximate tongue position for these two vowels.

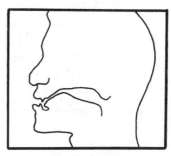

Figure 1

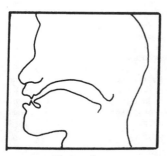

Figure 2

12

C. /a/(short) is produced with the tongue still farther from the roof of the mouth than /e/ and /ē/. The tongue is bunched under the center of the roof of the mouth and the lips are unrounded. Figure 3 shows the tongue position for /a/. Qualitatively Hausa /a/ is somewhere between the vowel in English but and the vowel in English father.

D. /ā/(long) is produced with the tongue flat in the mouth; the blade of the tongue may actually have slight depression. Qualitatively Hausa /ā/ is like the vowel in English father. Figure 4 shows the tongue position.

E. /o/(short) and /ō/(long) are formed with the back of the tongue raised and the lips rounded. Hausa (short)/o/ is often quite similar to Hausa (short)/a/. For Hausa (long)/ō/ the tongue is somewhat lower in the mouth than for the vowel in French peau. Figure 5 shows the approximate tongue position for these vowels.

F. /u/(short) and /ū/(long) are formed by raising the back of the tongue until it is close to the roof of the mouth. The lips are quite rounded. Hausa (short)/u/ is similar to the vowel in English put. For (long)/ū/ the tongue is slightly lower in the mouth than for the vowel in French fou. Figure 6 shows the approximate tongue position for these two vowels.

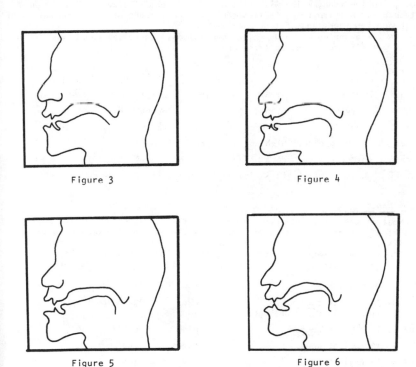

Figure 3   Figure 4

Figure 5   Figure 6

Hausa has two diphthongs (combinations of two vowels). These will be symbolized /ai/ and /au/. Production of these two sounds involves movement of the tongue from one position to another. The diphthong /ai/ is similar to the sound in English <u>bite</u>; the tongue moves from the position for Hausa (short)/a/ to a high shortened version of the vowel in English <u>bit</u>. In /au/, which is similar to the vowel in English <u>out</u>, the tongue moves from the position for Hausa (short)/a/ to a position close to the one which the tongue assumes in the production of the vowel in English <u>put</u>.

III. Tone

For the language learner, one of the most important phonological facts about Hausa is that every word has its particular tones. By this we mean that each syllable of a word has a relative pitch with respect to the other syllables in that word. Two different words may consist of identical vowels and consonants, their difference in meaning resulting from dissimilar tone patterns. It is very easy to see how erroneous production of tones could result in native speakers' having great difficulty understanding a student of Hausa, and to avoid this you should strive for accurate production of tone from the moment you begin speaking the language.

There are two basic tones in Hausa: high tone, which is unmarked in this book, and low tone, which will have a grave accent /ˋ/, over the vowel where it occurs. A third tone, falling tone, may be thought of as a combination of high and low tone, and will be marked /ˆ/.

A few examples of words which have (almost) identical vowels and consonants but different tone patterns are:

wà	'who?'	lo	wâ	'elder brother'	falling
mātā	'wives'	hi-hi	màtā	'wife'	lo-hi
kūkā	'crying'	hi-hi	kūkà	'baobab tree'	hi-lo
sakà	'put on'	hi-lo	sàkā	'release'	lo-hi
marinā	'dyeing place'	hi-hi-hi	marìnā	'dyers'	hi-lo-hi
dāmā	'chance'	hi-hi	dama	'worry'	lo-hi	dāmâ	'mix'	hi-lo
farī	'white'	hi-hi	fari	'ogling'	lo-hi	farī	'dry spell'	hi-lo

IV. Consonants

A. Most of the consonant sounds in Hausa will be no problem for the English speaking student, since they are virtually the same as the ones used in English. For this reason they are simply listed below with an example of an English and a Hausa word containing them. Those consonants which are harder for English speakers to produce correctly are given a fuller treatment.

/b/ as in English <u>be</u>	bàba	'father'
/ʧ/ as in English <u>church</u> (written <u>c</u> in Hausa orthography)	cāca	'gambling'
/d/ as in English <u>dead</u>	dōdō	'goblin'
/g/ as in English <u>gone</u>	gōgè	'rub'
/h/ as in English <u>help</u>	hūhū	'lungs'
/j/ as in English <u>judge</u>	jā	'rid'

14

/k/ as in English kick	kūkā	'crying'
/l/ as in Engligh light	lallē	'for sure'
/m/ as in English memory	màmā	'breast'
/n/ as in English noon	nūnà	'show'
/s/ as in English sissy	sōsai	'completely'
/š/ as in English shut (written sh in Hausa orthography)	shā	'drink'
/t/ as in English tart	tūtà	'flag'
/w/ as in English will	wàwā	'fool'
/y/ as in Engligh yoyo	yàyà	'how'
/z/ as in English zebra	Zazzāu	'the town of Zaria'

B. Hausa /f/

/f/ is not really like English f. To make it correctly you should place your two lips close together and expell air out of the narrow slit that separates them. The lips are unrounded for this sound.

C. Hausa /r/

Hausa has two sounds represented by the symbol r. For purposes of distinguishing between the two sounds in our description the symbols /r/ and /ř/ will be used, but we will follow the practice of standard Hausa orthography and write both of them r in this text.
/r/ is unlike English r. It is made by pointing the tip of the tongue towards the roof of the mouth and then moving it forward so that it taps against the ridge behind the upper teeth.
/ř/ is similar to the r in Spanish pero 'but' or perro 'dog'. It is made by tapping, or sometimes vibrating, the tip of the tongue against the ridge behind the upper teeth.

D. Glottalized Consonants

/'/: The sound written ' represents the stoppage of the voice heard between the two oh's in English "Oh oh!". In Hausa, this sound, usually called a "glottal stop", can occur within a word, for example sana'a 'occupation'. It is also pronounced at the beginning of every word which is spelled with an initial vowel, for example aikì 'work' is pronounced /'aikì/. It is produced by drawing the vocal cords together so that no air escapes through them. Pressure is built up in the lungs below the vocal cords, they are released, and the sudden escape of the air produces the characteristic sound.
/ɓ/: The remaining "glottalized" consonants are not found in most European languages. /ɓ/ is the glottalized counterpart of plain /b/. It is sometimes called an implosive b because air "implodes" into the mouth rather than being expelled as for plain /b/. The lips are closed as for plain /b/, but unlike the mechanism for plain /b/, the vocal cords are also closed. This creates a closed cavity between the lips and the vocal cords. The larynx ("Adam's apple"), where the vocal cords are located, is drawn downwards, creating a suction in the cavity just mentioned. Then the closure at the lips is released and air rushes into the cavity, causing a characteristic "implosive" sound. If you have difficulty imitating this sound as spoken by a Hausa speaker, you might try swallowing and pronouncing /b/ at the same time.

15

/ɗ/: This is the glottalized counterpart of plain /d/, and like /ɓ/, is also called "implosive". The tongue touches inside the mouth at the same position as for plain /d/. The manner of producing /ɗ/ is the same as for producing /ɓ/, the only difference being that for /ɓ/ the lips are closed, for /ɗ/ the tongue touches behind the teeth.

/ƙ/: This is the glottalized counterpart of plain /k/. Its manner of production differs from that of /ɓ/ and /ɗ/ by being "ejective" rather than "implosive". /ƙ/ is produced by placing the tongue as for plain /k/. The vocal cords are also closed as for /ɓ/ and /ɗ/. However, instead of lowering the larynx, it is <u>raised</u>. This compresses the air between the closed vocal cords and the closure formed in the mouth by the tongue. The tongue closure is then released, producing the characteristic "ejective" sound.

/ts/: This is the glottalized counterpart of /s/. The sound /ts/ is an "ejective" like /ƙ/, so the manner of producing the two sounds is the same. The only difference is that for /ts/ the tongue is placed as for a plain /s/ and the air is allowed to escape more slowly than with /ƙ/. NB: REGARDLESS OF SPELLING, THE HAUSA SOUND REPRESENTED BY /ts/ IS ENTIRELY DISTINCT FROM <u>ts</u> AS IN ENGLISH 'mats'.

/'y/: This is the glottalized counterpart of /y/. As with the other glottalized sounds, the vocal cords are drawn together. As they are released in the manner of a glottal stop /'/, the tongue moves as if to pronounce /y/.

E. Long Consonants

Hausa has long (doubled) consonants which are held longer when spoken than regular consonants. There are even a few words which are distinguished solely on the basis of them, for example:

kulè̱	'cat'	kullè̱	'lock'
manà	'to us'	mannà	'glue to'

F. Labialization and Palatalization of Consonants

The consonants /b/, /ɓ/, /k/, /ƙ/, and /g/ are pronounced with lips rounded before /o/, /ō/, /u/, and /ū/. Thus in words like buhū 'bag', bōkō 'deceit', gudu 'running', and gōrō 'kola nut', the /b/, /k/, and /g/ would have lip-rounding so that they are pronounced something like [bwuhū], [bwōkwō], [gwudu], and [gwōrō].

The consonants /k/ and /g/ are palatalized before /i/, /ī/, /e/ and /ē/. By this we mean that the tongue moves forward with relation to the hard palate in the same way that it does when /y/ is produced so that /k/ and /g/ have some of this quality. Thus, bakī 'mouth' would be pronounced [bakyī] and gida 'compound' would be [gyidā].

G. Nasals Changing to [ŋ]

/n/ is pronounced [ŋ] (like the ng in <u>ring</u>) before /k/, /ƙ/, /g/, and /'/. Thus, gwankī 'roan antelope' is pronounced [gwaŋkī], dankō 'rubber' is pronounced [daŋkō], and bango 'wall' is pronounced [baŋgō].

/n/ written at the end of a word is pronounced [ŋ], for example nan 'here' is pronounced [naŋ]. /m/ written at the end of a word is often pronounced this way as well, for example <u>kullum</u> 'always' is often pronounced [kulluŋ].

16

H. Intonation

The placement of individual words in a sentence results in the arrangement of the relative height of individual high and low tones throughout the sentence. This arrangement of tones over the length of an utterance is called its intonation pattern.

Hausa is characterized by what is referred to as a "downdrift" intonation pattern. This means that the pattern of high and low which stretches over the length of a sentence moves steadily downward. An unbroken string of high tones (as in the sentence yā kāwō ruwā 'he brought water') or low tones remains on one level, with perhaps slight lowering of the voice from one end of the sentence to the other. However, in a sentence where there are both high and low tones, a high tone following a low will have a lower pitch than a high preceding that low tone. The low tones remain on about the same pitch until the end of the sentence where they tend to go lower. The following sentence and diagram will illustrate how this works[1]:

Balā dà Shēhù zā sù zō dà   'Bala and Shehu will come with
mutānensù   their people'

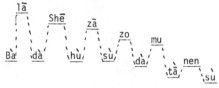

Question intonation follows the basic statement contours with two differences: (1) the overall pitch of the sentence is raised with less lowering of the voice on successive highs following lows than is found in statements; (2) the last high syllable is raised to a level which is higher than an ordinary high tone would be, and if there is a low following that high, it does not drop as far as an ordinary low tone would. If no low tone follows, the last high tone is raised as expected but drops off like a falling tone. The following diagrams illustrate question intonation:

Balā dà Shēhù zā sù   'will Bala and Shehu come
zō dà mutānensù?   with their people?'

yanā aikì nē?   'is he
                  working?'

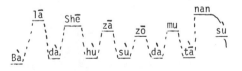

[1] This sentence and the corresponding question below are taken from Jean-Marie Hombert, 'Universals of Downdrift: Their Phonetic Basis and Significance for a Theory of Tone', *Studies in African Linguistics*, Supplement 5, pp. 169-183 (1974). The diagrams are an adaptation of the actual pitch curves as given by Hombert.

UNIT I

Malam Musa is on his way to work at about seven o'clock in the morning. Just outside his office he runs into Malam Audu and greets him in passing.

Mūsā:	Inā kwānā?	How did you pass the night?
Audù:	Lāfiyā lau.	Very well.
Mūsā:	Yàyà yârā?	How are the children?
Audù:	Lāfiyā lau.	Very well.
Mūsā:	Màdàllā. Sai an jumà.	Good. See you later.
Audù:	Sai an jumà.	See you later.

Vocabulary

an jumà	'one (an) has passed time (jumà)'			
inā	'how?'		sai	'until'
kwānā	'passing the night'		yârā	'children'
lāfiyà	'good health'		yàyà	'how?'
lau	(with laflya) 'good, well'			
màdàllā	(as interjection) 'good, fine'			

GRAMMAR

1.1 A Warning on Linguistic and Cultural Differences

In studying Hausa, a language unrelated to English and spoken in a culture very different from our own, we must constantly be on guard against allowing our cultural or linguistic habits to impose themselves on the way we use Hausa. In the introductory section on the Hausa sound system, the student was cautioned against trying to "sound natural" to himself In his attempt to speak Hausa.

In the dialogue of this unit, we begin to see that we must also be aware that In a culture as different from our own as is that of the Hausas, we must also learn new styles of saying and doing things. The numerous greetings and types of greetings, some of which we will concentrate on in the first three units of this book, may seem excessively formal or otherwise unusual to us, but certain habits of ours would certainly be viewed as strange by the Hausa person. For example, to him our tendency to get down to business after a quick 'Hello' would seem intolerably abrupt.

Greetings form an important part of any Hausa conversation, and in some social contexts a long series of greetings may constitute the entire conversation. It is therefore extremely important that the student master the more commonly used greetings. These will be practiced in Units II and III.

In studying Hausa, do not attempt to equate everything you learn with something in American culture or English speech patterns. Rather, try to become familiar with the dialogues and the types of situations in which they are used. If Hausa expressions in some cases are much like English, certainly make use of your knowledge of English to help you. If not, forget trying to seek an English equivalent and think in Hausa.

19

1.2 Length of Vowels at the End of a Word

The length of vowels occurring in the middle of words is usually easily distinguished as being long or short, both by the actual length of the vowel and by the qualitative differences between the long and short correspondants. However, at the end of a word pronounced in isolation or as the final word in an utterance, discernment of vowel length, especially on low tone, presents one of the more difficult problems in the Hausa sound system.

In final position a short vowel will often be followed by a glottal stop. For example, zo! 'come here!' is phonetically [zo']. Final long vowels, however, will never be followed by a glottal stop. It is thus not necessary to write zo' since the vowel written short is enough to indicate that the glottal stop may be heard after it. On the other hand, final vowels which can be analyzed as short by other means are not always followed by glottal stop, and in such cases final long and short vowels are very similar, if not identical, in pronunciation.

A few pairs of words contrasting only in final vowel length can be found, e.g. dāmā 'opportunity'--dāma 'right hand.' Very commonly, proper names are derived by shortening the final vowel of a word, e.g. bāko 'stranger'--Bāko a man's name, tsōhō 'old'--Tsōho a boy's name, kākā 'harvest time'--Kāka name given to a girl born during kākā.

Because of the difficulty in discerning the length of vowels at the end of words, in all the drills for long and short vowel distinction, we will be using bisyllabic words and will be concentrating only on the vowel in the first syllable.

DRILLS

1. Consonants

Repetition Drill - Listen to your informant say the following words. Then go through each list one or more times, repeating the words after him and trying to imitate his pronunciation in every detail.

/f/

fīlī	'open field'	kīfī	'fish'
fātà	'hide'	fàru	'happen'
zāfī	'heat'	fìta	'go out'
tàfi	'leave'	dafà	'cook'
fāfè	'split	sāfē	'morning'

/ɓ/

ɓāwō	'bark (of tree)'	ɓācì	'spoil'
ɓaunā	'water buffalo'	ɓōyè	'hide'
lēɓè	'lip'	ɓatà	'get lost'
haɓà	'chin'	taɓà	'touch'
ɓērā	'rat'	tūɓè	'undress'

/ɗ/

ɗāki	'hut'	ɗagá	'lift'
ɗaya	'one'	ɗaukã	'pick up'
kuɗī	'money'	ɗinki	'sewing'
kwāɗō	'toad'	fāɗi	'fall'
dauɗá	'dirt'	daɗé	'spend a long time'

II. Vowel Length

Repetition Drill - Follow the directions for consonant repetition drills above. Pay special attention to the vowel in the first syllable (see grammar section 1.2).

/a/

tarà	'nine'	zàtō	'thinking'
farī	'white'	yànzu	'now'
kashé	'kill'	sàyā	'buy'
karā	'stem'	barcī	'sleeping'
kawài	'only'	hankàlī	'good sense'

/ā/

gāshi	'hair'	kāwō	'bring'
sābō	'new'	sā'á	'luck'
fātá	'skin'	bàkī	'mouth'
jàkī	'donkey'	rānā	'sun'
kāmá	'catch'	màmākī	'astonishment'

Contrast Drill - Listen to the informant repeat the following pairs of words. They differ principally in the length of the vowel in the first syllable. Then go through the list again, repeating each pair of words after him.

'town'	gàrī	gārī	'flour'
'go'	tàfi	tāfī	'palm of hand'
'shatter'	fasá	fāsá	'postpone'
'sack'	jàkā	jākā	'female donkey'
'nine'	tarà	tārá	'collect'

Discrimination Drill - Now listen to the following pairs of words. Repeat each pair after the informant and say whether they are the same or different with respect to the length of the vowel in the first syllable.

'town'	gàrī	tarà	'nine'
'mouth'	bàkī	hakà	'like that'
'catch'	kāmá	kawài	'only'

21

'sack'	jàkā	jàkā	'female donkey'
'thinking'	zàtō	karā	'stem'
'palm'	tāfī	barcī	'sleep'
'postpone'	fāsà	rānā	'sun'
'now'	yànzu	bàkī	'mouth'
'kill'	kashè	kāwō	'bring'
'hoping'	fātā	farā	'white'

Repetition Drill - Follow the directions for the consonant repetition drill above. Pay special attention to the vowel in the first syllable (see grammar section 1.2)

/i/

cikì	'stomach'		irì	'seed'
gidā	'compound'		shìga	'enter'
fìta	'go out'		birnī	'walled city'
jirā	'wait for'		bìkī	'celebration'
jinī	'blood'		cìnikī	'bargaining'

/ī/

kīfī	'fish'		tīlàs	'by necessity'
rībà	'profit'		cīwò	'pain'
rīgā	'gown'		hīrā	'conversation'
sīsi	'sixpence'		jīkà	'grandchild'
rīmī	'kapok tree'		gīgìcē	'become flustered'

Contrast Drill - Follow the instructions for the contrast drills for /a/ and /ā/ above.

'pass time'	jimà	jīmà	'tanning'
'do first'	rigā	rīgā	'gown'
'knock over'	kifè	kīfī	'fish'
'eye'	idò	īkò	'power'
'dying'	rini	rīmī	'kapok tree'
'celebration'	bìkī	bīkò	'trying to reconciliate'

Discrimination Drill - Now listen to the following pairs of words. Repeat each pair after the informant and say whether they are the same or different with respect to the length of the vowel in the first syllable.

'fish'	kīfī	kīfī	'fish'
'eye'	idò	irì	'seed'
'gown'	rīgā	bìkī	'celebration'
'go out'	fìta	jinī	'blood'

22

'kapok tree'	rīmī	birnī	'walled city'
'sixpence'	sīsī	kīfī	'fish'
'blood'	jinī	gidā	'compound'
'power'	īkŏ	jirā	'wait for'
'stomach'	cikĭ	cīwŏ	'pain'
'gown'	rīgā	shìga	'enter'

Repetition Drill - Follow the directions for consonant repetition drills above. Pay special attention to the vowel in the first syllable (see grammar section 1.2)

/u/

dubū	'thousand'	wùyā	'difficulty'
mutù	'die'	kusa	'near'
bùhū	'bag'	gùdā	'unit'
dukà	'all'	ukù	'three'
kunyà	'modesty'	sùrukī	'in-law'

/ū/

sūnā	'name'	shūkà	'sow'
tùlū	'jug'	hūtà	'rest'
dūbā	'looking at'	kūrā	'hyena'
kūkā	'crying'	tūba	'repent'
hùlā	'cap'	sùrūtù	'gabbiness'

Contrast Drill - Follow the instructions for the contrast drills for /a/ and /ā/ above.

'all'	dukà	dūkà	'beating'
'contradict'	musà	Mūsā	'Moses'
'thousand'	dubū	dūbā	'looking at'
'unit'	gùda	gùgā	'well bucket'
'you (pl) '	kukà	kūkà	'baobab tree'

Discrimination Drill - Now listen to the following pairs of words. Repeat each pair after the informant and say whether they are the same or different with respect to the length of the vowel in the first syllable.

'contradicting'	musù	Mūsā	'Moses'
'crying'	kūkā	bùhū	'bag'
'three'	ukù	hùlā	'cap'
'mortar'	turmī	wùyā	'difficulty'
'jug'	tùlū	hūtà	'rest'
'thousand'	dubū	gudù	'run'

23

'sow'	shūkà	cuku	'cheese'
'repent'	tūba	gùdā	'unit'
'modesty'	kunyà	cūtā	'cheat'
'scratch'	sūsà	mutù	'die'

III. Tone

<u>Repetition Drill</u> - Repeat each word after your informant, paying close attention to the tone. Then repeat the words again while the informant checks your pronunciation.

<u>Tone Drill 1</u> - Single falling tone, single high tone, single low tone.

kâi	'head'	kai	'you' (masc. sing.)
fâm	'pound (money)'	shā	'drink'
râi	'life'	sai	'until'
sâ	'bull'	mè	'what?'
kyâu	'goodness'	wà	'who?'

<u>Tone Drill 2</u> - High-low tones.		<u>Tone Drill 3</u> - High-high tones.	
watà	'moon'	gidā	'compound'
gabàs	'east'	jinī	'blood'
jiyà	'yesterday'	fushī	'anger'
cikì	'stomach'	nīsā	'distance'
yārò	'boy'	ruwā	'water'

<u>Tone Drill 4</u> - Low-high tones.		<u>Tone Drill 5</u> - Falling-high tones.	
kàrē	'dog'	kûnnē	'ear'
kwàdō	'toad'	kyânwā	'cat'
àmin	'amen'	lâifī	'fault'
yànzu	'now'	yâuwā	reply to greeting
rìgā	'gown'	yâmmā	'west'

<u>Discrimination and Tone Identification Drills</u> - Without looking at your book, listen to your informant pronounce the following pairs of words. As soon as he has uttered a given pair, you should indicate whether the two words have the same tones by saying "same" or "different." The informant will then say the words again; this time you will say what the tone of each of the two words is, e.g. if he says yī, bī, you will say "high, high." Each student will identify a given pair of words in this manner. Remember, this exercise should be performed with the students' books closed while they listen to the informant.

Tone Drill 1

'you' (masc. sg. fut.)	kâ	kā	'you' (masc. sg. completive)
'what?'	mè	dâ	'formerly'
'she' (completive)	tā	tâ	'she' (fut.)
'with'	dà	dà	'if it were that'
'bull'	sâ	sû	'fishing'
'they' (indep. pron.)	sū	sū	'they'
'you' (f. sg. ind. pr.)	kē	mè	'what?'
'pound' (money)	fâm	fam	'securely'
'who?'	wà	wâ	'elder brother'
'naked'	tik	tìk	'bang' (noise of something falling)
'is'	nē	nî	'I' (indep. pron.)
'oil'	mâi	kai	'you' (m. sg. indep. pron.)
'sound of frogs'	kur	mas	'giddap!'
'gum'	gâm	gam	'green grasshopper'

Tone Drill 2

'inside'	cikī	cikì	'stomach'
'spears'	māsū	māsu	'possessors'
'enter!'	shìgo	shìgo	'enter!'
'wideness'	fādî	fādì	'fall'
'how'	yàyà	yàyā	'elder brother'
'package of kolas'	hūhù	hūhū	'lungs'
'bed'	gadō	gādō	'inheritance'
'point out'	nūnà	nūna	'ripen'
'return'	kōmō	kōmō	'return'
'crying'	kūkā	kūkà	'baobab tree'
'children'	yārā	kunnē	'ear'
reply to greeting	yâuwā	yâmmā	'west'
'take it!'	dàuki	sauka	'get down'
'forget'	mântā	mànna	'press it!'
'inform'	shâidā	lâifî	'fault'
'come back'	dāwō	dūbà	'look at'
'arm'	hannū	kaifî	'sharpness'
'women'	mātā	kashē	'kill'
'liver'	hantà	mântā	'forget'
'boy'	yārò	rainà	'despise'

25

B. Kande, on her way home from market, sees Hadiza inside her compound and
   stops to greet her.

Kànde:	Sànnu dà aikì.	Greetings on your work.
Hàdîzà:	Yâuwā.	Hello.
Kànde:	Inā wunî?	How's the day been?
Hàdîzà:	Lāfiyà lau.	Fine.
Kànde:	Inā gàjiyà?	How's the tiredness?
Hàdîzà:	Bābù gàjiyà.	There is no tiredness.
Kànde:	Tò màdàllà.	Good.
	Sai gòbe.	Until tomorrow.
Hàdîzà:	Sai gòbe.	Until tomorrow.

Vocabulary
(see also vocabulary for C)

bābù	=bâ (see Dialogue A)	tò/tô	'Ok, all right' (falling tone used where there is a pause following the tô)
dà	'with'		
sànnu	'hi, hello'	wunî	'passing the day'
		yâuwā	'hello' (in reply to certain greetings)

C. Aliyu is working in his field and Yusufu, who is passing by, stops to
   greet him. (NB: àmin follows any greeting phrase containing Allā 'God.')

Yùsufù:	Sànnu dà aikî	Greetings on your work.
Àliyù:	Yâuwā.	Hello.
Yùsufù:	Inā gàjiyà?	How's the tiredness?
Àliyù:	Bābù gàjiyà.	There's no tiredness.
Yùsufù:	Yàyà aikìn gōnā?	How's the farmwork?
Àliyù:	Mun gōdè Allā.	We thank God (for its productivity).
Yùsufù:	Tô, màdàllà.	Well, fine.
	Sai gòbe.	Until tomorrow.
Àliyù:	Sai gòbe.	Until tomorrow.

Vocabulary

aikì	'work'	gōnā	'farm'
Allā	'God'	mun gōdè	'we (mun) thank (gōdè)'
gòbe	'tomorrow'	sànnu	'hi, hello'

D. This dialogue is appropriate for either men or women.

   (Men) Adamu on his way home from work in the afternoon comes upon Hasan
   and greets him.

   (Women) Amina on her way home from the market in the afternoon comes upon
   Halima and greets her.

Adamu/Amina:	Barkà dà yâmmā.	Greetings in the (late) afternoon.
Hasàn/Hàlîmà:	Barkà kàdai. Ìnā	Greetings.
	wunî?	How's the day been?
A:	Lāfiyà lau.	Fine.
H:	Ìnā gidā?	How's the family?
A:	Lāfiyà.	Fine.
H:	Ìnā yârā?	How are the children?
A:	Sunà lāfiyà.	They're fine.
H:	Tō mādàllā.	Good.

Vocabulary

barkà	'hi, hello, greetings'	yâmmā	'late afternoon and early evening'
sunà	'they are'		

GRAMMAR

2.1 The Diphthong /ai/

In this unit we will have drills on the diphthong /ai/. This diphthong has two rather distinct pronunciations but is written only as ai for at least two reasons: (1) one can generally predict which words will have one pronunciation and which the other; and (2) there are no two words which are differentiated on the basis of these two pronunciations.

One of the pronunciations can be indicated [ɛy] and has as the closest English counterpart the vowel sound in a word like 'say' (note that this is not a "pure" vowel in English, but is diphthongized). The pronunciation of /ai/ is generally used directly after dental consonants, i.e. those consonants where the tongue touches just behind the upper teeth (in Hausa they are t, d, ɗ, s, z, sh, ts, l, r). See the repetition drill on /ai/ for examples.

The second pronunciation can be indicated as [əy] and has as its closest English counterpart the vowel sound in 'buy,' though it must be emphasized that this is only an approximation and you should listen carefully to the informant to get the correct pronunciation. This pronunciation of /ai/ is generally used after consonants other than dentals. See the drill on /ai/ for examples.

It should be emphasized again: NEITHER OF THE PRONUNCIATIONS OF /ai/ NECESSARILY SOUND LIKE ANY SOUND IN ENGLISH. Imitate as closely as possible the way your informant produces the sound in any given context.

DRILLS

I. Consonants

Repetition Drill - Listen to your informant say the following words. Then go through each list one or more times, repeating the words after him and trying to imitate his pronunciation in every detail.

/ƙ/

ƙōfà	'doorway'	ƙafà	'foot'
ƙauyè	'village'	ƙōshi	'be full'
bàƙō	'stranger'	tūƙà	'drive'

29

/ō/

zōbè	'ring'	nōmā	'farming'
gòbe	'tomorrow'	dōyà	'yam'
dōkì	'horse'		

/au/

saurō	'mosquito'	aurē	'marriage'
zaurè	'entrance hut'	aunà	'weigh'
nauyì	'heaviness'	gautā	'a type of vegetable'
sàuka	'get down'	saurì	'haste'
zaunà	'sit down'	ɗaukà	'pick up'

Contrast Drill - Follow the directions for the contrast drills for /ē/ and /ai/ above.

'square house'	sōrō	saurō	'mosquito'
'dig up'	tōnà	taunà	'chew'
'fry'	tōyè	tauyè	'shrink'
'a cult'	bōrì	baurì	'bitterness'
'exceed slightly'	gōtà	gautā	'a type of vegetable'

Discrimination Drill - Now listen to the following pairs of words. Repeat each pair after the informant and say whether they are the same or different with respect to the diphthong or vowel in the first syllable.

'weigh'	aunà	ōdà	'order'
'tie up'	ɗaurè	aurē	'marriage'
'car'	mōtà	nōmā	'farming'
'buffalo'	ɓaunà	bōrì	'a cult'
'come here!'	zō nàn	zaunà	'sit down'
'pick up'	ɗaukà	dōkà	'type of hair-do'
'mosquito'	saurō	saurì	'haste'
'chase off'	kòrā	kōmà	'return'
'type of vegetable'	gautā	gōnà	'farm'
'fear'	tsòro	tsaurì	'hardness'

III. Tone

Reproduction Drills - Repeat each word after your informant, paying close attention to the tone. Then repeat the words again while the informant checks your pronunciation.

Tone Drill 1 - High-high-high

gaisuwā	'greetings'	tasōshī	'dishes'
mōtōcī	'cars'	kēwayō	'come around again'
gishirī	'salt'		

32

Tone Drill 2 - High-high-low		Tone Drill 3 - High-low-high	
lāfiyà	'greetings'	kujèrā	'chair'
bindigà	'gun'	itàcē	'tree'
gāfarà	'forgiveness'	gidàjē	'compounds'
inuwà	'shade'	mutànē	'people'
fartanyà	'hoe'	tsuntsàyē	'birds'

Tone Drill 4 - Low-low-high		Tone Drill 5 - Low-high-high	
àmfānī	'usefulness'	cinikī	'trading'
tàkàlmī	'shoe'	kàsuwā	'market'
tàlàtin	'thirty'	shìnkāfā	'rice'
gònàkī	'farms'	àbinci	'food'
àshìrin	'twenty'	dàriyā	'laughter'

Tone Drill 6 - Low-high-low		Tone Drill 7 - Low-low-low and low-low-falling	
sàbulū	'soap'	àyàbà	'banana'
dàlīlì	'reason'	àkwàtì	'box'
màganà	'word'	Lìttinîn	'Monday'
làbārì	'news'	àsùbâ	'dawn'
bùkātà	'need'	Àlhàmîs	'Thursday'

33

A. Nuhu comes to visit Hasan at his compound. The following exchange of
greetings takes place.

Nūhù:	Sàlāmù àlaikùm.	May I come in?
Hasàn:	Àmin, àlaikà sàlāmù.	Come on in.
	Barkà dà zuwà.	Greetings on your coming.
Nūhù:	Yâuwā, barkā kàdai.	Greetings in return.
Hasàn:	Kā zō lāfiyà?	Have you come in good health?
Nūhù:	Lāfiyà lau.	Just fine.
Hasàn:	Gidā lāfiyà?	Is the family well?
Nūhù:	Lāfiyà ƙalau.	Very well.
Hasàn:	Ìnā lābārī?	What's the news?
Nūhù:	Làbārī sai àlhērī.	The news is good.
Hasàn:	Mādàllā.	Good.

Vocabulary

àlhērī	'good fortune'	ƙalau	= lau
kā zō	'you have (kā) come (zō)'	làbārī	'news'
		sai	'(nothing) except'

B. Kande is passing by. She sees Amina inside the compound pounding millet.
Kande stops at the entrance of the compound, greets her, and goes on her
way.

Kànde:	Gāfarà dai.	Hello in there.
•Amīna:	Yâuwā, maràbā.	Welcome.
Kànde:	Ìnā gàjiyà?	How's the tiredness?
Amīna:	Gàjiyā dà sauƙī.	The tiredness is light.
Kànde:	Mādàllā. Ìnā làbārī?	Good. How's the news?
Amīna:	Làbārī sai àlhērī.	The news is good.
Kànde:	Tō sai wani lōkàcī.	OK. Until another time.
Amīna:	Allà yà kai mù.	May God take us (to that time).
Kànde:	Àmin.	May it be so.

Vocabulary

| lōkàcī | 'time' | wani | 'another' |
| sauƙī | 'lightness, ease' | yà kai mù | 'may he (yà) take (kai) us (mù)' |

C. (Women) Mairo is selling <u>furā</u> in the market. Her friend, Aisha, who
is shopping there, stops and greets her.

(Men) Muhammadu is selling leather goods in the market. His friend,
Adamu, who is a broker there, stops and greets him.

Hausa greetings are often adaptable to the situation as exemplified
by <u>yàyà cìnikī</u> where Aisha or Adamu ask about the state of his or her
friend's business.

Ā'Ìsha/Ādàmu:	Sànnu dà aikī.	Greetings at your work.
Màiro/Mùhammadù:	Sànnu kàdai.	Greetings to you.
A:	Ìnā gùmī?	How's the heat?
M:	Ai lōkàcinsà nē.	Well, it's the time for it.
A:	Yàyà cìnikī?	How's trading?
M:	Àlhamdù lìllāhì.	Fine (lit.: praise God).
A:	Tò mādàllā. Sai an jumà̄.	Good. See you later.
M:	Yâuwa, sai an jumà̄.	Right, see you later.

Vocabulary

ai   'well ...'

àlhamdù
  lìllāhì 'praise God' (This expression, like <u>sàlāmù àlaikùm</u> and a number
          of others, is borrowed directly from Arabic as a fixed expression
          and cannot be grammatically analyzed in terms of Hausa grammar.)

cìnikī   'trading'

gùmī   'sweat, (metaphorically) hot weather'

lōkàcinsà 'time (<u>lokaci-</u>) for it (<u>-n-sa</u>)'

nē   'it is'

D. Lawal is returning from the field. Bello is alongside the road adjust-
ing a load on his donkey and greets Lawal as he approaches.

Bellò:	Sànnu.	Hi.
Lawàl:	Yâuwā, sànnu kàdai.	Hello.
Bellò:	Ìnā aikī?	How's the work?
Lawàl:	Aikī dà sauƙī.	The work's light.
Bellò:	Yàyà ruwā?	How's the rain.
Lawàl:	Ruwā yā yi gyārā.	The rain does good.
Bellò:	Yàyà ìyālì?	How's the family?
Lawàl:	Lāfiyà lau.	Very well.
Bellò:	Tò mādàllā.	Good.

Vocabulary

gyārā	'repairing'	ruwā	'water, rain'
ìyālì	'family'	yā yi	'it (<u>ya</u>) does (<u>yi</u>)'

3.1. The two "r's" of Hausa

There is a contrast in Hausa between two sounds which can be indicated /r/ and /ř/; that is to say there are words which consistently have one or the other of these sounds and there is no way to predict in many cases which of the two a word will contain.

In terms of articulatory phonetics, /r/ is an alveolar retroflex flap, /ř/ is an alveolar tongue trill or tap. The former is produced by passing the tongue rapidly across the alveolar ridge (the hump in the palate just behind the teeth) as it moves back to front. The latter is produced by "throwing" the tongue from a position of rest at the alveolar ridge, producing a tap. These two "r's" have a very similar acoustic effect and for this and other reasons (outlined in the drill on these two sounds) students will not be expected to consistently reproduce it. The two "r's" are not distinguished in the standard orthography.

In final position in a word, only /ř/ is found. This means that in words which change such that an /r/ which was in the middle of a word comes to be at the end of a word, this /r/ becomes /ř/:

tēbùř	'table'
màtâř	'the woman'
nā bař shi	'I left him"

Bař in the last example is from the verb barī 'leave', which loses its final ī when followed by an object.

The sound /r/ occurs only at the beginning or in the middle of words and occurs in these positions far more frequently than /ř/, but since /ř/ can also be found in these positions, we must say the two are contrastive.

	raba̍	'divide'
	kàrē	'dog'
but also	řùbūtū	'writing'
	kàřàtū	'reading'

DRILLS

1. Consonants

/b/ - /ɓ/

Contrast Drill - Listen to the informant repeat the following pairs of words, most of which differ only in that one has /b/ where the other has /ɓ/. Then go though the list again repeating each pair of words after him.

'a line'	bātā̀	ɓātā̀	'spoil'
'young dum palm'	kabā̀	kaɓā̀	'put to lips'
'come, come!'	habà̍	haɓà̍	'chin'
'guinea fowl'	zàbī	zàɓi	'choose!'
'locust'	bābè̍	ɓāɓè̍	'quarrel'

Discrimination Drill - Now listen to the following pairs of words. Repeat each pair after the informant and say whether the "b's" in the two words are the same (both /b/ or both /ɓ/) or different (one of each).

'bark (of tree)'	ɓāwȍ	bāwȁ	'slave'
'divide'	rabȁ	habȁ	'come,come!'
'front'	gàbā	ɓōyȅ	'hide'
'rat'	ɓērā	tūɓȅ	'undress'
'chin'	haɓȁ	bisȁ	'on, about'
'guinea fowl'	zȁɓā	biyā	'pay'
'get lost'	ɓatȁ	ɓaunā	'buffalo'
'half'	rabȉ	zȁɓȁ	'choose'
'lip'	lēɓȅ	bàkā	'bow'

/d/ - /ɗ/

Contrast Drill - Follow the directions given above for the contrast drill on /b/ - /ɓ/.

'mix'	dāmȅ	ɗāmȅ	'tighten belt'
'emir's palace'	fādȁ	fāɗȁ	'fall into'
'pound grain'	dakȁ	ɗakȁ	'in the hut'
'correct'	daidai	ɗaiɗai	'one by one'
'David'	Daudȁ	daudȁ	'dirt'

Discrimination Drill - Follow the directions for the discrimination drill above on /b/ - /ɓ/.

'take'	ɗaukȁ	dōyȁ	'cassava'
'crocodile'	kadȁ	faɗȁ	'fighting'
'unit'	gùdā	ɗaya	'one'
'coldness'	ɗȁrȉ	kuɗȉ	'money'
'open'	būɗȅ	dūbȁ	'look at'
'night'	darē	gidā	'compound'
'remove'	ɗȉbȁ	kwȁɗȍ	'toad'
'pound (grain)'	dakȁ	ɗagȁ	'lift'
'hill'	tudȕ	tāɗȉ	'conversation'
'width'	fāɗȉ	dōkȉ	'horse'

/k/ - /ƙ/

Contrast Drill - Follow the directions given above for the contrast drill on /b/ - /ɓ/.

'mouth'	bȁkȉ	bȁƙȉ	'guests'
'establish'	kafȁ	ƙafȁ	'foot, leg'
'like that'	hakȁ	haƙȁ	'dig'

'lock'	kullḕ	ƙullà̰	'knot'
'change'	sākḕ	sāƙḕ	'weave all of'

Discrimination Drill - Follow the directions for the discrimination drill on /b/ - /ɓ/.

'foot'	ƙafà̰	kàrē	'dog'
'fish'	kīfī	haƙà̰	'dig'
'mouth'	bā̰kī	ƙàrà̰	'increase'
'doorway'	ƙōfà̰	baƙī	'black'
'stranger'	bà̰ƙō	kusa	'near'
'catch'	kāmà̰	bìkī	'celebration'
'pleasant smell'	ƙanshī	zāƙī	'sweetness'
'calling'	kirà̰	ƙàfō	'horn'
'all'	dukà̰	mìƙḕ	'hold out'
'message'	sà̰ƙō	kōmà̰	'return'

/s/ - /ts/

Contrast Drill - Follow the directions for the contrast drill on /b/ - /ɓ/.

(NB: Even though the second sound here is spelled ts, it is not pronounced at all like the English 'mats,' etc. It is a glottalized "s", just as /ƙ/ is a glottalized "k."

'emir'	sarkī	tsarkī	'cleanliness'
'slash'	sārḕ	tsārḕ	'arranged completely'
'a type of pastry'	māsà̰	mātsà̰	'squeeze'
'quickness'	saurī	tsaurī	'hardness'
'scratch'	sūsà̰	tsūtsà̰	'worm'

Discrimination Drill - Follow the directions for the discrimination drill given above on /b/ - /ɓ/.

'sourness'	tsāmī	sārḕ	'slash'
'name'	sūnà̰	kitsḕ	'fat'
'near'	kusa	tsōhō	'old'
'worm'	tsūtsà̰	mātsà̰	'squeeze'
'rock'	dūtsḕ	sāmù	'get'
'scratch'	sūsà̰	nīsā	'distant'
'expensiveness'	tsà̰dā	tsuntsū	'bird'
'emir'	sarkī	tsayà̰	'stop'
'on, about'	bìsa	yātsà̰	'finger'
'a type of hair-do'	kitsō	samà̰	'sky'

39

/r/ - /r̃/

This distinction was explained in 3.1. Only a contrast drill is included below so that the student may hear the difference. However, this distinction will not be further drilled for several reasons: 1) in many cases there is variation from speaker to speaker as to which "r" is used; 2) these sounds are phonetically very similar, the distinction often hard to hear, even for a trained phonetician; and 3) there are virtually no words where this distinction is crucial to differentiate them from other words (many speakers will not show a contrast in the minimal pairs listed below).

'servant'	barā̀	bar̃ā̀	'begging'
'kind of dried fish'	sà̄rō	sà̄r̃ō	'type of gown'
'small glass bottle'	ƙarau	ƙar̃au	'thoroughly (ideophone)'
'sleeping'	barcī̄	bà̄r̃ shi	'leave it'!
'chase away'	kōrè̄	kōr̃è̄	'green'
'stalk'	karā̄	kà̄r̃ā̀tū	'reading'
'distributors'	marà̄bā̄	mar̃à̄bā̄	'welcome'

Short and Long Consonants

Contrast Drill - Listen to the informant repeat the following pairs of words which differ principally in that the second contains a long consonant where the first has a short one. Then, go through the list again, repeating each pair of words after him.

'hammer'	hamā̀	hammā̀	'yawning'
'prevent'	hanā̀	hannū̄	'hand'
'for us'	manà̄	mannā̀	'press against'
'contradicting'	musū̀	mussà̄	'cat'

Discrimination Drill - Now listen to the following pairs of words. Repeat each pair after the informant and say whether the words are the same or different with respect to the length of the consonant in the middle of the words.

'animal'	dabbā̀	tūba	'repent'
'sky'	samā̄	hammā̀	'yawning'
'on, about'	bisà̄	mussà̄	'cat'
'west'	yâmmā̄	tsûmmā̄	'rag'
'observing'	kallō̄	tùlū	'jug'
'crocodile'	kadā̀	gidā̄	'compound'
'this one'	wannà̄n	sà̄nnu	'greetings'
'hut'	bukkā̀	bà̄kā̄	'bow'
'prayers'	sallà̄	ƙyā̄lè̄	'disregard'
'prevent'	hanā̀	hannū̄	'hand'

II. Vowel Length

<u>Discrimination Drill</u> - (/a/ - /ā/). Listen to each of the following words, pronounce it, then say whether the vowel in the first syllable is long or short.

'catch'	kàmā	barcⵜ	'sleeping'
'prevent'	hanā	kāyā	'baggage'
'donkey'	jàkⵜ	farā	'white'
'hoping'	fātā	zàtō	'thinking'
'night'	darē	rānā	'sun'
'kill'	kashē	gārⵜ	'flour'
'female donkey'	jàkā	fārā	'start'
'theft'	sātā	hakà	'like that'
'bring'	kāwō	tàfⵜ	'palm of hand'

<u>Discrimination Drill</u> - (/i/ - /ī/). Follow the directions for the drill above.

'sixpence'	sīsⵜ	jimā	'pass time'
'kapok tree'	rīmⵜ	jikⵜ	'body'
'walled city'	birnⵜ	cīwō	'illness'
'fish'	kīfⵜ	tīlàs	'by necessity'
'build'	ginā	sīsⵜ	'sixpence'
'celebration'	bìkⵜ	binnē	'bury'
'eye'	idō	irⵜ	'kind'
'gown'	rīgā	jirā	'wait for'
'blood'	jinⵜ	rībā	'profit'
'conversation'	hīrā	ⵜkō	'power'

<u>Discrimination Drill</u> - (/u/ - /ū/). Follow the directions for the drill above.

'well bucket'	gùgā	hūlā	'cap'
'crying'	kūkā	mùtûm	'person'
'three'	ukù	kunyā	'modesty'
'looking at'	dūbā	hūtū	'resting'
'close'	kusa	tunā	'remember'
'run'	gudū	wùyā	'difficulty'
'mortar'	turmⵜ	sūnā	'name'
'jug'	tūlū	dukà	'all'
'thousand'	dubū	wucē	'pass'
'hyena'	kūrā	hūrā	'blow'

III. Tone

Discrimination and Tone Identification Drills - Without looking at your
book, listen to your informant pronounce the following pairs of words. As
soon as he has uttered a given pair, you should indicate whether the two
words have the same tone patterns by saying "same" or "different." The
informant will then say the words again; this time you will say what the
tone pattern is, e.g. if he says littāfī you will say "high-high-low," and
if he says Àlhàmîs you will say "low-low-falling." Each student is to
identify a pair of words in this manner. Remember, this exercise should
be done with closed books.

'meaning'	azancī	fuskōkī	'faces'
'roads'	hanyōyī	kēwayō	'come around again'
'well-being'	lāfiyà	igiyà	'rope'
'eyes'	idànū	littāfī	'book'
'tree'	itācē	makòyī	'learner'
'laughter'	dàriyā	shèkàrū	'years'
'leader'	shùgàba	tàlàtin	'thirty'
'help'	tàimakō	kàsuwā	'market'
'need'	bùkātà	inuwà	'shade'
'trouble'	wàhalà	màganà	'speech'
'investigation'	bìncìkē	àmfànī	'usefulness'
'year'	shèkarà	gāfarà	'forgiveness'
'pocket'	àljīhū	gānuwā	'rampart around town'
'hoe'	fartanyà	shìnkāfà	'rice'
'dawn'	àsubâ	shùgàba	'leader'

IV. Greetings[1]

barkà/sànnu   yâuwā or (yàuwā) barkà/sànnu (kàdai)

These two greetings can be, and often are, followed by the preposition dà
plus expressions of the following two types:

(1) The activity of the person being greeted (aikī 'work', hūtāwā 'resting',
zamā 'sitting', zuwà 'arrival', cìnikī 'trading', etc.);

(2) The period of the day (hàntsī 'late morning', rāna 'midday', yâmmā
'late afternoon', darē 'night', etc.). Barkā is the more commonly used
of the two with these expressions.

Any one of these greetings may be answered by any of the combinations on
the right above. ( ) means optional, / means one or the other, with the
restriction that a greeting with sànnu cannot be answered with barkā or
vice versa.

---

[1] Since there is no set answer for this type of drill, these drills are not
on tape. They should be used with an informant or instructor.

Question and Answer Drill - Give an appropriate response to each of the following greeting phrases.

sànnu	sànnu dà zuwà
barkà da yâmmā	barkà dà zuwà
sànnu dà aikī̀	barka dà rānā
sànnu dà hūtàwā	barkà dà aikī̀
barkà	sànnu dà cinikī̀
barkà dà hàntsī̀	barkà dà zamā

yàyà ìyālī?[2]	lāfiyà (lau/Ƙalau); sunà lāfiyà
yàyà/inā gùmī̀	ai, lōkàcinsà nē

The words yàyà or inā can be used followed by

(1) Refefence to the family or household of the person being greeted (yârā 'children', ìyālī̀ 'family', gidā 'household', the name of some member of the household, etc.). The response can be any of those on the right hand side of the first example above. The word sunà is a pronominal form used where more than one person is referred to; when one masculine person is referred to, substitute yanà, for one feminine person, tanà.

(2) Reference to the type of weather prevalent at the time (gùmī̀ 'hot weather', sanyī 'damp cold', ɗārī̀ 'dry cold', ruwā 'rain', zāfī̀ 'heat', etc.). The appropriate answer is on the right hand side of the second example. Ruwā 'rain' has the further standard response ruwā yā yi gyārā meaning something like 'the rain is good for the crops.'

Question and Answer Drill - Give an appropriate response to each of the following greeting phrases.

inā gidā?	yàyà Hàdizà?
yàyà yârā?	inā ruwā?
yàyà ruwā?	inā ɗārī?
inā Mammàn?	yàyà gidā?
inā sanyī?	inā Màryamà?
yàyà ìyālī?	inā zāfī?
inā gùmī?	yàyà Àli?

<hr/>

[2] The term ìyālī̀ refers to one's dependents (wife and children) only, NEVER to one's parents. Another term, iyàyē, is used to refer to one's parents, but this term is seldom used in greetings.

UNIT IV
DIALOGUES

A. Mālàm: Mḕnē nḕ wannàn?   What's this?
 Ɗālìbī: Bàn sanī ba. Mḕne nè?   I don't know. What is it?
 Mālàm: Wannàn littāfī̀ nē.   This is a book.
 Ɗālìbī: Wannàn tēbùr nē?   Is this a table?
 Mālàm.   Ā'ā̰, wannàn kujḕrā cè.   No, this is a chair.
           Gā̀ tēbùr nân.   Here is the table.

Vocabulary

ā'ā̰	'no'	littāfī̀ n.m.	'book'
bàn sanī ba	'I don't know' (I-not know not)	(lìttàttàfai pl.)	
		mḕnē nḕ	'what is it?'
cē/cè	'it is' (used with feminine nouns)	(masculine or gender unknown)	
		mālàm n.m.	'teacher; (as term
ɗālìbī n.m.	'student (male)'	(màlàmai pl.)	of address) sir'
ɗālìbā n.f.	'student (female)'	nân	'here'
(ɗàlìbai pl.)		ne̅/nè	'it is' (used with
gā̀	'here ... is, there ... is' (=French voilà)		masculine nouns)
		tēbùr n.m.	'table'
		(tēburōrī pl.)	
kujḕrā n.f.	'chair'	wannàn dem. pron.	'this (one)'
(kùjērū pl.)			

B. Mālàm: Ìnā idṑ?   Where is the eye?
 Ɗālìbī: Gā̀ shi nân.   Here it is.
 Mālàm: Hakà nē. Mḕnē nḕ wannàn.   So it is. What is this?
 Ɗālìbī: Wannàn fuskà cē?   Is that the face?
 Mālàm: Ā'ā̰. Wannàn ƙafà cē.   No. That is the foot.
           Gā̀ fuskà.   Here is the face.

Vocabulary

fuskà n.f.	'face'	ìnā	'where, where is?'
(fuskōkī pl.)		ƙafà n.f.	'foot; leg'
hakà	'thus, like that'	(ƙafafuwà pl.)	
idṑ n.m.	'eye'	shi object pro.	'him; it (m)'
(idānū pl.)			

Further practice - Construct your own dialogues by substituting the following nouns for the nouns in dialogues A and B.

gāshī̀ n.m.	'hair'	kûnnē n.m.	'ear'
hancī n.m.	'nose'	yātsà n.m.	'finger'
hannū n.m.	'hand; arm'	àgōgo n.m.	'watch'
kâi n.m.	'head'	àlƙalàmī n.m.	'pen'

45

jàkā n.f.	'bag'			
kudī n.m.	'money'	tākàlmī n.m.	'shoe, sandal'	
mabūdī n.m.	'key'	takàrdā n.f.	'paper'	
tagùwā n.f.	'shirt'	wàndō n.m.	'pants'	

C. If you have not already done so, everyone in the class should adopt a Hausa name. In dialogue C., once you become familiar with the expressions, substitute the names of class members.

Màlàm:	Wànē nè wannàn?	Who is this?
Dàlibī:	Shī Audù nè.	He's Audu.
Màlàm:	Kai, wànē nè?	Who are you?
Dàlibī:	Nī Hasàn nè.	I am Hasan.
Màlàm:	Inà Sālisù?	Where is Salisu?
Dàlibī:	Gà shi nân.	Here he is.
Màlàm:	Màdàllà. Wannàn wàcē cè?	Good. Who is this?
Dàlibī:	Ita Halīmà cē.	She's Halima.

Vocabulary

ita	indep. pron.	'she, her'		shī	indep. pron.	'he, him'
kai	indep. pron.	'you (m.sg.)'		wàcē cè		'who is (it - fem. person)?'
ni	indep. pron.	'I, me'		wànē nè		'who is (it - masc. person)'

D. This dialogue takes place between two students.

Abdù:	Su wànē nè?	Who are they?
Bellò:	Sū dàlìbai nè.	They are students.
Abdù:	Shi dàlibī nè?	Is he a student?
Bellò:	À'à, shī màlàmī nè.	No, he's the teacher.
Abdù:	Kai dàlibī nè?	Are you a student?
Bellò:	Ī, nī dàlìbī nè.	Yes, I am a student.
Abdù:	Tô, dà kyâu.	OK, good.

Vocabulary

ī		'yes'		sū indep. pron	'they, them'
kyâu n.m.		'goodness'		su wànē nè	who are they?'
dà kyâu		'good, that's fine'			

Further Practice - Construct your own dialogues by substituting the following nouns for the nouns in dialogues C. and D..

Bàhaushè n.m.	'Hausa man'	Bàtūrìyā n.f.	'European woman'
Bàhaushìyā n.f.	'Hausa woman'	Tūràwā n.pl.	'Europeans'
Hausàwā n.pl.	'Hausa people'	màcè n.f.	'woman'
Bàtūrè n.m.	'European' (normally used for anyone of European or American origin)	(màtā pl.)	
		mutûm n.m. (mutànè pl.)	'man; person'

46

yārinyà n.f.   'girl'
('yam màtā pl.)

yārò n.m.   'boy'
(yārā pl.)

yârā n.pl.   'children'
(boys or boys and
girls together)

GRAMMAR

4.1 Gender

Nouns in Hausa are either masculine or feminine gender. Almost all feminine nouns end in -a or -ā, a notable exception being màcè 'woman.' There is a fair number of masculine nouns which end in -ā however, so it is very important to learn the gender of a noun as you learn the noun.

kujèrā (feminine noun)   'chair'

littāfī (masculine noun)   'book'

gidā (masculine noun ending
in -a)   'compound, household'

4.2 Independent pronouns

The independent pronouns are as follows:

Singular		Plural	
nī	ne	mū	us
kai	you (m)		
kē	you (f)	kū	you
shī	him		
ita	her	sū	them

These pronouns have several usages. One is with the identifier nē/cē (see grammar 4.3).

shī nè   'it's him'
kē cè   'it's you (f.sg.)'
sū nè   'it's them'

Other uses of these pronouns will be pointed out as they arise.

4.3 The Identifier nē/cē

Hausa has no single equivalent of the English verb "be." One use of "be" in English is that of a linking verb as exemplified in the following sentences:

He is my teacher.

That is a book.

We are students.

This concept is expressed in Hausa by the particles nē or cē:

wannàn littāfī nē   'that is a book'   ƙōfà cē   'it's a door'

shī Audù nē   'he is Audu'   nī cè   'it's me' (woman speaking)

mū dàlibai nè   'we are students'   nī nè   'it's me' (man speaking)

ita Halìmà cē   'she is Halima'

47

There are several things to be remembered about nē and cē:

1) nē is used with masculine nouns or pronouns and plural nouns (even if the plural refers to feminine things or persons), cē is used with feminine nouns or pronouns;

2) the tone of nē or cē is always opposite of that of the preceding syllable;

3) nē or cē usually comes at the end of the sentence.

N.B.: NĒ AND CĒ ARE NOT VERBS. At the moment this may not seem very important, but it should always be kept in mind since when we do get to real verbs no attempt should be made to identify nē and cē with them.

4.4 "What is it?", "Who is it?"

mēnē nè?	'what is it?'
mēnē nè wannàn?	'what is this?'

This is the common way to ask what something is. You will note the word nē in the expression. These expressions are used if the gender of the thing in question is not known, but the answer will have nē or cē depending on what the gender is.

Even though mēnē nē contains the masculine identifier, nē, mēnē nè is normally used to refer to any noun, even if the noun happens to be feminine and the questioner knows this.

mēnē nè?	'what is it?'		
littāfì nē	'it's a book'	mēnē nè wannàn?	'what is this?'
mēnē nè wannàn?	'what is this?	wannàn kujèrā cē	'this is a chair'
wannàn littāfì nē	'this is a book'		

Analogous to these expressions used with non-human objects, there are these expressions:

wànē nè?	'who is it?' (masculine person)
wàcē cè?	'who is it?' (feminine person)
su wànē nè?	'who are they?'

4.5 "Where is X?"; "here X is", "there X is"

We have seen inā used in greetings like inā gàjiyà? and inā aikì? where the meaning of this interrogative word is 'how?.' In this unit we see it followed by a noun in sentences like inā Audù where it means 'where is Audu?'

The word gā 'here ... is', 'there ... is' may be equated with the French voici or voilà. Gā may be followed by a noun or one of the set of direct object pronouns which will be studied in detail in a later unit. The third person forms are shi 'him', ta 'her', and su 'them.' These three forms will be used in drills in this unit.

The determination of 'here ... is' as opposed to 'there ... is', if context does not make it clear which is intended, is done by the addition of nân or cân respectively. Thus, gā shi cân can only mean 'there he is' whereas gā shi alone could mean 'here he is' or 'there he is' depending on the context.

48

Examples of ìnā and gà are

ìnā Audù?	'where is Audu?'
gà shi cân	'there he is'
ìnā littāfî dà fensìr	'where are the book and pencil?'
gà su ñân	'here they are'
gà ƙōfà	'there's the door' or 'here's the door'

PRONUNCIATION

Question Intonation

In the greetings of the first three units we have seen questions formed in two basic ways:

1) Questions introduced by a question word such as ìnā or yàyà, where the intonation pattern is similar to a statement (with possibly overall higher pitch and/or a short drop of the voice on the last syllable):

ìnā wunì?	'how did you pass the day?'
yàyà yârā?	'how are the children?'

2) Questions formed like a statement but with special question intonation:

kā zō lāfiyà?	'did you come in good health?'

These are often called "yes-no" questions because they can be answered "yes" or "no." In English they are usually marked by the auxiliary verb 'do' at the beginning and a rising intonation.

In Hausa, there is no such auxiliary as 'do' and it is with the question intonation alone that we indicate that we are asking a question. The basic "rule" for question intonation is that THE LAST HIGH TONE SYLLABLE IN THE QUESTION IS RAISED TO A PITCH WHICH IS HIGHER THAN AN ORDINARY HIGH TONE WOULD BE, and any following low tone syllables do not drop as low as an ordinary low tone would be. If there is no low tone syllable following the final high tone syllable (i.e., if the high tone syllable is final) the pitch first goes higher than a normal high tone but then falls off slightly like a falling tone.

The following drill is in three parts. In the first part, all the utterances end on a high tone. In the second part, the last two syllables are high-low. Be especially careful here to raise the HIGH tone to an extra high pitch, NOT the low tone. The third part of the drill has sentences ending in a mixture of tone patterns.

Part 1

Questions ending in high tone - On the left is a sentence with normal statement intonation. On the right is the same utterance changed into a question by using question intonation. Repeat the statement, then the question, after the informant, making an effort to imitate every detail of his intonation.

aikì nē	'it's work'	aikì nē?
yā dāwo	'he has come back'	yā dāwo?

49

'yarkà cē	'it's your daughter'	'yarkà cē?
kā ci tuwō	'you ate food'	kā ci tuwō?
tanà dà shī	'she has it'	tanà da shī?
kin gānè shi	'you (f) understood it'	kin gānè shi?
sunà gidā	'they are at home'	sunà gidā?
yā yi tsàdā	'it's expensive'	yā yi tsàdā?
bài yi barcī ba	'he didn't sleep'	bài yi barcī ba?
bâ shi dà gidā	'he has no home'	bâ shi dà gidā?

Part 2

Questions ending in a low tone - Follow the directions for the drill above.

lāfiyà	'good health'	lāfiyà?
gōnā cè	'it's a farm'	gōnā cè?
yârā nè	'they're children'	yârā nè?
yā kàwō shi	'he brought it'	yā kàwō shi?
gàskiyā nè	'it's the truth'	gàskiyā nè?
yanà zuwà	'he's coming'	yanà zuwà?
gōnātā cè	'it's my farm'	gōnātā cè?
kā hau dōkī	'you rode a horse'	kā hau dōkī?
kanà lāfiyà	'you are in good health'	kanà lāfiyà?
yā ga yārinyà	'he saw the girl'	yā ga yārinyà?

Part 3

Mixed tone patterns - Follow the instructions for the drills above.

ita cè	'it's her'	ita cè?
yanà nân	'he's here'	yanà nân?
bābu shī	'there is none of it'	bābu shī?
an kāwo	'it has been brought'	an kāwo?
zâ a gidā	'one is going home'	zâ a gidā?
inà sônsà	'I like it'	inà sônsà?
bâ shi dà shī	'he doesn't have it'	bâ shi dà shī?
sun tàfi gidā	'they went home'	sun tàfi gidā?
kàsuwā cè	'it's a market'	kàsuwā cè?
sun shā miyà	'they "ate" (drank) sauce'	sun shā miyà?
sun ci tuwō	'they ate mush'	sun ci tuwō?
mutànen Kanò	'people of Kano'	mutànen Kanò?
bâ lâifinsà ba	'it's not his fault'	bâ lâifinsà ba?

sun yi dàriyā   'they laughed'   sun yi dàriyā?
yanā gidansà   'he's at his home'   yanā gidansà?

GRAMMATICAL DRILLS

Drill 1 - Replace the nouns in the following exercises by the appropriate independent pronouns. Replace the second person pronouns by the appropriate first person pronoun, and the first person pronoun by the appropriate second person pronoun. For example:

Cue:	màcè cē	Cue:	kē cè
Student response:	ita cè	Student response:	nī cè

1. littāfī nē	5. mū nè	9. kujèrā cè	12. Bàhaushè nē
2. ƙafà cē	6. takàrdā cè	10. nī nè	13. kū nè
3. dàlibai nè	7. kai nè	11. nī cè	14. yārinyā cè
4. tèbùr nē	8. mutànē nè		

Drill 2 - Answer the question mènē nè wannàn? by putting the cue word into the pattern sencence wannàn X nē/cē. For example:

Question:	mènē nè wannàn?	Question:	mènē nè wannàn?
Cue:	littāfī	Que:	taguwā
Student response:	wannàn littāfī nē	Student response:	wannàn taguwā cè

Question	Cue	Question	Cue
1. mènē nè wannàn?	idò	6. mènē nè wannàn?	mabūdī
2. mènē nè wannàn?	yātsà	7. mènē nè wannàn?	àgōgo
3. mènē nè wannàn?	fensìr	8. mènē nè wannàn?	jàkā
4. mènē nè wannàn?	tèbùr	9. mènē nè wannàn?	gōnā
5. mènē nè wannàn?	takàrdā	10. mènē nè wannàn?	kujèrā

Drill 3 - The cue is a question of the form wannàn X nē/cē? The response is simply ī, X nē/cē. Be very careful to give proper question intonation and statement intonation. The drill should be done between two students who switch roles on the second repetition of the drill so that each student uses both types of intonation. For example:

Cue: wannàn tèbùr nē?
Student response: ī, tèbùr nē

1. wannàn ƙafà cē?	6. wannàn yārinyà cē?
2. wannàn mabūdī nē?	7. wannàn àgōgo nè?
3. wannàn tàkàlmī nē?	8. wannàn taguwā cè?
4. wannàn yàtsà nè?	9. wannàn takàrdā cè?
5. wannàn wàndō nè?	10. wannàn littāfī nē?

Drill 4 - This drill can be used by two students alone, or by an instructor
giving the cue, one student giving the first response, and a second student
giving the answer to that response. Remember that the third person
pronouns used with gā are shi (m.sg.), ta (m.sg.), and su (pl.). (See 4.5,
second paragraph). For example:

        Cue: inā tēbur?

        Student response: bàn sanì ba

        Answer: gā shi nân

1. inā jàkā?
2. inā kuɗī?
3. inā takàrdā?
4. inā kujèrā?
5. inā yârā?

6. inā àgōgo?
7. inā littāfī?
8. inā yārinyà?
9. inā màlàmai?
10. inā taguwā?

Drill 5 - Answer the questions wànē nè?, wàcē cè?, and su wànē nè?, with the
pattern sentences as shown in the examples.

Question: kū su wànē nè? | Question: kē wàcē cè?

Cue: dàlibai? | Cue: Hàlīmà

Student response: mū dàlibai nè | Student response: nī Hàlīmà cē

Question	Cue	Question	Que
1. su wànē nè?	màlàmai	6. kai wànē nè?	Mùhammadù
2. wànē nè?	màlàmī	7. wàcē cè?	Aishà
3. wàcē cè?	Bintà	8. su wànē nè?	yârā
4. wànē nè?	Lawàl	9. kē wàcē cè?	Mèro
5. kū su wànē nè?	dàlibai	10. su wànē nè?	'yam mātā

Drill 6A and 6B - You will hear a question of the form inā X? Go through
the drill twice:

6A The first time, give the answer gā X nân. For example:

        Question: inā Audù?

        Student response: gā Audù nân

6B The second time, instead of repeating the noun, substitute the appropriate direct object pronoun (shi, ta, su). For example:

        Question: inā Audù?

        Student response: gā shi nân

1. inā tēbur?
2. inā yārinyà?
3. inā Mammàn?
4. inā kujèrā?
5. inā dàlibai?

6. inā takàrdā?
7. inā littāfī?
8. inā Hàlīma?
9. inā taguwā?
10. inā mālàm?

Drill 7 - Answer the questions by putting the cue word into the pattern
sentence ā'ā, X Y nē/cē. For example;

Question: kē Bàhaushìyā cè?
Cue: Bàtūrìyā
Student response: ā'ā, nī Bàtūrìyā cè

Question	Cue	Question	Cue
1. kū Hàusāwā nè?	Tūrāwā	6. shī Bàhaushē nè?	Bàtūrè
2. shī mālàm nē?	yārò	7. kū ɗàlìbai nè?	mālàmai
3. ita Bàtūrìyā cè?	Bàhaushìyā	8. kai Hasàn nē?	Sàlisù
4. kai mālàmī nè?	ɗàlìbī	9. ita Hàlīmà cē?	Maryamà
5. sū mātā nè?	'yam mātā	10. shī Mūsā nè?	Abdù

53

C. Mālàm:	Mēnē nè cikin littāfī̀?	What's in the book?
Ɗālibī̀:	Takàrdā cè.	It's paper.
Mālàm:	Ìnā littāfī̀?	Where's the book?
Ɗālibī̀:	Gā̀ shi nân à kân kujèrā.	Here it is on the chair.
Mālàm:	Tô, fensìr fà?	OK, what about the pencil?
Ɗālibī̀:	Gā̀ shi cân à ƙàrƙashin tēbùr.	There it is (over there) under the table.

Vocabulary

à prep.	'at'		(à) kân	'on top of'
(à) cikin	'in, inside'		(à) ƙàrƙashin	'underneath'

D. Mālàm:	Ìnā Shēhù?	Where is Shehu?
Ɗālibī̀:	Gā̀ shi cân kusa dà Àli.	There he is close to Ali.
Mālàm:	Tô, wācē cè bāyan Maryamà?	OK, who is it behind Maryama?
Ɗālibī̀:	Ita Fāti cè.	She is Fati.
Mālàm:	Gàban Fāti fà?	And in front of Fati?
Ɗālibī̀:	Ai, Maryamà cē.	Uh, it's Maryama.

Vocabulary

(à) bāyan	'behind'	kusa dà	'near'
(à) gàban	'in front of'		

Further practice - Substitute nouns used in the dialogues of Units IV and V into dialogues C and D to construct your own dialogues. Use the Hausa names of class members in dialogue D.

GRAMMAR

5.1 Demonstratives in Hausa

In the dialogues of Units IV and V we have seen the following demonstratives used:

wannàn	wancàn/waccàn
waɗànnân	waɗàncân
nân	cân

Their use will be more fully explained in 5.2, but before going on to this, a few words should be said about their meanings.

The immediate tendency is to identify those on the left with English 'this', 'these', and 'here', and those on the right with 'that', 'those', and 'there'. This will give an inaccurate view of the way these words are applied in context.

a) Hausa tends to use <u>wannàn</u> to refer to any <u>single object</u> which is fairly close to the speaker, even objects far enough away that we might use 'that/those' to designate them in English. <u>Wancàn/waccàn</u> is restricted to objects at a fairly great physical distance from the speaker.

b) When indicating two or more objects which can be touched, <u>wannàn</u> is used for all of them. If the objects are at such a distance that they cannot be touched, but still are not at a great distance,

56

wannàn is used for the first one indicated and wancàn/waccàn for the others.
c) When referring to a concept, idea, statement, etc. about to be presented
or just presented, wannàn is used. Wancàn/waccàn is restricted to the
more remote past. Note that English usually uses 'this' to refer to such
concepts, ideas, statements, etc. being presented or about to be presented,
but 'that' is used in reference to things presented in past time, no matter
how recent, e.g., 'that's right' in Hausa is wannàn gàskiyā nè.

Very generally then, wannàn (wadànnân, nân) is normally used whenever
'this' (these, here) is used in English, but it overlaps a great deal with
English 'that' (those, there). Wancàn/waccàn (wadàncàn, càn) are largely
restricted to great physical distance or remote past.

5.2 Demonstrative pronouns

Following are the Hausa demonstrative pronouns listed in paradigm form
(for convenience, they have been translated using 'this', that', etc., but
keep in mind that these translations will not always be equivalent to the
Hausa meanings):

Singular		Plural	
wannàn	'this' (referring to any single object)	wadànnân	'these'
wancàn	'that' (referring to a single object of masculine gender)	wadàncàn	'those'
waccàn	'that' (referring to a single object of feminine gender)		

These demonstrative pronouns have been well illustrated in the dialogues of
Units IV and V in such sentences as

wānē nè wannàn	'who is this?'
wannàn littāfī nè	'this is a book'
wadàncàn kùjērū nè	'those are chairs'

Sometimes these demonstratives will correspond to English 'this one',
'that one', etc. Note that English uses "one" with demonstratives in this
way only when an opposition with some other thing(s) is indicated. Hausa
would either simply stress the demonstrative or reword the sentence so as
to throw the emphasis on the word in question. Note the difference between
the following sentences in English and Hausa.

Q: Wannàn fensìr nē?	'Is this a pencil?'
A: Ā'à, wannàn àlƙalàmi nè.	'No, this is a pen.
Wannàn, shī nè fensìr.	This is a pencil.'

The last Hausa sentence could be literally translated 'this one, it is it
the pencil.'

57

5.3 Positional Words and Prepositions

In this unit we have encountered several words which resemble English prepositions in their translations. For example:

(à)	cikin littāfī̀	'in the book'
(à)	kân kujèrā̄	'on the chair'
(à)	k̀arkashin tēbùr	'under the table'

There is probably no harm in thinking of these words as prepositions at this early stage in your study of Hausa. A few facts about these words may be easier to understand, however, if the student is made aware of the fact that they are nouns which indicate position of one object with respect to another.

One thing that should be noted is that the true preposition à, which has a very general meaning of 'at (a place)' is frequently used with these positional nouns. Thus, one might think of à cikin littāfī̀ as meaning 'at the interior of the book'. The preposition à is almost always used with some positional words, especially with à kân 'on top of'.

A second way these positional words differ from prepositions is that they can appear alone with no noun following:

gà ta cân à cikī̀	'there she is inside'
gà shi nân kusa	'here it is close by'

The positional word kusa 'near' is somewhat different from the others found in Unit V since it must always be followed by the preposition dà when used with a noun.

gà shi cân kusa dà Abdù 'there he is over there near Abdu'

5.4 Negation of nē̄/cē̄

In Unit IV we have seen how nē̄ and cē̄ are used to identify masculine and feminine nouns. The negative of this identifying construction is formed by placing bà ... ba around the thing that is to be negated. This will usually correspond to the noun in the predicate in sentences like 'that is not my coat'.

bà littāfī̀ ba nē̄	'it's not a book'
bà kujèrā̄ ba cē̄	'it's not a chair'
wannàn bà àllō ba nē̄	'this is not a blackboard'
sū bà dàlībai ba nē̄	'they are not students'

Note that nē̄/cē̄ follows the second ba.

5.5 Plural of Nouns

Pluralization in Hausa is quite complex. Although there is system to their formation, i.e. some definite patterns can be recognized, the overall picture can be quite confusing for the beginning student. This being the case, the easiest way to tackle the plurals is simply to learn the plural form along with the singular.

Fortunately for the student, Hausa does not use plurals nearly as much as European languages do, e.g. with numbers greater than one. Thus, if the student learns some of the more commonly used plurals such as mutānē̄ 'people', mātā̄ 'women', yārā̄ 'children', and a few others, he may find it possible to simply note (rather than memorize) the plural forms of most nouns unless they are employed in the dialogues and exercises.

58

GRAMMATICAL DRILLS

Drill 1A - Using each of the pictures as a cue, one student should ask a
second student mēnē nē wannàn?, su wānē nè wadànnân?, wācē cē wannàn?, etc.
(using only the demonstratives ending in -nan). The second student then
answers wannàn/wadànnân X nē/cē. For example, the question for the first
picture is wānē nē?, the response is yārò nē.

Drill 1B - Follow the directions for 1A, but use the appropriate form
wancàn, waccàn, wadàncân. Note that the figures are more distant than in 1A.

Drill 2 - Answer the question mēnē nḕ cikin àkwàtì? with the sentence
X nḕ/cḕ/.

Question: mēnē nḕ cikin àkwàtì?
Cue: àlƙalàmī
Student response: àlƙalàmī nḕ

Question	Cue	Question	Cue
1. mēnē nḕ cikin àkwàtì?	kuɗì	6. mēnē nḕ cikin àkwàtì?	wàndō
2. mēnē nḕ cikin àkwàtì?	takàrdā	7. mēnē nḕ cikin àkwàtì?	jàkā
3. mēnē nḕ cikin àkwàtì?	mabūdī	8. mēnē nḕ cikin àkwàtì?	tagùwā
4. mēnē nḕ cikin àkwàtì?	tàkàlmī	9. mēnē nḕ cikin àkwàtì?	àgōgo
5. mēnē nḕ cikin àkwàtì?	takàrdā	10. mēnē nḕ cikin àkwàtì?	fensìr

Drill 3 - Substitute the expressions listed below into the pattern
sentence gà shi cân ...?

Cue: kusa dà bangō
Student response: gà shi cân kusa dà bangō?

1. bāyan kujḕrā   6. kusa dà hanyà
2. à ƙân kujḕrā   7. cikin gidā
3. à ƙàrƙashin tēbùr   8. à ƙàrƙashin mōtà
4. gàban Fāti   9. bāyan tāgà
5. cikin mōtà   10. gàban gidā

Drill 4 - Answer the question inā X? by putting the cues into the pattern
sentence gà shi/ta cân ... .

Question: inā àkwàtì?
Cue: à ƙàrƙashin tēbùr
Student response: gà shi cân à ƙàrƙashin tēbùr
Question: inā Hàlīmà?
Cue: kusa dà Maryamà
Student response: gà ta cân kusa dà Maryamà

Question		Question	
1. inā Audù?	à ƙân kujḕrā	6. inā hanyà?	bāyan gidā
2. inā mabūdī?	à ƙàrƙashin littāfì	7. inā àllō?	cikin ɗakì
3. inā Fàti dà Maryamà?	cikin mōtà	8. inā mōtà?	kusa dà bishiyà
4. inā wàndō?	à ƙân àkwàtì	9. inā tēbùr?	bāyan bangō
5. inā ɗàlìbai?	gàban ƙōfà	10. inā fensìr?	à ƙân takàrdā

61

Drill 5 - Answer the questions with a complete sentence of the pattern
waɗànnân/waɗàncân ... nē.

Question 1:   mènē nè waɗànnân?

Cue: fensìr dà littāfì

Student response: waɗànnân fensìr dà littāfì nē.

Question 2:   waɗàncân fà?

Cue: kùjèrū

Student response: waɗànnân kùjèrū nè.

Question	Cue		
1. mènē nè waɗàncân?	ƙōfà dà àllō	6. waɗànnân fà?	bangwàyē
2. waɗànnân fà?	alƙalumà	7. mènē nè waɗànnân?	àgōgo dà jàkā
3. mènē nè waɗànnân?	takàrdā dà mabūɗì	8. waɗàncân fà?	tākalmà
4. waɗàncân fà?	tāgōgì	9. mènē nè waɗànnân?	hancì dà hannū
5. mènē nè waɗàncân?	mōtà dà bishiyà	10. waɗàncân fà?	tàkàrdū

Drill 6 - Answer the questions in the negative as illustrated in the example.

Question: wannàn kujèrā cè?

Student response: ā'à, wannàn bà kujèrā ba cè

1. wannàn gidā nē?

2. wannàn ƙafà cē?

3. shì mālàm nē?

4. wannàn ƙōfà cē?

5. wannàn yārinyà cē?

6. waɗàncân tāgōgì nē?

7. wannàn tēbùr nē?

8. kai Bàhaushè nē?

9. kē Bàhaushìyā cè?

10. wannàn yārò nē?

11. wannàn tāgà cē?

12. wannàn littāfì nē?

13. sū Hàusàwā nè?

14. shì mài gidā nē?

15. wannàn jàkā cè?

Drill 7 - Using the pictures as cues, one student should ask a second student a question of the form ìnā littāfī? The second student gives an answer of the form gā shi nân à kân kujērā. Use the expressions kusa dà, ƙarƙashin, cikin, or a kân.

Drill 8A and 8B - Repeat the initial sentence, then substitute the first cue into the appropriate place in that sentence. As each cue is given, substitute it into the sentence formed from the previous cue, so that a new sentence is formed.

Initial sentence:	àkwai fensìr à kân littāfī̀
Cue 1:	gā̀
Student response:	gā̀ fensìr à kân littāfī̀
Cue 2:	kusa dà takàrdā
Student response:	gā̀ fensìr kusa dà takàrdā
Cue 3:	mềnē nề?
Student response:	mềnē nề kusa dà takàrdā.

8A Initial sentence: mềnē nề?

Cues	Student response
1. cikin littāfī̀	mềnē nề cikin littāfī̀?
2. gā̀ fensìr	gā̀ fensìr cikin littāfī̀
3. à kân kujèrā	gā̀ fensìr à kân kujèrā
4. mềnē nề?	mềnē nề à kân kujèrā?
5. gā̀ shi cân	gā̀ shi cân à kân kujèrā
6. bāyan Audù	gā̀ shi cân bāyan Audù
7. ìnā?	ìnā Audù?
8. dà Hàlīmà	ìnā Audù dà Hàlīmà?
9. gā̀	gā̀ Audù dà Hàlīmà
10. kusa da gida	gā̀ Audù dà Hàlīmà kusa dà gidā

8B Initial Sentence: wànē nề?

1. gàban Hàlīmà	wànē nề gàban Hàlīmà?
2. wàcē cè	wàcē cè gàban Hàlīmà?
3. gā̀ Fàti	gā̀ Fàti gàban Hàlīmà
4. kusa dà bangō	gā̀ Fàti kusa dà bangō
5. littāfī̀	gā̀ littāfī̀ kusa dà bangō/ gā̀ Fàti kusa dà littāfī̀
6. à k̃àrk̃ashin tēbùr	gā̀ littāfī̀ à k̃àrk̃ashin tēbùr/gā̀ Fàti à k̃àrk̃ashin tēbùr
7. mềnē nề?	mềnē nề à k̃àrk̃ashin tēbùr?
8. wadànnân	mềnē nề wadànnân?/ mềnē nề wadànnân à k̃àrk̃ashin tēbùr
9. cikin mōtā̀	mềnē nề cikin mōtā̀?
10. su wànē nề	su wànē nề cikin mōtā̀?
11. gā̀ dàlìbai	gā̀ dàlìbai cikin mōtā̀

PRONUNCIATION REVIEW

Vowel Length Discrimination

Identification Drill - On a sheet of paper, make two columns, one labelled "short vowel", the other "long vowel." Listen to the following words and put the number of the word in one column or the other depending on whether the vowel in the first syllable is long or short.

1. kāyā	'baggage'	11. k̀àshT	'bone'	21. jàkT	'donkey'
2. kTfT	'fish'	12. b̀àkT	'mouth'	22. fìta	'go out'
3. dukà	'all'	13. g̀àrT	'town'	23. t̀àfi	'leave'
4. sàyā	'buy'	14. ukù	'three'	24. idò	'eye'
5. sārà	'chopping'	15. d̀Tbà	'dip out'	25. kūrā	'hyena'
6. tùlū	'bottle'	16. birnT	'walled town'	26. mātsà	'squeeze'
7. rTmT	'kapok tree'	17. hTrā	'conversation'	27. gidā	'house'
8. mutù	'die'	18. karā	'stalk'	28. g̀àrT	'flour'
9. tarà	'nine'	19. kusa	'near'	29. bùhū	'sack'
10. hūtà	'rest'	20. b̀àd̀i	'next year'	30. k̀àrā	'increase'

Reproduction Drill - After correcting your paper, listen to the informant repeat each word again, repeating after him while making especially sure that you pronounce the vowel in the first syllable correctly.

GUIDED CONVERSATION

The student should now be ready to freely use the range of expressions illustrated in the dialogues of Units IV and V. Following are some suggestions for directed conversation using this material. It is suggested that such conversation be restricted to the grammatical patterns learned and that vocabulary not be extended appreciably beyond that already introduced.

1) Using two or three fixed expressions such as 'ask him', 'tell him', etc., the informant has students question each other. A few such expressions might be

tàmbàyè shi/tàmbàyè ta	'ask him/ask her'
gàyā masà/gàyā matà/qàyā mini	'tell him/tell her/tell me'
mè ya cè?/mè ta cè?	'what did he say?/what did she say?' [*]

[*] Used by the informant to get the student to tell him what another student has said.

2) The instructor points out a group of objects or persons and has one student ask another questions about them. For example:

On a chair there is a book with a piece of paper in it and a pencil.

Abdù:	Mènē nè wad̀ànnân?
Hasàn:	LittāfT dà takàrdā dà fensìr.
Abdù:	Inā takàrdā?
Hasàn:	G̀à ta cikin littāfT.
Abdù:	Fensìr fà?
Hasàn:	Ai, g̀à shi kusa dà littāfT.

65

3) Designating a group of objects or persons, the instructor has a student describe what he sees. For example:

The instructor has a student, named Hàwwa, stand in front of the door. Zàinabù describes the scene.

Zàinabù: Ita Hàwwa cē.

Gà ta cân gàban ƙōfà.

Wancàn àllō nè.

Gà Hàwwa kusa dà shī.

DIALOGUES

A. Yahaya is the houseboy in Malam Sa'idu's compound. Uwargida (Malam
Sa'idu's wife) has sent him to market around 3:00 P.M. to buy eggsᵜ and
a basket, with instructions to return home quickly. He buys the eggs
but has some small change of his own which is burning a hole in his
pocket. He sees some guavas for sale which strike his fancy.

Yàhàya:	Gwēbā̀ nawà nawà nḕ?	How much are the guavas each?
Màì sayàd dà gwēbā̀:	Ukù kwabō nḕ.	Three for a kobo.
Yàhàya:	Tô, bā̀ ni shidà.	OK, give me six.
MSG:	Tô, kā̀wō kuɗī.	OK, give me the money (bring money).
Yàhàya:	Kinā̀ dà lḕmō?	Do you have any oranges?
MSG:	Ā'à̀, bābù.	No, there aren't (any).
Yàhàya:	Tô, sai an jumā̀.	All right, see you later.

Vocabulary

bā̀	v.tr.	'give'	kwabō n.m.	'kobo' (=about 1.6¢)
bà		imperative of bā̀	lḕmō n.m.	any citrus fruit
bābù	n.f.	'there isn't/aren't any'	màì sayad dà	'one who sells ...'
gwēbā̀	n.f.	'guava'	nawà	'how much?'
kā̀wō	v.tr.	'bring'	shidà	'six'
kàwō		imperative of kawō	ukù	'three'
kuɗī	n.pl.	'money'		

B. Yahaya wanders on a bit further and stops at a cigaret seller's (ɗan tēbùr)
table to buy some cigarets.

Yàhàya:	Àkwai Màì Zōbè?	Are there any Three Rings (possessor of the ring)?
ᵭan Tēbùr:	Ī, àkwai Màì Zōbè da Falâis da Fai-Fài. Gà̀ gōrò kuma.	Yes, there are Three Rings, Flight, and Five Five Fives. Here are kola nuts too.
Yàhàya:	Màì Zōbè nawà nawà nḕ?	How much are the Three Rings (per pack)?
DT:	Sulè sulè nḕ.	A shilling each.
Yàhàya:	Tô, kā̀wō gudā̀. Agōgonkà yanā̀ dà kyâu. Kàrfè nawà yànzu?	All right, give me (bring) one ... Your watch is very nice looking (Your watch is with beauty). What time is it now?
DT:	Yànzu karfè ukù dà rabī.	It's now 3:30.
Yàhàya:	Kâi! Nā̀ yi lattì! Ìnā̀ màì sayad dà kwàndō?	Wow! I'm late! Where is the basket seller?
DT:	Yanā̀ cân.	He's over there.

67

Vocabulary

àkwai	'there is/are'	gùdā n.m.	'a unit; one'
ɗan tēbùr n.m.	small goods salesman	kyâu n.m.	'beauty; goodness'
(ʼyan tebur pl.)	who has his wares on display on a table in the street or market	ƙarfè n.m.	'metal; o'clock'
Fai-fài n.m.	'Five Five Five's' - a fairly good quality cigaret	Mài Zōbè n.m.	'Three Rings' (possessor of the ring) - a very cheap brand of cigaret
Falâis n.m.	'Flight'- an inexpensive brand of cigaret	nā yi latti	'I (nā) have done (yi) lateness (latti)', i.e. 'I'm late'
gōrò n.m.	'kola nut(s)'	rabī n.m.	'half'
kâi!	'wow!'	sulè n.m.	'shilling'(=10 kobo)
kwàndō n.m. (kwandunā pl.)	'basket'	yànzu	'now'

C. Yahaya hurries to the basket seller, knowing the consequences if he does not get home quickly. On the other hand, he knows the consequences if he pays too much for the basket, so he is forced to bargain for it.

Yàhàya:	Nawà nē kwàndō?	How much for a basket?
Mài sayad dà kwàndō:	Sulè gōmà.	Ten shillings.
Yàhàya:	Kâi! Sunà dà tsàdā. Zân biyā kà sulè ukù.	Wow! They're expensive (they are with costliness). I'll give you three shillings.
MSK:	Àlbarkà.	No thanks! (expression indicating flat refusal to consider the offer)
Yàhàya:	Tô, gà sulè bìyar.	All right, here's five shillings.
MSK:	Tô, kàwō kuɗī.	OK, it's a deal (bring money).

Vocabulary

àlbarkà	'no thanks' (said by a dealer refusing an offer)	zân biyā kà	'I (nā) will pay (biyā) you (kà).'
bìyar	'five'	tsàdā n.f.	'expensiveness'
gōmà	'ten'		

GRAMMAR

6.1 Continuative Pronouns - 'have', 'be in a place'

The continuative pronouns are shown in the table which follows with the word nân 'here' (the reason for calling them 'continuative pronouns' will become evident in a later unit).

Singular		Plural	
inã nân	'I am here'	munã nân	'we are here'
kanã nân	'you (m) are here'	kunã nân	'you are here'
kinã nân	'you (f) are here'		
yanã nân	'he is here'	sunã nân	'they are here'
tanã nân	'she is here'		
anã nân	'one is here'		

Note: Each of these pronoun forms ends in the syllable -nã and from an analytical point of view this might best be considered a separate particle. However, the standard orthography represents the forms as shown above--minus tone and vowel length marking--and we have chosen to conform for pedagogical reasons.

We will be considering two uses of this set of pronouns in this unit:

a) In unit four we saw that one use of 'be' in English, i.e. 'be something/someone', was expressed by the identifier nē/cē. Another use of 'be' in English is to express 'being in a place', for example:

> he is here
>
> he is at home

This concept is expressed in Hausa with the continuative pronoun followed directly by the location. Examples are:

yanã cân	'he/it is over there'
Mammàn yanã gidã	'Mamman is at home'
sunã Kanò	'they are in Kano'

b) There is no verb 'to have' in Hausa. This concept is expressed by the continuative pronoun plus the preposition dà 'with' followed by a noun or one of the independent pronouns (4.2). Examples are:

yanã dà àlƙalàmī	'he has a pen'	tanã dà sū	'she has them'
yanã dà shī	'he has it'	Mammàn yanã dà rīgã	'Mamman has a gown'
tanã dà alƙalumã	'she has pens'	Mammàn yanã dà ita	'Mamman has it'

c) Continuative pronouns followed by nouns of quality are equivalent to the English construction is/are + predicate adjective, for example he is big/strong/fat, etc.. We find an example of this in Dialogue B in the sentence Sunã dà tsãdã, tsãdã being a noun of quality meaning 'expensiveness'. Although the sentence is an example of the 'have' construction discussed in 2), we will naturally translate it as 'they are expensive' rather than 'they have expensiveness'. Other examples of nouns of quality in this construction are:

girmã n.m.	'bigness'
bishiyã tanã dà girmã	'the tree is big'(the tree has bigness)

69

6.5 Telling time

The word for "o'clock" in Hausa is ƙarfè. The literal meaning of this word is 'metal', referring to gongs used in schools or on railroad work gangs to signal the time. The hours are expressed by ƙarfè plus the number indicating the hour.

ƙarfè ɗaya   'one o'clock'

ƙarfè biyu   'two o'clock'

ƙarfè gōmà   'ten o'clock'

The half hour is indicated by rabī 'half', the quarter hour by kwatà, other minutes by mintī.

ƙarfè ukù dà rabī   '3:30'

ƙarfè huɗu dà kwatà   '4:15'

ƙarfè biyar dà
     mintī biyar   '5:05'

If the time has passed the half hour, the word bâ 'without' can be used as we use 'til' in English.

ƙarfè ukù bâ kwatà   'quarter 'til three'

ƙarfè huɗu bâ mintī biyar   'five 'til four'

At this point you have only learned the numbers 1-10. Higher numbers, which will be introduced in the next unit, are applied to give time like 12 o'clock, 20 minutes after 1, etc. in the same way as 1-10.

'At' used in time expressions as in 'they came at three o'clock' is expressed in Hausa by dà.

munā makarantā dà ƙarfè takwàs   'we are at school at 8:00'

mutānē sun zō dà ƙarfè tarà dà rabī

                                        'the people came at 9:30'

GRAMMATICAL DRILLS

Drill 1 - Answer the questions by replacing the noun by the appropriate independent pronoun. If the question is in the first person, change it to the second person, if it is in the second person, change it to the first person.

Question: yanā dà kāyā?   Question: kanā dà gwēbà

Student response: Ī, yanā dà sū   Student response: Ī, inā dà ita

1. yanā dà kwabò?   7. yanā dà sulè?

2. kanā dà kwàndō?   8. kunā dà kwandunā?

3. kinā dà gwēbà?   9. sunā dà gōnā?

4. tanā dà tābà? (tābà n.f. 'cigarets, tobacco') 10. munā dà lèmō?

5. sunā dà littàttàfai?   11. tanā dà fensìr?

6. inā dà kuɗī?   12. kanā dà sulè?

72

Drill 2 - After hearing the cue sentence of the form màcè cḕ, form a new sentence with the continuative pronoun followed by dà kyâu, that is, tanā̀ da kyâu 'she is attractive/good'.

Cue sentence: mutā̀nē nḕ

Student response: sunā̀ dà kyâu

Cue sentence: takàrdā cḕ

Student response: tanā̀ dà kyâu

1. dā̀llbai nḕ   6. dáʼlìbⲦ nḕ
2. tēbùr nē   7. 'yam mātā nḕ
3. ƙōfā̀ cē   8. yārinyā̀ cē
4. mutā̀nē nḕ   9. Bàhaushḕ nē
5. fensìr nē   10. màcè cē

Drill 3 - You will recall that the Hausa construction, continuative pronoun plus dā̀ meaning 'have', when followed by a noun of quality, is best translated '...is good/beautiful/strong' etc. Keep this translation in mind while doing the following drill.

The cues are nouns designating some concrete object followed by some noun of quality. Using these cues, form sentences as illustrated in the example. This drill may be done with the books open so that you can see the cues.

Cue: kwandunā̀/tsā̀dā

Student response: kwandunā̀ sunā̀ dà tsā̀dā

1. bishiyā̀/girmā 'hugeness'   6. Kànde/ƙibā̀ 'fatness'
2. jàkā/tsā̀dā   7. gidā̀jē/girmā
3. àgōgo/kyâu   8. lḕmō/tsā̀dā
4. Bellò/ƙarfⲦ 'strength'   9. ƙōfā̀/kyâu
5. fensìr/àmfānⲦ 'usefulness'   10. Audù/ƙibā̀

Drill 4A - 4E - Use the cue questions of this drill for five different drills as explained in A - E.

4A Change the question of the form àkwai X? to a statement of the form àkwai followed by the direct object pronoun corresponding to X.

Cue question: àkwai kujḕrā?

Student response: àkwai tà

4B Change the question of the form àkwai X? to a negative statement of the form bābù X.

Cue question: àkwai kujḕrā?

Student response: bābù kujḕrā

4C Change the question of the form àkwai X? to a negative statement of the form bābù followed by the pronoun corresponding to X. Remember that after bābù the independent pronouns, not the direct object pronouns, are used.

Cue question: àkwai kujḕrā?

Student response: bābù ita

73

Drill 8 - Ask the question ƙarfè nawà yànzu? while pointing at one of
the illustrations below. Another student should supply the answer
yànzu ƙarfè (time).

Student 1: (pointing to picture) ƙarfè nawà yànzu?

Student 2: yànzu ƙarfè ukù

1.   2.   3.   4.   5.

6.   7.   8.   9.   10.

11.   12.   13.   14.   15.

Drill 9A - 9C - Repeat the initial sentence, then substitute the first
cue into the appropriate place in that sentence. As each cue is given,
substitute it into the sentence formed from the previous cue, so that
a new sentence is formed. (See Unit V, Drill 8 for example)

9A Initial Sentence: àkwai gwēbà

Cues	Student response
1. cân	àkwai gwēbà cân
2. à kàntT n.m. 'shop'	àkwai gwēbà (cân) à kàntT
3. bàbù	bàbù gwēbà (cân) à kàntT
4. tābà	bàbù tābà (cân) à kàntT
5. irT-irT	bàbù tābà irT-irT (cân) à kàntT
6. gà	gà tābà irT-irT (cân) à kàntT
7. àkwai	àkwai tābà irT-irT (cân) à kàntT

9B Initial Sentence: kwabò kwabò nē

1. gōrò	gōrò kwabò kwabò nē
2. à kàsuwā	gōrò kwabò kwabò nē à kàsuwā
3. nawà nawà	gōrò nawà nawà nē à kàsuwā?
4. wajen ɗan tēbùr	gōrò nawà nawà nē wajen ɗan tēbùr? (wajen 'at' used
5. Mài Zōbè	Mài Zōbè nawà nawà nē wajen ɗan tēbùr? with persons)
6. sulè sulè	Mài Zōbè sulè sulè nē wajen ɗan tēbùr
7. à kàntT	Mài Zōbè sulè sulè nē à kàntT.

9C Initial Sentence: sunà nân

1. kàsuwā	sunà kàsuwā
2. mutànē	mutànē sunà kàsuwā
3. yàrà	yàrà sunà kàsuwā
4. makarantā	yàrà sunà makarantā
5. dà ʄarfè tarà	yàrà sunà makarantā dà ʄarfè tarà
6. takwàs	yàrà sunà makarantā dà ʄarfè takwàs
7. màlàm	màlàm yanà makarantā dà ʄarfè takwàs
8. dà rabT	màlàm yanà makarantā dà ʄarfè takwàs da rabT

77

PRONUNCIATION REVIEW

I. Tone Identification - On a sheet of paper, number from 1 to 25. Listen to the following words and write on your paper what the tone pattern is using H for high, L for low, and F for falling. For example, when you hear the word k̄ōfā, you should write HL.

1. kāyā	'load'	9. ruwā	'water'	18. àbù	'thing'
2. rīgā	'gown'	10. kûnnē	'ear'	19. kwàd̄ō	'frog'
3. lâifT	'fault'	11. tsòrō	'fear'	20. fushT	'anger'
4. yàushè	'when'	12. yārò	'boy'	21. habâ	'chin'
5. gidā	'compound'	13. màcè	'woman'	22. yârā	'children'
6. mùtûm	'person'	14. k̄ùrā	'dust'	23. barcT	'sleeping'
7. k̄afâ	'foot'	15. tsuntsū	'bird'	24. fùrē	'flower'
8. kàrē	'dog'	16. k̄yûyā	'laziness'	25. k̄ōfâ	'doorway'
		17. gāshT	'hair'		

Reproduction Drill - When you have corrected your paper, listen to the words again, repeating each after your informant.

II. Question Intonation - Listen to your informant repeat each of the following sentences. As he repeats each one, make it into a question by repeating the same sentence with question intonation. Correct your pronunciation as the informant repeats the question. Don't be satisfied by simply raising your voice to a higher pitch at the end of the sentence. Rather, note carefully on which syllable your informant raises his voice.

1. yanā dà tsādā
2. àkwai lēmō nân
3. tanā dà sulè
4. waccàn tāgā cē
5. kanā dà mōtà.
6. wannàn littāfī nē
7. yanā dà kwandunā
8. àkwai sulè hud̃u

9. tanā dà kujērā
10. Abdù yanā nân
11. yanā k̄àrk̄ashin tēbùr
12. bābù k̄àsuwā à gàrT
13. Bàtūrè yanā dà shT
14. yā bā kà sulè ukù
15. àkwai lēmō à kàntT

GUIDED CONVERSATION

1) A market situation may be set up with one student taking the part of a buyer, the other of a seller. Choose small items that would reasonably be priced below 10 shillings, for example, cigarets (in West Africa, a a d̃an tēbùr will even have a pack of cigarets open so that single cigarets can be sold), fruit (plastic fruit can be brought to class), pencils or pens, etc.

   Bargaining will be treated again more extensively in a later unit, so these conversations here should be kept very simple and short, being restricted to the expressions in the dialogues. The students should know beforehand pretty much what they are going to say as to prices and exact form the bargaining will take.

Example conversations:

a) The seller will quote a price much too high, creating the situation
   where the buyer will object to the expense.

Buyer:	Nawà nē lēmō?	How much are the oranges?
Seller:	Biyu sulè nē.	Two for a shilling.
Buyer:	Kâi! Sunà dà tsàdā! Zân biyā kà kwabō bakwài.	Wow! They're expensive. I'll give you 7 kobo.
Seller:	Àlbarkà.	No thanks.
Buyer:	Tô, gà kwabò gōmà.	OK, here's 10 pence.
Seller:	Tô, kāwō kudī.	OK, give (me) the money.

b) The buyer is shopping around to find out prices of various items
   before buying.

Buyer:	Nawà nawà nē àyàbà?	How much are the bananas.
Seller:	Biyu kwabō biyar.	Two for 5 kobo.
Buyer:	Gwēbà fà?	How about guavas?
Seller:	Uku kwabò.	Three for a penny.
Buyer:	Tô, bà ni gwēbà shidà.	OK, give me six guavas.

) Using a cardboard clockface with adjustable hands (or if you don't have one,
a piece of paper with a circle on it and pencils for clock hands), the
teacher, informant of another student can make different times and a second
student give the times indicated.

Also, the teacher or informant can give times in Hausa, and a student
can form the times using the clock face. In this unit, times using numbers
above 10 should be avoided.

79

UNIT VII

DIALOGUES

Malam Abubakar is a census taker in the Katsina area. In the village of Doro, he arrives at Malam Sa'idu's compound where he asks about the people living there and the extent of Malam Sa'idu's livestock (which are counted for purposes of taxation).

Àbūbakàr:	Kū nawà nē à gidā?	How many of you live here (you are how many in the compound?)
Sà'Tdù:	Mū bakwài nē.	There are seven of us. (We are seven.)
Àbūbakàr:	Yârankà nawà?	How many children do you have? (Your children are how many?)
Sà'Tdù:	Yârana sun kai bìyar.	There are five children. (My children reach five.)
Àbūbakàr:	Bàbù tsōhonkà à nân?	Your father isn't here?
Sà'Tdù:	Ī, bābù. Sai nī dà uwargidā dà yârā.	No, he's not. Just me, the wife, and the kids.
Àbūbakàr:	Kanà da tumākT nawà?	How many sheep do you have?
Sà'Tdù:	Ai, sun kai wajen shâ biyu.	Well, there are about 12. (Well, they reach about twelve.)
Àbūbakàr:	Ìnā su kè?	Where are they?
Sà'Tdù:	Gâ ƙu cân bāyaŋ wancàn dâkT. Àkwai zàbT dà kâjT cikin dâkìn kumā.	There they are behind that hut. There are guinea fowl and chickens in the hut as well.

Vocabulary

gidā n.m. (gidājē pl.)	'compound'		tsōhō n.m. (tsôfàffT or tsòffT pl.)	'old man; father'
kai v.tr.	'reach, attain'		tunkìyā n.f. (tumākT pl.)	'sheep'
kāzā n.f. (kâjT pl.)	'chicken'		uwargidā n.f.	'first (or only) wife'
kumā adv.	'as well, morcover'		wajen	'about'
sai prep.	'only, just'		zàbō ŋ.m. (pl. zàbT)	'guinea fowl'

Having completed the census taking, Malam Abubakar notes that Malam Sa'idu is wearing an exceptionally fine rīgā. Being surprised that one might buy such a rīgā in a village the size of Doro, he asks where Malam Sa'idu might have gotten it.

Àbūbakàr:	Rīgarkà tanà dà kyâu.	Your gown is very beautiful.
Sà'Tdù:	Hakà nē.	That it is.
Àbūbakàr:	Ìnā akà ɗinkà ta?	Where was it sewn? (Where did one sew it?)

81

It is extremely important that you pronounce these with proper tones and vowel length, for if you don't, the sentence could mean something entirely different from what you have in mind.

In this unit we have seen several examples of the completive aspect. In all cases the action can be interpreted as having been completed, even though the time of reference is not in the past.

nā kāwō rīgā dàgà Kàtsinà   'I brought the gown from Katsina'

yârā sun kai bìyar   'there are five children' (lit: the
                                   children have reached five)

7.3 Relative Completive and Relative Continuative

Corresponding to the continuative pronouns given in 6.1 and the Completive Aspect pronouns given in 7.2 there are two further pronoun sets which we will call the "Relative Continuative" and the "Relative Completive". The Relative Continuative is illustrated with īnā 'where?', the Relative Completive with īnā and the verb tàfi 'go'.

Relative Continuative

Singular		Plural	
īnā na kè (or ni kè)?	'where am I?'	īnā mu kè?	'where are we?'
īnā ka kè?	'where are you?'(m)	īnā ku kè?	'where are you?'
īnā ki kè?	'where are you?'(f)		
īnā ya kè?	'where is he?'	īnā su kè?	'where are they?'
īnā ta kè?	'where is she?'		
īnā a kè?	'where is one?'		

The element kè here is parallel in function to -nà in the continuative paradigm of 6.1. In conformity to the standard orthography used in most published literature, we are writing kè separated from the pronoun but -nà attached to it.[1]

Relative Completive

Singular		Plural	
īnā na tàfi?	'where did I go?'	īnā mukà tàfi?	'where did we go?'
īnā ka tàfi?	'where did you go?'(m)	īnā kukà tàfi?	'where did you go?'
īnā kikà tàfi?	'where did you go?'(f)		
īnā ya tàfi?	'where did he go?'	īnā sukà tàfi?	'where did they go'
īnā ta tàfi?	'where did she go?'		
īnā akà tàfi?	'where did one go?'		

[1] The element kè seen in the paradigm has a short vowel at the end of a sentence, that is, the phrases in the paradigm are pronounced, īnā ya kè?, etc. If anything follows, kè has a long vowel, for example wā ya kè nan? 'who is here?'.

The Relative forms of the subject pronouns are used in place of the corresponding pronouns of 6.1 and 7.2 in certain grammatical environments. One such environment is in a question WHEN A QUESTION WORD COMES AT THE BEGINNING OF THE SENTENCE.

but	ìnā akà ɗinkà ta?	'where was it sewn?'
	an ɗinkà ta à Kàtsinà	'it was sewn in Katsina'
but	mē sukà kāwō?	'what did they bring?'
	sun kāwō rīgā	'they brought a gown'
but	wā ya yi aikī?	'who did work?'
	Abūbakàr yā yi aikī	'Abubakar did work'
but	ìnā su kè?	'where are they?'
	sunà nân	'they are here'
but	wā ya kè cikin ɗâkī?	'who's in the hut?'
	Sà'īdù yanà cikin ɗâkī	'Sa'idu is in the hut'

Another use of the Relative forms is illustrated in the sentence

à can akà yī tà   'one made it there/it was there that
                      one made it'

of Dialogue B of this Unit. It is a very common practice in Hausa to emphasize some part of a sentence by placing it at the beginning of the sentence. When a word or phrase is emphasized in this way, the Relative form must be used if the sentence is in the Completive or Continuative. This "fronting" locution is similar to our way of stressing some part of a sentence by using "it was so and so that ... ", for example, 'It was in Katsina that I bought it', etc., but in Hausa this locution tends to be used more frequently than the corresponding English one.

At this stage only the use of the Relative form after question words will be stressed, but keep your ears open for the usage after emphasized constructions too, and try to develop a "feel" for them.

7.4 Wannàn, wancàn, etc. as Demonstrative Adjectives

In 5.2, the use of the words wannàn, wancàn, and their corresponding feminine and plural forms as demonstrative pronouns was explained. These words can be used as demonstrative adjectives to modify nouns as well. When used this way, they directly precede the noun they modify and must agree with it in number and gender.

bāyan wancàn ɗâkī   'behind that hut'

an ɗinkà wannàn rīgā à Kàtsinà   'this gown was sewn in Katsina'

waɗànnân kwandunā nawà nawà nē?   'how much are these baskets each?'

7.5 dà Meaning 'and'

Dà can be used between nouns (never between verbs or sentences) to mean 'and'. If there are more than two nouns in a series, dà is usually placed between all nouns. If the series of nouns stands at the very beginning of a sentence, dà may appear before the first noun as well.

85

sai nī dà uwargidā dà yârā mu kè nan   'only me, the wife, and kids
                                              are here'

nā kāwō tēbùr dà kujērā dà littāfī   'I brought a table, a chair,
                                             and a book'

dà nī dà kai dà shī, mū àbōkai nè   'he, you, and I, we are friends'

Note that when the first person singular appears as one of a series, it
is always the first mentioned.

7.6 Use of an 'one'

In the aspect pronoun paradigms of 6.1, 7.2, and 7.3, we find the
pronoun forms anā, an, akà, and a kè which have been translated as 'one'.
These pronouns are used in a way very similar to the French on or the German
man to denote what is often expressed by the passive or the impersonal
"they" in English as in 'they say the moon is made of green cheese.'

        an ɗinkà rīgā à Kàtsinà   'the gown was sewn at Katsina'

        an kirā shì   'he was called'

Though sentences using an, etc. often correspond to English passives,
they are also frequently used where it would be difficult to give a passive
rendering in English, as with intransitive verbs.

        an tàfi jiyà   'one left yesterday', "there
                                    was a departure yesterday"

      anā nân   'one is here', "people/someone
                                    are/is here"

Finally, note that with 'one' in English, we can say 'one' in the
first clause of a sentence and then use 'he' in the second clause to
refer to 'one', for example "one must study a lot if he hopes to learn
Hausa well." This is not possible in Hausa. If an is used in the first
clause, a form of an must also be used in the second clause.

        in anā dà rīgā, anā sâ ta   'if one has a gown, he (one) puts it on'
It would have been entirely wrong to have said yanā sâ ta in the second clause.

7.7 'Yes' and 'no' Answers to Questions

Answers to negative questions in Hausa (and other African languages)
are a source of confusion to European students since the procedure is
opposite from European languages. When asked a question such as 'didn't
you do your work?', the Hausa answer is ī 'yes' if he did not do the work,
i.e. 'yes, (what you say is correct) I did not do it.' Likewise, if he did
do his work, he would answer in Hausa ā'à 'no', i.e. 'no, (what you say is
wrong) I did do it.'

      Q: bābù tsōhonkà à nân?   'isn't your father here?'

      A: ī, bābù   'no, he isn't' (yes, it's true that
                                      he isn't here)

      Q: wannàn bā zābō ba nè?   'isn't that a guinea fowl?'

      A: ā'à   'on the contrary' (it is a guinea fowl)

7.8 Numbers 11-20

The numbers 11-19 are formed by adding gōmà shâ or simply shâ before the numbers 1-9 (see 6.4).

11. (gōmà) shâ ɗaya	16. (gōmà) shâ shidà
12. (gōmà) shâ biyu	17. (gōmà) shâ bakwài
13. (gōmà) shâ ukù	18. (gōmà) shâ takwàs
14. (gōmà) shâ huɗu	19. (gōmà) shâ tarà
15. (gōmà) shâ biyar	20. àshìrin

An alternative way of saying 18 and 19 is to say "twenty minus two" and "twenty minus one" using the word bābù in the following way:

18. àshìrin biyu bābù

19. àshìrin ɗaya bābù

The student is advised to use the pattern preferred by his informant for these two numbers.

As with the numbers 1-10 (and all higher numbers as well), the numbers 11-20 always directly follow the noun they modify and the noun is usually in the singular.

GRAMMATICAL DRILLS

Drill 1 - Answer the questions as in the example.

Question:	kā zō lāfiyà?
Student response:	Ī, nā zō lāfiyà

1. kin zo?		6. kā tàfi Kanò?	'go'
2. kā kāwō kuɗī?		7. nā yi wannàn?	
3. sun yi aikī?		8. mun kāwō kāzā?	
4. yā ɗinkà rīgā?		9. tā tàfi gàrī?	
5. an yī tà à Kàtsinà?		10. kun yi aikī?	

Drill 2 - You will be given a pattern sentence in the completive aspect followed by a series of cue words. If the cue is an independent pronoun, simply substitute the corresponding completive aspect pronoun in the pattern sentence. If the cue is a noun, use it as the subject of the pattern sentence. (Of course, if the subject of the sentence is a noun, you must still use an appropriate completive aspect pronoun.)

Pattern sentence:	an zō jiyà
Cue 1:	nī
Student response:	nā zō jiyà
Cue 2:	Mammàn
Student response:	Mammàn yā zō jiyà

Pattern sentence: an zō lāfiyà

Cues:	1. nī	3. Àli	5. sū	7. kē	9. mātā
	2. kai	4. mùtûm	6. mutànē	8. Hàdīzà	10. mū

87

Repeat the drill using the same cues with the following pattern sentences:

an tàfi Kanò   an kāwō kāyā

an ɗinkà rīgunā̀   an yi aikī̀

Drill 3A - 3D (Drills on Relative forms)

3A Example: Cue: àkwai lìttàttàfai

                  Student response: inā̄ su kè?

1. àkwai ɗàkī	6. àkwai kà̀jī
2. àkwai kàzā	7. àkwai gàrī
3. àkwai fensìr	8. àkwai rīgā
4. àkwai takàrdā	9. àkwai lèmō
5. àkwai ɗàlìbai	10. àkwai kwàndō ukù

3B Use the appropriate relative form in the response mḕ ___ kāwō?
'what did ___ bring?'. Substitute second person for first and first for
second.

                Cue: Àli yanà̀ nân

                Student response: mḕ ya kāwō?

1. mài gidā yanà̀ nân	6. munà̀ nân
2. yā̂rā sunà̀ nân	7. kunà̀ nân
3. inà̀ nân	8. sunà̀ nân
4. uwargidā tanà̀ nân	9. kanà̀ nân
5. kinà̀ nân	10. ɗan tēbùr yanà̀ nân

3C Answer the cue questions with the sentence ___ kāwō tà dàgà Kàtsinà[1]
'___ brought it from Katsina.'

                Cue: dàgà ìnā mài gidā ya kāwō rīgā?

                Student response: yā kāwō tà dàgà Kàtsinà

1. dàgà ìnā ya kāwō takàrdā?	6. dàgà ìnā Yàhàya ya kāwō tābà̄?
2. dàgà ìnā na kāwō rīgā?	7. dàgà ìnā mukà kāwō mōtā̀?
3. dàgà ìnā mātā sukà kāwō kàzā?	8. dàgà ìnā ta kāwō kàzā?
4. dàgà ìnā akà kāwō tunkìyā?	9. dàgà ìnā mutànē sukà kāwō rīgā?
5. dàgà ìnā ka kāwō gwēbà̄?	10. dàgà ìnā kikà kāwō tunkìyā?

---

[1]A more idiomatic and natural answer would be to put dàgà Kàtsinà at the
beginning of the sentence, retaining the Relative Completive, so you may
want to practice it this way as well. Note that when we answer a question
word in English, we stress the word which corresponds to the question
word, for example in answer to the question 'where did he bring the gown from?',
we would stress the place where he brought it from in the answer, that is,
'he brought it from <u>Katsina</u>.' Hausa does this by fronting, as explained in
7.3.

3D Answer the cue question with ___ -nā̀ nân using the appropriate continuative pronouns.

Cue: ìnā Àli ya kề?

Student response: yanā̀ nân

1. ìnā Maryamà ta kề?
2. ìnā dàlibai su kề?
3. ìnā ka kề?
4. ìnā dàkī ya kề?
5. ìnā mu kề?
6. ìnā rīgā ta kề?
7. ìnā na kề?
8. ìnā a kề?
9. ìnā ki kề?
10. ìnā ku kề?

Drill 4 - Each of the following cue sentences has a demonstrative adjective wannàn, wancàn, etc. If the adjective is one of the -nan forms, change it to the corresponding -can form, it is is a -can form, change it to a -nan form.

Cue: nā kāwō wannàn kujềrā

Student response: nā kāwō waccàn kujềrā

Cue: wadànnân tākalmā̀ sunā̀ dà kyâu

Student response: wadàncân tākalmā̀ sunā̀ dà kyâu

1. kā dinkà wannàn rīgā?
2. yā ƙirgà wadàncân kājī 'count'
3. nawà nē wannàn zàbō?
4. kā kāwō wadànnân kāyā?
   n.pl. 'goods, baggage'
5. mālàm yā yankà wannàn kàzā
   'slaughter'
6. wadàncân tumākī sun kai wajen gōmà
7. àkwai kājī cikin wannàn dàkī
8. waccàn jàkā tanā̀ dà kyâu
9. gà àgōgo à wannàn kàntī
10. wadànnân zàbī sun kai wajen gōmà

Drill 5 - Answer the question kū nawà nē à gidā? with the pattern sentence mū ... nē, supplying the numbers below into the blank.

1. 19
2. 8
3. 12
4. 14
5. 11
6. 17
7. 14
8. 7
9. 16
10. 8
11. 15
12. 20

Drill 6A and 6B - Do this drill twice. The cues are all negative questions. The first time answer by Ī 'that's right' followed by the negative changed to a statement.

6A Cue: wannàn bà zàbō ba nề? 'isn't this a guinea fowl?'

Student response: Ī, bà zàbō ba nề   'no, it's not a guinea fowl'

Cue: bābù gwēbā̀?   'aren't there any guavas?'

Student response: Ī, bābù   'no, there aren't'

The second time, answer the question by ā'ā̀ 'on the contrary' followed by the appropriate affirmative statement.

6B Cue: wannàn bà zàbō ba nề? 'isn't this a guinea fowl?'

Student response: ā'ā̀, zàbō nē   'on the contrary, it is a guinea fowl'

Cue: bābù gwēbā̀?   'aren't there any guavas?'

Student response: ā'ā̀, àkwai   'on the contrary, there are'

89

Cues:

1. wannàn bā rīgā ba cē?
2. bābù tābā?
3. wadànnân bā tumākī ba nē?
4. waccàn bā ƙōfā̀ ba cē?
5. bābu tsōhonkà à nân?

6. wannàn gàrī bā Kàtsinà ba nē?
7. wadànnân bā tākalmā̀ ba nē?
8. bābù kājī cikin dàkī?
9. bābù lèmō à kàsuwā?
10. wannàn bā kujērā ba cē?

Drill 7 - From the sentences of the form nā zō tàre dà Audù 'I came with Audu' (tàre dà 'together with' must be used when talking about one person accompanying another), construct sentences of the form dà nī dà Audù munà nân.

Cue: Audù yā zō tàre dà Hasàn

Student response: dà Audù dà Hasàn sunà̀ nân

1. yā zō tàre dà ita
2. nā zō tàre dà tsōhō
3. Hàlīmà tā zō tàre dà Maryamà
4. uwargidā tā zō tàre dà yầrā
5. tā zō tàre dà Shēhù

6. kun zō tàre dà ita
7. nā zō tàre dà Sà'īdù dà Garbà
8. Fàti tā zō tàre dà Kànde dà Aishà
9. Mammàn yā zō tàre dà yầrā
10. nā zō tàre dà kai dà Mammàn

Drill 8 - Give the correct answers to the following arithmetic problems as illustrated in the example.

Question: takwàs dà takwàs nawà kḕ nan? (8 + 8 = ?)

Student response: takwàs dà takwàs shầ shidà kḕ nan (8 + 8 = 16)

1. 2 + 11 = ?
2. 8 + 7 = ?
3. 12 + 6 = ?
4. 10 + 7 = ?
5. 9 + 8 = ?

6. 13 + 3 = ?
7. 7 + 7 = ?
8. 6 + 6 = ?
9. 12 + 8 = ?
10. 9 + 10 = ?

Drill 9 - Answer the questions of the type kunà̀ dà X? with the pattern sentence Ī, nā kāwō shi/tà/sù dàgà Kàtsinà as shown in the example.

Cue: yanà̀ dà rīgā?

Student response: Ī, yā kāwō tà dàgà Kàtsinà

Cue: kunà̀ dà akwātunà̀?

Student response: Ī, mun kāwō sù dàgà Kàtsinà

1. sunà̀ dà mōtà?
2. kunà̀ dà rīgunà̀?
3. yanà̀ dà tākalmà̀?
4. kunà̀ dà kwàndō?
5. kunà̀ dà lìttàttàfai?

6. tanà̀ dà tagùwā?
7. kunà̀ dà àgōgo
8. sunà̀ dà kwàndō?
9. tanà̀ dà jakunkunà̀?
10. yanà̀ dà àkwiyā̀?

90

Drill 10A and 10B - Repeat the initial sentence, then substitute the first cue into the appropriate place in that sentence. As each cue is given, substitute it into the sentence formed from the previous cue, so that a new sentence is formed.

10A __Initial sentence:__ yârā nawà à nân?

Cues	Student response
1. tumākī	tumākī nawà à nân?
2. wajen bìyar	tumākī wajen bìyar à nân
3. à bāyan ɗākī	tumākī wajen bìyar à bāyan ɗākī
4. gōmà shâ bìyar	tumākī wajen gōmà shâ bìyar à bāyan ɗākī
5. wancàn ɗākī	tumākī wajen gōmà shâ bìyar à bāyan wancàn ɗākī
6. cikin wancàn ɗākī	tumākī wajen gōmà shâ bìyar cikin wancàn ɗākī
7. sū	(tumākī,) sū wajen gōmà shâ bìyar cikin wancàn ɗākī

10B __Initial Sentence:__	rīgā tanā dà tsādā
1. kyâu	rìgā tanā dà kyâu
2. yārinyà	yārinyà tanā dà kyâu
3. mùtûm	mùtûm yanā dà kyâu
4. dà rīgā	mùtûm yanā dà rīgā
5. yā ɗinkà	mùtûm yā ɗinkà rīgā
6. kāwō	mùtûm yā kāwō rīgā
7. dàgà Kàtsinà	mùtûm yā kāwō rīgā dàgà Kàtsinà
8. dàgà cân	mùtûm yā kāwō rīgā dàgà cân
9. kāwō tà	mùtûm yā kāwō tà dàgà cân

PRONUNCIATION REVIEW

__Consonant Identification__ - On a sheet of paper make two columns, one labelled glottalized consonant (i.e. ɓ, ɗ, ƙ, ts), the other plain (i.e. b, d, k, s). Listen to the following words and put the number of the word in one column of the other depending on whether the word contains a glottalized consonant or not.

1. fadà	'quarreling'	10. tsōhō	'old man'	19. dōyà	'cassava'
2. kāmà	'catch'	11. bàra	'last year'	20. biyā	'pay'
3. sàmù	'get'	12. ƙōfà	'doorway'	21. kirà	'calling'
4. lēɓè	'lip'	13. ɓōyè	'hide'	22. ɗarī	'coldness'
5. tādī	'conversation'	14. tudù	'hill'	23. yàtsà	'finger'
6. nīsā	'distant'	15. ƙàfō	'horn'	24. hakà	'like that'
7. ƙafà	'foot'	16. bāwà	'slave'	25. haɓà	'chin'
8. sàyā	'buy'	17. ɗùmī	'sound of voices'		
9. fàda	'emir's palace'	18. tsayà	'stop'		

__Reproduction Drill__ - After correcting your paper, listen to each word again and repeat after your informant.

GUIDED CONVERSATION

1) Using the expression found in dialogue A of this unit, one student may
   ask another about things he has in the classroom.

Student 1:	Kanà dà littāfì nawà à nân?	How many books do you have here?
Student 2:	Sai littāfì biyu.	Only two books.
Student 1:	Bābù àl̃kalàmì?	No pens?
Student 2:	Ì, sai fensìr ukù.	That's right, just three pencils.
Student 1:	Àkwai kuɗì dà yawà cikin wannàn jàkā, kō?	There's a lot of money in this (hand)bag, isn't there?
Student 2:	Kâi! Bābù!	Ha! There's none!

Alternatively, a hypothetical situation can be set up where one student
visits another at his house and asks about his family. If there is a good
artist in the class, a Hausa compound similar to the accompanying illustration
might be sketched on the blackboard and one student might take the role of
mài gidā and another ask him about his compound, family, etc.

92

2) One student may compliment another on some personal article of his,
for example some article of clothing, a handbag, etc.

Student 1: Tākalmànkà sunā̀ dà   Your shoes are very attractive.
            kyâu.

Student 2: Hakà ŋē, àmmā sunā̀   Right, but they were expensive.
            dà tsādā.

Student 1: Nawà nē?   How much?

Student 2: Bàn sanī̀ ɓa.   I don't know.
            Wajen dālā̀ àshìrin.   About $20.

Student 1: Tô, bâ lâifī.   Well, there's nothing wrong with that.

3) One student may ask another to cout various objects around the classroom
by asking such questions as

                ɗàlìbī nawà nē à nân?

                tāgā̀ nawà nē cikin wannàn ɗākī?

                kujèrā nawà nē bāyan tēbùr?

You may find it useful to count the things out loud so as to become
more familiar with the numbers in sequence.

DIALOGUES

A. Hasan/Halima has just bought a hoe/wooden spoon at the market. On his/her way home he/she passes through an area on the edge of the market where there are many small sheds. These serve as shops for small goods vendors. Here one can purchase everything from can openers to home-made kerosene lamps. Suddenly Hasan's/Halima's friend Mudi/Mero, a hardware vendor, calls out.

Mūdi/Mēro:	Sànnu dà zuwā Hasàn/HàlTmà!	Welcome Hasan/Halima!
Hasàn/HàlTmà:	Sànnu dai. Yàyā cinikT?	Hello. How's business?
M:	Alhamdù lìllāhT! Kā/Kin ci kāsuwā?	Thanks be to God. Have you been to the market?
H:	T, fartanyātā/ƙoshiyātā tā karyē., Gā sābuwā nân. Nā jē wajen STdì ammā bā shi dà ita.	Yes, my hoe/spoon broke. Here's a new one. I went to Sidi's place, but he didn't have one.
M:	Bābu wajensà?!	He didn't have any?! (There were none at his place)
H:	NT mā nā yi mạ̄mākT. Kullum yanā dà ita. Kâi wuƙàƙenkà/kì sunā dà kyâu.	I was really surprised. He always has it (in stock). Hey, your knives are nice (with goodness).
M:	Hakà nē. Kanā/kinā sô?	That's right. Do you want (one of them)?
H.	T, àmmā bâ ni dà kudT yànzu. Bàri sai an jumā.	Yes, but I don't have any money now. Better wait till later.
M:	Tô, sàuka lāfiyà.	OK, arrive safely.
H:	Āmin.	Amen.

Vocabulary

àmmā	'but'		kullum	'always'
barT	v.tr.	'to leave'	mā	(after a noun or pronoun)
bari		imperative of barT - often translated as "better to ...", "why not ...?"		'as for'
			māmakT	n.m. 'surprise'
			yi māmakT	'be surprised'
ci	v.tr.	'eat'	sābuwā	adj.f. 'new (one)'
ci kāsuwā		'do marketing'	(sābō m., sàbabbT/sàbbT pl.)	
fartanyā	n.f.	'hoe'	sàuka	v.intr. 'get down, arrive (at a place to stay)'
(fartanyōyT pl.)				
jē	v.intr.	'go'	sô	v.n.m. 'wanting'
karyē	v.intr.	'break, snap in two' (a stick, etc.)	wajē	n.m. 'place, direction'
ƙoshiyā	n.f.	'large, wooden spoon'	wuƙā	n.f. 'knife'
(ƙoshiyōyT pl.)			(wuƙàƙē pl.)	

B. Abdu is sitting in front of his compound when he notices his friend Lawali trudging by, his eyes fixed on the ground.

Abdù:	Inā gaisuwā, Lawàli.	I greet you Lawali.
Lawàli:	Yâuwā, sànnu.	Greetings.
Abdù:	Kanā lāfiyà?	Are you well?
Lawàli:	Wàllāhì! Bā ni dà lāfiyà!	Ohhh man! I'm not so well (I am not with health)!
Abdù:	Mè ya sāmē kà?	What's wrong (what has taken you)?
Lawàli:	Inā cīwòn kâi don nā yi aikī dà yawà jiyà.	My head aches (I'm aching of head) because I worked hard yesterday.
Abdù:	Aikìn mè ka yi?	What work (work of what) did you do?
Lawàli:	Mânyan mōtōcī sun zō dàgà Jàs cìke dà ƙayan àbinci. Nā saukè dōyā dà yawà dàgà mōtōcîn.	Some trucks (big cars) came from Jos full of foodstuffs. I unloaded a lot of yams from the trucks.
Abdù:	Lallē, aikìn nan yanā dà wuyā.	That work is really hard (for sure that work is with difficulty).
Lawàli:	Gàskiyā nè. Duk nā gàji.	That's true. I'm all tired out.
Abdù:	Allàh yà bā kà lāfiyà.	May God give you good health.
Lawàli:	Āmin.	Amen.

Vocabulary

cìke (dà)	'full (of)'	lallē	'for sure'
cīwò n.m.	'pain, illness'	mânyā adj.pl.	'big (ones)'
cīwòn kâi	'headache'	mânyan mōtōcī	'trucks' (big "cars")
dōyā n.f.	'yam(s)'	don/dòmin	'because'
duk/dukà	'all; completely'	sāmē	from sāmu v.tr. 'get, obtain, take'
gaisuwā n.f.	'greeting'	mè ya sāmē kà	"what's the matter with you?"
gàskiyā n.m.	'truth'		
jiyà	'yesterday'	wàllāhì	'by God" (exclamation to stress truth of somethin
kâi n.m. (kāwunà pl.)	'head'		
		wuyā n.f.	'difficulty'
saukè v.tr	'unload'	yawà n.m.	'abundance'
		dà yawà	'a lot, much, many'

COMPREHENSION PRACTICE

Without looking at your books, listen to the passage as you informant reads it through once, pausing to explain (in Hausa) the meaning of any new words or expressions. Your informant will read through the passage a second time at normal conversational speed and then ask you the oral questions which follow. Answer in complete sentences in Hausa.

Mèro à Kàsuwā

Jiyà nā ga[1] Mèro à kàsuwā. Tā ci kàsuwā. Ƙòshiyàrtà tā karyè.
Tā jē wajen STdì àmmā bâ shi dà ita. Mèro tā yi màmākì don kullum
yanà dà ita. Bāyan tā jē wajen STdì tā zō kàsuwā. Can àkwai ƙòshiyōyT
dà yawà. Tā sàyā². Nā ga sābuwar ƙòshiyàrtà. Ita kuma, tā gá wuƙàƙēnā
sunà dà kyâu. Tanà sô àmmā bâ ta dà kudT. Sabò dà³ hakà tā barT sai
an jumà.

[1] ga   v.tr.   'see' (form used before nouns); before pronouns
                  one uses gan, and when no object follows, ganT
                  (see question 7)

²sàyā   v.tr.   'buy'   tā sàyā   'she bought (one)'
³sabò dà   'because (of)'   sabò dà hakà   'because of that'

TambayōyT

1. Yàushè na ga Mèro à kàsuwā?   yàushè?   'when'
2. Tā ci kàsuwā, kō?
3. STdì yanà dà ƙòshiyà?
4. Don mè Mèro ta yi màmākT?
5. Bāyan Mèro tā jē wajen STdì, ìnā ta jē?
6. Àkwai ƙòshiyà à kàsuwā?
7. Mè Mèro ta ganT à wajēna?   (see note 1 above)
8. Don mè Mèro ta barT sai an jumà?

Aikìn Lawàli

NT Lawàli nē. Yànzu duk nā gàji.   Ìnā ciwòn kâi don nā yi aikT
dà yawà à kàsuwa. Jiyà nā jē kàsuwā nā ga mōtōcT cìke dà dōyà. Sun zō
dàgà Jàs. Nā saukè kāyan àbinci dàgà mōtōcìn. Lallē aikìn nan yanà dà
wùyā!

TambayōyT

1. Lawàli yanà làfiyà?
2. Mè ya sàmē shi?
3. Don mè Lawàli ya kè ciwòn kâi?
4. Mè Lawàli ya yi à kàsuwā?
5. Dàgà ìnā mōtōcìn sukà zo?
6. Lawàli yā saukè kāyan àbinci dàgà mōtōcìn?
7. Yàyà aikìn nan ya kè?

97

GRAMMAR

8.1 Negative of the Continuative Pronouns

The continuative pronouns (see 5.1) have a special negative form. The complete paradigm is shown below.

Singular		Plural	
bā nà̃	'I am not ...'	bā mà̃/mwà̃/mũ̀	'we are not ...'
bā kà̃	'you(m) are not ...'	bā kwà̃/kũ̀	'you are not ...'
bā kyà̃	'you(f) are not ...'		
bā yà̃	'he is not ...'	bā sà̃/swà̃/sũ̀	'they are not ...'
bā tà̃	'she is not ...'		
bā ã̀	'one is not ...'		

A few examples of these forms in sentences are:

bā mà̃ dà arzikī̃	'we don't have wealth'
bā yà̃ nân	'he isn't here'
bā sà̃ gidā	'they aren't at home'

The forms listed above exemplify Kano Hausa, which has been chosen as "standard" Hausa. This is the dialect set forth in this book, but you should be aware of other versions of this paradigm that are commonly used, even within Kano. One frequently used variant of these forms, normally used with dà to form the "have" construction, is the following. Note that the pronouns here are exactly like the direct object pronouns (see 4.5 and 11.2).

Singular		Plural	
bâ ni dà shī̃	'I don't have it'	bâ mu dà shī̃	'we don't have it'
bâ ka dà shī̃	'you(m) don't have it'	bâ ku dà shī̃	'you don't have it'
bâ ki dà shī̃	'you(f) don't have it'		
bâ shi dà shī̃	'he doesn't have it'	bâ su dà shī̃	'they don't have it'
bâ ta dà shī̃	'she doesn't have it'		
bâ a dà shī̃	'one doesn't have it'		

Examples are:

bâ shi dà kuɗī̃	'he doesn't have (any) money'
bâ ni dà awākī̃	'I don't have (any) goats'

There are a few other minor variations found in one or both of these paradigms. The student is advised to find out which forms the informant for his class uses both with locative nouns (nân, gidā, etc.) and with the "have" construction. Copy these forms into the paradigms above, and practice them. substituting them for those given in the book where necessary.

8.2 The Possessive Link or Linker: -n/-r

Possession and other types of close association between nouns is shown by linking the two nouns by what we will refer to as the "linker". In order to remember the proper word order, it might be helpful to think of the linker as meaning 'that of'.

98

kuɗi-n Audù	'Audu's money' (money-that of Audu)
mutàne-n gàrī	'the townspeople' (people-those of town)
rīga-r Mammàn	'Mamman's gown' (gown-that of Mamman)

(The linker is normally written directly attached to the possessed noun but it has been separated here to show the grammatical construction.)

The important facts about the linker are:

a) It has the form -n when the possessed noun is masculine or plural, and the form -r when the possessed noun is feminine.

b) When the linker is added, the final vowel of the possessed noun is always shortened, for example the possessed nouns the the examples above when pronounced alone would be kuɗī, mutānē, rīgā; when the linker is attached to a noun ending in a diphthong, the final -i or -u of the diphthong is dropped as in

kâi	'head'	kân sarkī	"stamp" ('head of king' - referring to picture on the stamp)
kyâu	'beauty'	kyân yàrinyà	'beauty of the girl'

c) Very frequently, the feminine linker -r will not be pronounced as "r", but as the first sound of the following word; thus, instead of

rīgar Mamman	'Mamman's gown'
gōnar Sālisù	'Salisu's farm'

you will hear a lengthened "m" in the first example and a lengthened "s" in the second:

rīgam Mammàn

gōnas Sālisù

d) The masculine linker -n is pronounced -m before labial consonants, that is b, ɓ, f, m. It is pronounced as the -ng in 'sing' before g, k, ƙ.

kuɗin Mammàn (pronounced kuɗim Mammàn) 'Mamman's money"

mutànen gàrī (pronounced mutàneng gàrī) 'townspeople'

(Since this change in the pronunciation is completely predictable it does not need to be written. Thus the above examples will consistently be written as they are at the left even though they will be consistently pronounced as indicated inside the parentheses.)

A special marker, ɗin (ɗī- before first person singular posssessive pronouns) is often used instead of the normal linker after foreign borrowings ending in a consonant.

nawà nē karàs ɗinki?	'how much are your carrots?'
ìnā tēbùr ɗīna?	'where is my table?'

99

8.3 Possessive Pronouns

The possessive pronouns are given below, exemplified with a masculine and a feminine noun.

Masculine Noun		Feminine Noun	
kuɗī-n-ā[1]	'my money'	mōtà-t-ā[1]	'my car'
kuɗi-n-kà	'your(m) money'	mōtà-r-kà	'your(m) car'
kuɗi-n-kì	'your(f) money'	mōtà-r-kì	'your(f) car'
kuɗi-n-sà	'his money'	mōtà-r-sà	'his car'
kuɗi-n-tà	'her money'	mōtà-r-tà	'her car'
kuɗi-n-mù	'our money'	mōtà-r-mù	'our car'
kuɗi-n-kù	'your(pl) money'	mōtà-r-kù	'your(pl) car'
kuɗi-n-sù	'their money'	mōtà-r-sù	'their car'

With the partial exception of the first person singular, the noun-plus-possessive-pronoun constructions are exactly like the noun-plus-noun constructions. The same assimilatory changes of the linker take place as well (-r may become the same as a following consonant and -n becomes -m before labials, -ng before velars).

(written) kuɗinmu is pronounced kuɗimmù	'our money',
(written) kuɗinkù is pronounced kuɗingkù	'your money',
(written) motàrkà may be pronounced motàkkà	'your car',
(written) motàrsà may be pronounced motàssà	'his car', etc.

You may wish, for practical purposes, to remember the first person singular possessive pronouns as -na for masculine nouns and -ta for feminine nouns. However, as you can see by the paradigms above, they are perfectly parallel to other possessive pronoun constructions with the following qualifications:

a) While the masculine linker is -n, as with other pronouns and nouns, THE FEMININE LINKER IS -t, NOT -r. This apparent aberrancy is easily explained by the history of Hausa sounds. At one time, the feminine linker was -t in all constructions, for example Hausa speakers would have said rīga-t Mamman and riga-t-sa, and indeed this pronunciation is still heard some places. However, by a very regular historical process, all t's (and as a matter of fact all other dental consonants) which fell immediately before another consonant or at the end of a word became -r. Only in the first person singular where the possessive pronoun did not begin in a consonant was the -t retained.[2]

---

[1] The -a is short at the end of a sentence but is long otherwise, for example:
kuɗīnā nè.

[2] The observant student will ask why the feminine linker is not -t before nouns beginning in a vowel, for example, why does one say rīga-r Audù, not rīga-t Audù? The answer is that all nouns written with an initial vowel are actually pronounced with an initial glottal stop ('), which functions as a consonant in Hausa. Hence, rīga-r Audù may be heard as rīga' 'Audù.

dákīnā	(dákī-n-ā)	'my hut'
rīgátā	(riga-t-ā)	'my gown'

b) Before first person singular possessive pronouns, all nouns have a long final vowel, even if the final vowel of the noun in isolation is short.

shúgàbānā	(from shúgàba)	'my boss'
àkwàtīnā	(from àkwàtì)	'my box'

8.4 The Linker Used to Mean "the one in question"

Where one wants to clearly indicate that reference is being made to a previously mentioned or implied item, the linker can be added alone to a noun. This usage resembles in some ways the use of the definite article, 'the', in English, but it's use is optional is Hausa (note that in English we must use the definite article when making such references), moreover, it often would be much more like a demonstrative 'this' or 'that' than simply the article.

For nouns ending in a low tone, the appropriate linker (-n for masculine nouns, -r for feminine) is simply added to the noun. If the noun ends in a high tone, it changes to falling tone.

gà sābuwàr nân	'here's the new one (that we've been talking about)'
nā sauke dōyā dàgà mōtōcîn	'I unloaded yams from the trucks (that I just mentioned)'
A: fartanyā tā karye?	'the hoe has broken'
B: ìnā fartanyàr?	'where's the hoe (that you're talking about)?'

8.5 Palatalization of Consonants

The consonants t, d, s, and z change to c, j, or sh if they precede i or e. Such changes are found in words having more than one form, for example, singulars and plurals of nouns. In one form of the word, t, d, s, or z may precede a, o, or u, but in another form they may precede i or e. For example, in this unit we have the singular mōtā 'car, truck' where t precedes a. The t changes to c before the i in the plural form mōtōcī. Another example is the word kāzā 'chicken', the plural of which is kājī. This change is called "palatalization".

d and z become j before i or e

t becomes c before i or e

s becomes sh before i or e

These changes are very regular and are found in situations other than the formation of plurals. We will refer back to this section when other examples of palatization are encountered.

8.6 Time Concepts (jiyà, gòbe, etc.)

Besides words for 'today', 'yesterday', and 'tomorrow', Hausa has words for two, three, and four day periods.

shēkàràn jiyà	'day before yesterday'
jiyà	'yesterday'
yâu	'today'

101

gŏbe	'tomorrow'
jⁱbi	'day after tomorrow'
gātà	'three days hence'
città	'four days hence'

GRAMMATICAL DRILLS

<u>Drill 1</u> - Answer the following questions in the negative as illustrated in the example.

Cue question: Àli yanà̄ nâṇ?

Student response: ā'à̄, Àli bā̄ yà̄ nâṇ

1. yanà̄ cân?
2. wuƙā tanà̄ nâṇ?
3. sunà̄ ƙàrƙashin tēbùr?
4. kanà̄ kusa dà mōtà̄?
5. mài gidā yanà̄ nâṇ?

6. kinà̄ gàban ɗàkⁱ?
7. uwargidā tanà̄ gidā?
8. Àli yanà̄ wajen Sⁱdì?
9. mōtōcⁱ sunà̄ kà̄suwā?
10. kunà̄ kusa dà gōnā?

<u>Drill 2A - 2B</u> - Do this drill twice, answering the questions in the negative as explained in A and B.

2A Answer the question of the form <u>anà̄ dà X?</u> with a negative sentence <u>ā'à̄,</u> <u>bā̄ a dà X.</u>

Question: sunà̄ dà awākⁱ? 'goats'

Student response: ā'à̄, bā̄ su dà awākⁱ

2B Answer the question of the form <u>anà̄ dà X?</u> with a negative sentence <u>ā'à̄,</u> <u>bā̄ a dà</u> followed by the independent pronoun corresponding to X.

Question: sunà̄ dà awākⁱ?

Student response: ā'à̄, bā̄ su dà sū

1. tanà̄ dà lèmō?
2. kunà̄ dà dōyà̄?
3. sunà̄ dà yà̄rā?
4. kinà̄ dà ƙōshiyà̄?
5. yanà̄ dà mōtà̄?

6. munà̄ dà tumākⁱ?
7. kanà̄ dà mātā hudu?
8. tanà̄ dà littāfⁱ?
9. kinà̄ dà gwēbà̄?
10. kinà̄ dà awākⁱ dà yawà̄?

<u>Drill 3</u> - Change the pattern sentences of the form 'Ali has money' to sentences of the form 'it's Ali's money' as in the example.

Pattern sentence: Àli yanà̄ dà kuɗⁱ

Student response: kuɗin Àli nè̄

1. màcè tanà̄ dà ƙwai ƙwai n.m. 'egg(s)'
2. Shēhù yanà̄ dà rⁱgā
3. yà̄rā sunà̄ dà gwēbà̄
4. Zàinabù tanà̄ dà tàttàsai tàttàsai n.m. 'peppers'
5. mālàm yanà̄ dà àgōgo
6. ɗan tēbùr yanà̄ dà tābà̄

102

7. mutā̀nē sunā̀ dà tumākī
8. Hasàn yanā̀ dà wukā̄
9. Maryamà tanā̀ dà tunkìyā̄
10. yārò̄ yanā̀ dà sulè̀

Drill 4 - Change the noun possessor to the corresponding pronoun possessor.

Cue sentence: kuɗin Àli nè̀
Student response: kuɗinsà nē

1. ƙwan màcè nē
2. rìgar Shēhù cē
3. gwēbàr yā̂rā cè̀
4. tàttā̀san Zàinabù nē
5. àgōgon mālàm nē

6. tābàr ɗan tēbùr cē
7. tumākin mutā̀nē nè̀
8. wuƙar Hasàn cē
9. tunkìyar Maryamà cē
10. sulè̀n yārò̄ nē

Drill 5 - Answer the question by changing the second person possessive pronoun to first person of the first person to second person as in the examples.

Question: wannàn littāfìnkà nē?
Student response: Ī, littāfìnā̄ nè̀
Question: wannàn tābàtā cè̀?
Student response: Ī, tābàrkà cē

1. wannàn gàrinkù nē?
2. wannàn gōrò̄nā nè̀?
3. wannàn tābàrkà cē?
4. wannàn kuɗinkì nē?
5. wannàn kujè̀rātā cè̀?

6. wannàn qōnarkà cē?
7. wannàn kwàndonmù nē?
8. wannàn tàttā̀sankù nē?
9. wannàn takàrdātā cè̀?
10. wannàn ƙwalnā̀ nè̀?

Drill 6 - From a sentence of the form nā̄ kā̄wō̄ wuƙā̄ 'I brought a knife', form a question of the form ìnā̄ wuƙàr? 'where is the knife (that you mentioned)?' using the linker as described in 8.4 to mean "the one in question".

Cue sentence: nā̄ kā̄wō̄ kuɗī (from cue kuɗī)
Student response: ìnā̄ kuɗìn?

1. zàbō̄
2. fartanyà̄
3. kwabò̄
4. kà̄zā̄
5. dōyà̄
6. kāyā̄
7. rìgā̄
8. kwàndō̄
9. gōrò̄
10. ƙōshiyà̄

Drill 7 - Form the pattern sentence wannàn ... -sà/-tà/etc., àmma wancàn ... -sà/-tà/etc. In each case your cue will be the continuative pronouns in the cue sentences as shown below.

Cue sentence: yanā̀ dà kè̀kē, tanā̀ dà wuƙā̄ 'bicycle'
Student response: wannàn kè̀kensà nē, àmmā waccàn wuƙartà cē
Cue sentence: kinā̀ dà littāfī, inā̀ dà kujè̀rā̄
Student response: wannàn littāfìnkì nē, àmmā waccàn kujè̀rātā cè̀

103

1. inā dà àlƙalàmī, sunā dà littāfī
2. kinā dà àgōgo, yanā dà rīgā
3. munā dà tēbùr, inā dà takàrdā
4. kunā dà tàttàsai, tanā dà àlƙalàmī
5. inā dà hūlā, kanā dà mōtā   n.f. 'cap'
6. sunā dà kwàndō, munā dà rīgā
7. yanā dà gidā, kunā dà yārō
8. kinā dà tābà, tanā dà tunkiyā

<u>Drill 8A - 8B</u> - In drills 8A and 8B repeat the initial sentence, then as an independent pronoun is given as a cue, substitute the corresponding completive aspect pronoun as subject of the sentence and the corresponding possessive pronoun on the direct object of the verb.

Initial sentence: yā ɗinkà wàndonsà

Cue 1:   nī

Student response: nā ɗinkà wàndōnā

Cue 2:   kai

Student response: kā ɗinkà wàndonkà

8A <u>Initial sentence</u>: yā karyà ƙōshiyàrsà   karyā v.tr. 'break, snap in two

1. kai   5. shī
2. sū   6. kū
3. mū   7. ita
4. nī   8. kē

8B <u>Initial sentence</u>: yā kāwō kāyansà

1. sū   5. nī
2. kē   6. ita
3. shī   7. kū
4. mū   8. kai

<u>Drill 9A - 9B</u> - Use the following cues for two drills as described in 9A and 9B.

9A Substitute the cue noun into the pattern sentence <u>lallē wuƙàƙenkà sunā dà kyâu</u>. In each case use the 2nd person singular possessive pronoun.

Cue: mōtā

Student response: lallē mōtàrkà tanā dà kyâu

9B Substitute the cue noun into the pattern sentence given in 9A and change the sentence to the negative.

Cue: mōtā

Student response: lallē mōtàrkà bâ ta dà kyâu

1. fartanyā 3. gōnā 5. ƙōshiyā 7. aikī 9. rīgā
2. gidā   4. gāshī 6. hūlā   8. zàbī 10. mōtōcī

Drill 10 - Insert the noun or pronoun cues into the pattern sentence yā jē
wajen ... àmmā bā yà gidā 'he went to ...'s place but ... wasn't home.'
If an independent pronoun is given as a cue, use the corresponding possessive
pronoun with wajen.

	Cue:	Shēhù
	Student response:	yā jē wajen Shēhù àmmā bā yà gidā
	Cue:	nī
	Student response:	yā jē wajēnā àmmā bā nà gidā

1. MūdT	6. ita	11. sū
2. shī	7. Hasàn	12. Àli
3. mālàm	8. kai	13. kē
4. Mèro	9. Bintà	14. mū
5. kū	10. nī	15. wadànnân mutānē

Drill 11 - We have seen the word wajen in Units VII and VIII in two different
uses, one meaning 'about' as in tumākī wajen shā biyu nē 'there are about 12
goats', and the other meaning 'place of, toward' as in nā jē wajen STdì 'I went
to Sidi's place'. In the following drill, you will be given a series of nouns.
Substitute the cue noun into one of the two pattern sentences depending on
which is more appropriate: a) inā dà ... wajen gōmà 'I have about 10 ...', or
b) nā jē wajen ... 'I went to ...'s place.'

	Cue:	tumākī
	Student response:	inā da tumākī wajen gōmà
	Cue:	Shēhù
	Student response:	nā jē wajen Shēhù
	Cue:	shī
	Student response:	nā jē wajensà

| 1. Àli | 3. kai | 5. Hasàn | 7. ita | 9. mânyan mōtōcī |
| 2. kàjī | 4. awākī | 6. zàbī | 8. Ƙōshiyōyī | 10. Shaibù |

Drill 12A - 12C - Repeat the initial sentence, then substitute the first cue
into the appropriate place in that sentence. As each cue is given, substitute
it into the sentence formed from the previous cue, so that a new sentence is
formed.

12A Initial sentence: yanà dà Ƙoshiyà

Cues	Student response
1. Sīdì	Sīdì yanà dà Ƙoshiyà
2. fartanyà	Sīdì yanà dà fartanyà
3. kullum	kullum STdì yanà dà fartanyà
4. dà ita	kullum STdì yanà dà ita
5. jiyà	jiyà STdì yanà dà ita
6. bà shi	jiyà STdì bà shi dà ita
7. Hàlīmà	jiyà Hàlīmà bà ta dà ita

105

12B __Initial sentence:__ Shēhù yā zō

1. shēkaràn jiyà — Shēhù yā zō shēkaràn jiyà
2. mōtā̀ — mōtā̀ tā zō shēkaràn jiyà
3. mânyan mōtōcT̄ — mânyan mōtōcT̄ sun zō shēkaràn jiyà
4. dàgà cân — mânyan mōtōcT̄ sun zō dàgà cân shēkaràn jiyà
5. Jàs — mânyan mōtōcT̄ sun zō dàgà Jàs shēkaràn jiyà
6. cìke dà dōyā̀ — mânyan mōtōcT̄ sun zō dàgà Jàs cìke dà dōyā̀ shēkaràn jiyà
7. kāyan àbinci — mânyan mōtōcT̄ sun zō dàgà Jàs cìke dà kāyan àbinci shēkaràn jiyà

12C __Initial sentence:__ inā̀ ciwṑ

1. Lawàli — Lawàli yanā̀ ciwṑ
2. ciwòn kâi — Lawàli yanā̀ ciwòn kâi
3. don yā yi aikT̄ — Lawàli yanā̀ ciwòn kâi don yā yi aikT̄
4. dà yawā̀ — Lawàli yanā̀ ciwòn kâi don yā yi aikT̄ dà yawā̀
5. yā saukè dōyā̀ — Lawàli yanā̀ ciwòn kâi don yā saukè dōyā̀
6. dà yawā̀ — Lawàli yanā̀ ciwòn kâi don yā saukè dōyā̀ dà yawā̀
7. dàgà mōtōcîn — Lawàli yanā̀ ciwòn kâi don yā saukè dōyā̀ dà yawā̀ dàgà mōtōcîn

PRONUNCIATION REVIEW

__Tone descrimination__ - On a sheet of paper, number from 1 to 25. Listen to the following words and write on your paper what the tone pattern for each word is, for example, the word __lāfiyā̀__ has the tone pattern HHL.
   Correct your paper.
   Listen to the words again, repeating each word after the informant.

1. tàmbayā̀	'question'		14. tàkàlmT̄	'shoe'
2. àmfànT̄	'usefulness'		15. jàwābT̄	'reply'
3. gujiyā̄	'peanuts'		16. dūnìyā̀	'world'
4. tsuntsàyḕ	'birds'		17. gaisuwā̄	'greeting'
5. kuskurè	'mistake'		18. ùngùlū	'vulture'
6. gàskiyā̄	'truth'		19. māgànT̄	'medicine'
7. lōkàcT̄	'time'		20. ƙòƙarT̄	'effort'
8. tārīhì	'history'		21. kùnāmā̀	'scorpion'
9. àbōkT̄	'friend'		22. kujèrā̄	'chair'
10. hayāƙT̄	'smoke'		23. jàma'à̄	'the public'
11. àyàbà	'banana'		24. àkwātì	'box'
12. fartanyā̀	'hoe'		25. shēkarā̀	'year'
13. gàtarT̄	'axe'			

GUIDED CONVERSATION

1) Two students play the roles of two people meeting on the street. One may
have just bought something, failed to buy it, or be on his way to buy it.
It may be necessary to introduce a new verb or two, but this should be kept
to a minimum. These conversations should be used as an opportunity to use
greetings.

Example conversation:

Student 1:	Audù, barkà dà kwānā.	Audù, greetings in the morning.
Student 2:	Barkà kàdai. Yàyà gùmī?	Greetings. How's the heat?
1:	Ai, lōkàcinsà nē.	Well, it's the time for it.
2:	Ìnā iyālī?	How's the family?
1:	Sunà lāfiyà.	They're well.
2:	Mādàllā. Mēnē nè wannàn?	Good. What's that?
1:	Tagùwātā cè. Duk tā ɓàci.	It's my shirt. It's completely ruined.
2:	An ɗinkà sābuwā?	Has a new one been sewn.
1:	Ī, gà ta nân.	Yes, here it is.
2:	STdì yā ɗinkà ta?	Did Sidi sew it?
1:	Ā'à, Yàhàya yā ɗinkà ta.	No, Yahaya sewed it.
2:	Tô, bâ lâifī.	Well, there's nothing wrong with that.
	Sai an jumà.	See you later.
1:	Yâuwā, sai an jumà.	Right, see you later.

2) One student may play the role of a trader, laborer, etc. and another
student may play the part of his friend passing by. Carefully establish
the situation and don't try to make the conversation long.

Example dialogues:

A. Student one is a visitor to a town a little way from his own and has
just arrived in a truck. He approaches a trader friend of his in the
market.

Student 1:	Sànnu Garbà. Yàyà cìnikī?	Greetings Garba. How's business.
Student 2:	Àlhamdù lìllāhī.	Praise be to God.
	Kā zō dàgà gàrinkù?	Have you come from your town?[1]
1:	Ī, gà ni nā zō wajen	Yes, here I am, I arrived about
	ƙarfe ukù dà rabī.	3:30.
2:	Kā zō cikin mōtà?	Did you come in a car/truck?
1:	Ī, nā zō cikin mōtà cìke	Yes, I came in a truck loaded with
	dà dōyà.	yams.
2:	Tô mādàllā. Barkà dà zuwà.	Well fine. Greetings on your
		arrival.

---

[1] Only an Emir or chief of a town can say garīnā 'my town' and only to him
can one say gàrinkà 'your(sg) town'. For everyone else, singular or plural,
one says gàrinmù/ gàrinkù/ gàrinsù 'our/your/their town'.

107

B. Student one encounters his friend, student two, who is setting up chairs for a meeting.

Student 1: Lawàli, sànnu dà aikì.　Lawali, greetings at work.

Student 2: Yâuwā, sànnu.　Greetings.

1: Kâi, kā yi aikì dà yawà.　Wow, you have done a lot of work.

2: Gàskiyàrkà. Àkwai tằrō̃ à ƙarfḕ takwàs. Sabō̃ da hakà mun sằ duk wadànnân kùjḕrū à nân.　You're right. There's a meeting at 8:00. That's why (because of this) we have put all these chairs here.

1: An kāwō̃ sù dà mōtằ?　Were they brought (here) by car?

2: Ā'ằ, mun kāwō̃ sù dàgà wancàn gidā̃.　No, we brought them from that building.

1: Tỗ, aikìnkù yanằ dà kyâu.　Well, your work looks good.

UNIT IX

DRILLS FOR REVIEW

This unit consists of drills designed to reinforce the material covered in Units I - VIII. The student should work through each drill several times until he can reply to the cues quickly.

Drill 1 - Supply an appropriate reply to the greetings listeḍ below.

Cue: Sànnu.

Student response: Yâuwā, sànnu.

1. Salāmù àlaikùm. (men)
2. Gāfarā dai. (women)
3. Barkā dà zuwā.
4. Sànnu dà aikī.
5. Inā kwānā?
6. Inā wunī?
7. Inā gaisuwā.
8. Barkā dà rāna.
9. Sànnu dà hūtāwā.
10. Inā iyālī?
11. Yàyà sanyī? 'cold weather'
12. Yàyà ruwā?
13. Inā làbārī?
14. Sàuka làfiyà.
15. Sai an jumā.
16. Allāh yà kai mù.

Drill 2 - Answer the question mēnē nè wannàn? with the sentence wannàn ... nē/cē.

Cue: mēnē nè wannàn?/wuƙā

Student response: wannàn wuƙā cē

1. fartanyā
2. littāfī
3. ƙōfā
4. hūlā
5. zābō
6. ƙōshiyà
7. kàzā
8. gidā
9. àlƙalàmī
10. fensìr

Drill 3 - Answer the questions with the appropriate responses as shown in the examples.

Cue: wānē nè?/Audù

Student response: shī Audù nē

Cue: kē, wācē cē?/Halīmà

Student response: nī Halīmà cē

Cue: su wānē nè?/màlàmai

Student respones: sū màlàmai nē

1. wānē nè?/Mammàn
2. wācē cē?/Zàinabù
3. su wānē nè?/Audù dà Bellò
4. kai, wānē nè?/Īsa
5. kē, wācē cē?/Aishà
6. kū, su wānē nè?/dàlìbai
7. su wānē nè?/'yan tèbùr
8. wānē nè?/nī
9. wācē cē?/Hàwwa
10. kai, wānē nè?/màlàm

109

Drill 4 - Answer the question àkwai .,.? with the sentence ā'ā, bābù ... .
In each case bābù should be followed by the appropriate pronoun.

Cue question: àkwai lìttàttàfai?

Student respones: ā'ā, bābù sū

Cue question: àkwai tābà?

Student response: ā'ā, bābù ita

1. àkwai lèmō?   6. àkwai tēburōrī?
2. àkwai gōrò?   7. àkwai gidàjē?
3. àkwai Mài Zōbè?   8. àkwai mōtà?
4. àkwai hūlunà?   9. àkwai gōnà?
5. àkwai gwēbà?   10. àkwai ruwā?

Drill 5 - Change the following affirmative sentences to negative as
illustrated.

Cue sentence: munà dà ƙwai dà yawà

Student response: bâ mu dà ƙwai dà yawà

1. sunà dà kudī dà yawà   7. kanà dà kwabò ukù
2. munà dà lìttàttàfai   8. kinà dà gōrò
3. kinà dà lèmo   9. Hàlīmà tanà dà tàttàsai
4. tanà dà fensìr   10. mutànē sunà dà fartanyōyī
5. inà dà takàrdā   11. munà dà kwandunà
6. kinà dà aikī   12. kunà dà yârā dà yawà

Drill 6 - Transform the following negative sentences to affirmative
sentences as shown in the example.

Cue: bâ ka dà àlƙalàmī

Student response: kanà dà àlƙalàmī

1. bâ ki dà làbārī   6. bâ su dà kudī
2. bâ ni dà kwabò   7. bâ ta dà ƙwai
3. bâ shi dà kwandunà   8. bâ ka dà dōyà
4. bâ mu dà kudī   9. bâ ni dà takàrdā
5. bâ shi dà ruwā   10. bâ ki dà tābà

Drill 7A - 7B - Use the following cues to do drills 7A and 7B.

7A Place the noun cue in the frame wannàn ... nē/cē. Make sure to use nē
for masculine nouns, cē for feminine nouns, and make sure also that you
are giving nē and cē the tone opposite the preceding syllable.

Cue: gidā

Student response: wannàn gidā nè

Cue: fartanyà

Student response: wannàn fartanyà cē

7B Place the noun cue in the frame wannàn bà ... ba nè/cè. Again, you will
have to use the correct form depending on gender, but nē and cē will be
low in each case since they follow high tone ba.

Cue: gidā

Student response: wannàn bā gidā ba nè

1. ƙòfà
2. bangō
3. itàcē
4. tābà
5. kàntī
6. takàrdā
7. tunkìyarkì
8. gàrinmìi
9. zābonsà
10. tābàtā

11. Bàhaushìyā
12. wàndōnā
13. fartanyàtā
14. Bàhaushè
15. hanyàr Kàtsinà
16. àbincinkù
17. ƙòshiyàr Mèro
18. kàzar Maryamà
19. tsōhon Sà'īdù
20. tàkàlmin mài gidā

Drill 8 - You will hean a cue sentence of the form gà ... nā/tā/mù nân 'here
is my/our ...'. Respond with the question ka/kin/kun kāwō shì/tà/sù dàgà
Kanò? 'did you bring it/them from Kanò?' using the direct object pronoun
appropriate to the noun in the cue sentence. For cues 1 - 6, use kā in the
response, in 7 - 12 use kin, and in 13 - 18 use kun.

Cue sentence: gà rìgātā nân

Student response: kā kāwō tà dàgà Kanò?

Cue sentence: gà zanènā nân n.m. 'woman's body cloth'

Student response: kin kāwō shì dàgà Kanò?

Cue sentence: gà awākinmù nân

Student response: kun kāwō sù dàgà Kanò?

kā	kin	kun
1. gà wàndōnā nân	7. gà ƙòshiyàtā nân	13. gà lìttàttàfanmù nân
2. gà tàkalmànā nân	8. gà tākalmànā nân	14. gà kujèrarmù nân
3. gà lìttāfīnā nân	9. gà àdīkònā nân 'headscarf'	15. gà kàjinmù nân
4. gà fartanyàtā nân	10. gà ƙwainā nân	16. gà hūlunànmù nân
5. gà àgōgōnā nân	11. gà kwàndōnā nân	17. gà kàyanmù nân
6. gà taguwàtā nân	12. gà wuƙàtā nân	18. gà kwàndonmù nân

Drill 9 - Following each sentence of the form "is this so and so's thing?",
you will be given a noun or independent pronoun cue. Give the response
"no, it's (cue)'s thing".

Question: wannàn tàkàlminkà nē?

Cue: Audù

Student response: ā'à, tàkàlmin Audù nē

111

	Question:	wannàn hū̀lar Mammàn cē?
	Cue:	nī
	Student response:	ā'ā, hū̀lātā cḕ

1. wannàn tābàrkà cē?/Hàlīmà
2. wadànnân zàbin yārò nē?/yàrinyà
3. wannàn gònar Garbà cē?/nī
4. wannàn gidan STdì nē?/Sà'īdù
5. wannàn hanyàr Kanò cē?/Kàtsinà
6. wannàn wàndonkà nē?/shī
7. wadànnân kàjin Aishà nē?/Zàinabù
8. wannàn tunkìyarsà cē?/ita

9. wannàn kàntin Abūbakàr nē?/nī
10. wadànnân tumākin mài gidā nē?/uwargidā
11. wannàn kwainà nē?/Hàdīzà
12. wannàn gàrinkù nē?/sū
13. wadànnân mōtōcin Àli nē?/Lawàli
14. wannàn kòshiyàr Mḕro cē?/Hàlīmà
15. wannàn tàttàsankì nē?/ita
16. wadànnân wukāken Hasàn nē?/Mūdī

Drill 10 - Each of the sentences in this drill contains a single noun someplace. Replace the noun in each case with a pronoun. It might be useful to
review the places where an independent pronoun must be used and the places
where a direct object pronoun must be used. If the noun to be replaced is
the subject of a continuative pronoun or a verb in the completive aspect,
simply drop the noun since the pronoun is already there.

	Cue sentence:	Hàlīmà cḕ
	Student response:	ita cḕ
	Cue sentence:	inà̄ dà kudī
	Student response:	inà̄ dà sū
	Cue sentence:	Mūdī yā dìnkà̄ ta
	Student response:	yā dìnkà̄ ta

1. àkwai wukā
2. gà̄ tumākī cân
3. kanà̄ dà tàttàsai?
4. kàsuwā cḕ
5. Mḕro tā jē wajensà
6. an yi kòshiyà̄ à nân
7. gà̄ mālàm cân
8. bà̄ mōtōcī ba nḕ
9. àkwai àbincin gwan-gwan
10. tanà̄ dà wukā

11. bābù kwai
12. Hàlīmà tanà̄ dà sū?
13. Lawàli yā saukè ta
14. Sà'īdù nḕ
15. mōtōcī sun zō dàgà cân
16. àkwai tumākī
17. gà̄ kòfà̄ cân
18. bābù gwēbà̄
19. yanà̄ dà wukākē
20. bà̄ dàlìbai ba nḕ

112

Drill 11 - Give reasonable answers to the questions accompanying the pictures. Make sure that you use i̲ and ā̲'ā̲ correctly when answering negative questions. Review 7.7 if necessary.

lìttattāfai bā sū
ƙàrƙashin tēbùr?

mêne nè à hannun Abdù?

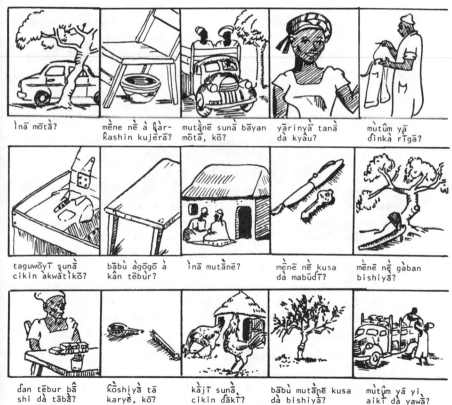

ìnā mōtà?

mēne nē à ƙàr-
ƙashin kujērā?

mutā̀nē sunà bāyan
mōtā, kō?

yārinyà tanà
dà kyâu?

mùtûm yā̀
ɗinkà rīgā?

taguwōyī̀ ṣunà
cikin àkwātìkō?

bābù àgōgō à
kân tēbùr?

ìnā mutā̀nē?

mēnē nḕ kusa
dà mabūdī?

mēnē nḛ̀ gàban
bishiyā?

ɗan tēbur bā̀
shi dà tābà?

ƙòshiyà tā
karyē, kō?

kàjī sunà
cikin ɗākī?

bābù mutā̀nē kusa
dà bishiyā?

mùtûm yā yi
aikī dà yawà?

113

Drill 12 - Change the following sentences to the negative.

Cue:	wannàn idǒ nḗ
Student response:	wannàn bā̀ idǒ ba nḕ
Cue:	àkwai tsōhonsà à nân
Student response:	bābù tsōhonsà à nân
Cue:	inā̀ dà kuɗī̀
Student response:	bâ ni dà kuɗī̀

1. sū ɗàlìbai nḕ
2. àkwai aikī̀ yâu
3. yanā̀ dà tàttàsai
4. àkwai mutānē dà yawā̀
5. tsōhōnā yanā̀ gidā
6. waɗànnân tumākī nḕ
7. waccàn tāgā̀ cē
8. 'yam mātā sunā̀ dà kyâu
9. àkwai wuƙā wajensà
10. shī mài gidānā nḕ

11. àkwai mânyan mōtōcī à kāsuwā
12. rīgā tanā̀ dà tsādā
13. àkwai kā̀jī cikin wancàn ɗàkī
14. wannàn mùtûm mālàminmù nḕ
15. mài gidā yanā̀ Kàtsinà yâu
16. uwargidā tanā̀ dà ƙōshiyā̀
17. wannàn fartanyàr Àbūbakàr cē
18. àkwai tumākī dà yawā̀ à gàrinmù
19. waɗàncân zābī nḕ
20. wuƙarkì tanā̀ cikin gidā

Drill 13 - Change the following sentences to the corresponding affirmative.

Cue:	wannàn bā̀ idǒ ba nḕ
Student response:	wannàn idǒ nḕ
Cue:	bābù tsōhonsà à nân
Student response:	àkwai tsōhonsà à nân
Cue:	bâ ni dà kuɗī̀
Student response:	inā̀ dà kuɗī̀

1. sū bā̀ ɗàlìbai ba nḕ
2. bābù aikī̀ yâu
3. bā̀ shi dà tàttàsai
4. bā̀ mutānē dà yawā̀
5. tsōhōnā bā̀ yā̀ gidā
6. waɗànnân bā̀ tumākī ba nḕ
7. waccàn bā̀ tāgā̀ ba cē
8. 'yam mātā sunā̀ dà kyâu
9. bābù wuƙā wajensà
10. shī mài gidānā nḕ

11. bābù mânyan mōtōcī à kāsuwā
12. rīgā bā̀ ta dà tsādā
13. wannàn mùtûm bā̀ mālàminmù ba nḕ
14. bā̀ kā̀jī cikin wancàn ɗàkī
15. mài gidā bā̀ yā̀ Kàtsinà yâu
16. uwargidā bā̀ ta dà ƙōshiyā̀
17. wannàn bā̀ fartanyàr Àbūbakàr ba cē
18. bā̀ tumākī dà yawā̀ à gàrinmù
19. waɗàncân bā̀ zābī ba nḕ
20. wuƙarkà bā̀ tā̀ cikin gidā

Drill 14 - Perform the addition as indicated in the examples.

Problem:	shā̂ biyu dà takwàs nawā kḕ nan? (12 + 8 = ?)
Student response:	shā̂ biyu dà takwàs àshìrin kḕ nan (12 + 8 = 20)

114

1. 2 + 1 = ?   6. 10 + 4 = ?
2. 3 + 5 = ?   7. 7 + 10 = ?
3. 5 + 5 = ?   8. 10 + 8 = ?
4. 6 + 6 = ?   9. 10 + 10 = ?
5. 5 + 9 = ?   10. 15 + 4 = ?

Drill 15 - Give the Hausa for the following times.

Cue: 3:12
Student response: ƙarfè ukù dà mintì gõmà shâ biyu

1. 1:00   5. 6:10   9. 6:03   13. 12:12
2. 2:15   6. 12:00   10. 5:30   14. 10:43
3. 7:45   7. 9:18   11. 8:55   15. 11:16
4. 4:30   8. 2:40   12. 10:45   16. 9:50

Drill 16A - 16B

16A Cover up the right hand column and change the direct object noun or
    locative expression (or subject noun if there is neither a direct object
    or locative) into a question word, making other necessary changes.

16B Cover up the left hand column and replace the question word with the
    cue noun or locative expression. The left hand column gives you the
    answers.

16A Cue:	sun ci àbinci	16B Cue:	mè sukà ci?/àbinci
Response:	mè sukà ci?	Response:	sun ci àbinci
Cue:	nā tàfi gidā	Cue:	inā ka tàfi?/gidā
Response:	ina ka tàfi?	Response:	nā tàfi gidā

1. yā ci gōrò	1. mè ya ci?/gōrò
2. nā tàfi Kàtsinà	2. inā ka tàfi?/Kàtsinà
3. fartanyà tā karyè	3. mè ya karyè?/fartanyà
4. mutānē sun saukè dōyà	4. mè mutānē sukà saukè?/dōyà
5. an bā nì kuɗī	5. mè akà bā kà?/kuɗī
6. kā sàuka à gidan àbōkinkà	6. inā na sàuka?/gidan àbōkinkà
7. mōtōcī sun zō dàgà Jàs	7. dàgà inā mōtōcī sukà zō?/Jàs
8. kin jē kàsuwā	8. inā na jē?/kàsuwā
9. mātātā tā yi àbinci	9. mè màtarkà ta yi?/àbinci
10. nā ɗinkà rīgunà dà yawà	10. mè ka ɗinkà?/rīgunà dà yawà
11. kun ci kàzā	11. mè mukà ci?/kàzā
12. mun kāwō kāyan àbinci	12. mè kukà kāwō?/kāyan àbinci
13. Lawàli yā gàji	13. wā ya gàji?/Lawàli
14. kā tàfi wajen Sīdì	14. inā na tàfi?/wajen Sīdì
15. nā yi aikī dà yawà	15. mè ka yi?/aikī dà yawà

115

Drill 17A - 17B

17A Cover up the right hand column and change the locative expression or the object of dà to a question word. If the word to be changed is the object of dà, you will have to repeat the pronoun shī after dà because dà cannot appear without an object. Thus, the answer is literally 'what does he have it?', etc.

17B Cover up the left hand column and replace the question word by the noun of locative expression given as a cue.

17A Cue:	Audù yanā̀ dà dōyā̀	17B Cue:	mḕ Audù ya kḕ dà shī?/dōyā̀
Response:	mḕ Audù ya kḕ dà shī?	Response:	Audù yanā̀ dà dōyā̀
Cue:	inā̀ nân	Cue:	inā̀ ka kḕ?/nân
Response:	inā̀ ka kḕ?	Response:	inā̀ nân

1. dōyā̀ tanā̀ Jàs	1. inā̀ dōyā̀ ta kḕ?/Jàs
2. munā̀ dà kāyan àbinci	2. mḕ ku kḕ dà shī?/kāyan àbinci
3. Sà'Tdù yanā̀ gidā	3. inā̀ Sà'Tdù ya kḕ?/gidā
4. kunā̀ dà kā̀jī dà yawà	4. mḕ mu kḕ dà shī?/kā̀jī dà yawà
5. inā̀ dà kwabò ukù	5. mḕ ka kḕ dà shī?/kwabò ukù
6. Hàlīmà tanā̀ dà wukā̀k̃ē	6. mḕ Hàlīmà ta kḕ dà shī?/wukā̀k̃ē
7. kinā̀ bāyan tēbùr	7. inā̀ na kḕ?/bāyan tēbùr
8. mōtōcī sunā̀ kàsuwā	8. inā̀ mōtōcī su kḕ?/kàsuwā
9. kanā̀ cikin d̃akī	9. inā̀ na kḕ?/cikin d̃akī
10. STdì yanā̀ dà fartanyā̀	10. mḕ STdì ya kḕ dà shī?/fartanyā̀
11. munā̀ nân	11. inā̀ ku kḕ?/nân
12. d̃ā̀lìbai sunā̀ makarantā	12. inā̀ d̃ā̀lìbai su kḕ?/makarantā
13. kanā̀ dà kud̃ī dà yawà	13. mḕ na kḕ dà shī?/kud̃ī dà yawà
14. inā̀ cikin mōtā̀tā	14. inā̀ ka kḕ?/cikin mōtā̀tā

Drill 18 - Practice using numbers by asking each other questions about numbers of things around you which you can count. Count the things or persons one by one to practice the numbers in sequence. Some possible questions are given below.

        kanā̀ dà littāfī nawà à nân?

        mabūd̃ī nawà nē à cikin àljThunkà?   àljThū n.m. 'pocket'

        tāgā nawà cikin wannàn d̃akī?

        d̃ā̀lìbai nawà à nân?

        kwabò nawà nē à cikin àljThunkà?

        kanā̀ dà àlk̃alàmī dà fensìr nawà à nân?

        kujḕrā nawà nē cikin wannàn d̃akī?

- Repeat the initial sentence, then substitute the first cue into the appropriate place in that sentence. As each cue is given, substitute it into the sentence formed from the previous cue, so that a new sentence is formed.

19A <u>Initial sentence</u>: yā zō

Cues	Student response
1. Aishà	Aishà tā zō
2. Bellò	Bellò yā zō
3. yi rīgā	Bellò yā yi rīgā
4. aikī	Bellò yā yi aikī
5. dàlibī	dàlibī yā yi aikī
6. yārò	yārò yā yi aikī
7. wannàn yārò	wannàn yārò yā yi aikī
8. wancàn	wancàn yārò yā yi aikī
9. saukè kāyā	wancàn yārò yā saukè kāyā
10. dōyà	wancàn yārò yā saukè dōyà
11. wannàn mùtûm dà wancàn yārò	wannàn mùtûm dà wancàn yārò sun saukè dōyà
12. dà yawà	wannàn mùtûm dà wancàn yārò sun saukè dōyà dà yawà
13. kāyā	wannàn mùtûm dà wancàn yārò sun saukè kāyā dà yawà

19B <u>Initial sentence</u>: tanà nân

1. Aishà	Aishà tanà nân
2. Hàlīmà	Hàlīmà tanà nân
3. Shēhù	Shēhù yanà nân
4. yā zō	Shēhù yā zō
5. sàuka	Shēhù yā sàuka
6. à gàrī	Shēhù yā sàuka à gàrī
7. gidā	Shēhù yā sàuka à gidā
8. gidanmù	Shēhù yā sàuka à gidanmù
9. wajen ƙarfè biyu	Shēhù yā sàuka à gidanmù wajen ƙarfè biyu
10. gōmà shâ biyu	Shēhù yā sàuka à gidanmù wajen ƙarfè gōmà shâ biyu
11. dà rabī	Shēhù yā sàuka à gidanmù wajen ƙarfè gōmà shâ biyu dà rabī

19C Initial sentence: mū nawà nē à nân?

1. sū   sū nawà nē à nân?
2. à gàr⊤   sū nawà nē à gàr⊤?
3. wancàn gàr⊤   sū nawà nē à wancàn gàr⊤?
4. gidā   sū nawà nē à (wancàn) gidā?
5. wannàn gidā   sū nawà nē à wannàn gidā?
6. kū   kū nawà nē à wannàn gidā?
7. dàlìbai   dàlìbai nawà nē à wannàn gidā?
8. yârā   yârā nawà nē à wannàn gidā?
9. gōmà   yârā gōmà à wannàn gidā
10. gōmà shâ bìyar   yârā gōmà shâ bìyar à wannàn gidā
11. nā ƙirgā
     'counted'   na kirga yara goma sha biyar a wannan gida
12. Àbūbakàr   Àbūbakàr yā ƙirgà yârā gōmà shâ bìyar à wannàn gidā
13. yànzu   yànzu Àbūbakàr yā ƙirgà yârā gōmà shâ bìyar à wannàn
                          gidā

118

DIALOGUES

A. Malam Haruna is looking for a gift for a friend who he intends to visit.
While in the market his eye falls on a group of colorful mats. He picks
one up and begins to examine it. The mat seller addresses him.

Mài Tàbarmā: Rânkà yà dadè. Mè zā kà sàyā?	May your life be prolonged. What are you going to buy?
Hārūnà: Nawà nē kuɗin tàbarmā?	How much is (the price of) a mat?
MT: Tàyā.	Make an offer.
Hārūnà: Nā tayà sulè gōmà.	I offer ten shillings.

MT (jerking the mat from Haruna's hands):
Habà! Bà kà san kântà ba. Kàwo!	Come on now! You don't know its value (its "head"). Give it here (bring)!
Hārūnà: Kâi, mālàm! TayT bà tōyT ba nè.	Hey, sir! No reason to get burned up just because a man makes an offer (lit: offering is not burning up/ being set fire to)!
MT: Ha ha! Tô, kuɗintà Nairā huɗu.	Ha ha! OK, its price is four Naira.
Hārūnà: Tô, nā ƙārà sulè takwàs.	OK, I increase (my offer by) eight shillings.
MT: Kàwō sulè tàlàtin, shT kè nan.	Give me (bring) thirty shillings and it's a deal.
Hārūnà: In kā ragè mini sulè biyar, nā yàrda.	If you reduce (your price) five shillings for me, I'll agree.
MT: À'à, kuɗintà sun fi hakà.	No, it's worth more than that (its price exceeds that way).

Hārūnà (turning to leave):
Tô nā tàfi.	OK, good-bye (I've left). [A common practice in bargaining is to walk off in hopes that the seller will call you back and accept your last offer.]
MT: Tô, kàwō kuɗT.	OK, let's have (bring) the money.

Vocabulary

dadè v.intr.	'last a long time, spend a long time'			râi n.m.	'life'
fi v.tr.	'exceed'			rânkà yà dadè	(greeting to a social superior) 'may your life be long'
habà	'come on, now!'			sàyā v.tr.	'buy'
in (or ɪdan)	'if; when'			shT kè nan	'that's that, there's nothing more to say'
ƙārà v.tr.	'increase'				
mini	'to/for me'			tàbarmā n.f. (tàbàrmT pl.)	'mat woven from palm fronds'
Nairā	'Naira' (= about $1.60)				
				tàlàtin	'thirty'
ragè v.tr.	'reduce, decrease'			tayà v.intr.	'make an offer'

119

tayⱦ n.m.	'making an offer'	yàrda v.intr. 'agree'
tòyⱦ n.m.	'setting fire to'	

B. Amina goes to the market to buy food for the family. She stops in front of a vegetable seller who has her wares arranged in small piles on a mat in front of her.

AmⱦInà: Nawà nawà nē kashìn tàttàsai?	How much for each pile of peppers?
Mài sayad dà kāyan làmbū:	
Wannàn sulè sulè; wannàn sⱦIsⱦI sⱦIsⱦI; wannàn kùwā kwabō kwabō	These (i.e. this size pile) are a shilling each; these are five kobo each; these are one kobo each.
AmⱦInà: Zā kì bar wannàn na sulè sulè à kân sⱦIsⱦI sⱦIsⱦI?	Will you let this one for a shilling each go for five kobo each?
MSKL: Ā'à, àlbarkà.	No, no sale.
AmⱦInà: Tô, zân biyā kwabō takwàs takwàs.	OK, I'll pay eight kobo each.
MSKL: Tô, nā bar mikì. Kāwō kuɗⱦI.	OK, I'll let you (have it). Give me the money (bring money).

Amina walks on a little further to a stall where a hawker has eggs and lettuce displayed.

AmⱦInà: Kwai nawa nawa ne?	How much are the eggs each?
Mài sayad dà ƙwai:	
Ukù sulè.	Three for a shilling.
AmⱦInà: Zā kì barⱦI huɗu sulè?	Would you make it four for a shilling (will you let [them go] four for a shilling)?
MSK: Tô, nā sallàmā.	All right, I agree.

Vocabulary

barⱦI v.tr. (bar before objects)	'leave, let go'	na (in the context here)	'for'
		sallàmā v.intr.	'agree to a price' (said by a salesman when the price quoted by a buyer is acceptable
kashⱦI n.m.	'small pile' (usually of items which are quite small, like chile peppers or peanuts, which are not sold individually)		
		sⱦIsⱦI n.m.	'five kobo'
		sulè n.m.	'shilling' (= 10 kobo)
ƙwai n.m.	'egg(s)'	tàttàsai n.m.	'chile peppers'
làmbū n.m.	'(irrigated) garden'		
kāyan làmbū	'vegetables''		

120

COMPREHENSION PRACTICE

Without looking at your books, listen to the passage as your informant reads through it once, pausing to explain in Hausa the meaning of any new words or expressions. Your informant will read the passage a second time at normal conversational speed and then ask you the questions which follow. Answer in complete sentences.

Mālàm Hārūnà Yā Ci Kàsuwā

Jiyà Mālàm Hārūnà yanā̀ kàsuwā yanā̀ dūban[1] kāyā. Àkwai tàbarmā mài kyâu à kàsuwā. Mài tàbarmā ya ga Mālàm Hārūnà yanā̀ dūban tàbarmarsà. Ya cȇ, "Rânkà yà daɗè! Mȇ zā kà sàyā?" Mālàm Hārūnà ya cȇ, "Nawà nē kuɗin tàbarmā?" Mài tàbarmā ya cȇ wà Mālàm Hārūnà yà tayā.[2] Mālàm Hārūnà kuma ya tayà sulè gōmà. Mài tàbarmā ya cȇ, "Habà!" Ya kāmà[3] tàbarmarsà. Mālàm Hārūnà ya yi māmākī. Ya cȇ, "Kâi, mālàm! Tayī bà tōyī ba nȇ!" Mài tàbarmā ya yi dàriyā[4]. Ya cȇ, "Tô, kuɗin tàbarmā Nairà huɗu." Mālàm Hārūnà dà mài tàbarmā suka yi cìnikī. Mālàm Hārūnà ya bā dà Nairà biyu dà sulè bìyar, mài tàbarmā ya sallàmā.

[1]dūbā̀ v.n.m.	'looking at, examining'
yanā̀ dūban kāyā	'he was looking at the goods'
[2]ya cȇ wà Mālàm Hārūnà yà tayà	'he said to Malam Haruna he should make an offer'
[3]kāmà v.tr.	'catch, seize'
[4]dàriyā n.f.	'laughter'
yi dàriyā	'laugh'

Tambayōyī

1. Jiyà ìnā Mālàm Hārūnà ya kȇ?
2. Zâi dūbà kāyan àbinci à kàsuwā?
3. Mài tàbarmā mȇ ya cȇ?
4. Mālàm Hārūnà, nawà ya tayā?
5. Bāyan Mālàm Hārūnà yā tayà sulè gōmà, mȇ mài tàbarmā ya yi?
6. Mālàm Hārūnà yā yi māmākī?
7. Mȇ Mālàm Hārūnà ya cȇ?
8. Bāyan Mālàm Hārūnà yā cȇ hakà, mài tàbarmā mȇ ya yi?
9. Mālàm Hārūnà dà mài tàbarmā sun yi cìnikī?
10. Nawà mài tàbarmā ya sallàmā?

GRAMMAR

10.1 Future Aspect

The pronouns of the future aspect, shown with the verb zō 'come' for illustrative purposes, are as follows:

Singular		Plural	
zân zō	'I will come'	zā mù zō	'we will come'
zā kà zō	'you(m) will come'	zā kù zō	'you will come'
zā kì zō	'you(f) will come'		
zâi zō	'he will come'	zā sù zō	'they will come'
zā tà zō	'she will come'		
zā à zō	'one will come'		

In 7.1 we explained at some length why we talk about the "aspect" rather than the "tense" of Hausa verbs, viz. we are not referring to a time when the action took place, but rather to something about the action itself - completed action, continuing action, etc.

The Future Aspect is no exception. It indicates an action which will have its inception after the point in time being referred to, whether this point in time is past, present, or future. Of course, very frequently the time of reference will be the present moment in which case the future aspect is much like our future tense, for example, in discussing work that is to be done tomorrow, the following utterances would be appropriate:

> zā kà saukè dōyà? 'are you going to unload yams?'
>
> zân yi aikī dà yawà 'I'll work very hard'

The utterances using future aspect in this unit refer to future time as well:

> mè zā kà sàyā? 'what are you going to buy?'

However, the future aspect can refer to an action which will have its inception after a time of reference in the past. A couple of examples from familiar Hausa stories can be used to illustrate this.

a) A jackal has been eating a chicken and a bone gets lodged in his throat. He sets out to find someone to dislodge it, and we find the following sentence:

> yā cè duk wândà ya cirè masà, zâi bā shì lādā
> 'he said whoever dislodged it, he would give him a reward'

b) A man complaining of his poverty asks that he be killed to put him out of his misery.

> zā à sārè shi, sai wani ya zō ya cè ...
> 'he was about to be decapitated, when a certain man came and said ...

10.2 The Imperative

The Imperative is the only case where a verb can be used with no subject pronoun to mark person, number, and aspect. Instead, the verb itself undergoe tone changes. THE IMPERATIVE CAN BE USED ONLY IN THE SINGULAR. (For plurals the subjunctive is used - see 12.1). The basic facts for imperative tones are as follows:

One syllable verbs have high tone in the imperative except before direct object pronouns, where the verb is low and the pronoun high.

> zō nân 'come here'
> bà ni shidà 'give me six'

122

Two syllable verbs always have low tone on the first syllable, regardless of the basic tone. This means verbs of which the basic tones are low-high retain their basic tone patterns. Verbs where the basic tones are high-low will have low-low before noun direct objects, but before no object or a pronoun object, the second syllable is raised to high. (Pronoun objects after these verbs have high tone.)

sàuka lāfiyá	'arrive safely'
sàukè dōyá	'unload the yams'
tàyā	'make an offer'
k̃irgā su	'count them'
(basic form of k̃irgà 'to count' has tones high-low)	

10.3 Length of Final Vowels in Verbs

The observant student will have noticed that the length of the final vowels of some verbs is not always the same. The full set of rules governing this feature of verbs is somewhat complex and will be covered more fully in later lessons. Very generally, transitive verbs other than those ending in -o have short final vowels before noun direct objects and long final vowels elsewhere. Verbs ending in -o have long final vowels everywhere except before a pause. In intransitive verbs not ending in -o, the final vowels are generally invariant, that is, long or short depending on basic form.

10.4 Numbers 20-100

The tens from 20 to 100 are

20.	àshìrin	70.	sàbà'in
30.	tàlàtin	80.	tàmànin
40.	àrbà'in	90.	tàsà'in or càsà'in
50.	hàmsin	100.	d̃arT
60.	sìttin		

The numbers in between are formed very simply by using the preposition dà 'with' (Note that shà̃--Section 7.8--is only used with the numbers 11-19; dà is used from then on.):

21. àshìrin dà d̃aya

32. tàlàtin dà biyu

43. àrbà'in dà ukù   etc.

An alternative way of saying 28 and 29, 38 and 39, etc. is to subtract two or one from the next highest ten in the same way as described for 18 and 19 in 7.8:

48. àrbà'in dà takwàs	or	hàmsin biyu bàbu
59. hàmsin dà tarà	or	sìttin d̃aya bàbu

It is recommended again that the student discover and learn the pattern preferred by his informant.

123

10.5 Bargaining

Throughout Africa, one of the principal day-to-day activities is bargaining. The price of virtually every commodity for sale in a market or by a trader is bargainable, and after greetings, the language of bargaining is probably the most useful skill that the student of Hausa can acquire. Following are some of the more necessary expressions for bargaining.

a) Money[1]

Nigeria now has a decimal currency system. Although the official units are <u>Naira</u> and <u>kobo</u> (100 kobo = 1 Naira), some terms in Hausa are retained from the old pound/shilling/pence system. In particular, the term <u>sulè</u> (from English 'shilling') is still in common use and refers to a ten kobo coin. <u>Sulè</u> will be translated 'shilling' even though the term "shilling" has no official status in the present monetary system. The term sĪsĪ (from English 'sixpence') is used to refer to the five kobo coin. This coin is the same size and is equivalent in value to the old sixpence coin.

Unit	Symbol	Hausa term	Approximate U.S. equivalent
Naira	₦1.00	Nairã	$1.60
10 kobo	₦.10 or 10k	sulè	16 cents
5 kobo	₦.05 or 5k	sĪsĪ	8 cents
kobo	₦.01 or 1k	kwabõ	1.6 cents
half kobo	½k	dàrĪ	

b) "price"

The word kuɗĪ 'money' is used to mean 'price':

kuɗin lèmõ	'the price of oranges'
kuɗinsà	'its price'

c) "each", "apiece"

To indicate that a certain commodity is so much for each one, the money unit is repeated twice. In like fashion, to ask how much some commodity is for each one, nawà 'how much?' is doubled.

nawà nawà nè kashin tàttàsai?	'how much is each pile of peppers?'
gõrõ kwabõ kwabõ nè	'the kola nuts are a kobo each'

If the price isn't statable in terms of a single monetary unit such as kwabõ, sulè, etc., but must be modified by a number, then the number is doubled, for example:

gwèbã kwabõ biyu biyu	'the guavas are two kobo each'

[1] In French speaking West Africa, the basic unit of money is the franc (50 CFA = 1 French franc). The unit of money used in quoting prices in Hausa in these countries is <u>dalã</u> which is 5 francs CFA (=app. $.025) since the five francs CFA piece is the smallest piece of money commonly used (the one franc CFA piece, called <u>tammã</u>, is no longer minted, though it is occasionally seen). The Nigerian money system is used in this book since it is expected that most of the Hausa speakers that American students will come contact with will be Nigerians.

d) "four for a shilling", etc.

When more than one item goes for a price statable as a unit, this is expressed by the number of items followed by the price stated once.

ƙwai nawà nawà nē?   'how much are the eggs each?'
huɗu sulè   'four for a shilling'

e) In the dialogues of this and previous units we have seen a few other words and expressions frequently encountered in bargaining.

nā sallàmā (said by the seller)   'I agree (to your offer)'

àlbarkà (said by the seller)   'no thanks, not enough'

kàwō kuɗī (lit: 'bring money')   'sold'

nā tayà...(said by the buyer,   'I'll offer...'
followed by the amount he
offers)

nawà ka hanà?   'what's the lowest price you'll
                                    take?' (how much do you refuse?)

sulè uku na hanà   'you'd have to offer more than 3s.
                                    (3 shillings [is what] I'd refuse)

GRAMMATICAL DRILLS

Drill 1 - This drill consists simply of questions in the future aspect. Answer the question by changing it to a statement. Change the second person to first person.

Cue: zā kà sàyi tàbarmā?   sàyi (form used before noun
Student response: Ī, zân sàyi tàbarmā   direct obj., from sàya)
Cue: zā sù tàfi gidā?
Student response: Ī, zā sù tàfi gidā

1. zā kà ƙārà sulè?   6. mài tàbarmā zâi ragè kuɗintà?
2. zā sù zō nân yâu?   7. zā mù bā shi sulè?
3. zâi ɗinkà taguwà?   8. Amīnà zā tà barī shidà sulè?
4. zā mù jē Kanò gòbe?   9. zā kà ragè minì sulè bìyar?
5. zā ki bar wannàn sīsī sīsī?   10. Lawàli zâi saukè dōyà ɗàyà motà?

Drill 2 - Transform the sentences below from the completive to the future aspect as shown in the examples.

Cue sentence: Audù yā yi aikī dà yawà
Student response: Audù zâi yi aikī dà yawà
Cue sentence: mun saukè dōyà dàgà motà
Student response: zā mù saukè dōyà dàgà motà

1. Màlàm Hārūnà yā kàwō sulè bìyar   6. kun tàfi wajen STdi
2. nā bar miki   7. kin sàyi kashin tàttàsai
3. tā barī shidà sulè   8. kà sàuka à Kàtsinà
4. mōtōcī sun zō dàgà Jàs   9. an kàwō rīgā dàgà Kanò
5. mun yi màmākī   10. mài tàbarmā yā ga Màlàm Hārūnà

125

Drill 3 - You will be given a sentence in the future aspect, second person singular. Change the sentence to the imperative.

    Cue: zā kà sàyi tàbarmā

    Student response: sàyi tàbarmā

1. zā kà bā nì kwabò   6. zā kà kāmà shi
2. zā kì kāwō kuɗī   7. zā kà ɗinkà wàndō
3. zā kà jē wajen Sīdì   8. zā kì yi àbinci
4. zā kà kāwō sù   9. zā kà saukè
5. zā kà saukè dōyà   10. zā kà yī shi

Drill 4 - Use the continuative pronoun in the pattern sentences as your cue in constructing the sentence in kā/kin/yā/tā/sun ragē sulè biyu, nā yàrda.

    Cue: tanà dà rīgā

    Student response: in tā rage sulè biyu, nā yàrda

    Cue: sunà dà rīgā

    Student response: in sun rage sulè biyu, nā yàrda

1. kunà dà rīgā   6. tanà dà dōyà
2. yanà dà rīgā   7. kanà dà dōyà
3. kanà dà rīgā   8. sunà dà dōyà
4. sunà dà rīgā   9. kinà dà dōyà
5. kinà dà rīgā   10. kunà dà dōyà

Drill 5 - You will be given a sentence of the form kuɗin ƙwai gùdā kwabò biyu nē 'the price of one egg is two pence'. Your response will be to give the price for each of a bunch of eggs (or whatever the item is) by doubling the price as illustrated in section c) of 10.5, in this case kuɗin ƙwai kwabò biyu biyu nē.

    Cue: kuɗin àlƙalàmī gùdā sulè nē

    Student response: kuɗin àlƙalàmī sulè sulè nē

    Cue: kuɗin gwēbà gùdā kwabò biyu nē

    Student response: kuɗin gwēbà kwabò biyu biyu nē

1. kuɗin gōrò gùdā kwabò nē
2. kuɗin zàbō gùdā sulè ukù nē
3. kuɗin kashìn tàttàsai gùdā sīsì nē
4. kuɗin ƙōshiyà gùdā kwabò biyu nē
5. kuɗin kwàndō gùdā kwabò biyar nē
6. kuɗin burōdì gùdā sulè nē   n.m.   'loaf of bread'
7. kuɗin gwēbà gùdā kwabò biyu nē
8. kuɗin kashìn tàttàsai gùdā kwabò huɗu nē

9. kuɗin lèmō gùdā kwabô nē

10. kuɗin kāzā gùdā sulê huɗu dà sīsī nē

Drill 6 - Answer the question X dà Y nawà kè nan? with the sentence X dà Y, Z kè nan as shown in the example.

Cue: àshìrin dà tàlàtin, nawà kè nan? (20 + 30 = ?)

Student response: àshìrin dà tàlàtin, hàmsin kè nan (20 + 30 = 50)

1. 21 + 21 = ?
2. 10 + 40 = ?
3. 15 + 20 = ?
4. 22 + 40 = ?
5. 15 + 15 = ?

6. 30 + 40 = ?
7. 19 + 10 = ?
8. 25 + 25 = ?
9. 60 + 30 = ?
10. 60 + 23 = ?

Drill 7 - In this drill you will be given as a cue a sum of money either in shillings or in Naira. If the sum is in shillings, your response will be sulê X, kwabō Y kè nan, if it is in Naira, your response will be Nairà X, sulê Y kè nan, that is, give the equivalent of shillings in kobo and the equivalent of Naira in shillings.

Cue: sulê shidà

Student response: sulê shidà, kwabō sìttin kè nan

Cue: Nairà huɗu

Student response: Nairà huɗu, sulê àrbà'in kè nan

1. sulê ɗaya
2. Nairà ɗaya
3. sulê biyu
4. Nairà biyu
5. Nairà bìyar

6. sulê huɗu
7. sulê bìyar
8. Nairà ukù
9. sulê ukù
10. Nairà huɗu

Drill 8 - Answer the question X à ɗebè Y, nawà kè nan? 'X take away Y is how much?' with the pattern sentence X à ɗebè Y, saurā Z 'X take away Y, (the) remainder (is) Z'. The expression à ɗebè literally means 'may one remove'.

Cue: hàmsin à ɗebè àshìrin nawà kè nan? (50 - 20 = ?)

Student response: hàmsin à ɗebè àshìrin, saurā tàlàtin (50 - 20 = 30)

1. 80 - 40 = ?
2. 100 - 70 = ?
3. 44 - 22 = ?
4. 50 - 23 = ?
5. 90 - 45 = ?

6. 70 - 30 = ?
7. 85 - 15 = ?
8. 36 - 16 = ?
9. 60 - 35 = ?
10. 47 - 17 = ?

127

Drill 9 - Answer the question, <u>nawà ne kuɗin X?</u> with the phrase <u>kuɗinsà/tà...</u>
with the price give as a cue put in the blank. Do this drill with the books
open so you can see the prices given as cues.

    Question: nawà ne kuɗin rĩgã?

    Cue: ₦11.80

    Student response: kuɗintà fâm bìyar dà sulè gõmà shâ takwàs

1. nawà nē kuɗin wuƙã?   30k
2. nawà nē kuɗin àlƙalàmī?   5k
3. nawà nē kuɗin hūlã?   ₦5.50
4. nawà nē kuɗin kwàndõ?   ₦1.70
5. nawà nē kuɗin littãfī?   ₦5.93
6. nawà nē kuɗin kēkē?   ₦45.00
7. nawà nē kuɗin àgõgõ?   ₦12.50
8. nawà nē kuɗin mõtà?   ₦850.00

Drill 10 - Repeat the initial sentence, then substitute the first cue into
the appropriate place in that sentence. As each cue is given, substitute it
into the sentence formed from the previous cue, so that a new sentence is
formed.

Initial sentence: nã bar mikì

Cues

1. Audù   Audù yã bar mikì

2. future aspect   Audù zâi bar mikì

3. Audù dà Mammàn   Audù dà Mammàn zā sù bar mikì

4. wannàn   Audù dà Mammàn zā sù bar mikì wannàn

5. na sĩsĩ sĩsĩ   Audù dà Mammàn zā sù bar mikì wannàn na sĩsĩ sĩsĩ

6. kashĩ   Audù dà Mammàn zā sù bar mikì (wannàn) kashĩ na sĩsĩ sĩs

7. à kân kwabõ   Audù dà Mammàn zā sù bar mikì (wannàn) kashĩ na sĩsĩ sĩs
    ukù ukù   à kân kwabõ ukù ukù

GUIDED CONVERSATION

    The drill section of this unit is not as extensive as in some of the
previous units so that more time can be given to the guided conversation.
A large proportion of the time spent on the unit should be passed in bargaining for various things. Everyone should have a chance to play the part
of both buyer and seller several times.
    You should be familiar with the bargaining expressions found in this
unit. You should also review the dialogues of Unit VI where a few other
such expressions are found. The various patterns that bargaining constructic
fall into are outlined in 10.5.
    To start with, the exact form the bargaining will take should be decidee
on beforehand, that is, the prices that the buyer and seller will volunteer
to start with should be fixed; the final price should be fixed; it should
be decided whether the buyer or seller will strenuously object to the other'
offer or whether they will come to rapid agreement on a price; it should be
decided whether the buyer will walk away and be called back or a decision

be reached on the spot; etc. After more familiarity with expressions is attained, the bargaining students can let the bargaining situation take its own course. Several items of the same kind but of varying quality might be brought to class so that the bargainers can use them for "leverage" by offering to buy or sell two items for a price less than the sum of the two separately, or by offering to buy or sell an item of slightly inferior quality for the price offered for a better one. Some suggestions are several pieces of handicraft such as small sculptures or pieces of jewelry, several pairs of sandals, several shirts, several knives, or several pens and pencils. Another possibility would be to bring plastic fruit of various kinds. You might want to decide beforehand what the highest price a buyer would want to pay for an item and what the lowest price the seller would let it go for would be. The idea of the bargaining would then be to achieve a compromise between these prices. Following are some examples:

	Seller	Buyer	
tàkàlmī	₦2.00	₦1.50	
wuⱤà	30k	20k	
àyàbà	3k	2k	'banana'
zōbè	₦8.00	₦5.00	'ring'
tagùwā	₦6.50	₦4.50	

kwāna	v.intr.	'pass the night'	tsīnī	n.m.	'sharp point'
Lārābā	n.f.	'Wednesday'	wàhalā	n.f.	'trouble'
ran Lārābā		'(the day of) Wednesday' (see 11.6)	wàyā	n.f.	'wire'
sàuka	v.intr.	'get dwon, stay (as a guest)'	wàtō		'that is to say'
			zamā	n.m.	'staying (in one place)'
shakkā	n.f.	'doubt'	zō	v.intr.	'come'
tàfiyà	n.f.	'travelling'			

B. Malam Amadu now invites Malam Shehu inside the house to chat.

Āmadù: Tô, bismillā, mù shìga zaurè. Kā gan shì, kō shārā bàbù.
Well, be my guest, let's go into the entrance hut. You see, it hasn't even been swept. (A standard apology offered when a guest enters the house.)

Shēhù: Ā'ā, ai bā kōmē.
It doesn't matter. (Standard reply to the above "apology".)

Āmadù: Inā lābārī?
What's the news?

Shēhù: Lābārī sai àlhērī.
The news is good.

Āmadù: Nā ji kā yi hadàrī dà mōtàrkà.
I heard that you had an accident with your car.

Shēhù: Ī, àmmā bàn yi ràunī ba.
Yes, but I didn't suffer any injuries.

Āmadù: An aunà arzìkī. Barkà!
You were lucky (one measured wealth). Congratulations!

Shēhù: Af! Nā ji mātarkà tā haihù.
Say! I heard your wife had a baby.

Āmadù: Ī, tā hàifi dā namijì.
Yes, she had a boy (male son).

Shēhù: Allāh yà rayā.
May God give (him) life.

Āmadù: Āmin.
Amen.

Vocabulary

af		interjection of surprise, often feigned	namijì	n.m.	'male (human or animal)'
arzìkī	n.m.	'wealth, good fortune'	ràunī	n.m.	'injury'
aunā	v.tr.	'weigh, measure'	(raunukā pl.)		
dā ('yā'yā pl.)	n.m.	'son'	yi ràunī		'get injured'
hadàrī	n.m.	'accident'	rayā	v.tr.	'give life to'
hàifi from hàifā	v.tr.	'give birth to'	shārā	n.f.	'sweeping'
haihù	v.intr.	'give birth, have a baby'	shìga	v.intr.	'enter'
ji	v.tr.	'hear'	zaurè (zaurukā pl.)	n.m.	hut or room at entrance of a compound - used by mai gidā to entertain his friends
kōmē		'anything, (with negative) nothing'			

COMPREHENSION PRACTICE

Without looking at your books, listen to the passage as your informant reads through it once, pausing to explain in Hausa the meaning of any new words or expressions. Your informant will read the passage a second time at normal conversational speed and then ask you the questions which follow. Answer in complete sentences.

Zìyārā[1] Kanò

Wata rāna[2] Màlàm Shēhù ya zō Kanò. Mōtàrsà ta ɓācì à daf dà Bauci àmmā bài yi ràunī ba. Ya kwāna à bārikìn Bauci. À Kanò ya sàuka à gidan Ìbrāhìm, mài ƙàtòn kâi dà tsīnin hancī. ShT mā, yanà aikī à Gidan Wayà. Wàshēgàrī[3] Màlàm Shēhù ya tàfi gidan àbōkinsà[4], Màlàm Àmadù. Màlàm Shēhù ya bâ Màlàm Àmadù làbārin tàfiyàrsà kumā sukà yàrda tàfiyā, tā fi zamā. Sukà shìga zaurē sukà ci gàbā[5] dà hīrā[6], sai[7] Màlàm Shēhù ya cè yā ji màtar Màlàm Àmadù tā haihù. Ai, wannàn gàskiyā nè. Tā hàifi ɗā namijì. Allàh yà rayà, àmin.

[1]zìyārā	n.f.	'visiting'	[5]ci gàbā	'continue' ("eat" ahead)
[2]wata rāna		'one day'	[6]hīrā n.f.	'chatting'
[3]wàshēgàrī		'the next day'	[7]sai	'when'
[4]àbōkī	n.m.	'friend'	[8]'yā màcè n.f.	'baby girl'

Tambayoyi

1. Ìnā Màlàm Shēhù ya tàfi?
2. Mè ya sàmē shì à daf dà Bauci?
3. Ìnā ya kwāna à Bauci?
4. Dà ya kai Kanò, ìnā ya sàuka?
5. Wànē nè Màlàm Ìbrāhìm? Yanà aikī à kàntī?
6. Wànē nè Màlàm Àmadù?
7. Màlàm Shēhù yā bâ Màlàm Àmadù làbārin bārikìn Bauci?
8. Ìnā Màlàm Shēhù dà Màlàm Àmadù sukà shìga?
9. Mè Màlàm Shēhù ya cè yā ji?
10. Gaskiyā màtar Màlàm Shēhù tā hàifi 'yā màcè[8]?

GRAMMAR

11.1 Negative Completive Aspect

The negative forms of the completive aspect pronouns (7.2) are shown in the table which follows. The verb zō 'come' is used to illustrate how these forms work.

133

Singular		Plural	
bàn zō ba	'I didn't come'	bà mù zō ba	'we didn't come'
bà kà zō ba	'you(m) didn't come'	bà kù zō ba	'you didn't come'
bà kì zō ba	'you(f) didn't come'		
bài zō ba	'he didn't come'	bà sù zō ba	'they didn't come'
bà tà zō ba	'she didn't come'		
bà à zō ba	'one didn't come'		

The negative completive is comprised of a short, low tone pronoun directly preceded by a short, low tone bà. A second short, high tone ba is placed at the end of the sentence. If there is a noun subject, it precedes the first bà.

No matter how long the sentence is, the second ba should come at the end except for a few adverbial expressions, usually indicating time, such as jiyà 'yesterday', yâu 'today', dà rāna 'at midday', etc. With these expressions, ba may either precede or follow. One word, tukùna 'not yet', always appears after the final ba.

Examples of the negative completive are

mōtà bà tà bā kà wàhalà ba?	'didn't your car give you any trouble?'
bàn fita nā ganī ba	'I didn't go out and see'
bài zō ba jiyà	
or	'he didn't come yesterday'
bài zō jiyà ba	
bài zō ba tukùna	'he hasn't come yet'

11.2 Direct Object Pronouns

In 4.5 and 6.3 we saw the pronouns shi, ta, and su used with the words gà and àkwai. These pronouns are part of the following set of direct object pronouns:

Singular		Plural	
ni/nì	'me'	mu/mù	'us'
ka/kà	'you(m)'	ku/kù	'you'
ki/kì	'you(f)'		
shi/shì	'him'	su/sù	'them'
ta/tà	'her'		

Two things should be noted about the use of these pronouns:

a) They have short vowels and "polar tone", that is, the tone is opposite the tone of the preceding syllable (there are two exceptions to this "polar tone" rule which will be covered in a later unit).

b) The pronouns are used only when they DIRECTLY FOLLOW TRANSITIVE VERBS or the words gà, àkwai, and bà (and gàrē which will be covered in 15.6).

Thus we have

      nā gan shì   'I saw him'

with the transitive verb <u>ganī</u> 'see' (the form <u>gan</u> is explained in 11.4), but in

      inà dà shī   'I have it'

where <u>dà</u> is not a verb, we must use the independent pronoun, <u>shī</u>.

    In 10.3 it was pointed out that the final vowel length of verbs varies according to various factors. You should note that with many transitive verbs, a final vowel will be long before a pronoun direct object and short before a noun direct object. This situation will be discussed more fully in a later unit, but it is best to form good habits as early as possible, so try to imitate your informant in this respect.

    IMPORTANT: In Hausa, when referring to a previously mentioned noun, it is not always necessary to use a direct object pronoun and sometimes it is absolutely wrong to use one. The direct object <u>pronoun is optional</u> with most verbs when you are referring to a previously mention <u>specific, concrete object</u>, that is when the pronoun would refer to a noun that would be modified in English by 'the', by a demonstrative pronoun, or would mean 'the one in question'.

    Q: kā kāwō wannàn tàbarmā?   'did you bring this mat?'

    A: Ī, nā kāwō
       or   'yes, I brought it'
       Ī, nā kāwō tà

    Q: Sīdi, yā ɗinkà wàndōn   'did Sidi sew the pants?'

    A: Ī, yā ɗinkà
       or   'yes, he sewed them'
       Ī, yā ɗinkà shi

The pronoun is preferably not used when referring to an inanimate object. It is normally used when referring to a human.

    The direct object <u>pronoun cannot be used</u> when the <u>object is not specific</u>, that is when the noun to which the pronoun would refer is used in a general way to refer to a type of thing rather than any specific object of that type. In English, the pronouns used in such cases will usually be 'one' or 'some' rather than 'he', 'she', 'it', etc. For example, the question 'did you get a hoe?' could be answered in English 'yes, I got one'; the question 'did you drink some water?' could be answered 'yes, I drank some'. Reference is not being made to any specific hoe or to any specific water.

    Q: kā yi tàbarmā?   'did you make a mat?' (i.e. a mat as opposed to a rug or some other type of object)

    A: Ī, nā yi   'yes, I made one'

    Q: tā fasà ƙwai?   'did she break any eggs?'

    A: Ī, tā fasà   'yes, she broke some'

    Some verbs, notably <u>sanī</u> and <u>ganī</u> 'know' and 'see', can be used with concrete, physical objects or with abstract facts or activities. When the object is a specific concrete person or thing, they <u>must</u> be followed by the direct object pronouns. With abstract facts or activities as objects, they take no pronoun.

Q:	kā san Ìbrāhìm?	'do you know Ibrahim?'
A:	Ī, nā san shì	'yes, I know him'
Q:	kin ga mātarsà?	'did you see his wife?'
A:	Ī, nā gan tà	'yes, I saw her'
Q:	kā san mōtātā tā ɓàci?	'did you know my car broke down?'
A:	bàn sanī ba	'I didn't know (that)'
Q:	kā ga sun tàfi?	'did you see that they had left?'
A:	Ī, nā ganī	'yes, I saw'

There are some other factors that play a role in whether or not a direct object pronoun will be used to refer to a noun. What is important, however, is not that you memorize the "rules" above in detail, but that you realize that at times where some sort of pronoun is needed in English, Hausa does not necessarily need any overtly expressed pronoun.

11.3 Continuative Pronouns with "Action Nouns"

In the dialogue of this lesson we see an illustration of a further use of the continuative pronouns (see 6.1) in the sentence

yanā aikì à Gidan Wayā   'he works at the Post Office'

The continuative pronouns can be used with "action nouns" such as aikì 'work, working'; maganà 'speech, speaking'; wāsā 'play, playing'; etc. These words are not verbs, but when used with the continuative pronouns, they function much as verbs. Further examples are

inā tsàmmānì kanà dà awākī   'I think you (must) have a lot
       dà yawā   of goats'

yanā barcī   'he's sleeping'

11.4 The Verbs 'see', 'know', and 'leave'

Most verbs in Hausa follow some very general patterns which will be described in later lessons. As in all languages, however, there are a few words which do not fall into the most general categories and must be described separately. Three such words are the verbs ganī 'see', sanī 'know', and barī 'leave'. They have the following forms (note that sanī and barī follow the same pattern while ganī differs in having two high tones and has different forms before nouns and pronouns):

	ganī 'see'	sanī 'know'	barī 'leave'
Form when no object follows	ganī	sanī	barī
Form when followed by a pronoun direct object	gan	san	bar (also before in-indirect objects – see Unit XII)
Form when followed by a noun direct object	ga	san	bar

136

Some examples using these verbs are

nā ganT	'I see'
kā ga awākTnā?	'did you see my goats?'
T, nā gan sù	'yes, I saw them'
bàn sanT ba	'I don't know'
kā san Ibrāhìm?	'do you know Ibrahim?'
T, nā san shì	'yes, I know him'
nā baɾ mōtằtā cân	'I left my car over there'
nā baɾ mikì kwabǒ kwabǒ	'I (will) let you have (it) for a kobo each' (I leave to you kobo-kobo)

11.5 The Verb bā 'give'

In English the thing given is the direct object of the verb 'give' and the recipient of this "gift" is the indirect object. In Hausa the situation is somewhat reversed. The use of bā 'give' is perhaps best illustrated with examples:

a) yā bā nì kudT   'he gave me money'

b) yā bā nì   'he gave me (some unspecified object)'

c) yā bā dà kudī   'he gave money'

In a) where both the recipient and gift are expressed, the recipient directly follows the verb, and is in fact the direct object. The gift then directly follows the recipient. In b) where no gift is overtly expressed, the recipient again directly follows the verb.

However, in c), where only the gift is expressed, the preposition dà must be used.

One further point is that when bā is followed by a direct object pronoun recipient, it has high tone and long vowel, but when followed by a noun recipient it has falling tone and long vowel.

nā bâ ɗan tēbùr sulè   'I gave the ɗan tebur a shilling'

nā bâ shì sulè   'I gave him a shilling'

11.6 The Days of the Week

The names for the days of the week in Hausa are:

Lahàdì	'Sunday'
Litinîn	'Monday'
Tàlātà	'Tuesday'
Làrabà	'Wednesday'
Àlhàmîs	'Thursday'
Jumma'à	'Friday'
Àsabàr; SātT	'Saturday'

The days of the week are frequently preceded by ran 'the day of' as illustrated in Dialogue A.

nā zō ran Làrabà   'I came on Wednesday'

137

GRAMMATICAL DRILLS

Drill 1 - Transform the affirmative sentences below to negative sentences as shown in the example.

Cue sentence: mōtā̀ tā bā kà wàhalā̀?

Student response: mōtā̀ bà tà bā kà wàhalā̀ ba?

1. kā̄ zō ran Lahàdì?

2. nā̄ zō à mōtā̀

3. yā̄ kwāna à bārikin Bauci

4. Audù yā̄ san shì

5. mōtā̀ tā ɓàcì à daf dà Bauci

6. kun yi hadàrī dà mōtàrkù?

7. nā̄ ragè sulè̄ bìyar

8. mun kāwō sulè̄ tàlātin

9. kuɗintà sun fi hakà

10. mōtōcī sun zō dàgà Jàs

Drill 2A - 2B

2A You will be given a cue of the form 'someone does not have ...'. Your response will be tô, zâi bā (pronoun)... . Supply the direct object pronoun which corresponds to the subject of the cue sentence followed by the noun of the cue sentence.

Cue sentence: Audù bā̂ shi dà gōrò

Student response: tô, zâi bā shì gōrò

Cue sentence: bā̂ ni dà gwēbā̀

Student response: tô, zâi bā kà gwēbā̀

2B Replace the recipient with a pronoun as in 2A, but this time drop the thing given completely.

Cue sentence: Audù bā̂ shi dà gōrò

Student response: tô, zâi bā shì

Cue sentence: bā̂ ni dà gwēbā̀

Student response: tô, zâi bā kà

1. yā̂rā bā̂ su dà gwēbā̀

2. Mammàn bā̂ shi dà fensìr

3. bā̂ ku dà kuɗī

4. bā̂ ki dà kòshiyà

5. mutā̀nen gàrī bā̂ su dà àbinci

6. bā̂ mu dà fartanyōyī

7. Hàlīmà bā̂ ta dà tābā̀

8. Mūsā bā̂ shi dà fartanyà̄

9. bā̂ ka dà lìttàttàfai

10. bā̂ ni dà àbinci

Drill 3 - You will be given a sentence of the form yā yi ... jiyà with an "action noun" in the space. Change this to a sentence of the form yanà̀ ... yànzu, using the appropriate continuative pronoun followed by the same action noun. Three nouns used in this drill that have not occurred so far in dialogues are màganà̄ 'speaking', wā̄sā 'playing', and barcī 'sleeping'.

Cue sentence: yā̂rā sun yi wā̄sā jiyà

Student response: yā̂rā sunà̄ wā̄sā yànzu

1. Ibrāhim yā yi aikī jiyà

2. mātātā tā yi shàrā̄ jiyà

3. nā̄ yi tàfiyà̄ jiyà

4. dà̄libai sun yi wā̄sā jiyà

138

5. kun yi màganā̀ jiyà
6. mutànē sun yi aikī̀ jiyà
7. nā̀ yi wā̀sā̀ jiyà

8. yā̀ yi barcī̀ jiyà
9. Hārūnà yā̀ yi tàfiyā̀ jiyà
10. uwargidā̀ tā̀ yi shā̀rā̀ jiyà

Drill 4A - 4C - This drill is for practice of the various forms of barī̀, sanī̀, and ganī̀.

4A Replacᶒ the underlined verb in the cue sentence with the proper form of barī̀.

Cue sentence: nā̀ yī̀ shì à gidā̀
Student response: nā̀ bar shì à gidā̀

1. yā̀ sà̀yi tà̀barmā̀ à kà̀suwā̀
2. bà̀ tà̀ yà̀rda ba
3. sun kà̀wō kùjèrū gà̀ban ɗàkī̀

4. tā̀ ga gidā̀ kō shā̀rā̀ bà̀bù
5. yā̀ zō gidā̀ wajen ƙarfè̀ ukù
6. bà̀n san shì ba

4B Replacᶒ the underlined verb in the cue sentence with the proper form of sanī̀.

Cue sentence: nā̀ gaishḕ shì
Student response: nā̀ san shì̀

1. yā̀ gaishḕ kà̀
2. kā̀ ga Ìbrāhìm?
3. nā̀ zō dà̀ mā̀lā̀min makarantā̀

4. kā̀ ga aikìn nan yanā̀ dà̀ wùyā̀
5. Ìbrāhìm yā̀ ganī̀
6. nā̀ ji mà̀tarkà̀ tā̀ haihù

4C Replace the underlined verb in the sentence with the proper form of ganī̀.

1. bà̀l sanī̀ ba
2. yā̀ gaishḕ kà̀
3. kā̀ bar shì à Gidan Wayā̀?

4. nā̀ yi ƙōshiyōyī̀ dà̀ yawā̀ jiyà
5. an bar nì kusa dà̀ gidankù
6. nā̀ ji wuƙà̀ƙensà̀ sunā̀ dà̀ kyâu

Drill 5 - Put the cues into the sentence nā̀ bā̀ ... 'I gave ...'. If the cue is a person or a pronoun, it should be the recipient of the giving. If the cue is a thing, it should be the thing given. If both a person and a thing are given as a cue, put them both into the sentence.

Cue: shī̀
Student response: nā̀ bā̀ shì̀
Cue: kuɗī̀
Student response: nā̀ bā̀ dà̀ kuɗī̀
Cue: Àmīnà̀, ƙwai
Student response: nā̀ bā̀ Àmīnà̀ ƙwai

1. À̀madù
2. sulè̀ biyu
3. ita, tà̀barmā̀

4. kū
5. Hārūnà̀
6. kà̀zā dà̀ zà̀bō

7. kḕ
8. kai, wàhalà̀
9. dōyā̀

10. ɗà̀libī̀, littāfī̀

139

Drill 6 - Answer the question yàushè zā sù zō? by substituting the cues below in the pattern sentence zā sù zō ran (day).

Cue: yàushè zā sù zō? (Monday)

Student response: zā sù zō ran Lìtìnîn

1. yàushè zā sù zō? (Friday)
2. yàushè zā mù zō? (Sunday)
3. yàushè zā tà zō? (Saturday)
4. yàushè zân zō? (Wednesday)
5. yàushè zā kà zō? (Monday)

6. yàushè zā kì zō? (Thursday)
7. yàushè zā sù zō? (Tuesday)
8. yàushè zâi zō? (Friday)
9. yàushè zā kù zō? (Sunday)
10. yàushè zâi zō? (Thursday)

Drill 7 - Answer the question yàushè zā à zō? 'when will one come?' with the sentence bà à bar gidā ba tùkùna 'one hasn't left the house yet'. Answer a question in the second person with the first person.

Cue question: yàushè zā kì zō?

Student response: bàn bar gidā ba tùkùna

1. yàushè zâi zō?
2. yàushè zā kù zō?
3. yàushè zā tà zō?
4. yàushè zā sù zō?
5. yàushè Âmadù zâi zō?

6. yàushè zā kà zō?
7. yàushè dàlìbai zā sù zō?
8. yàushè zā kì zō?
9. yàushè zā à zō?
10. yàushè uwargidā zā tà zō?

Drill 8A - 8B

8A Give an affirmative reply to the questions below. Your answers should contain the direct object pronoun that corresponds to the direct object noun in the question. Change the first person pronouns to second person and second person to first person.

Cue sentence: kā ga awākīnā?

Student response: Ī, nā gan sù

Cue sentence: sun san nì?

Student response: Ī, sun san kà

8B Follow the directions for 8A, but answer in the negative rather than in the affirmative.

Cue sentence: kā ga awākīnā?

Student response: ā'ā, bàn gan sù ba

Cue sentence: sun san nì?

Student response: ā'ā, bà sù san kà ba

1. Hàlīmà tā san Ìbrāhìm?
2. kin bar mōtàrkì cân?
3. mutànen Gidan Wayà sun gan kà?
4. Audù yā bar kuɗinsà?
5. kun ga zaurèn?

6. an bar kà à can?
7. sun bar lìttàttàfansù à gidā?
8. kā ga Audù à kàsuwā?
9. yā gan mù à Gidan Wayà?
10. mun bar alƙalumànmù can?

140

11. kā ga rĩgarsà?   13. an bar kù à ƙauyè?

12. Hàwwa tā san Hàlĩmà?   14. yā bā nì fâm biyu?

Drill 9A - 9B - Use the cues for two drills.

9A You'll be given a sentence of the form yâu ... nē wherę a day of the week
fills the blank. Respond with the sentence gòbe ... kē nan, using the
name for the proper day of the week in the blank.

   Cue: yâu SātĨ nḕ

   Student response: gòbe Lahàdì kḕ nan

9B Follow the directions for 9A, substituting jiyà for gòbe in the response.

   Cue: yâu SātĨ nḕ

   Student response: jiyà Jumma'ā̀ kḕ nan

1. Lìtinîn 3. Àsabàr 5. Jumma'ā̀ 7. Tàlātà̀

2. Àlhàmîs 4. Lahàdì 6. Làrabā

Drill 10 - Answer the following questions in the affirmative, either replacing the noun direct object by a pronoun or no object at all. This drill
might first be done with students asking the informant the questions to find
out which responses seem most natural to him.

   Cue question: kā aunà wannàn àkwâtì?

   Student response: Ĩ, nā aunà̀ or Ĩ, nā aunā̀ shi

   Cue question: kā ci àbinci?

   Student response: Ĩ, nā ci

1. yā ɗinkà wannàn wàndõ?   7. kin yi aikĩ?

2. tā sun Zàinabù?   8. tā karyà ƙoshiyā̀ yâu?

3. kun ci dõyā̀?   9. kun ji màganà̀ cikin ɗakĩ?

4. kā̀ bar wannàn kujèrā à gàban gidã? 10. yā ga Abdù à Gidan Wayà̀?

5. kā san mā̀tātà̀ tā haihù?   11. tā karyà ƙoshiyàrtà?

6. yā bar yā̀ransà à gidā?   12. kā aunà̀ ɗankà̀?

Drill 11A - 11C - Repeat the initial sentence, then substitute the first cue into
the appropriate place in that sentence. As each cue is given, substitute it
into the sentence formed from the previous cue, so that a new sentence is
formed.

11A Initial sentence: tā ɓàci

Cues	Student response
1. mõtā̀	mõtā̀ tā ɓàci
2. mõtātā̀	mõtātā̀ tā ɓàci
3. mõtàrkà	mõtàrkà tā ɓàci
4. bā dà wàhalā̀	mõtàrkà tā bā dà wàhalā̀
5. bā kà wàhalā̀	mõtàrkà tā bā kà wàhalā̀
6. daf dà Bauci	mõtàrkà tā bā kà wàhalā̀ daf dà Bauci

141

7. Kàtsinà	mōtàrkà tā bā kà wàhalā daf dà Kàtsinà
8. nā ji	nā ji mōtàrkà tā bā kà wàhalā daf dà Kàtsinà
9. an cê	an cê mōtàrkà tā bā kà wàhalā daf dà Kàtsinà
10. nā san	nā san mōtàrkà tā bā kà wàhalā daf dà Kàtsinà

11B <u>Initial sentence:</u> nā zō

1. Āmadù	Āmadù yā zō
2. Shēhù	Shēhù yā zō
3. ran Lahàdì	Shēhù yā zō ran Lahàdì
4. Lìtinîn	Shēhù yā zō ran Lìtinîn
5. Tàlātà	Shēhù yā zō ran Tàlātà
6. sàuka	Shēhù yā sàuka ran Tàlātà
7. à gidan Ìbrāhìm	Shēhù yā sàuka ran Tàlātà à gidan Ìbrāhìm
8. wajen ƙarfè huɗu	Shēhù yā sàuka ran Tàlātà à gidan Ìbrāhìm wajen ƙarfè huɗu
9. bìyar	Shēhù yā sàuka ran Tàlātà à gidan Ìbrāhìm wajen ƙarfè bìyar
10. dà kwatà	Shēhù yā sàuka ran Tàlātà à gidan Ìbrāhìm wajen ƙarfè bìyar dà kwatà

11C <u>Initial sentence:</u> tā yi cìnikī

1. aikìn gidā	tā yi aikìn gidā
2. shàrā	tā yi shàrā
3. Àmīnà	Àmīnà tā yi shàrā
4. màtarsà	màtarsà tā yi shàrā
5. màtarkà	màtarkà tā yi shàrā
6. haihù	màtarkà tā haihù
7. hàifi ɗà nimijì	màtarkà tā hàifi ɗà namijì
8. 'yā màcè n.f. 'baby girl'	màtarkà tā hàifi 'yā màcè
9. nā ji	nā ji màtarkà tā hàifi 'yā màcè

GUIDED CONVERSATION

1) Based on the expressions in dialogue A in this unit, two students may discuss a trip (real or imaginary) that a student has recently taken, or plans for a trip that he intends to take. Things that might be discussed are day of departure (use the names for the days of the weeks), day of arrival, place where one is staying, and type of transportation. The words for different types of transport are

> mōtà   n.f.   'car, bus, truck'
>
> jirgin samà   n.m.   'airplace' (vehicle of the sky)

142

jirgin ƙasà   n.m.   'train'   (vehicle of the land)

jirgin ruwā   n.m.   'boat'   (vehicle of the water)

The word jirgī means 'any vehicle inside which one can ride' (except a car). If it is understood that the vehicle is plane, train, or boat by context, jirgī alone may be used.

Example conversation:

Student 1: Inā zā kà jē gòbe?	Where are you going tomorrow?
Student 2: Zân tàfi gàrinmù.	I'm going to go to my home town.
1: Inā nè gàrinkù?	Where is your home town?
2: Gàrinmù New York kè nan.	My home town is New York.
1: Zā kà jē à jirgin samā?	Are you going to go by plane?
2: Ī, hakà nē.	Yes, that's right.
1: Zā kà ga bàbankà?	Will you be seeing your father?
2: Ā'à, bā yā New York yànzu. Yanā Chicago yanā aikī.	No, he's not in New York now. He's in Chicago working.

2) A person on a trip may stop at a hotel. One student takes the part of a traveler, another the part of the desk clerk. You probably have enough expressions at your disposal to do this either in the context of a Nigerian bārikī or an American hotel or motel.

Example conversation:

Student 1: Barkā dà zuwā.	Greetings on your arrival.
Student 2: Barkā kàdai.	Greetings to you.
1: Zā kà kwāna à nan?	Are you going to pass the night here?
2: Hakà nē. Nawà nē ɗakī?	That's right. How much is a room?
1: Kwānā ɗaya, Nairā shidà.	One night (one passing of the night) (is) ₦6.00.
2: Ai, bābù tsādā. Zân tàfi ran Jumma'à, wàtàu jībi.	Well, that's not too expensive. I'll be leaving Friday, that is, day after tomorrow.
1: Dà kyâu. Kanà dà kāyā?	Fine. Do you have luggage?
2: Bàn kāwō kāyā dà yawā ba. Sai wannàn jàkā.	I didn't bring much luggage. Just this bag.
1: Tô, yārò, kai jàkâr ɗakin Mālàm (name).	All right. Boy, take the bag to Mr. (name)'s room.

143

DIALOGUES

A. This dialogue describes the trouble Malam Shehu Abubakar had with his car on the way to Kano. As he is passing through a small village about thirty-five miles south of Bauchi, a loud roaring begins to issue from beneath his Peugeot 404. He stops the car, looks under it[,] and sees a large hole in his muffler. Rather than drive into Bauchi, he decides to try to have it repaired in the village. He goes in search of a black-smith.

Shēhù:	Sànnu dà aikĪ!	Greetings at work!
MaƙèrĪ:	Maràbā!	Welcome!
Shēhù:	Inà sô kà yĪ miɲì wani ɗan gyārā à mōtātā.	I want you to make a minor repair on my car.
MaƙèrĪ:	Wànè Irìn gyārā nè?	What kind of repair is it?
Shēhù:	Sàlansā tā hūjè.	The muffler has a hole in it (is pierced).
MaƙèrĪ:	Kanà sô ìn ĪΤƙè ta?	Do you want me to patch it?
Shēhù:	Ī, àmmā inà saurĪ.	Yes, but I'm in a hurry.
MaƙèrĪ:	Nâ kai har ƙarfè ukù kàfin ìn gamà.	It will take me until 3:00 to finish it (I'll reach 3:00 before I finish).
Shēhù:	Bà zā kà yi ƙòƙarĪ kà gamā zuwā ƙarfè biyu ba?	Won't you make an effort to finish by 2:00?
MaƙèrĪ:	Ai, sai nā sayō gawàyĪ.	Look, I have to go buy charcoal.
Shēhù:	Tô, yi hanzarĪ!	OK, hurry up.
MaƙèrĪ:	Ai gaggàwā bâ ta dà àmfānĪ.	"Haste makes waste." (Proverb: Haste has no usefulness.)

Vocabulary

àmfānĪ	n.m.	'usefulness'	ƙòƙarĪ n.m.	'effort'
gaggàwā	n.f.	'hastening'	ĪΤƙè v.tr.	'patch, plug (a hole)'
gamà	v.tr.	'finish'	maƙèrĪ n.m.	'blacksmith'
gawàyĪ	n.m.	'charcoal'	(maƙèrā pl.)	
gyārā	n.m.	'repair'	sàlansā n.f.	'muffler, exhaust pipe'

ɗan gyārā 'minor repair' (ɗan 'son of' can be used in this way with masculine nouns to mean 'small, insignificant'; with feminine nouns, 'yar 'daughter of' is used, for example 'yar wàhalà 'minor difficulty')

hanzarĪ	n.m.	'speed'	saurĪ n.m.	'quickness'
har		'until'	sayō v.tr.	'buy (and bring back)'
hūjè	v.intr.	'get pierced'	wànè adj.m.	'what?, which?'
irĪ	n.m.	'kind'	wani adj.m.	'some, a, a certain'
kàfin		'before'	zuwà (cf. zō 'come')	'by, up to, to'

B. Malam Shehu Imam is a school inspector attached to the Ministry of Education in Kaduna. One day he has to travel to Katsina to inspect several primary schools. Just outside of Funtuwa he stops and asks for directions.

Shēhù: Ìnā hanyàr zuwā Kàtsinà?

Where is the road to Katsina?

Wani mùtûm: Gà ta nân. Kanā sô ìn bā kà bayānī?

Here it is. Do you want me to give you directions?

Shēhù: Ī, mànà.

Yes, indeed.

Mùtûm: Tô, sai kà yī ta tàfiyà har kà jē Funtuwà. Kà bī ta dāmạ kà jē Malumfāshi, kà wucē har Yāshi.

Well, you keep on going until you get to Funtuwa. Turn right and go to Malamfashi, go past until (you reach) Yashi.

Shēhù: Dàgà Yāshi fà?

And after Yashi?

Mùtûm: À Yāshi àkwai hanyā dàgà kudù zuwā arēwa. Tô, sai kà bī ta hagu ɗin, kà yi arēwa har kà kai Kàtsinà.

At Yashi there is a road (running) from south to north. You turn left like this and go north till you reach Katsina.

Shēhù: Dàgà Yāshi zuwā Kàtsinà mīl nawà nē?

From Yashi to Katsina, how many miles is it?

Mùtûm: Ai mîl hàmsin dà ɗaya nè.

Oh it's fifty-one miles.

Vocabulary

arēwa	n.f.	'north'	hanyā	n.f.	'road'
bàyānī	n.m.	'explanation'	(hanyōyī pl.)		
bi	v.tr.	'follow'	kudù	n.f.	'south'
dāma	n.f.	'right, right hand'	jē	v.intr.	'go'

ɗin   'thus' (as used here, the speaker has probably extended his left arm and ɗin means "the way I am pointing")

mànà   emphasis particle, often used following Ī 'yes'; gives notion of "urgency" when used with a statement

hagu   n.f.   'left, to the left'

mîl   n.m.   'mile'

wucē   v.tr./intr. 'pass'

COMPREHENSION PRACTICE

Without looking at your books, listen to the passage as your informant reads through it once, pausing to explain in Hausa the meaning of any new words or expressions. Your informant will read the passage a second time at normal conversational speed and then ask you the questions which follow. Answer in complete sentences.

Mōtā Tā Bàci

Wata rāna Mālàm Shēhù Àbūbakàr yanà tàfiyà Kanò. Daf dà Bauci ya ji[1] mōtàrsà tanà wani irìn kūgī.[2] Ya tsayà,[3] ya fita[4] mōtà, ya ga sàlansà tā hūjē. Sabò dà hakà ya tàfi wajen maKērī à gàrîn. Can ya cē yanà sô maKērī yà yī masà wani ɗan gyārā à mōtàrsà. MaKērī ya tàmbayà irìn gyārā dà zâi yī wà mōtàr Mālàm Shēhù. Mālàm Shēhù ya cē sàlansà tā hūjē, yanà sô maKērī yà līKè ta. Ya cē kumā yanà saurī àmmā maKērī ya cē zâi kai har Karfè ukù kàfin yà gamā sabò dà bâ shi dà gawàyī. Sai yā sayō. Malam

146

Shēhù ya cè maƙèrī yà yi saurī, maƙèrī ya amsā[5] masa, "Ai gaggāwā bā ta dà àmfānī."

1. ji v.tr.   'hear, perceive'
2. ƙūgī n.m.   'roaring sound'   5. amsā v.tr.   'answer'
3. tsayà v.intr.   'stop'   6. lōkàcī n.m.   'time, hour'
4. fìta v.intr.   'go out'

Tambayoyi

1. Mālàm Shēhù yanà tàfiyà Kanò?
2. Daf dà Bauci, mè Mālàm Shēhù ya ji?
3. Bāyan Mālàm Shēhù yā ji ƙūgin, mè ya yi?
4. Mè ya ɓaci à mōtà?
5. Mè Mālàm Shēhù ya cè wà maƙèrī?
6. Mè maƙèrī zâi yī wà sàlansà?
7. Mālàm Shēhù yanà saurī?
8. Har ƙarfè nawà maƙèrī zâi kai kàfin yà gamà gyārā?
9. Don mè zâi kai har wannàn lōkàcī[6]?
10. Mè maƙèrī ya cè wà Mālàm Shēhù?

GRAMMAR

12.1 The Subjunctive Aspect

The subject pronouns for what we shall refer to as the subjunctive aspect are set forth in the following table, illustrated with the verb tàfi 'go (away)':

Singular		Plural	
in tàfi	'I should go'	mù tàfi	'we should go'
kà tàfi	'you(m) should go'	kù tàfi	'you should go'
kì tàfi	'you(f) should go'		
yà tàfi	'he should go'	sù tàfi	'they should go'
tà tàfi	'she should go'		
à tafi	'one should go'		

Note that all these pronouns have a low tone and short vowel.
Unlike the other aspects, it is difficult to give any simple, fairly general characterization of the meaning of the subjunctive such as completed action, progressive action, etc. Some of the more common uses are described below. Others will be encountered later.

a) Commands

The subjunctive can be used in the second person as a command. Hausa also has an imperative verb form (see 10.2), but the subjunctive can normally be used as an imperative with little or no change in meaning.

147

The second person plural subjunctive is the only way to form a plural imperative.

kà yi ƙòƙarī kà gamā   'make an effort to finish'

yârā, kù tàfi kàsuwā kù sàyi dōyā   'children, go to market and buy some yams'

b) "should", "must", "let's", etc.

The subjunctive corresponds to a variety of expressions in English which are obviously related in meaning but for which it is difficult to find a single suitable term. Generally, corresponding English expressions would have one of the words 'should', 'must', 'might', etc. in them and express the notion of obligation (moral or otherwise), desire, fittingness, etc. Examples, some of which have been seen in the dialogues, are

in tàfi kàsuwā?   'should I go to the market?'

mù shìga zaurē   'let's go into the entrance hut'

Allāh yà kai mù   'may God take us (that far)'

rânkà yà dadē   'may your life be prolonged'

yà yi hanzarī   'he should hurry'

The word <u>sai</u> is often used in these expressions with very little difference in meaning, except when used with second person, where it changes the expression into something like "you should ..." rather than a simple command.

sai mù sayō gawàyī   'we ought to buy some charcoal'

sai kà ragè minì kuɗintà   'you ought to reduce the price for me'

sai kà yī ta tàfiyà   'you should keep on going'

sai yà zō nân   'he should come here'

Finally, the imperative form of <u>barī</u> 'leave' can be used with a following verb in the subjunctive, usually in the first person, to mean something like "how about" but often with no real difference from the subjunctive alone.

bàri mù shìga zaurē   'let's go into the entrance hut'

bàri in kāwō makà kujèrā   'let me bring you a chair'

c) After an expression of desire

We have seen several examples of the form <u>inā sô</u> 'I want' followed by a sentence.

inā sô kà yī minì wani ɗan gyārā   'I want you to do a minor repair for me'

kanā sô in līƙè ta?   'do you want me to weld it?'

kanā sô in bā kà bàyanī?   'do you want me to give you an explanation?'

Sentences following such expressions of desire, hoping, etc. are always in the subjunctive aspect. One important thing to point out is that unlike English, French, or other European languages where an infinitive can be used following such expressions when the subject of the desire

148

clause and the subject of the second clause are the same, Hausa normally uses the subjunctive aspect in the second clause. Thus, in English
and French where we have 'I want to go to Katsina', 'he wants to buy
charcoal'; 'je veux aller à Katsina', 'il veut acheter du charbon de
bois' (the person wanting and the person doing the action of the infinitive are the same), in Hausa we find inā sō in tàfi Kàtsinà and yanā
sō yà gyàrà mōtā, which would have the literal translations 'I want I
(should) go to Katsina' and 'he wants he repair the car' respectively.

kanā sô kà kwāna à barikî?   'do you want to spend the night
                               at the rest house?'

yanā sô yà sayō qawàyī   'he wants to buy charcoal'

munā sô mù wucè har Yàshi   'we want to go on to Yashi'

d) "in order to", "so that"

The subjunctive is used with the conjunctive don or dōmin 'for, because'
in the second clause of a sentence to express the notion "in order to",
"so that" (note that in English the word 'to' alone will often be used
instead of the full phrase 'in order to', for example, I sent him to
chase away goats). No examples of this usage have been seen in this
unit, but the following sentence occurs in Unit 13:

nā àiki dānā gōnā don yà kōrē sù   'I sent my son to the farm to
                                     chase them off'

Further examples are:

kà bā nì kudī don in sayō qawàyī   'give me money so that I can
                                     buy charcoal'

yā kāwō mōtàrsà don in yī masà   'he brought his car so that I
gyārā   could do repairs for him'

Dōmin could have been used in place of don in any of these sentences.

e) After kāfin 'before'

When used as a conjunction, kāfin 'before' is always followed by the
subjunctive.

nā kai kàrfè ukù kāfin in gamā   'it will take me to three
                                     o'clock before I finish'

kāfin kà kai Kàtsinà, kā ga   'before you reach Katsina,
gōnàkkī dà yawā   you will see a lot of farms'

f) After the Future Aspect

When several coordinate sentences in the future aspect appear one directly after the other, the subjunctive pronouns are used in all but the
first sentence. Examples are:

bà zā kà yi kōkarī kà gamā zuwā   'won't you try and finish by
karfè biyu ba?   two o'clock'

zân wucè Yàshi in bi arēwa   'I'll pass Yashi and go north'

149

wasu mutā̃nē sun wucè nân   'some men passed by here'

b) "another, some more; other, others"

sai wani lōkàcī   'see you later (until another time)'

sai wata rāna   "au revoir" (until another day)

nā̃ gan shì à wani gàrī   'I saw him in some other town'

wasu sun zō, wasu bà sù zō ba 'some came, others didn't'

bā nā̃ sôn wannàn rīgā,   'I don't like this gown; bring
  à kāwō wata   another'

12.6 Points of the Compass

The names of the four points of the compass are:

arḕwa	'north'
kudù	'south'
gabàs	'east'
yâmma	'west'

These words are all feminine. To say 'north, south, east, west of x', the preposition da̠ is used:

yanā̃ arḕwa dà Kanò   'it is north of Kano'

GRAMMATICAL DRILLS

Drill 1A - 1B

1A Change the sentences in the future aspect below to a sentence in the subjunctive aspect introduced by sai ... .

Cue: zâi tàfi kā̀suwā

Student response: sai yà tàfi kā̀suwā

1B Give the negative future of the sentences.

Cue: zâi tàfi kā̀suwā

Student response: bà zâi tàfi kā̀suwā ba

1. zā kù bā mù bàyānī   6. zā kì kāwō jàkā
2. zā mù shiga zaurè   7. zā à līkè ta
3. zā kà sayō gawàyī   8. zā tà ragè mini kuɗintà
4. zā sù yī ta tàfiyā̀   9. zâi kwāna à bārikī
5. zâi zō nân   10. zā kù kāwō mini kujērā

Drill 2 - Complete the sentence nā̃ cê makà/mikì etc. ... yi ƙòƙarī ...
gamā̃ zuwā ƙarfè biyu, supplying the subjunctive aspect pronoun corresponding
to the dative pronoun in the blanks.

Cue: nā̃ cê masà

Student response: nā̃ cê masà yà yi ƙòƙarī yà gamā̃ zuwā̀ ƙarfè biyu

Cue: nā̃ cê makà

Student response: nā̃ cê makà kà yi ƙòƙarī kà gamā̃ zuwā̀ ƙarfè biyu

1. nā cê matà
2. nā cê mikì
3. nā cê muku̇
4. nā cê masà
5. nā cê wà mutânē

6. nā cê makà
7. nā cê musù
8. nā cê wà Kànde
9. nā cê wà 'yam mātā
10. nā cê wà makềrī

Drill 3 - Using the pairs of cue sentences below, construct a single
sentence on the pattern X bā Y kudῙ don Y sayō Z.

Cue sentences: Yā bā tà kudῙ. Tā sayō tàttàsai.

Student response: Yā bā tà kudῙ don tà sayō tàttàsai.

1. Mun bā kù kudῙ. Kun sayō kāyan aikῙ.
2. Nā bā sù kudῙ. Sun sayō kwai.
3. Kun bā nì kudῙ. Nā sayō gawàyῙ.
4. Yā bā kì kudῙ. Kin sayō tābā.
5. Tā bā shì kudῙ. Yā sayō dōyā.
6. Kā bā HàlῙmÀ kudῙ. Tā sayō dōyā.
7. Yā bā mù kudῙ. Mun sayō kāyan aikῙ.
8. Sun bā Audù dà Kànde kudῙ. Sun sayō lìttàttāfai.
9. Uwargidā tā bā Mammàn kudῙ. Yā sayō kōshiyā.
10. Nā bā Mūsā kudῙ. Yā sayō rēdiyò. rēdiyò n.m. 'radio'

Drill 4 - Change the pattern sentence so that it contains the appropriate
dative pronoun. In each case your cues will be the continuative pronoun
and the possessive pronoun on mōtā. Note that gyārā in the cue is a verb,
gyārā (all high tones) is a noun meaning 'a repair'.

Cue sentence: inā sô yà gyārà mōtàtā

Student response: inā sô yà yῙ mini wani dan gyārā à mōtàtā

Cue sentence: sunà sô yà gyārà mōtàrsù

Student response: sunà sô yà yῙ musù wani dan gyārā à mōtàrsù

1. tanā sô yà gyārà mōtàrtà
2. munā sô yà gyārà mōtàrmù
3. yanā sô yà gyārà mōtàrsà
4. kanā sô yà gyārà mōtàrkà
5. kunā sô yà gyārà mōtàrkù

6. sunā sô yà gyārà mōtàrsù
7. Shēhù yanā sô yà gyārà mōtàrsà
8. inā sô yà gyārà mōtàtā
9. Aishà tanā sô yà gyārà mōtàrtà
10. matàfiyā sunā sô yà gyārà mōtàrsù
matàfiyā n.pl. 'travelers'

Drill 5 - You will be given a sentence in the future aspect. Put the
sentence into the frame zān gamà aikῙ kāfin ... 'I will finish the work
before ...'. Remember that after kāfin the subjunctive aspect is always
used.

Cue sentence: zā kà zo

Student response: zān gamà aikῙ kāfin kà zo

153

1. zā à yi ruwā
   an yi ruwā 'it rained'
2. zâi bā kù bàyānī̀
3. yā̀rā zā sù zō dàgà makarantā
4. maƙḕrī̀ zâi gyārà mōtā̀
5. zā kà ci àbinci

6. zân gàji
7. uwargidā zā tà yi shā̀rā
8. zā kì kāwō minì ruwā
9. zā ƙù ga àbōkankù
   àbōkai n.pl. 'friends'
10. mài gidā zâi bar gidā

Drill 6 - As a cue you will be given two separate sentences in the future
aspect. Make them into a single compound sentence by changing the second
sentence to the subjunctive aspect (remember that when coordinate sentences
in the future aspect occur, only the first has the future aspect pronoun -
see 12.1, section f).

Cue: Zā kà yi ƙòƙarī̀. Zā kà gamā̀.

Student response: Zā kà yi ƙòƙarī̀ kà gamā̀.

1. Yâu zā mù tāshi. Zā mù jē Fùntuwā̀.   tāshi v.intr. 'set out'
2. Zâi sayō gawàyī̀. Zâi gyārà sàlansā̀.
3. Zā sù shìga zaurḕ. Zā sù yi màganā̀.
4. Zā kà yi haɗàrī̀ dà mōtàrkà. Zā kà yi ràunī̀.
5. Maƙḕrī̀ zâi yi hanzarī̀. Zâi lîƙè sàlansā̀.
6. Zā ƙù sayō yādī̀. Zā ƙù ɗinkà rîgā.   yādī̀ n.m. 'cloth, yard goods'
7. Mutā̀nē zā sù tàfi kā̀suwā. Zā sù saukè dōyā̀.
8. Zân bi wannàn hanyā̀. Zân kai Malumfāshi.

Drill 7 - Negate the affirmative sentences listed below. Do not look at
your books during this drill.

Cue sentence: zā tà yi ƙòƙarī̀

Student response: bà zā tà yi ƙòƙarī̀ ba

1. zā kà gamā̀ kā̀fin ƙarfè ukù
2. zā mù gamā̀ kā̀fin ƙarfè ukù
3. zā sù gamā̀ kā̀fin ƙarfè ukù
4. maƙḕrī̀ zâi gamā̀ kā̀fin ƙarfè ukù
5. zân gamā̀ kā̀fin ƙarfe ukù
6. zā tà gamā̀ kā̀fin ƙarfè ukù
7. zā ƙù gamā̀ kā̀fin ƙarfè ukù

8. zā à gamā̀ kā̀fin ƙarfè ukù
9. zā kà yi hanzarī̀
10. mutā̀nē zā sù yi hanzarī̀
11. zâi yi hanzarī̀
12. zā ƙù yi hanzarī̀
13. Hàdīzà zā tà yi hanzarī̀
14. zân yi hanzarī̀

Drill 8 - Expand the commands shown below into sentences of the pattern
in kā ragḕ (dative pronoun) sulḕ bìyar, (future pronoun) yàrda.

Cue sentence: ràgē masà sulḕ bìyar

Student response: in kā ragḕ masà sulḕ bìyar zâi yàrda

1. ràgē minì sulḕ bìyar
2. ràgē matà sulḕ bìyar

3. ràgē musù sulḕ bìyar
4. ràgē wà Bàtūrḕ sulḕ bìyar

154

5. ràgē wà Hārūnà sulè bìyar

6. ràgē masà sulè bìyar

7. ràgē wà Aishà sulè bìyar

8. ràgē manà sulè bìyar

9. ràgē wà mātā sulè bìyar

10. ràgē wà Ìsa sulè bìyar

<u>Drill 9</u> - In this drill there are two sets of sentences, one marked 'via', the other 'keep on doing'. In the group marked 'via', change the sentence by putting <u>ta</u> in a place appropriate to mean 'via' or 'by way of' a place or direction. In those marked 'keep on doing' insert <u>ta</u> in a place in the sentence appropriate to this meaning.

Cue: ('via') nā bi hanyàr Yāshi

Student response: nā bī ta hanyàr Yāshi

Cue: ('keep on doing') sun yi aikī

Student response: sun yī ta aikī

'via'

1. mù shìga zaurè

2. sai mù bi hanyàr Marāɗi

3. yā shìga ƙofàr

4. kà bi waccàn hanyà

5. bà zā mù jē Kàtsinà ba

6. sai in bi wannàn hanyà, kō?

'keep on doing'

1. yanà aikī à Gidan Wayā

2. mutànē sunà cìnikī har ƙarfè shidà

3. uwargidā tā yi shārā

4. maƙèrī yanà aikī

5. mun yi tàfiyà har mun jē Malumfāshi

6. yanà shìga ƙofàr

<u>Drill 10</u> - Supply the proper form of <u>wani</u>, <u>wata</u>, or <u>wasu</u> (or <u>waɗansu</u>) before the noun subject or object of the following sentences to give the meaning 'a/an', 'a certain', 'some'.

Cue: kà yī mini ɗan gyārā

Student response: kà yī mini wani ɗan gyārā

1. àkwai mùtûm gàban ƙofà

2. maƙèrī yā gyārà ta

3. mōtà tā ɓàci daf dà gàrinmù

4. nā ga zōbè cikin àkwàti

5. ɗàlibai bà sù zō makarantā ba yâu

6. mun ga gàrī dàgà nīsā   nīsā 'far off'

7. tā karyà ƙoshiyà

8. mutànē sun zō sù gaishè kà

9. màcè tā haihù à wannàn gidā

10. mùtûm mài ƙatòn kâi yanà aikī à Gidan Wayā

<u>Drill 11</u> - You will be given a sentence of the form bā nà sôn wannàn ... 'I don't like this ...'. Respond with the sentence <u>à kāwō wani/wata/wasu</u> (or <u>waɗansu</u>) 'bring another one/some others (let one bring another one/ some others)', using the form of <u>wani/wata/wasu</u> (or <u>waɗansu</u>) which agrees in gender and number with the noun in the cue sentence.

Cue: bā nà sôn wannàn taguwā

Student response: à kāwō wata

1. bā nà sôn wannàn tàbarmā

2. bā nà sôn wannàn lèmō

3. bā nà waɗànnân rīgunà

4. bā nà sôn wannàn rīgā

155

5. bā nà̰ són wadànnân kwandunā̰

6. bā nà̰ són wannàn wàndō

7. bā nà̰ són wannàn zōbḛ̀

8. bā nà̰ són wannàn dōyà̰

9. bā nà̰ són wadànnân littàttàfai

10. bā nà̰ són wannàn ƙoshiyà̰

Drill 12 - Using the names of the Nigerian towns listed below, answer the question dàgà X zuwā Y, mîl nawà nḛ̄? with the pattern sentence ai, mîl (number) nḛ̄. Pairs of students participate in this drill, one asking and the other answering the question as shown in the example. Ikko is 'Lagos', Gwàmbè is 'Gombe', and Jas is 'Jos'.

Cue:	Shāgāmù - Ikko (50)
Student 1:	dàgà Shāgāmù zuwā Ikko, mîl nawà nḛ̄?
Student 2:	ai, mîl hàmsin nḛ̄

1. Bauci - Gwàmbè (97)

2. Kàdūna - Zāriyà (49)

3. Malumfāshi - Yā̰shi (62)

4. Yā̰shi - Jibiyà (79)

5. Jàs - Bauci (82)

6. Kàtsina - Jibiyà (28)

7. Zāriyà - Fùntuwà (47)

8. Jàs - Zariya (157)

9. Kankìya - Kàtsina (36)

10. Yā̰shi - Kankìya (15)

Drill 13 - In the drill below you will have to make at least one and some-times two pronoun changes. Change both the indirect object and the direct object to the corresponding pronouns. Change all second person pronouns to first person and all first person to second person.

Cue sentence:	yà̰ kāwō manà gōròn?
Student response:	Ī, yā kāwō muku shĪ
Cue sentence:	yā̰rā sun kāwō wà Mammàn àbincîn?
Student response:	Ī, sun kāwō masà shĪ

1. yà̰ kāwō makà kwàndôn?

2. sun kāwō minì hūlàr?

3. tā kāwō mikì taguwâr?

4. sun kāwō wà Mammàn kuɗin?

5. yà̰ kāwō wà yā̰rā gwēbā̰?

6. Mālàm yā kāwō wà ɗàlibai littàttàfân?

7. Hàlīmà tā kāwō makà Mài Zōbè?

8. Mammàn dà Mūsā sun kāwō manà kāyā?

9. maƙērĪ yā kāwō wà Mālàm Shēhù sàlansàr?

10. yā kāwō manà fensirōrîn?

Drill 14 - Put the cue noun or pronoun into each of the frame sentences as an indirect object.

Example frame sentence:	nā sayō gawàyĪ
Example cues:	maƙērĪ, shĪ
Student responses after each cue:	nā sayō wà maƙērĪ gawàyĪ
	nā sayō masà gawàyĪ

Frame sentences: yā gayà̰ ... làbàrĪ

uwargidā tā kāwō ruwā̰

maƙērĪ yā lìƙè sàlansā̰

Cues: 1. shī   5. ita   9. kai
       2. kē   6. Shēhù   10. bàkṑ
       3. mài gidā̀ 7. nī   11. kū
       4. mū   8. sū   12. màtātā̀

Drill 15A - 15C - Repeat the intitial sentence, then substitute the first
cue into the appropriate place in that sentence. As each cue is given,
substitute it into the sentence formed from the previous cue so that a
new sentence is formed.

15A Initial sentence: makèrī yā gyārà mōtàr Mālàm Shēhù

Cues	Student response
1. kanà tsàmmānī	kanà tsàmmānī makèrī yā gyārà mōtàr Mālàm Shēhù
2. yi wani ɗan gyārā	kanà tsàmmānī makèrī yā yi wani ɗan gyārā
3. wà Mālàm Shēhù	kanà tsàmmānī makèrī yā yī wà Mālàm Shēhù wani ɗan gyārā
4. īīkè ta	kanà tsàmmānī makèrī yā īīkè ta
5. zâi	kanà tsàmmānī makèrī zâi īīkè ta
6. bā shì bàyānī	kanà tsàmmānī makèrī zâi bā shì bàyānī
7. kai Kàtsinà kàfin karfè ukù	kanà tsàmmānī makèrī zâi kai Kàtsinà kàfin karfè ukù
8. negative completive	kanà tsàmmānī makèrī bà zâi kai Kàtsinà kàfin karfè ukù ba

15B Initial sentence: kà jē

1. future aspect	zā̀ kà jē
2. gàrī	zā̀ kà jē gàrī
3. wànnan	zā̀ kà jē wànnan gàrī
4. wani	zā̀ kà jē wani gàrī
5. kai	zā̀ kà kai wani gàrī
6. wucè̀	zā̀ kà wucè̀ wani gàrī
7. kàfin kà bī ta hagu	zā̀ kà wucè̀ wani gàrī kàfin kà bī ta hagu
8. dāma	zā̀ kà wucè̀ wani gàrī kàfin kà bī ta dāma
9. kà kai Yàshi	zā̀ kà wucè̀ wani gàrī kàfin kà kai Yàshi
10. Kàtsinà	zā̀ kà wucè̀ wani gàrī kàfin kà kai Kàtsinà
	or
	zā̀ kà wucè̀ Kàtsinà kàfin kà kai Yàshi

15C Initial sentence: yā sayō sàlansà̀

1. Shēhù	Shēhù yā sayō sàlansà̀
2. makèrī	makèrī yā sayō sàlansà̀
3. karfè̀	makèrī yā sayō karfè̀
4. gawàyī	makèrī yā sayō gawàyī
5. kāwṑ	makèrī yā kāwṑ gawàyī

6. kai   maƙḕrī yā kai gawàyī

7. kai har ƙarfḕ biyu   maƙḕrī yā kai har ƙarfḕ biyu

8. ukù dà rabī   maƙḕrī yā kai har ƙarfḕ ukù dà rabī

9. zâi kai   maƙḕrī zâi kai har ƙarfḕ ukù dà rabī

10. future negative   maƙḕrī bà zâi kai har ƙarfḕ ukù dà rabī ba

GUIDED CONVERSATION

1) One person has something which has to be repaired which he takes to the proper person to do such a repair. They dicker over how much it should cost. Examples of things that might be repaired are a radio or other electrical appliance, a piece of furniture, an article of clothing, a car, etc.

Example conversation:

(After appropriate greetings)

Student 1: Gà ƙafàr wannàn kujḕrā tā karyḕ. Inà sō kà gyārà minì.	The leg of this chair is broken. I want you to fix it for me.
Student 2: Tô, bàrī ìn ganī.	Ok, let me see (it).
1: Nawà nē kuɗin gyārā?	How much is the price of the repair?
2: Ai, wannàn Naìrà biyu dà sulḕ bìyar nē.	Well, that'll be ₦2.50.
1: Haba!	Oh! Come on!
2: Yi hàƙurī. Sai nā sayō kātakō, kumā àkwai kuɗin gyārā.	Have patience. I have to buy the wood and then there's the labor charge.
1: Zân bā kà sulḕ shâ biyu.	I'll give you 12 shillings.
2: Àlbarkà!	No thanks!
1: Tô, sulḕ shâ ukù.	All right, 13 shillings.
2: Kàwō Naìrà biyu.	Give ₦2.00.
1: Gà Naìrà ɗaya dà sulḕ bìyar. ShĪ kḕ nan.	Here's ₦1.50. That's all (the more I'll give).
2: Tô, zân gamā gyārā gòbe.	OK, I'll be finished fixing it tomorrow.

2) Use the map for the suggested conversations or any others that you might think of.

    A. One student may ask another how far it is from one town to another. The second student should reply using the milages indicated.

    B. Give directions how to get to

       a) Biddà from Kwàntàgòra via Tègìnà/Zùngèrù

       b) Mìnà from Jaba

       c) Kadūna from Biddà via Kwàntàgòra/Sābon Birni

       d) Kwàntàgòra from Mìnà

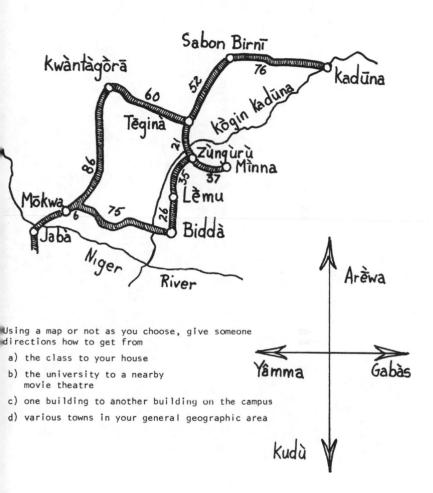

Kwàntàgòrā
Sabon Birnī
60
52
76
Kadūna
Tēginà
kògin kadūna
21
Zùngùrù
Mìnna
35
37
86
Lèmu
Mōkwa
75
6
26
Biddà
Jabà
Niger
River

Arèwa

Yâmma — Gabàs

Kudù

Using a map or not as you choose, give someone
directions how to get from

a) the class to your house
b) the university to a nearby
   movie theatre
c) one building to another building on the campus
d) various towns in your general geographic area

DIALOGUES

A. Malam Sa'idu Gwarzo pays a visit to the farm of his friend Yusufu Gobir.

Sà'Ïdù:	Barkā dà aikÏ. Bana kàm gōnarkā tā yi àlbarkà.	Greetings at work. This year your farm has flourished.
Yùsufù:	Ï, àlhamdù lìllāhÏ! Zō in nūnā makà ita.	Yes, praise be to God! Come, let me show it to you.
Sà'Ïdù:	Inā tsàmmānÏ kā k̃arā fād'intà.	I believe you have extended it (increased its breadth).
Yùsufù:	Gàskiyā nè. Nā s̃ari d̃ajin cân kumā nā shūkà dāwā.	You're right. I cleared that (area of) bush over there and planted guinea corn.
Sà'Ïdù:	À nân, gā shi kā shūkà audùgā.	Here I see you've planted cotton (here it is you've put cotton).
Yùsufù:	Ï, àmmā aikìntà yanā da wùyā. Nā nōmè ciyāwā kumā nā s̃ā tākÏ dà yawā.	Yes, but it is hard work. I hoed up weeds and put (i.e. spread) a lot of manure.
Sà'Ïdù:	Kai kad'ai ka yi duk wannàn aikÏ?	Did you yourself do all that work?
Yùsufù:	Ā'à, d̃anā Audù, yā tàimàkē nÏ.	No, my son, Audu, helped me.

Vocabulary

audùgā	n.f.	'cotton'	nōmè	v.tr.	'hoe, dug out with a hoe'
bana		'this year'	nūnā	v.tr.	'show'
ciyāwā	n.f.	'grass, weeds'	s̃ā	v.tr.	'put'
dājÏ	n.m.	'the bush'	s̃arā	(i/ē)v.tr.	'chop, cut down'
dāwā	n.f.	'guinea corn'	shūkà	v.tr.	'plant, sow'
fādÏ	n.m.	'breadth'	tàimakā	(i/ē)v.tr.	'help'
kad'ai		'just, only'	tākÏ	n.m.	'manure'
kàm		'as for, indeed'	tsàmmānÏ	n.m.	'thinking'

B. Malam Sa'idu and Malam Yusufu continue to discuss the latter's farm. Suddenly they are interrupted.

Yùsufù:	A'a, gā birÏ à gōnātā!	Oh, oh! There's a monkey on my farm.
Sà'Ïdù:	À inā?	Where?
Yùsufù:	Gā shi cân, kusa dà dāwā. Kadà yà b̃atā ta. D̃auki dūtsè kà jèfē shi.	There he is, near the guinea corn. Don't let him ruin it. Take a stone and throw (it) at him.
(Mālàm Yùsufù dà Mālàm Sà'Ïdù sun yi jÏfā).	(Malam Yusufu and Malam Sa'idu throw (the stones).)
Sà'Ïdù:	Tō, yā gudù.	OK, he's run away.
Yùsufù:	Tō, kā ga dabbōbÏ sunā bā nì wàhalà. Sunā shìgā gōnā sunā yÏ mini b̃arnā.	Well, you see (how) animals give me trouble. They enter the farm and do me damage.

161

2. Tone - NEARLY ALL VARIABLE VOWEL VERBS BEGIN WITH A LOW TONE SYLLABLE.

a) Almost all <u>two syllable</u> variable vowel verbs have the tone pattern low-high.

yā kòri birī̀	'he chased off the monkey'
yā kòrē shì	'he chased him off'
yā kòrā̄	'he chased (him) off'

There are three common verbs which have the tone pattern high-low when not followed by an object. These are ɗaukà 'take', ɗībà 'dip out, take out', and sāmù 'get, receive'. These verbs do have the pattern low-high when followed by objects, however. The verb ɗībà is also irregular in that the ī of the first syllable changes to ē when followed by an object.

yā ɗaukḕ shì	'he took it'
yā ɗaukā̀	'he took (it)'
tā ɗèbi ruwā̄	'she dipped out water'
tā ɗèbē shì	'she dipped it out'
tā ɗībā̀	'she dipped out'

b) <u>Three syllable verbs</u> which are variable vowel verbs invariably have the tone pattern low-high-low when not followed by a direct object. When followed by a direct object (noun or pronoun), the tone pattern becomes low-low-high with the appropriate final vowel changes.

nā tàmbàyi mālàm	'I asked the teacher'
nā tàmbàyē shì	'I asked him'
nā tàmbàyā̄	'I asked (him)'

c) <u>Tones before indirect objects</u>[1]

i) Two syllable variable vowel verbs switch their tone pattern to high-low before indirect objects.

nā kōrà masà awākī	'I chased the goats off for him'
yā ɗaukā̀ wà Yùsufù kāyā	'he carried the load for Yusufu'

ii) Three syllable variable vowel verbs have all high tones and add an <u>-r</u> before indirect objects (the <u>-r</u> often becomes <u>-m</u> before the <u>-m</u> of the indirect object pronouns).

---

[1]With some verbs different patterns can be found before indirect objects, though patterns outlined above are probably the more common. You may hear a pattern high-high with an added <u>-r</u> used with two syllable verbs (note the similarity with the three syllable pattern given here).

yā zāɓam masà dōkī	'he chose a horse for him'

With three syllable verbs, the pattern high-low-high with a final <u>-ā</u> may be heard.

yā tàmbàyā mini làbàrī	'he asked about the news for me'

Actually, most variable vowel verbs are only infrequently used with indirect objects, so we will spend very little time on them as so used. The patterns in 13.1 (1c) and this footnote are included for completeness.

yā tambayam mini maƙērī   'he asked the blacksmith for me'
nā tambayar wà Shēhù maƙērī   'I asked the blacksmith for Shehu'

3. Palatalization of consonants in variable vowel verbs - There are several
   variable vowel verbs which have t, d, s, or z as the consonant beginning
   the last syllable, for example

   sātā (i/ē)v.tr.   'steal'
   cīzā (i/ē)v.tr.   'bite'
   cūtā (i/ē)v.tr.   'cheat'
   isā (i/ē) v.tr.   'be sufficient for'

   Such verbs serve to illustrate the palatalization of these four consonants
   before i or ē that was explained in 8.5. When followed by objects, the
   consonants in the final syllables of these verbs are palatalized since the
   final vowel becomes i or ē depending on the object.

   an sāci kudīnā   'my money was stolen'
   kàrē yā cīje ni   'the dog bit me'
   maƙērī yā cūci Bàtūrè   'the blacksmith cheated the European'
   àbinci yā ìshē ni   'that's enough food for me'
                              ('the food is sufficient for me')

13.2 nan and can as Demonstrative Adjectives

   Before reading the remainder of this section, the student should re-read
   section 5.1 to refresh his memory on the differences of meaning between nan
   and can as opposed to the differences between 'this' and 'that' in English.
   An alternative to using wannàn, wancàn, etc. as demonstrative adjectives
   (7.3) to mean 'this/these' and 'that/those' is to attach nan and can after
   a noun by means of the linker (before nan, the feminine linker is invariably
   pronounced -n):

   dājin cân   'that bush area (over there)'
   dāwàr nân   'this guinea corn'
   (pronounced dāwàn nân)

   It is very important that you produce the correct tone patterns here.
   They are as follows:

   a) When the noun ends in a high tone, nàn and càn have a low tone.

   dabbōbin càn   'those animals (over there)'
   gōnar càn   'that farm (over there)'
   audùgar nàn   'this cotton'

   b) When the noun ends in a low tone, nân and cân have a falling tone.

   dūtsen cân   'that rock (over there)'
   nāmàn nân   'this meat'
   ciyāwàr nân   'this grass'

   These tone patterns apply to physical beings or objects that can be seen
   by the speaker. A different tone pattern using the same words but having
   a different meaning ('this/that one in question', 'this/that one we are
   talking about') will be seen in a later unit.

165

9. zā kà shā wannàn māgànT? 11. wā zâi kóri waɗancân dabbōbT?

10. maƙěrT yā gyārà wannàn mōtā 12. sai kù bi wannàn hanyā

Drill 11 - Using the cue sentences below, form responses on the pattern tố, bàri in nūnā followed by the dative pronoun and the direct object pronoun if appropriate. Remember that if the direct object pronoun follows the dative, the independent pronoun must be used.

Cue sentence: inā sô in dūbà kuɗinkà

Student response: tố, bàri in nūnā makà/miki (sū)

Cue sentence: yanā sô yà dūbà àgōgonkà

Student response: tố, bàri in nūnā masà (shT)

1. yanā sô yà dūbà mōtàrkà
2. sunā sô sù dūbà littàttàfankà
3. kunā sô kù dūbà birT
4. tanā sô tà dūbà gōnarkà
5. munā sô mù dūbà kāyankà

6. kinā sô ki dūbà nāmàn dājT
   nāmā n.m. 'animal'
7. yanā sô yà dūbà dabbōbinsà
8. sunā sô sù dūbà dāwā
9. munā sô mù dūbà aikinsà
10. tanā sô tà dūbà gawàyT

Drill 12 - Answer the questions below by saying ā'ā followed by the sentence in the negative.

Cue sentence: dabbōbT zā sù bā kà wàhalā?

Student response: ā'ā, bà zā sù bā ni wàhalā ba

Cue sentence: Hārūnà yā zō

Student response: ā'ā, bài zō ba

1. Mammàn, zā kà ƙārà fāɗin gōnarkà?
2. birT zâi shìga gōnā?
3. kin jěfē shì?
4. su Audù zā sù yi barcT à gōnā?
5. kun shūkà dāwā?

6. zā kà sā̂ tākT dà yawà?
7. zā mù nūnā masà gōnā?
8. sun sàri dājìn cân?
9. gōnā tā yi àlbarkā?
10. HàlTmà zā tà jē kàsuwā?

Drill 13A - 13C - Repeat the initial sentence, then substitute the first cue into the appropriate place in that sentence. As each cue is given, substitute it into the sentence formed from the previous cue, so that a new sentence is formed.

13A Initial sentence: HàlTmà tā dafà àbinci   dafà v.tr. 'cook'

Cues	Student response
1. Aishà	Aishà tā dafà àbinci
2. Lawàli	Lawàli yā dafà àbinci
3. shūkà dāwā	Lawàli yā shūkà dāwā
4. audùgā	Lawàli yā shūkà audùgā
5. sā̂	Lawàli yā sā̂ audùgā

172

6. tākī́	Lawàli yā sâ tākī́
7. dà yawà	Lawàli yā sâ tākī́ dà yawà
8. su Audù	su Audù sun sâ tākī́ dà yawà
9. negative completive	su Audù bà sù sâ tākī́ dà yawà ba
10. negative future	su Audù bà zā sù sâ tākī́ dà yawà ba

13B Initial sentence: yā jēfi birī́

1. ākwiyà	yā jēfi àkwiyà
2. yārò	yārò yā jēfi àkwiyà
3. subjunctive aspect	yārò yā jēfi àkwiyà
4. negative subjunctive	kadà yārò yà jēfi àkwiyà
5. ɓàtà gōnā	kadà yārò yà ɓàtà gōnā
6. dāwà	kadà yārò yà ɓàtà dāwà
7. audùgā	kadà yārò yà ɓàtà audùgā
8. birī́	kadà birī́ yà ɓàtà audùgā
9. dabbōbī́	kadà dabbōbī́ sù ɓàtà audùgā
10. minì	kadà dabbōbī́ sù ɓàtà minì audùgā
11. masà	kadà dabbōbī́ sù ɓàtà masà audùgā
12. wà Yùsufù	kadà dabbōbī́ sù ɓàtà wà Yùsufù audùgā

13C Initial sentence: yā bi Yùsufù

1. àikā	yā àiki Yùsufù
2. àiki Audù	yā àiki Audù
3. don yà kòri birī́	yā àiki Audù don yà kòri birī́
4. dabbōbī́	yā àiki Audù don yà kòri dabbōbī́
5. àiki yârā	yā àiki yârā don sù kòri dabbōbī́
6. àiki dàlìbai	yā àiki dàlìbai don sù kòri dabbōbī́
7. nḕmi dabbōbī́	yā àiki dàlìbai don sù nḕmi dabbōbī́
8. nḕmi mālàm	yā àiki dàlìbai don sù nḕmi mālàm
9. tàmbàyi mālàm	yā àiki dàlìbai don sù tàmbàyi mālàm
10. inà tsàmmānī́	inà tsàmmānī́ ya àiki dàlìbai don sù tàmbàyi mālàm

173

GUIDED CONVERSATION

1) Describe a place unfamiliar or only partially familiar to another student.
The easiest such place to discuss would probably be the scene outside your
classroom window. You might discuss new building being done, buildings
being torn down, use of buildings (class rooms, library, cafeteria, offices,
etc.), beauty or lack of beauty of various aspects of the scene, size and
alleged cost of facilities, etc. The words <u>ginā</u> 'build' and <u>rūshḕ</u> 'raze'
might be useful in such a conversation.

Student 1:	Nā ga an rūshḕ wani gidā cân.	I see that a building has been torn down over there.
Student 2:	Hakà nē. An rūshḕ shi don à k̃àrà girman gidan littāfī.	That's right. It was torn down so the library (house of book) could be en-larged (increased in size).
1:	Littàttàfai sun yi yawà, kō?	There were too many books, were there?
2:	Gàskiyarkà. Kā ga k̃atòn gidā cân?	That's right. Do you see that huge building over there?
1:	Ī, mḕnē nḕ?	Yes, what is it?
2:	Wannàn gidan ōfiṣōshin màlàmai. An ginā shi bāra.	That is a professors' office building. It was built last year. (<u>bāra</u> 'last year')
1:	Inā tsàmmānī kuɗinsà sun yi yawà, àmmā bā shi dà kyâu.	I imagine it cost a lot (its money did much), but it's ugly.

An alternative situation would be for one student who has recently visit-
ed the old <u>alma mater</u> to discuss changes or lack of change with a former
classmate.

Other such scenes which could be discussed in much the same way are an
airport (discuss expanding extent, building a new terminal, increased number
of planes, large numbers of people, etc.); a shopping center (increased
parking facilities, new structures added, types of stores, prices relative
to another place, etc.); a recreational facility or park (trees planted,
grass planted, or on the other hand, trees or grass removed, new structures
added, animals found there, numbers of people that visit it).

Some additional vocabulary might be useful:

fīlin jirgin samà	'airport'
tashàr jirgin samà	'air terminal'
tashàr mōtà	"bus station" (in West Africa, a large, open area where motor vehicles of all types pick up and leave passengers and goods)
fīlin mōtà	'parking lot'
fāsinjà n.m.,f., pl.	'passenger(s)'

2) Discuss frustrations encountered from pests such as insects or birds. Example
of situations might be the planting of a vegetable garden (discuss the preparation of the ground, use of fertilizer, types of vegetables planted, types
of pests confronted - birds, insects, etc.); the creation of a flower garden
(the same things may be discussed as for the vegetable garden).

Some additional vocabulary might be useful:

dàsā v.tr.		'plant, transplant'
àskḕ v.tr.		'clip, trim'
fḕsā v.tr.		'spray'
fḕsà māgànin k̃wằrT		'spray insecticide'
bā dà ruwā		'water, irrigate'
tākin zāmànT		'chemical fertilizer' (manure of modern times)
tsuntsū̱ n.m. (tsuntsāyḕ pl.)		'bird'
k̃wằrT n.pl.		'insects'
k̃udā̱ n.f. (k̃udājḕ pl.)		'fly'
fùrē n.m. (fùrànnT pl.)		'flower'
kàrâs n.m.		'carrot(s)'
lḕtàs n.m.		'lettuce'
tùmātùr n.m.		'tomato(es)'
dànkalT n.m.		'sweet potato; potato'

Example conversation:

Student 1: Kinā̃ dà fùrànnT à gidankì? — Do you have flowers at your house?

Student 2: Ā'à̱, àmmā̱ nā yi k̃ō- k̃arT ìn sā̃ à gàban gidā. — No, but I have tried to put them in front of the house.

1: Kin barT, kō? Don mḕ? — You left off (trying), huh? Why?

2: Don k̃wằrT sun ɓàtà fùrànnT. — Because insects ruined the flowers.

1: Bā̂ ki dà māgàninsù? — Don't you have any insecticide (medicine for them)?

2: Nā fḕsà māgànin k̃wằrT àmmā kullum sunā̃ ta ɓàrnā. — I sprayed on insecticide, but they kept on ruining (the flowers).

1: Àsshā! — That's too bad!

DIALOGUES

A. Malam Isa Hashim and Malam Na'ibi Banu, both residents of Zaria, decide to
take an after dinner stroll along the banks of the river.

Isa:	NŤ kàm jnā̀ jîŋ dāɗin yāwòn nân à bàkin kōgŤ.	As for me, I really enjoy this walk along the river bank.
Nā'ibi:	Kâi, gà̀ zābŤ cân sunā̀ tāshŤ! Kā̀ gan sù?	Hey! There are some guinea fowl flying up! Did you see them?
Tsa:	Ā'à̀, bàn gan sù ba. Inā̀ kàllon mà̀i gōnar càn yanā̀ hùɗar dōyā̀.	No, I didn't see them. I was looking at that farmer hilling up yams.
Nā'ibi:	Mù tàfi mù yi màganā̀ dà shŤ.	Let's go over and have a talk with him.

I and N:	Barkā̀ dà aikŤ!	Greetings at work!
Mà̀i gōnā̀:	Yâuwa, sànnu dà zuwā̀.	Welcome!
I and N:	Yàyā̀ dàminā̀?	How's the wet season?
Mà̀i gōnā̀:	Kayya! Ai bana an yi farŤ!	Alas! There is a drought this year (this year one did dryness)!
N and I:	Duk shūkàrkà̀ tā būshè̀, kō?	All your plants have dried up, have they?
Mà̀i gōnā̀:	Ā'à̀, sunà̀ dà sauran lalmà̀.	No, they still have some moisture.
I and N:	Tô, Allàh yà kāwō ruwā̀!	May God bring rain!
Mà̀i gōnā̀:	Āmiŋ! Āmin!	Amen! Amen!

Vocabulary

bàkŤ n.m. (bàkunā̀ pl.)	'mouth'	kayya	'alas!'
(à) bàkin	'alongside of'	kōgŤ n.m. (kōgunā̀ pl.)	'river'
būshè̀ v.intr.	'dry up'	laimà̀ n.f.	'dampness'
dāɗŤ n.m.	'pleasure'	màganā̀ n.f.	'words, speech'
dàminā̀ n.f.	'rainy season'	saurā n.m.	'remainder, the rest'
farŤ n.m.	'long, dry spell during the rainy season'	shūkà̀ v.tr. (shūkā̀ v.n.f.)	'plant, sow'
hùɗā̀ v.tr. (hùɗā̀ v.n.f.)	'hoe, bank up'	tāshi, v.intr. (tāshŤ v.n.m.)	'stand up, rise up'
kallō n.m.	'looking at, observing'	yāwò n.m.	'strolling'

B. A few months later at harvest time, Malam Isa is walking by the river again,
this time alone, when he sees the same farmer working in one of his fields.
Malam Isa decides to find out how his crops have fared.

177

nā dai ci tumù   'I've tasted the new millet, though'

nā fa biyā kà!   'why, I paid you!'

Of course these particles can occur places in a sentence other than between the person aspect pronoun and the verb.

bana kàm gōnarkà tā yi àlbarkã   'this year your farm has flourished'

shī nè kùwā   'indeed it's him'

nī dai bã ni dà lāfiyà   'well I don't feel so good'

nā sàri dājìn cân kuma nā shūkà   'I cleared that bush area and then
    dāwã   I planted guinea corn'

yàyà dōyã dai bana?   'and how are the yams this year?'

GRAMMATICAL DRILLS

Drill 1 - Change the sentences below from the completive to the continuative aspect.

    Cue sentence: makèrī yā līkè

    Student response: makèrī yanà līkèwā

1. sun kāwō   5. mun zō   9. sun sàrā

2. yā gamã   6. sun sã   10. yā kai

3. tā dadè v.intr. 'dally'   7. nā shìga   11. kun kōrā

4. kin tàfi   8. mun nūnã   12. tā būshè

Drill 2A - 2B - Change the sentences in the completive aspect into the continuative aspect. All the sentences of part 2A have verbs with -wā verbal nouns, all those in 2B have non -wā verbal nouns. If you are not sure what the verbal nouns are, look them up.

2A   Cue: yārō yā kāwō minì ruwā

    Student response: yārō yanà kāwō minì ruwā

1. tsuntsàyē sun βàtà hatsī   7. bàn fārà ba

2. makèrī yā līkè ta   8. an kāwō ruwā mù shā

3. mãsu gōnakī sun sã tākìn zāmànī   9. sun βàtà kudī à gàrī
    tākìn zāmànī 'chemical fertilizer'   (βàtà here means 'waste')
    (manure of modern times)
    10. mãsu gōnakī sun fārã?

4. fartanyãtā tā karyè   11. kōgī yā kāwō jirgin ruwā

5. makèrī yā sayō gawàyī   12. dabbōbī sun βàtã ta

6. duk shūkàrkà tā būshè?

2B   Cue: mãsu gōnakī sun shūkà dāwã

    Student response: mãsu gōnakī sunã shūkàr dāwã

1. sun tàfi   4. makèrī yā sàyi gawàyī

2. sun bi hanyà dàgà Yàshi zuwā   5. Āmadù dà Shēhù sun shìga zaurè
    Malumfāshi   6. bà sù zō ba

3. nā sō shì

7. nā ga kōgī dàgà dūtsèn nân
8. uwargidā tā bar ɗantà yà yi hakà
9. bài gyārà mōtà ba

10. bài sāmē shi ba
11. kā sàri itàcen nàn?
12. su Audù sun tàimàki ùbansù

Drill 3 - Answer the questions, changing the noun objects to pronouns or leaving out an overt object completely, whichever is appropriate.

Cue: yanà kāwō kuɗī?
Student response: yanà kāwôwā
Cue: mài gōnā yanà kiràn ɗansà?   kirā n.m. 'calling'
Student response: mài gōnā yanà kirànsà

1. mutānē sunà sâ rīgunànsù?
2. su Audù sunà tàimakon ùbansà?
3. munà nōmè wannàn cìyāwàr banzā?
   banzā n.f. 'worthless'
4. sunà kallon mài gōnā?
5. kanà gyāran mōtà?
6. makèrī yanà līkè garwā?
   garwā n.f. 'kerosene can'
7. maràsā hankàlī sunà karyà kōshiyà?
8. kunà ganin awākī dàgà dūtsè?

9. su Audù sunà kōrar tsuntsāyē?
10. 'yan tēbur sunà kāwō tēburōrinsù?
11. yanà barìn yārā sù yi hakà?
12. màsu gōnàkī sunà shūkàr dāwà?
13. sunà nūnà gōnàkinsù?
14. kunà sâ tākìn zāmànī?
15. bā kā sôn Yàhàya?
16. kōgī yanà kāwō jirgin ruwā?

Drill 4 - Change the sentences which use the completive aspect pronouns to create mài/màsu forms as shown in the example.

Cue: sunà dà dāwà
Student response: sū màsu dāwà nē

1. Audù yanà dà gōnā
2. sunà dà arzikī
3. Hàlīmà tanà dà tsīnin hancī
4. Mammàn yanà dà màtā huɗu
5. yanà hùɗar dōyà

6. sunà dà dawākī   dōkī n.m. 'horse'
                    (dawākī pl.)
7. tanà sayad dà ƙwai
8. yanà yī minì kiwò
   kiwò n.m. 'tending animals'
9. yanà dà gidā
10. tanà dà kwandō

Drill 5 - Negate the sentences below.

Cue sentence: sun gan shi
Student response: bà sù gan shi ba

1. zân gan sù
2. zābī sunà tāshì
3. mutānē sun ga zābī

4. Hàlīmà tanà màganà dà mài gōnā
5. kà tàfi kàsuwā
6. Audù yā gan tà

185

13A <u>Initial sentence:</u> yanà̰ jîn dāɗin yāwǒ

<u>Cues</u>

1. yāwòn nân   yanà̰ jîn dāɗin yāwòn nân
2. à bākin hanyà̰   yanà̰ jîn dāɗin yāwòn nân à bākin hanyà̰
3. kǒgī   yanà̰ jîn dāɗin yāwòn nân à bākin kǒgī
4. Īsa   Īsa yanà̰ jîn dāɗin yāwòn nân à bākin kǒgī
5. Hàlīmà   Hàlīmà tanà̰ jîn dāɗin yāwòn nân à bākin kǒgī
6. inà̰ jîn dāɗin   inà̰ jîn dāɗin yāwòn nân à bākin kǒgī
7. nī kàm   nī kàm inà̰ jîn dāɗin yāwòn nân à bākin kǒgī
8. jîn dāɗin ganin zàbī   nī kàm inà̰ jîn dāɗin ganin zàbī (à bākin kǒgī)
9. ganin mài gōnā   nī kàm inà̰ jîn dāɗin ganin mài gōnā (à bākin kǒgī)
10. negative   nī kàm bā nà̰ jîn dāɗin ganin mài gōnā (à bākin kǒgī)
    continuative

13B <u>Initial sentence:</u> zā sù fārà girbī

1. zâi   zâi fārà girbī
2. completive aspect yā fārà girbī
3. su Mùhammadù   su Mùhammadù sun fārà girbī
4. negative completive su Mùhammadù bà sù fārà girbī ba
5. ga zàbī   su Mùhammadù bà sù ga zàbī ba
6. dāwà̰ tā fid dà kâi su Mùhammadù bà sù ga dāwà̰ tā fid dà kâi ba
7. hatsī   su Mùhammadù bà sù ga hatsī yā fid dà kâi ba
8. munà̰ tsàmmānī   munà̰ tsàmmānī su Mùhammadù bà sù ga hatsī yā
                        fid dà kâi ba
9. tsuntsā̰yē sunà̰ ɓàrnā munà̰ tsàmmānī ṣu Mùhammadù bà sù ga tsuntsā̰yē
                        sunà̰ ɓàrnā ba
                or
                        munà̰ tsàmmānī tsuntsā̰yē sunà̰ ɓàrnā
10. dabbōbī   munà̰ tsàmmānī ṣu Mùhammadù bà sù ga dabbōbī
                        sunà̰ ɓàrnā ba
                or
                        munà̰ tsàmmānī dabbōbī sunà̰ ɓàrnā

13C <u>Initial sentence:</u> tā yi àlbarkà̰

1. gōnā   gōnā tā yi àlbarkà̰
2. bana kàm   bana kàm gōnā tā yi àlbarkà̰
3. kyâu   bana kàm gōnā tā yi kyâu
4. hatsī   bana kàm hatsī yā yi kyâu
5. dāwà̰   bana kàm dāwà̰ tā yi kyâu
6. yawà̰   bana kàm dāwà̰ tā yi yawà̰
7. wùtā̰-wutā̰   bana kàm wùtā̰-wutā̰ tā yi yawà̰
8. gà̰ mu dai,   gà̰ mu dai, bana kàm wùtā̰-wutā̰ tā yi yawà̰

1) In Nigeria the weather is not the subject of conversation <u>par excellence</u> that it is in America. However, we have learned a number of weather terms now, so it can properly serve as a vehicle for guided conversation in the classroom. Some suggestions for situations are: a Nigerian student discussing the differences between his country and the US (different seasons, degree of heat or cold, precipitation); two people remarking on the weather as a way to pass the time of day; one person describing the weather in one part of the country or the world to another (temperatures, precipitation, compensations made for weather such as extra clothes, fans, etc.). Some words and expressions will be useful:

d̄arī n.m.	'coldness (due to wind)'			
sanyī n.m.	'coldness (due to wind or wet)'			
zufā n.f.	'hot weather'	yâu anā zufā	'it's hot today'	
zāfī n.m.	'heat'	rānā tā yi zāfī yâu	'the sun is hot today'	
iskā n.f./m.	'wind'			
hadarī n.m.	'storm'	an yi hadarī jiyà	'there was a storm yesterday'	
ruwā n.m.	'water, rain'	an yi ruwā	'it rained'	
		anā ruwā	'it's raining'	
ƙankarā n.m.	'ice, any icy precipitation (snow, hail, etc.)'			
girgijē n.m. (gizāgizai pl.)	'storm cloud'			

sanyī yā⎤
zufā tā ⎬ yi 'the ⎡cold ⎤ is not too bad (made lightness)'
etc. ⎦ saukī ⎣hot weather⎦
⎣etc. ⎦

sanyī yā⎤
zufā tā ⎬ ƙarē 'the ⎡cold ⎤ is over/has finished'
etc. ⎦ ⎣hot weather⎦
⎣etc. ⎦

sanyī yā harbē ni   'I've caught a chill (the cold has kicked me)'

mahūcī n.m.   'fan'

Example conversations:

a) Student 1 is an American student and student 2 is a Nigerian student attending the same school:

Student 1:	Kâi, yâu anā zufā!	Good grief it's hot today!
Student 2:	Wannàn bā zufā ba cē! Sai kà zō Nījēriyā.	This isn't hot weather! You should come to Nigeria.
1:	Ashē?! A wànè lōkàcī zufā ta yi yawā?	Really?! At what time do you have very hot weather?
2:	Ai, à lōkàcin bazarā zufā tā yi yawā, àmmā à lōkàcin dāminā tā yi sauƙī.	Well, during <u>bazara</u> it is really hot, but during <u>damina</u> it is not too bad.

189

1:	Mềnē nề "bazarā" dà "dầminā"?	What are bazara and damina?
2:	Bazarā, ita cề wajen lōkàcin "Spring" ɗinkù, dầminā, lōkà- cin "Summer".	Bazara is about your Spring, damina is Summer.
1:	Don mề bā à zufầ lōkàcin dầminā?	Why isn't it hot during damina?
2:	Don anầ ruwā. Wànnan yā sầ sanyᴛ mài dādᴛ.	Because it rains. That causes cool weather (cold possessor of pleasure).

b) Two students meet and comment on the weather.

Student 1:	Ìnā zufầ?	How's the how weather (treating you)?
Student 2:	Kâi, zufầ tā yi yawầ!	Boy, it's really hot!
1:	Gàskiyā nề, àmmā gầ girgijề yā sàuka à arềwa.	That's right, but there's a rain- cloud which has built up (come down) in the north.
2:	Kanầ tsầmmānᴛ zā à yi ruwā yâu?	Do you think it will rain today?
1:	Inầ fầtā zā à yi.	I hope so.
2:	Nᴛ mā hakà. Ruwā zâi kāwō sanyᴛ.	Me too. The rain will bring some cool weather.

2) Needless to say, there are great differences between the traditional farming methods of northern Nigeria and those of the United States. One student should play the role of a Hausa man discussing differences between tradition- al African and American farming methods with an American. Following are several suggestions for areas that might be discussed. Keep the conversations very general and short. Do not attempt to discuss the fine points of any aspect of farming in either culture.

Different crops - Most of the crops found in one of the two countries are also found in the other, but different crops have different degrees of importance. Some of the main crops which differ are listed here with their suggested counterparts in each country.

Nigeria		United States		
dāwầ	n.f.	'sorghum'	alkamầ n.f.	'wheat'
hatsᴛ	n.m.	'guinea corn'	masàrā n.f.	'corn'
dōyầ	n.f.	'yams'	dànkalᴛ n.m.	'potato' (lit: sweet potato)

Equipment used - Traditionally, farming in Africa was all done by hand, though some animal drawn equipment is coming into use. Some of the things used in the two countries follow.

Nigeria		United States	
fartanyầ n.f. 'small hoe' (used for weeding (nōmề v.tr.) or for banking up rows (hūɗầ v.tr.))		injᴛ n.m. injin nōmā	'machine' 'tractor, farm machinery'

gàrmā̃ n.f.   'large hoe'
(used for preparing field for
planting (hūɗā̃); ox drawn plows
called gàrmar shānū (plow of
cattle are now used in some
areas)

shānū sunà̃ jân gàrmā̃ 'the cattle are pulling the plow'

sùngumT̃   hoe with a long handle used
               to make depressions in which
               to sow guinea corn

The various operations of farming that are done by hand in Nigeria but by
machine in the United States are

shūkā̀ v.tr.   'plant, sow'
(shūkā̃ v.n.f.)

hūɗā̀ v.tr.   'plow; bank up rows'
(hūɗā̃ v.n.f.)

nōmè̃ v.tr.   'weed'

girbT̃ n.m.   'harvesting grain, reaping'

Weather - Preparation of the field and planting in Nigeria begins at
the first rains (in late May - early June) and the success of the crop is
entirely dependent on the rain since only smaller vegetable gardens
(làmbū n.m.) are irrigated. In drier areas of the United States, irrigation is used.

an yi ruwā̃/anà̃ ruwā̃   'it rained/it is raining'

an bā̃ da ruwā̃   'irrigation has been done (one gave water)'

Insecticides and fertilizers - Use of insecticides is unknown in traditional African agriculture. Manure is used for fertilizer, as it is in
the United States, but chemical fertilizers have only recently begun to be
used in some areas of Nigeria.

māgànin k̃wārT̃   'insecticide' (medicine of bugs)

tākT̃ n.m.   'manure (used as fertilizer)'

tākin zàmànT̃   'chemical fertilizer' ("manure of modern times")

Increasing the size of a farm - Traditionally a farmer in Nigeria who
wanted to increase the size of his farm had to do nothing more than put forth
the effort to clear some unused land (yā̃ sāri dājT̃). In the United States,
somebody owns all the land, so a farmer who wishes to increase the size of
his holdings must buy new land (sai yà sàyā̃).

Example dialogue: a Nigerian (Student 2) and an American (Student 1) have
gone for a ride in the country in the Spring. As they pass a field where
a farmer is plowing, they discuss some differences between Nigerian and
American farming techniques.

Student 1: Gà manŏmī, yanà   There's a farmer plowing with a
           hùɗā dà injin nŏmā.   tractor. Do they use tractors in
           Anā àmfânī dà injī   your country?
           à ƙasarkù?

Student 2: Ā'à, anà aikī dà kā-   No, they use hand equipment and some
           yan hannū ƙumā wasu   farmers use animals.
           manŏmā sunā àmfânī
           dà dabbōbī.

1:         Wàtŏ su shānū, kŏ?   That is, (animals like) cattle, huh?

2:         Hakà nē. Anā àmfânī dà That's right. Cattle and donkeys
           shānū dà jàkkai.   are used. (jākī n.m. 'donkey',
                                  jàkkai pl.)

1:         Inā tsàmmānī zâi shūkà I think he's going to plant wheat
           alkamā à nân. Kunà cîn here. Do you eat wheat too?
           alkamā kū mā?

2:         Sai kàɗan. Àbincinmù shī Just a little. Our food is guinea
           nē hatsī.   corn.

1:         Kunà shūkàr hatsī dà fartanyà? Do you plant guinea corn with a
                                          (small) hoe?

2:         Ā'à, anà shūkà dà sùngumī. No, a sungumi is used. Weeding is
           Anà nŏmā dà fartanyà.   done with a hoe.

192

UNIT XV

DIALOGUES

A. The main cash crop of northern Nigeria is peanuts. A tax official pays a friendly call on a peanut buying agent who he suspects may be paying fewer taxes than he should.

Mài Hàràjî:	Màj gidā, barkà dà aikī. Inā fātā kā sāmi gyàɗā mài yawā bana.	Greetings at work, sir. I hope you've gotten plenty of peanuts this year.
Mài Gyàɗā:	Barkà kàdai. Bana kàm àlhamdù lìllāhì, gyàɗā tā sāmu sōsai.	Greetings. Thanks be to God there are plenty of peanuts this year.
Mài Hàràjî:	Nā zō don ìn ji yaddà ka kē tafiyad dà cinikin gyàɗarkà. Yàushè ka kē fārāwā?	I have come to hear how you carry on your peanut trade. When do you start?
Mài Gyàɗā:	Bā nā fārà cinikī sai an bùɗè fulōtī. 'Yan aikīnā kē jāwō hankàlin māsu gyàɗā sù zō rumfātā.	I don't begin trade until the trading area is opened. My workers draw the attention of the peanut farmers (owners) so that they come to my shed.
Mài Hàràjî:	'Yan aikìnkà har nawà nē?	How many employees do you have?
Mài Gyàɗā:	Sū gōmà shā ɗaya nē.	There are eleven of them.
Mài Hàràjî:	À ìnā dà ìnā su kē yī makà aikī?	In what areas (from where to where) do they work for you?
Mài Gyàɗā·	Duk à ƙasar Bici dà Dawāki su kē yī mini aikī.	Throughout the Bici and Dawaki area they work for me.
Mài Hàràjî:	'Yan aikìnkà, nawà nawà ka kē biyànsù, kuma sunā sāmùn kàmashō?	(About) your workers, how much do you pay them each, and do they get a commission?
Mài Gyàɗā:	Kōwā yanā sāmùn àlbāshin Nairā gōmà, kàmashon sule gùɗā gà kōwànè bùhū.	Everyone receives a salary of ten Naira and a commission of one shilling on each bag.

Vocabulary

àlbāshī	n.m.	'salary'	gà/gàrē	'in the presence of, at, for' (see 15.5)
biyā	v.tr.	'pay'		
(biyā	v.n.m.)		gyàɗā n.f.	'peanut, peanuts'
bùɗè	v.tr.	'open'	hankàlī n.m.	'attention; good sense'
bùhū	n.m.	'large bag'	jāwō n.tr.	'pull toward, draw'
(buhunā pl.)			kàmashō n.m.	'commission'
fātā	n.f.	'hoping'	kōwā	'everyone, each one'
fulōtī	n.m.	'buying area'		

(this area is opened for peanut buying by the Government from sometime in November through the winter months)

193

ìnā ka kè kai gyàɗā?	'where do you take the peanuts?'
nawà nawà ka kè biyànsù?	'how much do you pay them each?'
yàushè a kè būɗè fulōtī?	'when is the (peanut trading) area opened?'

b) When some element - an object, an adverb, a "prepositional phrase", etc. - is placed at the beginning of a sentence for emphasis. This usage corresponds to English sentences such as 'it's peanuts that I want' where the direct object of want is actually peanuts, but it has been moved to the front of the sentence. Moving an element to the beginning in Hausa also corresponds to simply stressing the corresponding element in English, for example 'I want peanuts'. Often nē or cē (depending on the gender of the noun involved) is used after the word that has been moved to the beginning. This parallels the English 'it's ... ' in the illustration above.

Note that if the subject of the sentence is to be emphasized, since it is already at the beginning of the sentence, a simple change from Continuative to Relative Continuative (with or without nē/cē inserted after the subject) shows emphasis. If the subject is a pronoun, the independent pronoun is repeated before the Relative Continuative.

'yan aikīnā (nè) su kè jāwō hankàlin màsu gyàɗā	'my workers draw the attention of the peanut owners'
nī (nè) na kè jāwō hankàlin màsu gyàɗā	'it's I who draw the attention of peanut owners'
sàlansà (cē) ya kè līkèwā	'it's a muffler he's repairing'
mū (nè) su kè àikā	'it's us they are sending'
barcī ya kè	'sleeping (is what) he is (doing)'
(à) gidā mu kè	'at home is where we are'
duk à ƙasar Bicì ɗà Dawāki su kè yī minì aikī	'throughout all the Bici and Dawaki area they work for me'
hakà a kè aunà gyàɗā	'it's like this that peanuts are weighed'

An indirect object can also be put at the beginning of a sentence to question or emphasize it. This is done by taking the indirect object noun, the independent pronoun corresponding to the indirect object pronoun, or the question word, and placing it at the beginning of the sentence. The particle wà is then placed directly after the verb to show that it is the indirect object which is emphasized or questioned, and not some other constituent.

Shēhù nē na kè kāwō wà kāyan gōnā	'it's Shehu I'm bringing the farm goods to'
(cf. inā kāwō wà Shēhù kāyan gōnā	'I'm bringing the farm goods to S.')
kū nè nà kè kāwō wà kāyan gōnā	'it's you I'm bringing farm goods to'
(cf. inā kāwō mukù kāyan gōnā	'I'm bringing you farm goods')
wā zā kà sayā wà àgōgon nàn?	'who are you going to buy this watch for?'

196

Certain adverbs, especially adverbs of time, can come at the beginning of the sentence without being emphasized. With such adverbs, it is the use of the Relative aspects, rather than the neutral Continuative or Completive, that indicates that the adverb is emphasized.

yâu mōtōcī dà yawā su kḕ wuc̣ḕwā   'today a lot of cars are passing'
(cf. yâu mōtōcī dà yawā sunā   'today a lot of cars are passing')
wuc̣ḕwa)

c) **In relative clauses.** Relative clauses will be discussed in detail in Unit XVI. The only example of a relative clause in the dialogues of this unit is

nā̀ zō don in̊ ji yâddà ka kḕ   'I've come to hear how you carry
tafiyar dà cìnikin gyàḍarkā   on your peanut trade'

The word yâddà here, which is related to yā̀yā̀ 'how?' could be translated 'the way in which'. There is also an example of a relative clause in the comprehension passage:

wurā̀rên dà 'yan aikīnā kḕ yī   'the places where my workers do
minì aikī   work for me'

15.2 nā̀ and kḕ alone after a Noun

In dialogue A of this unit we find the sentence

'yan aikīnā kḕ jāwō hankàlin   'my workers draw the attention
māsu gyàḍā sù zō rùmfātā   of the peanut owners to my shed'

Following the rules laid down so far, one would have expected 'yan aikīnā su kḕ ... However, in the third person, it is quite common for the part of the continuative pronoun indicating number and gender (ya, ta, su) to be dropped when preceded by a noun, since the noun itself is sufficient to show number and gender and the nā̀ or kḕ shows that it is continuative aspect.

Mūsā nā̀ zuwā̀ (=Mūsā yanā̀ zuwā̀)   'Musa is coming'

mài hàrājī nā̀ màganā̀   'the tax collector is speaking'

dawā̀ cḕ mài gōnā̀ kḕ shūkā̀   'it's guinea corn that the farmer
                                   is planting'

15.3 The ma- Agentive Nouns

"Agentive nouns" can be formed from many verbs and some action nouns by the addition of the prefix ma- to the verb root and the addition of certain suffixes and tone changes. Following are some of such agentive nouns with the verbs they are derived from:

Verb		Masc.Sing.	Fem.Sing.	Plural	
bi	'follow'	mabìyī	mabiyìyā	mabìyā	'follower(s)'
kēra̋	'forge'	makḕrī	makēriyā	makēra̋	'blacksmith(s) 'blacksmith's wife (wives)'
rubū̀tā	'write'	marùbūcī	marubūciyā	marubū̀tā	'writer(s)
tàfi	'go'	matàfìyī	mataf(iy)ìyā	matàfìyā	'traveller(s)'
tàmbaya̋	'ask'	matàmbàyī	matambayìyā	matàmbàyā	'asker(s)'

197

The rules for forming these nouns are as follows:
    The final vowel of the verb is dropped (except monosyllabic verbs or verbs ending in -i), then the prefix ma- is added.
    Masculine and plural: the verb root has low tone and a high tone -ī is added for masculine singular, high tone -ā for plural (-yī or -yā after a root ending in -i);
    Feminine singular: the verb root has all high tone and the suffix -īyā is added (-yīyā after a root ending in -i).

    Note that a root ending in t, d, s, or z undergoes palatalization (see 8.5) before the suffixes -ī or -īyā. Thus, from rubūtā 'write', we get marùbùcī and marubūcìyā.

15.4 Interrogative Adjectives

    The interrogative adjectives have the following forms:

         wànè + masculine noun   wànè gidā?   'which house?'
         wàcè + feminine noun   wàcè mōtà?   'which car?'
         wàďànnè + plural noun   wàďànnè mōtōcī? 'which cars?'

Remember that after all interrogative words, the relative form of the continuative aspect (15.1) must be used. The relative form of the completive (see 16.1) must also be used, but other aspects remain unchanged.

    wànè manòmī ya kè aikī à gōnarsà?   'which farmer is working in
                                          his field?'

    à wàcè ƙasā su kè yī makà aikī?   'in what area are they working
                                          for you?'

    wàďànnè yârā su kè barcī?   'which children are sleeping?'

    When used with the noun irī 'kind', the interrogative adjectives agree in gender and number with the noun modified by irī, not with irī itself.

    wànè irìn sufùrī ka kè àmfànī   'what kind of transportation
    dà shī?   do you use?'

    wàcè irìn dāwà zā kà shūkà?   'what kind of guinea corn are
                                          you going to plant?'

    wàďànnè irìn mōtōcī su kè   'which kind of trucks carry
    kai gyàďarkà?   your peanuts?'

15.5 Review of Questions

    Up to this point, we have seen three ways in which questions are formed in Hausa, each of which has its characteristic intonation. Although there were drills on question intonation in the early units of this book, we feel that proper use of question intonation is important enough in arriving at a native-like command of Hausa and difficult enough for most English speaking students to warrant a review at this point.

a) Yes-no questions

    These questions, so-called because they can be answered "yes" or "no", are constructed like declarative sentences but have question intonation. Question intonation involves raising the last high tone syllable (which is not necessarily the last syllable) to an extra high pitch. If this syllable is the last syllable in the sentence, the pitch falls sharply.

If low tone(s) follow(s), the low tone syllable is somewhat lower that
the extra high pitch preceding it, but not as low as the final low tone
of a normal declarative sentence. The pitch falls sharply on the final
syllable when it is low as well. Following are examples graphically
contrasting the same sentences with declarative and question intonation.

kā ga zābī.   'You saw the guinea fowl.'

kā ga zābī?   'Did you see the guinea fowl?'

shūkàrkà tā būshē   'your plants have dried up.'

shūkàrka tā būshē?   'have your plants dried up?'

b) Questions containing a "question word"

Questions containing a question word do not have question intonation.
A high tone on the final syllable of such questions falls in pitch somewhat, but it is not raised to the extra high pitch found in real question intonation nor does it fall as sharply. The interrogative words seen
so far with examples are

wānē nē (m)/wācē cē (f)/su wānē nē (pl)?   'who is it?'

wānē nē mài gidankà?   'who is your master?'

mēnē nē (m)/mēcē cē (f)?   'what is it?'

mēnē nē māgànin birī?   'what is good for getting
                                             rid of monkeys?' (medicine
                                             of monkeys)

wā?   'who?'

wā ya kē tàimakonkà?   'who's helping you?'

mē?   'what?'

mē ya sā ka kē tàmbàye-tàmbàyē hakà?   'what causes you to ask all
                                             these questions?'

īnā?   'where?'

īnā nē ka kē ajìyè gyàɗarkà?   'where do you store your
                                             peanuts?'

yàushè?   'when?'

yàushè ka kē fārà cìnikī?   'when do you start trading?'

yàyà?   'how?'

yàyà dōyà dai bana?   'how are the yams this year?'

nawà?   'how much?'

nawà nawà ka kē biyàn yārankà?   'how much do you pay your
                                             workers apiece?'

wànè(m)/wàcè(f)/wàɗànnè(pl)?   'which?'

wàcè hanyā zàn bi?   'which road should I follow?'

c) Questions ending in kō or kō bà hakà ba

The word kō or the more complete phrase kō bà hakà ba 'or isn't it thus?' added to the end of a statement gives a sentence equivalent to English "tag" questions ending in 'didn't you?', 'did you?', etc. Whereas English will use a different "tag" depending on the person, tense, and whether or not the question is negative, Hausa uses kō (bà hakà ba) at the end of any such question, much as French uses 'n'est-ce pas?'. In these questions, the question itself has normal statement intonation, but the added kō (bà hakà ba) has question intonation as described in a) above.

duk shūkàrkà tā būshē, kō?	'all you plants have dried up, haven't they?'
cunà sāmùn kàmashõ, kō?	'they get a commission, don't they?'

15.6 gà/gàrē 'in the presence of'

This preposition of very common use has the form gà before nouns, gàrē before pronouns (the direct object pronouns (11.2) are used). Its range of meanings is difficult to capture with any single English word. Perhaps the closed equivalent in a European language is French chez.

It can mean 'in one's house', 'in one's company', 'in one's possession', 'physically or mentally associated with one'.

yārõ yanà gà Hàlīmà	'the child is at Halima's, in Halima's care'
sunà gàrē nì	'they're at my house, in my company'
mun tàfi gà mài gyàɗā	'we went to the peanut salesman's'
àkwai saurī gàrē shì	'he is very quick' (there is quickness associated with him)

This last sentence is an example of how gà/gàrē can be used as an alternative to the expression already learned for 'have'. Instead of saying yanà dà kuɗī 'he has money', we can say àkwai kuɗi gàrē shì. Àkwai may be omitted if a pronoun follows gàrē, giving kuɗī gàrē shì. Dà can also be substituted for àkwai when either a noun or pronoun follows gà/gàrē, but it would be wrong to say kuɗī gà Mūdī with neither dà nor àkwai before gà when it is followed by a noun.

kyâu gàrē tà	
àkwai kyâu gàrē tà	'she is beautiful' ((there is) beauty associated with her)
dà kyâu gàrē tà	
àkwai ƙarfī gà Mūdī	'Mudi is strong' (there is strength associated with Mudi)
dà ƙarfī gà Mūdī	
mōtā gàrē shì	
àkwai mōtā gàrē shì	'he has a car' ((there is) a car in his possession)
dà mōtā gàrē shì	

Gà/gàrē may also mean 'as for', 'in the case of', 'pertaining to',
'linked to'.

lâifT gà mahàifT   'a crime against the father'
gàrē nì, bài kàmàtà ba   'to my mind, it isn't right;
                                     it's not a suitable way to act'
sunā sāmùn kàmashòn sulē gōmà   'they re getting a one shilling
gà kōwànè bùhū   commission for each bag'

GRAMMATICAL DRILLS

Drill 1A - 1B

1A Put the direct object or action noun at the beginning of the sentence
for emphasis. Nē and cē can optionally be used after the object.

Cue: yanā 1Tkè sàlansā

Student response: sàlansā (cē) ya kē 1Tkèwā

Cue: yanā 1Tkè ta

Student response: ita (cē) ya kē 1Tkèwā

Cue: sunā aikT

Student response: aikT su kē

1. inā sāmùn gyàdā mài yawā   6. inā sā ta à sìtō
2. inā fārà clnikT   7. kanā sôn àyàbà?
3. sunā barcT   8. sunā sāmùn kàmashòn sulē gùdā
4. kanā ganin kōgT dàgà cân?   9. uwargidā tanā kāwō shi
5. yanā nūnà gōnarsà   10. yârā sunā kòrar tsuntsàyē

1B Put the indirect object at the beginning of the sentence for emphasis.
Nē and cē can optionally be used after the indirect object.

Cue: yanā 1Tkè wà Shēhù sàlansā

Student response: Shēhù (nē) ya kē 1Tkè wà sàlansā

Cue: yanā 1Tkè masà sàlansā

Student response: shT (nē) ya kē 1Tkè wà sàlansā

1. sunā yT minì aikT   5. mài hàrājT yaṇā tambayar wà gwamnatT
2. makērT,yanā 1Tkè wà Shēhù   gwamnatT n.f. 'government'
   sàlansā   6. munā shūkā mukù hatsT
3. su Audù sunā kōrā masà dabbōbT 7. sun gayā wà mài gyàd̃à làbārT
4. manòmT yanā nūnā wà Īsa gōnā   8. mài gidā yanā nūnā manà mōtàrsà

Drill 2 - Form complex sentences that contain a relative clause introduced
by yaddà 'how' with the relative continuative aspect as shown in the examples.

Cue: sunā hùd̃ar dōyā

Student response: nā zō don in ga yaddà su kē hùd̃ar dōyā

201

Cue sentence: Audù ya kè kāwō gyàɗā   (wà)
Student response: wà ya kè kāwō gyàɗā?
Cue sentence: gyàɗā na kè ajìyêwā à sìtōnā   (mè)
Student response: mè ka kè ajìyêwā à sìtonkà?

1. bāyan an būɗè fulōtT na kè fārà cìnikT (yàushè)
2. sulè bìyar su kè biyànsù (nawà nē)
3. à kàsuwā ta kè (ìnā)
4. gyàɗā su kè kāwôwā (mè)
5. tābā ya kè sayē (mè)
6. 'yan aikT nē su kè jāwō hankàlin màsu gyàɗā (wà)
7. tashàr jirgin ƙasà à Kanò ya kè kai gyàɗā (ìnā)
8. kàmashòn sulè bìyar su kè sāmū gà kòwànè bùhū (nawà nē)
9. Hukūmàr CìnikT ta kè bā mù buhunā (wà)   Hukūmàr CìnikT 'Marketing Board'
10. duk à ƙasar Bicì dà Dawāki su kè yT minì aikT (ìnā)

Drill 8 - Another way to express the notion "have" is by the use of gà/gàrē
as shown in the examples. This can be done both with sentences such as 'he
has a book' and 'he has strength' (i.e., he is strong). Change the sentences
using the continuative pronoun to sentences using gà/gàrē as illustrated.

Cue: Àli yanā dà ƙarfT
Student response: àkwai ƙarfT gà Àli
Cue: tanā dà littāfT
Student response: àkwai littāfT gàrē tà

1. tanā dà kyâu   6. inā dà sulè gōmà
2. mùtumìn nân yanā dà ƙarfT   7. gōnarkà tanā dà fadT
3. sunā dà mōtōcT   8. mài gidā yanā dà mōtà mài kyâu
4. Hadiza tana da kyau   9. munā dà buhun gyàɗā
5. jākT yanā dà ƙarfT

Drill 9 - The word gà/gàrē can be used to mean 'in somebody's presence', or,
if the context warrants, 'in somebody's care'. In this drill, you will hear
a question of the form inā X ya/ta/su kè? 'where is/are X?' followed by a
noun or independent pronoun. Respond with a sentence of the form gà/gàrē ...
X ya kè/ta kè/su kè 'X is with/in the care of ...' with the noun or pronoun
in the space. Be sure to use the object pronoun after gàrē if the cue is a
pronoun.

Cue: inā yārā su kè? (ita)
Student response: gàrē tà su kè
Cue: inā ku kè? (Mùhammadù)
Student response: gà Mùhammadu mu kè

204

1. ìnā mài hàrājī̀ ya kè? (mài gyàɗā) 6. ìnā su kè? (shī)
2. ìnā ya kè? (àbōkinsà) 7. ìnā īsa ya kè? (manòmī)
3. ìnā Sà'īdù ya kè? (kai) 8. ìnā su Audù su kè? (uwargidā)
4. ìnā Aishà ta kè? (ita) 9. ìnā ku kè? (sū) ::
5. ìnā bàbankà ya kè? (Abūbakàr) 10. ìnā yārinyà ta kè? (kē)

Drill 10 - In each of the sentences below, prepose the "prepositional phrase" to the front of the sentence and make the necessary change from the continuative aspect to the relative continuative aspect. Note that nīsā 'far', dàgà 'from', and kusa 'near' do not have à preceding them when preposed to initial position ín a sentence. The à is optional in all of the other cases in this drill.

Cue: yanà kân tēbùr
Student response: à kân tēbùr ya kè
Cue: tanà nīsā dà gàrinkù
Student response: nīsā dà gàrinkù ta kè

1. tanà kusa dà Hàlīmà 6. kunà bāyan ōfìshinmù
2. sunà yāwò à bàkin kògī 7. sunà ƙàrƙashin kujèrarkì
3. inà tàfiyà dàgà Zāriyà zuwà Kanò 8. kanà bāyan mōtà
4. yanà nīsā dà ƙauyènmù 9. munà bàkin hanyà
5. munà gàban Gidan Wayà 10. kàzā tanà cikin ɗākī

Drill 11 - Reply to statements patterned on gà su cân, sunà sāran dājī with sentences patterned on bà sù san yaddà a kè sāran dājī ba.

Cue: gà ta cân tanà ɗ'inka rīgā
Student response: bà tà san yaddà a kè ɗ'ink'a rīgā ba
1. gà shi cân yanà hùɗar dōyà 6. gà shi cân yanà sà tākī
2. gà mu nân munà sà buhunà à mōtōcī 7. gà ta cân tanà ɗībàr ruwā
3. gà ni nân inà shūkà dāwà 8. gà su cân sunà kòrar dabbōbī
4. gà su cân sunà ɗaukàr gyàɗā 9. gà ni nân inà sāran dājī
5. gà mu nân munà aunà gyàɗā 10. gà̀ su cân sunà jāwò hankàlin màsu gyàɗā

Drill 12 - In this drill you will be given a sentence that contains a ma-"agentive noun" and then asked to form a sentence that contains the verbal root from which the agentive noun was formed.

Cue: Shī mabìyin Sarkī nē. Mè ya kè yî? Sarkī n.m. 'emir'
Student response: Yanà bîn Sarkī.
Cue: Ita mataimakìyarmù cē. Mè ta kè yî?
Student response: Tanà tàimakonmù.

205

1. ShT manômT nè. Mề ya kề yî?
2. Ita maɗinkìyar tufāfî cē. Mề ta kề yî?
3. Ita masōyìyar Audù cē. Mề ta kề yî?
4. ShT masàyin gyàɗā nè. Mề ya kề yî?
5. Sū makềrā nè. Mề su kề yî?
6. Sū matàfìyā nề. Mề su kề yî?
7. Sū matàmbàyā nề. Mề su kề yî?
8. Ita mataimakìyar yârā cề. Mề ta kề yî?
9. Hàlîmà masayìyar kwandunâ cē. Mề ta kề yî?
10. ShT mashâyin giyâ nē. Mề ya kề yî?   giyâ n.f. 'beer'

Drill 13 - Answer the question yârankà har nawà nề? with the pattern sentence sū (number) nề.

    Cue: yârankà har nawà nề? (18)
    Student response: sū gōmà shâ takwàs nē

1. yârankà har nawà nề? (12)   6. 'yan aikìnkà har nawà nề? (51)
2. kàjinkà har nawà nề? (9)   7. zàbinkà har nawà nề? (27)
3. awākinkà har nawà nề? (22)   8. tàbàrminkà har nawà nề? (33)
4. bùhunkà har nawà nề? (46)   9. Ʀwankà har nawà nề? (64)
5. mōtōcinkà har nawà nề? (17)   10. tumākinkà har nawà nề? (14)

Drill 14 - Reply with a complete negative sentence to the questions below.

    Cue: kanà àmfànT dà mânyan mōtōcT?
    Student response: ā'à, bā nà àmfànT dà mânyan mōtōcT

1. kunà àmfànT dà mânyan mōtōcT?   6. kanà àmfànT dà mânyan mōtōcT?
2. tanà àmfànT dà mânyan mōtōcT?   7. yanà àmfànT dà mânyan mōtōcT?
3. su Īsa sunà àmfànT dà mânyan   8. anà àmfànT dà mânyan mōtōcT?
   mōtōcT?   9. mài hàrājì yanà àmfànT dà mânyan
4. munà àmfànT dà mânyan mōtōcT?   mōtōcT?
5. kinà àmfànT dà mânyan mōtōcT?   10. màsu gyàɗà sunà àmfànT dà mânyan
                                        mōtōcT?

Drill 15 - Repeat the initial sentence, then substitute the first cue into the appropriate place in that sentence. As each cue is given, substitute it into the sentence formed from the previous cue so that a new sentence is formed.

15A Initial sentence: nā fārà aikT

Cues   Student response
1. continuative aspect   inà fārà aikT
2. cìnikT   inà fārà cìnikT

206

3. yanā̀   yanā̀ fārà cìnikᴛ

4. mài gyàɗā   mài gyàɗā yanā̀ fārà cìnikᴛ

5. negative continuative   mài gyàɗā bā̄ yā̀ fārà cìnikᴛ

6. sai an būɗe fulōtᴛ̀   mài gyàɗā bā̄ yā̀ fārà cìnikᴛ sai an būɗè fulōtᴛ̀

7. sai 'yan aikìnsā̀ sun   mài gyàɗā bā̄ yā̀ fārà cìnikᴛ sai 'yan aikìnsà sun
    jāwō hankàlin mā̄su   jāwō hankàlin mā̄su gyàɗā
    gyàɗā

8. sai mā̄su gyàɗā sun zō   mài gyàɗā bā̄ yā̀ fārà cìnikᴛ sai mā̄su gyàɗā sun zō

9. sai mā̂nyan mōtōcᴛ sun   mài gyàɗā bā̄ yā̀ fārà cìnikᴛ sai mā̂nyan mōtōcᴛ
    zō   sun zō

10. sai an kāwō masà   mài gyàɗā bā̄ yā̀ fārà cìnikᴛ sai an kāwō masà
     gyàɗā   gyàɗā

15B **Initial sentence:**   yā̄ sā̀mē shì

1. continuative aspect   yanā̀ sāmùnsà

2. kōwā̄   kōwā̄ yanā̀ sāmùnsà

3. kàmashṑ   kōwā̄ yanā̀ sāmùn kàmashṑ

4. kàmashòn sᴛsᴛ̀   kōwā̄ yanā̀ sāmùn kàmashòn sᴛsᴛ̀

5. gà kōwànè bùhū   kōwā̄ yanā̀ sāmùn kàmashòn sᴛsᴛ gà kōwànè bùhū

6. kàmashòn sulè̀ gùdā   kōwā̄ yanā̀ sāmùn kàmashòn sulè̀ gùdā gà kōwànè bùhū

7. gà kōwànè Nairā̀   kōwā̄ yanā̀ sāmùn kàmashòn sulè̀ gùdā gà kōwànè Nairā̀

8. nā̄ ji   nā̄ ji kōwā̄ yanā̀ sāmùn kàmashòn sulè̀ gùdā gà
                     kōwànè Nairā̀

9. inā̀ fātā   inā̀ fā̀tā kōwā̄ yanā̀ sāmùn kàmashòn sulè̀ gùdā gà
                     kōwànè Nairā̀

10. nᴛ dai   nᴛ dai, inā̀ fātā kōwā̄ yanā̀ sāmùn kàmashòn sulè̀
                     gùdā gà kōwànè Nairā̀

15C **Initial sentence:**   hatsᴛ yā̄ fid dà kâi

1. yā̄ yi àlbarkā̀   hatsᴛ yā̄ yi àlbarkā̀

2. kyâu   hatsᴛ yā̄ yi kyâu

3. yawā̀   hatsᴛ yā̄ yi yawā̀

4. yā̄ sā̀mu   hatsᴛ yā̄ sā̀mu

5. dā̄wā̀   dā̄wā̀ tā̄ sā̀mu

6. gyàɗā   gyàɗā̀ tā̄ sā̀mu

7. negative completive   gyàɗā bà tà sā̀mu ba

8. bana kàm   bana kàm gyàɗā bà tà sā̀mu ba

9. kàyya!   kàyya! bana kàm gyàɗā bà tà sā̀mu ba

207

1) One student takes the part of a person engaged in some business and the
   other someone discussing the conduct of the business with him. Suggestions
   are

   grocery, clothing, or book business - Discuss the types of products
   sold, source of the products (bought from the manufacturer, brought from
   warehouses, made in the store), volume of business (best seasons for various
   products, present state of business - good or bad), number of employees,
   how the employees are paid (salary, commission, etc.).

   door to door salesman - Discuss the products sold (for example, mùjallà
   'magazines', burōshī dà tsintsiyā 'brushes and brooms', etc.), the way the
   product is sold (salary or commission), reception people give to the product (sunā sàyē kō bā sā sàyē), area covered (duk à gàrin nàn 'everywhere
   in town' or in a certain area - unguwā n.f. 'quarter, district').

   The following is an example conversation about newspaper delivery:

   jàrīdā n.f. 'newspaper
   (jàrīdū pl.)

   rarrabā v.tr. 'distribute (things to various places)'

Student 1:	Inā ʂō in ji yaddà ka kē rarràba jàrīdù.	I want to hear how you distribute newspapers.
Student 2:	Sai in tāshì wajen ƙarfè huɗu don ìn gamà aikī kàfin mutànē sù tāshì.	I have to get up about 4:00 so that I can finish work before people have gotten up.
1:	Awà nawà ka kē yī kanà rarràbàwā?	How many hours do you distribute?
2:	Inā gamāwā wajen ƙarfè shidà dà rabī sai ran Lahadì. Ƙàn nan inā gamàwā wajen ƙarfè bakwài.	I have finished by about 6:30 except on Sunday. That day I finish about 7:00.
1:	Kanā àmfànī dà mōtàrkà?	Do you use your car?
2:	Hakà nè. Kā san inā rarràbàwā duk à unguwar nan.	That's right. You know, I deliver in this entire district.
1:	Yàyà a kē biyànkà?	How are you paid?
2:	Inā sāmun àlbāshī kumā àkwai kàmashòn gà kōwànè mài sàyen jàrīdā.	I get a salary and there is a commission for each subscriber.

2) One student plays the part of a tax consultant who is trying to straighten
   out the tax affairs of a second student. In doing so, the first student
   must question the second student about his financial affairs including
   income, investments, and possible tax deductable items. You may want to
   establish a fictitious situation or use the true situation of the student
   being questioned.

Example conversation:

Student 1:	Inä dà wasu tàmbàye-tàmbàyē.	I have a few questions.
Student 2:	Tô, mẽnē nè?	All right, what are they?
1:	Dàgà ìnā ka kē sāmùn kud̃ī?	Where do you get your money?
2:	Inä sāmųn kud̃ī dàgà wajen Gwamnatī.	I get money from the Government.
1:	Wàtō, kanä dà sìkōlàshif?	That is, you have a scholarship?
2:	Ī, àmmā inä˛tsàmmāni bā nä biyàn hàrājī dàgà kud̃ìn.	Yes, but I don't think I am paying taxes on that money.
1:	Kanä dà wasu kud̃ī?	Do you have any other money?
2:	Ī, nä yi aikì dà dāminä kumā àkwai wasu kud̃ī˛à bankī. Inä sāmùn ruwā.*	Yes, I worked during the summer and there is also some money in the bank. I'm getting interest.
1:	Tô, dōlè kà biyā hàrājī dàgà kud̃ìn aikìnkà kumā dàgà kud̃ìn ruwā.	Well, you must pay (it is required that you pay) taxes on the money from your work and on your interest money.

*ruwa (=ruwan kud̃ī) n.m. 'interest (on money)'
bankī n.m. 'bank'

sâ n.m.	'bull'	shaidà n.f.	'evidence'
sāniyā n.f.	'cow'	tàre dà	'together with'
shānū n.pl.	'cattle'	tsinkē v.tr. or intr.	
sā'à n.f.	'time'		'break loose; snap
sāwū n.m.	'tracks'		in two (rope, etc.)'

B. Having completed the inspection of the allegedly ravaged farm, the assessor returns with Umaru and Beti.

AlƙalĪ:	MuhùtĪ, yàyà kĪmàr Bàrnar Ùmarù ta kē?	Assessor, what is the assessment of Umaru's damage?
MuhùtĪ:	Ai, damĪ gōmà shānun Bètì sukà Bàtà?	Well, it was ten bundles that Beti's cattle destroyed.
AlƙalĪ:	Ùmarù, kā san kō nawà nē kud'in damĪ gōmà?	Umaru, do you know how much ten bundles cost?
Umaru:	Ī, kōwànè damĪ Nairà biyu dà sulè biyu nē.	Yes, each bundle is two Naira two shillings.
AlƙalĪ:	Tô, Betì, zā kà biyā tàrar Nairà takwàs.	All right, Beti, you'll pay a fine of eight Naira.
Umaru:	Rânkà yà dad'e! Nā cê kud'in kōwànè damĪ Nairà biyu dà sulè biyu nē!	May your life be prolonged! (But) I said the price of each bundle is two Naira two shillings.
AlƙalĪ:	Ī, nā ji. Dà kā yi ƙaryā gàme dà Bàrnâr kumā kā yi hakà yanzu. Saƙō dà hakà zā kà sàmi Nairà bakwài, a kai ràgōwàr Nairà gudā bàitulmālĪ.	Yes, I heard. Before you lied about the damage and you've done the same now (i.e. he lied about the price). Because of that you'll get seven Naira and the remaining Naira is to be taken to the Treasury.
Bètì:	Allàh yà gàfàrtà Mālàm! NĪ fàkĪrĪ nē. Bà ni dà fâm hud'u à nân. À yardam minì ìn jē gidā ìn d'auko?	Please sir! I am a poor man. I don't have four pounds here. Would it be permissable for me to go home and bring it back?
AlƙalĪ:	Tô, yi suarĪ!	All right, hurry up!

Vocabulary

bàitùlmālĪ n.m.	'Treasury'	gàme dà	'concerning, about'
dâ	'formerly, before'	kĪmà n.f.	'estimate'
d'aukō v.tr.	'go and bring back'	ƙaryā n.f.	'lie'
fàkĪrĪ n.m. (fàkĪrai pl.)	'destitute person'	tàrā n.f.	'fine (of money)'
		ràgōwà n.f.	'remainder'
gàfàrtā v.tr.	used in (Allàh yà) gàfàrtà Mālàm, a respectful way of addressing an educated person		

COMPREHENSION PRACTICE

Without looking at your books, listen to the passage as your informant reads through it once, pausing to explain in Hausa the meaning of any new words or expressions. Your informant will read the passage a second time at normal conversational speed and then ask you the questions which follow. Answer in complete sentences.

212

À Fādàr[1] Àlƙālī

Àbù nē mài ban shà'awā[2], mùtûm yà zìyàrci fādàr àlƙālī. Dòmin
kōyàushē[3] àlƙālī yanā sāmùn ƙàràrrakī irī̀-irī̀[4] dà zâi yi shàrī̀'ā[5] à
kânsù. Waɗansu ƙàràrrakîn gàme dà aurē[6] nē, waɗansu gàme dà faɗā̀[7],
waɗansu kùwā gàme dà gādò[8] nē. Gà mā mìsālī̀[9] ɗaya dàgà cikin irìn
ƙàràrrakîn dà àlƙālîn ya kè jînsù.

Wani manòmī, Ùmarù, yā yi ƙàrar wani Bàfillācè, Bētì, wai shānun
Bētì sun shìga gōnarsà sukà ɓātā masà hatsī. Ùmarù ya cè yā san shānun
Bētì nē sabò dà yā bi sāwansù har gidan Bētì. Bētì ya mai dà[10] jàwābī̀
cêwā[11] shānûn sun tsinkè sā̀'àd dà mài yī masà kīwò kè barcī. Ùmarù ya
cè Bàrnâr tā kai damī̀ àshìrin àmmā Bētì bài yàrda ba. Sabò dà hakà
àlƙālī ya àiki muhùtī gōnar Ùmarù tāre dà Bētì dà Ùmarù don yà kimmàntà
ɓàrnâr.

Dà sukà dāwō, muhùtī ya faɗā̀ wà àlƙālī cêwā damī̀ gōmà shānûn sukà
ɓātā. Àlƙālī ya cè Bētì zâi biyā Nairā̀ takwàs, Ùmarù yà sàmi Nairā̀ bakwài,
à kai sauran kudîn bàitùlmālī̀.

[1]fādà n.f.	'chambers, hearing room (of a judge)'	[7]faɗā̀ n.f.	'quarrel, fight'
[2]ban shà'awā	'pleasant, giving pleasure'	[8]gādò n.m.	'inheritance'
		[9]mìsālī̀ n.m.	'example'
[3]kōyàushē	'always'	[10]mai dà v.caus.	'reply'
[4]irī̀-irī̀	'of different kinds'	[11]cêwā	'that (after verb of saying or telling)'
[5]shàrī̀'ā n.f.	'justice, judgement'		
yi shàrī̀'ā à kân X	'pass judgement on X'		

TambayōyĪ

1. Don mè zìyāràr fādàr àlƙālī àbù mài ban shà'awā nē?

2. Wàɗànnè irìn ƙàràrrakī àlƙālī ya kè shàri'ā à à kânsù?

3. Mè ya sā Ùmarù ya yi ƙàrar Bētì Bàfillācè?

4. Mēnē nè shaidàr Ùmarù cêwā shānun Bētì nē sukà yi ɓàrnâr?

5. Bētì yā yàrda dà àbîn dà Ùmarù ya cè?

6. Yàushè shānûn sukà tsinkè?

7. Mè Ùmarù ya cè gàme dà yawàn Bàrnâr?

8. Don mè àlƙālī ya àiki muhùtī gōnar Ùmarù?

9. Dà muhùtī ya dāwō, mè ya faɗā̀ wà àlƙālī?

10. Ùmaru yā sàmi Nairā̀ takwàs wajen Bētì?

213

GRAMMAR

16.1 Relative Clauses

Nouns may be modified by relative clauses. If the verb in the relative clause is completive or continuative, the <u>relative</u> completive or
<u>relative</u> continuative must be used. Relative clauses can be introduced
in two different ways:

a) The short form, using the marker <u>dà</u>

The marker <u>dà</u> may be used to introduce a relative clause. <u>Dà</u> is not
actually a relative pronoun like 'who' or 'whom', though it would probably not do any great harm to think of it as such. The word that the
relative clause modifies (its antecedent) usually adds final <u>-n</u> or <u>-r</u>
meaning "the one in question" (review section 8.4). This is <u>not</u> the
linker used to connect two nouns.

ɓàrnâr dà shānū sukà yi	'the damage that the cattle did'
àlƙālîn dà ya ji ƙārā	'the judge who heard the complaint'
Bàfillācèn dà ya kè kīwòn shānū	'the Fulani man who was tending cattle'
sā'àr dà mài yī minì kīwŏ kè barcī	'while (the time at which) my herdsman was sleeping'

The word <u>àbù</u> 'thing' has a special form <u>àbi-</u> used before <u>-n</u>. In the
relative construction we always find <u>àbîn dà</u> 'the thing which, that,
what'.

àbîn dà ya fàɗā gàskiyā nè	'what (the thing which) he said is true'
kā ji àbîn dà Ùmarù ya yi ƙārarkà?	'did you hear what (the thing which) Umaru's complaint against you is?'

b) The long form, using <u>wândà</u>, etc.

Relative clauses may be introduced by the following forms:

wândà	(referring to a masculine noun)
wàddà/wâccè	(referring to a feminine noun)
waɗàndà	(referring to a plural noun)

Some speakers use different tone patterns for these forms. You should
discover the tone pattern and the form of the relative marker which
your informant prefers and practive using these forms.

These forms do not differ in meaning from the short form, but the
antecedent with these forms does not add <u>-n</u> or <u>-r</u>. These forms are
not normally used with abstract nouns such as <u>ɓàrnā</u>, <u>lōkàcī</u>, etc.

àlƙālī wândà ya ji ƙārā	'the judge who heard the complaint'
Filànī waɗàndà su kè kīwòn shānū	'the Fulanis who were tending cattle'

These "long forms" can also be used alone to mean 'the one who ...',
'the ones who ...'.

wândà ya yi ƙaryā yā biyā tàrar Nairà gōmà	'the one who lied paid a fine of #10'

The construction meaning 'to have' may occur in a relative clause, but the preposition dà used in this construction cannot stand alone without some object. Hence, a pronoun referring to the antecedent must be placed after dà. Whereas in English we say 'the cattle that I have', the Hausa construction would be literally translated 'the cattle which I am with them'.

shānûn dà na kè dà sū   'the cattle which I have'

dāwàr dà ya kè dà ita   'the guinea corn which he has'

16.2 Indirect Questions

Corresponding to questions such as 'what is that?' are phrases called indirect questions such as the underlined part in the sentence 'I don't know what that is'. In English, the word introducing an indirect question is usually the same as the corresponding question word, that is what in the examples given here. In Hausa, this is not always the case. The question words that we have seen and their corresponding indirect question words are given below. Note that an indirect question has the form of a relative clause.

Question word		Indirect question word	
wà?	'who?'	wândà, wâddà, wadàndà	'who, the one who'
mè?	'what?'	àbîn dà	'what, the thing which'
ìnā?	'where?'	Indà	'where, the place where'
yàyà?	'how?'	yaddà/yandà	'how, the way in which'
yàushè?	'when?'	lōkàcîn dà/sā'àr dà	'when, the time at which'
don mè?	'why?'	dàlīlìn da	'why, the reason (for) which'

| wà ya zō? | 'who came?' |
| bàn san wândà ya zō ba | 'I don't know who came' |

| mè ka kè sô? | 'what do you want?' |
| zân bā kà àbîn dà ka kè sô | 'I'll give you what you want' |

| ìnā a kè shân giyà? | 'where does one drink beer?' |
| mù jē indà a kè shân glyà | 'let's go where they drink beer' |

| yàyà ya kè yîn wànnan? | 'how does he do that?' |
| inà sô în ji yaddà ya kè yîn wànnan | 'I want to hear how he does that' |

| yàushè sukà zō? | 'when did they come?' |
| bàn san lōkàcîn dà sukà zō ba | 'I don't know when they came' |

16.3 Relative Completive in Consecutive Action

When a series of completed actions follow one after the other, the relative completive is used in place of the regular completive. We have seen this usage in many of the comprehension passages and in dialogue A of this unit:

215

<pre>
    nā biyō sāwùn sukà kùwa zō har   'I followed the tracks and they
        gidan Bētī   led up to Beti's house'
</pre>

Narrative will be almost exclusively in the relative completive.

A common consecutive action construction is seen in the comprehension passage of this unit:

<pre>
    dà sukà dāwō, muhùtī ya fadà   'when they came back, (then) the
        wà Alkālī ...   assessor said to the judge ...'
</pre>

Dà introduces a clause in the relative completive, translatable as 'when ..', and the second clause, in the relative completive (and often introduced by sai), can usually be translated in English by 'then ...'.

16.4 Some Uses of the Word kō

A word of very frequent occurence in Hausa is kō. Following are some, by no means all, of the uses of this word.

a) "or"

In this use, kō can link nouns or whole sentences. It is commonly placed before each of the items so linked, including the first one. The kō coming before the first of sentences linked in this way means 'whether', before the first of two or more nouns it means 'either'.

<pre>
    kō nī kō kai   'either you or I'

    kō kā zō, kō bà kà zō ba,   'whether you come or not (or you
        duk ɗaya nē   don't come), it's all the same'
</pre>

b) "even", "not even"

Whereas in English, in the negative 'not' is put with 'even', in Hausa, the sentence itself is put in the negative and kō is used exactly as in the affirmative.

<pre>
    kō kusa, bà sù kai damī àshìrin   'it wasn't even close to 20 bundles'
        ba   (not even near do they equal 20
                                                  bundles)

    kā gan shì kō shārā bābu   'you see it's not even swept'
                                              (you see it, not even sweeping
                                                  is there)

    kō nī, nā sàmi kuɗī dà yawà   'even I received a lot of money'
</pre>

c) Introducing a question

Note that kō must be used in examples like the third and fourth where a question follows a verb like sanī 'know', tàmbayà 'ask'. The portions introduced by kō in these sentences are called "indirect questions" (cf. 16.2) since they are not being asked directly as questions but are being reported as questions that were asked or are being asked as part of another question.

<pre>
    kō Audù nē ya gyārà sàlansà?   'was it Audu who repaired the
                                                  muffler?'

    kō kā sàmi gyàɗà mài yawà?   'did you get a lot of peanuts?'

    kā san kō nawà nē kuɗin damī   'do you know how much (how much
        gōmà?   is the money of) ten bundles are?'
</pre>

nā tàmbàyē shì kō yā biyā 'yan   'I asked him if he paid his
    aikìnsà   workers'
d) "isn't that so?"

This use of kō (or the phrase kō bà hakà bā) was described in 15.5.

kā sàmi gyàdā mài yawà, kō?   'you received a lot of peanuts,
                                          didn't you?'
tanā dà tsādā, kō?   'it was expensive, wasn't it?'
e) kōwànè/kōwàcè/kōwàdànnè 'each'; 'every'

kō- can be prefixed to the interrogative adjective described in 15.4,
wànè 'which(m)?', wàcè 'which(f)', wàdànnè 'which(pl)?' to mean 'each'
or 'every'. It must agree in number and gender with the noun it modifies.

kōwànè damì Nairā biyu da sulè   'each bundle (is worth) two Naira and
    biyu nè   two shillings'
anā sā gyàdà mài yawā à kōwàcè   'many peanuts are put in every
    mōtā   truck'

16.5 More on Verbs Before Indirect Objects

    In this unit we find the sentence

    à yardam minì ìn jē gidā?   'could I be permitted to go home?'

This form of yàrda 'agree, agree to' is the same as the form of variable
vowel verbs mentioned in the footnote to section 13.1 with all high tones
and added -r before indirect objects (-r becomes -m before the following
m- of the indirect object pronoun). All variable vowel verbs are transitive while yàrda is intransitive. However, it has the same tone pattern
as variable vowel verbs and shares some of their characteristics.

16.6 The Bà.../...-āwā Formation

    Nouns which designate people from a particular place may be formed in
Hausa by adding certain affixes to the noun which indicates the place in
question. If the noun to which the affixes are added designates a tribe
or sect, then the new formations name the members of that tribe or sect.
    The basic rules for these formations are: a) for both masculine and
feminine singular, a low tone prefix, Bà-, is added to the noun indicating
place or ethnic group; b) the plural is formed by adding the suffix -āwā.
    If the noun to which the above affixes are added ends in -ā, this
vowel is replaced by -ē in the masculine singular and by -ìyā in the feminine singular, and the place or ethnic noun takes on high tone. A noun
which ends in a consonant sometimes adds an -ī suffix to form the masculine singular, and the feminine singular is formed with -ā instead of -ìyā.
The plurals often have high tone throughout, although for some words,
the root as well as the first -ā suffix has low tone. The palatalization
rule (8.5) applies in these formations. The table below illustrates these
formations:

Noun of place or group		Masculine	Feminine	Plural
Tūrai	'Europe'	Bàtūrē	Bàtūrìyā	Tùràwā
Hausa	'Hausa tribe'	Bàhaushè	Bàhaushìyā	Hàusàwā

217

3B Follow the same instructions as in 3A, but use the short form of the relative marker, dà.

Cue sentence: Yā kòri birȋ. Birȋ yā shȋga gōnā.

Student response: Yā kòri birȋn dà ya shȋga gōnā.

1. Mun yi k̃ārar Bàfillācè. Bàfillācè yanà k̃Twòn shānū.

2. Nā gai dà Filànȋ. Filànȋ sunà k̃ētàrè hanyà. k̃ētàrē v.tr. 'cross'

3. Kā tàmbàyi mak̃èrȋ. Mak̃èrȋ yā gyàrà mōtàtā.

4. Sun ga zàbȋ. Zàbȋ sunà tàshȋ.

5. Bētȋ zâi bâ àlk̃āȋȋ kudȋ. Bētȋ yanà kāwō kudȋ dàgà gidansà.

6. Kun saukè dōyà dàgà mōtōcȋ. Mōtōcȋ sun zō dàgà Jàs.

7. Kin shȋga mōtà. Yā sàyi mōtà.

8. Mun yi àmfànȋ dà gawàyȋ. Mun sayō gawàyȋ.

9. Tā sàyi tābà. Munà sôn tābà.

10. Yā d̃ãuki bùhū. Sun yi bùhū.

Drill 4 - Join the pairs of sentences below into one complex sentence that contains a relative clause. Use the short form of the relative marker.

Cue: Mun ga b̃àrnā. Shānū sun yi b̃àrnā.

Student response: Mun ga b̃àrnâr dà shānū sukà yi.

1. Nā ga Filànȋ. Filànȋ sunà k̃Twòn shānū.

2. Tā ji k̃ārā. Ùmarù yā yi k̃ārā.

3. Muhùtȋ yā kimmàntà b̃àrnā. Shānū sun yi b̃àrnā.

4. Àbōkȋnā yā nūnà minȋ gidā. Yanà sàyen gidā.

5. Mun ga shānū. Shānū sun tsinkè.

6. Nā kirà mài yȋ minȋ k̃Twò. Mài yȋ minȋ k̃Twò yanà barcȋ.

7. Nā biyō sāwun shānū. Sāwun shānū sun zō har gidan Bētȋ.

8. Ùmarù yā gai dà mùtûm. Mùtûm yanà hùd̃ar dōyà à gōnâr.

9. Tanà d̃ȋnkà rȋgā. Shēhù zâi sà rȋgā.

10. Mun ga dabbōbȋ. Dabbōbȋ sun b̃àtà manà hatsȋ.

11. Mun yi màganà dà àlk̃āȋȋ. Àlk̃āȋȋ yā ji k̃āramù.

12. Shānûn sun tsinkè à lōkàcȋn. Mài yȋ minȋ k̃Twò yanà barcȋ à lōkàcin.

Drill 5 - Your cues will be sentences of the forms 'he has X' or 'he uses X'. Form a new sentence of the form 'we saw the X that he has' or 'we saw the X that he uses'. Review the end of section 16.1 for use of pronouns with the proposition dà in relative clauses.

Cue: yanà dà shānū

Student response: mun ga shānûn dà ya kè dà sū

1. yanà àmfàni dà mânyan mōtōcȋ

2. sunà dà gyàdā

3. Filànȋ sunà dà shānū

4. tanà dà kāyan àbinci

220

5. yanà àmfànī dà sufurī
6. tanà dà kàjī
7. Ùmarù yanà dà mōtà

8. mài gyàdā yanà àmfànī dà jirgin ƙasà
9. mutānē sunà dà dabbōbī
10. sunà àmfànī dà rùmfā

<u>Drill 6</u> - Your cue will be a question followed by a noun or independent pronoun. Respond with <u>kō (noun or pronoun cue)</u> followed by a negative statement as shown in the examples.

Cue: kā san shānū sun ɓàtà hatsī? (Ùmarù)
'did yóu know the cattle ruined the guinea corn?'

Student response: kō Ùmarù bài sanī ba 'not even Umaru knows'

Cue: yā gan kà cân? (shī) 'did he see you there?'

Student response: kō shī bài gan nì ba 'not even he saw me'

1. yā fàɗi gàskiyā? (Ùmarù)
2. kā sanī? (nī)
3. dōyà tā yi kyâu? (hatsī)
4. àbōkinkà yā tàimàkē kà? (shī)
5. dāwà tā fid dà kâi? (hatsī)

6. kā san yā yi ƙaryā? (àlƙalī)
7. kā sàmi àlbàshinkà? (nī)
8. gōnarkà tā yi àlbarkà?
   (gōnàkin ƙasar Zāriyà)
9. kā yi ƙārar Bètì? (Ùmarù)
10. shānunkà sun tsinkè? (shānun Bètì)

<u>Drill 7</u> - Using the cue sentences, form indirect questions patterned on the sentence <u>nā tàmbàyē shì/tà/sù etc. kō ...</u> as shown in the examples.

Cue: mài gyàdā yanà dà sìtō?

Student response: nā tàmbàyē shì kō yanà dà sìtō

Cue: Ùmarù dà Bètì sun biyō sawun shānū?

Student response: nā tàmbàyē sù kō sun biyō sāwun shānū

1. mài gyàdā yā ɓā 'yan aikìnsà kàmashò?
2. tanà dà shaidà?
3. kin fārà cinikī?
4. Ùmarù yā san kuɗin damī gōmà?
5. kanà àmfànī dà mànyan mōtōcī?

6. sunà sāmùn kàmashòn sulè bìyar gà kōwànè bùhū?
7. yā yi saurī?
8. Kànde tā biyā tàrar Nairā shidà?
9. su Mammàn sunà kōrar tsuntsàyē?
10. Hàlīmà tanà ƙārar Bètì Bàfillàcè?

<u>Drill 8</u> - Form sentences with <u>kōwànè</u> and <u>kōwàcè</u> on the pattern <u>tô, kuɗin kōwànè/kōwàcè ... (price) nē</u> as shown in the example.

Cue: zân sàyi àgōgo (₦8)

Student response: tô, kuɗin kōwànè àgōgo Nairà takwàs

1. zân sàyi bùhū shidà (₦2)
2. zân sàyi ƙoshiyā (₦1.10)
3. zân sàyi àlƙalàmī (60k)
4. zân sàyi taguwà (₦1.50)
5. zân sàyi fartanyà (80k)

6. zân sàyi wandō (₦3)
7. zân sàyi littāfī (20k)
8. zân sàyi hùlā (70k)
9. zân sàyi tàbarmā (₦2.20)
10. zân sàyi damī gōmà (₦1.80)

221

Drill 9 - Construct Bà- .../...-āwā nouns from the pattern sentences as shown in the examples.

    Cue: yanā jîn Hausa
    Student response: shī Bàhaushḕ nē
    Cue: an hàifē tà à Amìrkà
    Student response: ita Bà'amirkìyā cḕ

1. an hàifē kà à Gōbir
2. an hàifē kì à Sakkwatō
3. an hàifē tà à Rashà (Russia)
4. yanā jîn Filātancī
   Filātancī n.m. 'Fulani language'
5. an hàifē sù à Tūrai

6. an hàifē mù à Indìyà
7. tanā jîn Yarabancī
   Yarabancī n.m. 'Yoruba (language)'
8. an hàifē shì à Fàransà (France)
9. an hàifē tà à Masàr
   Masàr n.f. 'Egypt'
10. an hàifē kù à Ingìlà

Drill 10 - You will be given a sentence followed by an English cue such as 'next week', 'last month', etc. Repeat the cue sentence with the proper Hausa time expression added to the end.

    Cue: zân kōmā̀ gàrinmù (next week)   kōmā̀ v.intr. 'return'
    Student response: zân kōmā̀ gàrinmù mākòn gòbe

1. shānunsà sun shìga gōnātā̀ (last month)
2. zân sàyi mōtā̀ (month after next)
3. ìnā ka kḕ? (day before yesterday)
4. bàbansà zâi zō (day after tomorrow)
5. bā mā̀ aikī̀ (this week)
6. nā biyā tàrar Nairā̀ shidà (last week)
7. zā à būɗḕ fulōtī̀ (three days hence)
8. ìnā zā kà jē? (next month)

Drill 11 - Change the statements below to questions of the pattern (item) nawà kukà/kikà etc. (verb)? as shown in the example.

    Cue: kun kāmà kīfī   kāmà v.tr. 'catch'
                                               kīfī n.m. 'fish'
    Student response: kīfī nawà kukà kāmā̀?

1. shānū sun ɓātà damìn hatsī
2. kun yi bùhū
3. mun ga mōtà
4. tā sàyi kujḕrā
5. kā sāmi fartanyà

6. kin ɗinkà taguwā
7. sun kāwō littāfī̀
8. kun sayad dà kwàndō
9. Ùmarù yā ɗauki dōyā̀
10. mun hàrbi zàbō   hàrbā (i/ē) v.tr. 'shoot'

Drill 12 - Answer each of the questions below with the pattern sentence
bàn san yaddà/àbîn dà/indà/wândà/lōkàcîn dà ... .

    Cue: înā ya kè?

    Student response: bàn san indà ya kè ba

    Cue: yàyà kukà yi aikìn nân?

    Student response: bàn san yaddà kukà yi aikìn nân ba

1. înā ya kè ajîyè gyàɗarsà?
2. mè ta kè sô?
3. wà ya tàimàkē sù?
4. yàyà a kè tafiyad dà cìnikin gyàɗā?
5. mè ya fàru? fàru v.intr. 'happen'

6. wàcē cè ta kè sàyen hùlar nàn?
7. yàushè ya kè fàrà cìnikinsà?
8. mè ya gayà wà àlkàlī?
9. înā ya kè?
10. yàushè ta kè barcī?

Drill 13 - Substitute the figures below in the pattern sentence kā san kō nawà nē kuɗin damī gōmà?

    Cue: 17 (gōmà shâ bakwài)

    Student response: kā san kō nawà nē kuɗin damī gōmà shâ bakwài?

1. 18	4. 42	7. 74	10. 100
2. 22	5. 57	8. 86	11. 59
3. 39	6. 65	9. 91	12. 30

Drill 14 - Substitute the items listed below in the pattern sentence nā cê kuɗin kōwànè damī sulè àshìrin dà biyu nē. The number in parentheses which follows each item should be substituted in the last part of the sentence as shown in the example.

    Cue: rīgā (₦8)

    Student response: nā cê kuɗin kōwàcè rīgā Nairà takwàs nē

1. kwàndō (₦1.46)
2. taguwā (₦1.90)
3. kèkē (₦10) n.m. 'bicycle'
4. tàbarmā (₦2.60)
5. fartanyà (₦3.00)

6. wàndō (₦1.10)
7. hūlā (90k)
8. tèbùr (₦5)
9. ƙoshiyà (66k)
10. àgōgo (₦42)

Drill 15A - 15C - Repeat the initial sentence, then substitute the first cue into the appropriate place in that sentence. As each cue is given, substitute it into the sentence formed from the previous cue so that a new sentence is formed.

15A Initial sentence: zābī sun tāshì

Cues	Student response
1. gudù	zābī sun gudù
2. birī	birī yā gudù

223

3. shānū   shānū sun gudù

4. tsinkḕ   shānū sun tsinkḕ

5. sā'ad dà na kḕ gidā   shānū sun tsinkḕ sā'ad dà na kḕ gidā

6. na kḕ nan   shānū sun tsinkḕ sā'àd dà ne kḕ nan

7. mài yT minì kTwṑ   shāhū sun tsinkḕ sā'àd dà mài yT minì kTwṑ
         ya kḕ nan

8. ya kḕ barcT   shānū sun tsinkḕ sā'àd dà mài yT minì kTwṑ
         ya kḕ barcT

9. don mḕ   don mḕ shānū sųkà tsinkḕ sā'àd dà mài yT minì
         kTwṑ ya kḕ barcT?

10. mḕ ya sâ   mḕ ya sâ shānū sukà tsinkḕ sā'àd dà mài yT
         minì kTwṑ ya kḕ barcT?

15B Initial sentence: mun jē gàrT

1. kàsuwā   mun jē kàsuwā

2. gōnā   mun jē gōnā

3. subjunctive aspect   mù jē gōnā

4. don mù shūkà dāwḕ   mù jē gōnā don mù shūkà dāwḕ

5. don mù nōmḕ cìyāwḕ   mù jē gōnā don mù nōmḕ cìyāwḕ

6. gá Ɓàrnā   mù jē gōnā don mù ga Ɓàrnā

7. Ɓàrnar birT   mù jē gōnā don mù ga Ɓàrnar birT

8. Ɓàrnar shānū   mù jē gōnā don mù ba Ɓàrnar shānū

9. Ɓàrnâr dà birT ya yi   mù jē gōnā don mù ga Ɓàrnâr dà birT ya yi

10. shānū   mù jē gōnā don mù ga Ɓàrnâr dà shānū sukà yi

15C Initial sentence: inā Ƙārā

1. yanā̀   yanā̀ Ƙārā

2. Ùmarù   Ùmarù yanā̀ Ƙārā

3. completive aspect   Ùmarù yā yi Ƙārā

4. Ƙārar Bētì   Ùmarù yā yi Ƙārar Bētì

5. gàban àlƙālT   Ùmarù yā yi Ƙārar Bētì gàban àlƙālT

6. yi Ƙaryā   Ùmarù yā yi Ƙaryā gàban àlƙālT

7. gàme dà àlbâshinsà   Ùmarù yā yi Ƙaryā gàme dà àlbâshinsà (gàban àlƙālT)

8. Ɓàrnā   Ùmarù yā yi Ƙaryā gàme dà Ɓàrnā (gàban àlƙālT)

9. Ɓàrnar shānū   Ùmarù yā yi Ƙaryā gàme dà Ɓàrnar shānū (gàban àlƙālT)

10. kuɗin damìn hatsT   Ùmarù yā yi Ƙaryā gàme dà kuɗin damìn hatsT (gàban
         àlƙālT)

GUIDED CONVERSATION

1) Use a courtroom situation as the basis for dialogues. Several students may take the parts of the judge (àlƙàlī), the court clerk (àkāwu), the arresting officer (ɗàn sàndā), and the plaintiff(s). Do not try to make a long, elaborate play out of the situations. Rather, keep the situations simple and the dialogues short. Decide beforehand the course the dialogue will take and the basic things the various participants are going to say.

Innumerable situations can be based on traffic court. Examples are the appearance of a person stopped for speeding, running a stop sign, illegal turn, etc. You may want to work in the story of the arresting officer (time of arrest, speed defendant was traveling, how quickly he stopped, whether or not he had his licence); the story of the defendant (there was no sign, he didn't see a sign, he doesn't think he was speeding, he pleads guilty or innocent); decision of the judge (found guilty or innocent, fined, given warning). Other situations might be an arrest for jay walking (time of arrest, traffic conditions, other factors such as those just given for traffic violations); arrest for drunkenness (anā shân giyā 'one was drinking' - where and when the arrest took place, damage done by defendant, defendant's story, judgement).

Useful vocabulary:

tūƙà (mōtà) v.tr. 'drive (a car)'

tsayā v.intr. 'stop' yā tsayā 'he stopped'
(tsaiwā v.n.f.)

tsai dà v.tr. 'stop' nā tsai dà shī 'I stopped him'

jūyà v.tr. or
  intr. 'turn' yā jūyà indà 'he turned where
     akà hanā it wasn't permitted'

lāsìn n.m. 'license'

kwanà n.f. 'corner'

lambà n.f. '(road) sign'

tikìtì n.m. 'ticket'

gàrgàɗī n.m. 'warning' an yi masà 'he was given a
     gàrgàɗī warning'

tārā n.f. 'fine'

ƙārā n.f. 'complaint; an yi ƙārarsà 'a complaint has been
    accusation' made against him'

lâifī n.m. 'fault, crime'

shàrī'à n.f. 'court, judgement'

shàrī'à { tā sāmē shì dà lâifī 'the court finds him guilty'

{ bà tà sāmē shì dà lâifī ba 'the court finds him innocent'

Example conversation: A defendant who has allegedly run a stop sign is brought before the judge.

B. Mālàm A.: Kâi! B.! Kàrenkà yā
ɓātà furànnīnā!

Mālàm B.: Yàyà ka san kàrēnā nè?

Mālàm A.: Don nā ga hàlāmàr k̃àtòn
sāwunsà nân.

Mālàm B.: Tǫ̀ shᴛ kè̃ nan. Kàrē kàrē
nè̃. Kō yā saŋ wannàŋ
furànnī nè̃, bà̃ cìyāwà ba
nè̃?

Mālàm A.: Dūbi, in nā gan shì à nân
kuma zân hàrbē shì!

Hey! B.! Your dog has ruined my flowers!

How do you know it was my dog?

Because I saw (the sign of) his enormous tracks here.

Well all right. A dog's a dog. Does he know these are flowers and not weeds?

Look, if I see him here again, I'll shoot him!

228

UNIT XVII

DRILLS FOR REVIEW

This unit contains drills designed to reinforce the material covered
in Units X - XVI. The student should work through each drill several times
until he can respond to the cues quickly and without looking at the book.
The drills may be used in the language laboratory as well as in class.

Drill 1 - Negate the sentences below.

　　　Cue sentence:　　　kù tàfi gidanmù

　　　Student response:　kadà kù tàfi gidanmù

　　　Cue sentence:　　　Audù zâi zō gôbe

　　　Student response:　Audù bà zâi zō gôbe ba

1. nā gan shì jiyà dà yâmma

2. makèrī zâi gyārà minì mōtā

3. kà yi wannàn

4. kù fārà girbī

5. sunà sāmùn àlbāshin Nairā biyar

6. tā tàfi kàsuwā tà sayō gawàyī

7. àkwai gyàdā màsu yawà cikin
　　rumfarsà

8. Bàrnâr tā kai damī àshìrin

9. mun tafiyad dà cìnikin gyàdār

10. inà sô yà yī minì wani ɗan gyārā
　　à mōtātā

11. Filànin nàn sunà dà shānū dà yawà

12. shānūn zā sù tsinkè

13. àkwai zābī à dājìn cân

14. tsuntsàyē sunà Bàrnā

15. don mè ku kè aikī yànzu?

Drill 2A - 2B

2A Change the sentences in the continuative aspect below to the completive
aspect, making any changes that may be necessary.

　　　Cue sentence:　　　sunà ɗaukàr kāyā

　　　Student response:　sun ɗauki kāyā

2B Do the drill as in 2A, but replace the direct object noun with a pronoun or delete the object, whichever is appropriate.

　　　Cue sentence:　　　sunà ɗaukàr kāyā

　　　Student response:　sun ɗaukà

1. manōmā sunà sāran dājìn

2. munà ganin zābī

3. tanà kòrar birī

4. bā yà sāmùn takàrdâr?

5. manōmā sunà sā tākī

6. kunà cìn àbinci?

7. Hàlīmà bā tà ɗinkin rīgunà

8. Mammàn dà Mūsā sunà hùɗar dōyà

9. ruwā bā yà Bàtà rīgar nàn

10. munà tàimakon Mūsā

11. inà cirè cìyawà

12. Mālàm Shēhù yanà bìn hanyàr

13. màsu gyàdā sunà kāwō tàkàrdū

14. Hàusàwā bā sà shân giyà

229

Drill 3 - Substitute the sums of money listed below in the pattern sentence
zàn ba kà (sum).

        Cue: ₦9.09

        Student response: zan ba ka Naira tara da kwabo tara

1. 20½k   3. ₦2.06   5. 61k   7. ₦129.00   9. ₦76.00

2. 49k   4. ₦1.83   6. ₦87.00   8. ₦88.79   10. ₦51.14

Drill 4 - Join the pairs of sentences with the conjunction don and change
the second sentence to the subjunctive.

        Cue sentences: Nā àiki Hàlīmà gōnā. Tā kòri dabbōbī.

        Student response: Nā àiki Hàlīmà gōnā don tà kòrī dabbōbī.

1. Nā àiki su Audù gōnā.   Sun shūkà dāwā̀.

2. Nā àiki Hàlīmà gidā.   Tā dafà̀ àbinci.

3. Nā bā̂ Mammàn kudī.   Yā sàyi fartanyà.

4. Nā àiki Mūsā dà Sulè tashàr jirgin kasà.   Sun kāwō kāyā.

5. Nā àiki Kànde wajen Sīdì.   Tā sàmi kòshiyà.

6. Nā àiki Bellò wajen makērī.   Yā sayō gawàyī.

7. Nā àiki makērī wurin mōtàtā.   Yā gyārà̀.

8. Nā àikē kù gidā.   Kun tàimàki uwargidā.

9. Nā bā kì kudī.   Kin sàyi dāwā̀.

10. Nā àikē kù gōnā.   Kun gamà aikìn.

Drill 5A - 5B

5A Change the following questions, which are all in the completive aspect,
to sentences in the continuative aspect with yànzu added as shown in the
examples. Use the correct pronoun forms for verb objects, etc.

        Cue: Fìrìmiyā̀ yā yi màganā̀ dà sāfe? Fìrìmiyā̀ n.m.
                                                  'Premier'
        Student response: yanā̀ màganā̀ yànzu

        Cue: an hūɗà̀ dōyā̀ dà sāfe?

        Student response: anā̀ hūɗā̀ yànzu

5B Change the questions to completive negative and add tùkùna.

        Cue: Fìrìmiyā̀ yā yi màganā̀ dà sāfe?

        Student response: bài yi màganā̀ ba tùkùna

        Cue: an hūɗà̀ dōyā̀ dà sāfe?

        Student response: bà à hūɗā̀ ba tùkùna

1. an būɗè fulōtī jiyà?   5. kun nūnā̀ wà mutànē gidankù?

2. mànyan mōtōcī sun zo?   6. Filānī sun wucè dà sāfe?

3. mutànē sun sàmi àlbâshinsù?   7. kā sā̀ tākī à gōnarkà jiyà?

4. yā yi cìnikī dà sāfe?   8. màsu gyàɗā sun zō rùmfarkà?

230

9. Lawàli yā ɗàuki kāyā? 11. yârā sun yi wàsā?

10. kun ci àbincîn dà na kāwō? 12. an tàimàkē tà?

Drill 6 - Move the objects or "prepositional phrases" to the beginning of
the sentences below and make the necessary changes from the continuative
aspect to the relative continuative aspect as shown in the examples.

Cue sentence: munā màganā

Student response: màganā mu kè

Cue sentence: yanā kusa dà tābā

Student response: kusa dà tābā ya kè

1. yanā tàfiyā dàgà kudù zuwā arèwa
2. munā hùɗar dōyā
3. inā kai tà kusa dà tashàr jirgin
   Kasà
4. inā ganin zābT
5. sunā Kàrkashin tēbùr
6. kunā yT masà aikT duk à Kasar
   Bicì dà Dawāki

7. manōmā sunā sā̂ tākT
8. munā yāwō à bàkin kōgT
9. yanā barcT
10. inā yîn ɗan gyārā
11. ɗàlìbai sunà barìn fensirōrinsù
12. inā biyō sāwun shānun Bētì

Drill 7A - 7B

7A Put the direct object or "prepositional phrase" at the beginning of
the sentence for emphasis and make other necessary changes. If there
is both a direct object and a "prepositional phrase", repeat the sentence twice, preposing one, then the other.

Cue: shānun Bētì sun Bàtà gōnātā

Student response: gōnātā shānun Bētì sukà Bàtā

Cue: nā sàyi tābā wajen ɗan tēbùr

Student response 1: tābā cē na sàyi wajen ɗan tēbùr

Student response 2: wajen ɗan tēbùr na sàyi tābā

1. muhùtT yā kimmàntà Bàrnar shānū
2. an tàimàkē nì
3. nā ga zābT cân
4. matàfìyā sun tāshì dàgà bārikT
5. kā bā shì?

6. kun sàyi kāyā màsu kyâu
7. maràr lāfiyā yā shā māgànT
8. nā san mālàmin nàn
9. an nèmi kuɗT wajen Tùràwā
10. mun gan sù

7B Put the indirect object at the beginning of the sentence for emphasis.

Cue: sun faɗà minì làbārì

Student response: nT nè sukà faɗà wà làbārì

1. an ɗaukà minì kāyan nàn
2. yā sayō mukù zōbè

3. an Kārā wà Bàtūrè kuɗìn kāyā
4. Yùsufù yā nūnā wà Sà'Tdù gōnarsà

231

5. mun nḕmā̀ matà k̇òshiyā̀   7. sun fad̦ā̀ wà àlk̇aɪ̄ɪ k̇ārā

6. sun nūnā̀ manà makarantarsù   8. nā̀ kāwō masà kujḕrā

Drill 8 - Perform the calculations listed below as shown in the examples.

Cue: shâ takwàs dà tàlātin nawà kè̄ nan? (18 + 30 = ?)

Student response: shâ takwàs dà tàlātin, àrbà'in dà takwàs kè̄ nan
                                                    (18 + 30 = 48)

Cue: hàmsin à d̦ēbè tàlātin dà biyu, nawà kè̄ nan?
                                                    (50 - 32 = ?)

Student response: hàmsin à d̦ēbè tàlātin dà biyu, shâ takwàs kè̄ nan
                                                    (50 - 32 = 18)

1. 30 - 20 = ?	5. 70 - 20 = ?	8. 90 - 45 = ?
2. 55 + 15 = ?	6. 37 + 30 = ?	9. 80 + 20 = ?
3. 82 - 12 = ?	7. 60 - 15 = ?	10. 20 + 50 = ?
4. 45 + 13 = ?		

Drill 9 - Using the cue sentences below, form sentences on the pattern
sai kà ragè̄ (dative noun or pronoun) kud̦intà as shown in the examples.

Cue: bā̄ nā̀ sàyen wannàn àgōgo

Student response: sai kà ragè̄ minì kud̦insà

Cue: Mūsā bā̄ yā̀ sàyen wad̦annân kwandunā̀

Student response: sai kà ragè̄ wà Mūsā kud̦insù

1. bā̄ tā̀ sàyen wannàn wàndō   7. Àbūbakàr bā̄ yā̀ sàyen wannàn mōtà

2. bā̄ mā̀ sàyen wannàn tābā̀   8. bā̄ tā̀ sàyen wannàn jàkā

3. d̦ālìbɪ̄ bā̄ yā̀ sàyen wannàn birò   9. bā̄ nā̀ sàyen wannàn sàlansà
   birò n.m. 'ballpoint pen'   10. uwargidā bā̄ tā̀ sàyen wannàn àgōgo

4. bā̄ sū̀ sàyen wannàn rɪ̄gā   11. bā̄ mù sàyen wannàn gidā

5. bā̄ yā̀ sàyen wad̦annân hūlunā̀   12. màlàmai bā̄ sū̀ sàyen wad̦annân

6. bā̄ nā̀ sàyen wannàn gōrò   littattàfai

Drill 10 - In response to statements containing a noun modified by one of
the indefinite adjectives, wani/wata/wasu (or wad̦ansu), ask a question by
using one of the interrogative adjectives, wànè/wàcè/ wàd̦ànnè, to modify
the same noun that was modified by the indefinite adjective.

Cue: wani mùtûm yanā̀ gàban k̇ōfà

Student response: wànè mùtûm ya kè̄ gàban k̇ōfà?

Cue: nā̀ ga wata bùdurwā mài kyâu   bùdurwā n.m. 'young
                                                        unmarried woman'
Student response: wàcè bùdurwā mài kyâu ka ganɪ̄?

Cue: an kāmā̀ wasu mutā̀nē kasō   kasō n.m. 'prison'
                                                        kāmā̀ ... kasō 'put
Student response: wàd̦ànnè mutā̀nē akà kāmā̀ kasō?   in prison'

232

1. wani Bàfillācè̄ yā wucè̄ dà shānunsà
2. yā sā̂ gyàɗā̀ à wata rùmfā
3. wasu mutā̂nē sun zō sù gan kù
4. wani manṑmT yanā̀ aikT à gōnarsà
5. nā ji shānū sun Ɓātà wata gōnā
6. nā ci àbinci maràr kyâu à wani bārikT
7. wasu dabbōbT sunā̀ ta Ɓātà hatsT
8. ruwan nàn yā zō dàgà wani kōgT
9. nā ji anā̀ cîn nāmàn àladè̄ à wata ƙasā   nāmā̀ n.m. 'meat', àladè̄ n.m. 'pig'
10. wani māgànT yā bā shì cTwòn cikT

Drill 11A - 11B - Join the pairs of sentences below to form one long, complex sentece containing a relative clause.

11A Use the long forms of the relative markers (wândà/wâddà/waɗàndà).

Cue sentences: Mun ga mōtōcT. MōtōcT sun zō dàgà Bauci.

Student response: Mun ga mōtōcT waɗàndà sukà zō dàgà Bauci.

11B Do the same drill a second time using the short form of the relative marker , dà.

Cue sentences: Mun ga mōtōcT. MōtōcT sun zō dàgà Bauci.

Student response: Mun ga mōtōcîn dà sukà zō dàgà Bauci.

1. Tanā̀ sàyen tābà̀. Inā̀ sôn tābà̀.
2. Sun sā̀mi buhunā̀. Māsu gyàɗā̀ sun kāwō buhunā̀.
3. Yā bi hanyā̀. Hanyā̀ tanā̀ zuwā̀ Kanȯ̂.
4. Nā biyā 'yan aikT. 'Yan aikT sun yT masà aikT duk à ƙasar Bicì dà Dawāki.
5. Kun ga manṑmT. ManṑmT yanā̀ aikT à gōnarsà.
6. Kin dafà àbinci. Zā kù ci àbinci.
7. Nā sàyi sà̀lansā̀. Maƙè̄rT yā gyārà sà̀lansā̀.
8. Kā tàmbàyi mùtûm. Mùtûm yā bā mù bàyānT.
9. Kun sàyi kwàndō. HàlTmà tanā̀ sôn kwàndō.
10. Yā yi haɗàrT à gàrT. Inā̀ gàrT.
11. Nawà nē tābarmā? Kanā̀ sôn tàbarmā.
12. Nā sàuka à gidan mùtûm. Mùtûm yanā̀ aikT à Gidan Wayā̀.
13. Nā shā māgànT. An bā nì māgànT à asìbitì.   asìbitì n.m. 'hospital'
14. Mun tàimàki manṑmT. ManṑmT yā gàji.
15. Nā yi màganā̀ dà manṑmT. ManṑmT zâi tàimàkē mù.

233

Mammàn:	Bàn sanī ba. Har yànzu iyāyen yārinyā bà sù yankà sàdākìn ba.	I don't know. Up till now the girl's parents haven't fixed the brideprice.
Cìrōmà:	Kā kai gaisuwar iyāyē?	Have you taken the parents' "greetings"?
Mammàn:	Ī, nā kai musù Nairā takwàs.	Yes, I took them eight Naira.
Cìrōmà:	Yàushe zā à yi baiwā?	When will the betrothal take place (when will one do the betrothat)?
Mammàn:	Làrābā nè zā à yi.	It will be on Wednesday.
Cìrōmà:	Ai Mammàn, zā kà àuri bùdurwā kō bàzawàrā?	Hey Mamman, are you going to marry a virgin or a divorcee?
Mammàn:	Ā'à! bùdurwā zân àurā!	Hey! I'm going to marry a virgin!
Cìrōmà:	Tō, Allāh yà bā dà zaman lāfiyā.	Good, may God give a peacful life (living in health).
Mammàn:	Àmin!	Amen!

Vocabulary

àniyā n.f.	'zeal'	iyāyē n.pl.	'parents'
aurē n.m.	'marriage'	nēmā (i/ē) v.tr.	'look for'
baiwā n.f.	'betrothal' (setting of the marriage date)	(nēmā v.n.m.)	
		sàdākī	
		(or sàdākī) n.m.	'brideprice'
bàzawàrā n.m. (zawarāwā pl.)	'divorced woman'		(money given by the groom to the bride's parents to buy her sheep, a goat, a neck-
bùdurwā n.f. (budurwōyī pl.)	'unmarried girl of marriageable age, virgin'		lace, etc.)
		tōshī n.m.	'present to win a person over'
gaisuwā n.f.	'offering made to secure something' (here, money given to bride's parents to curry their favor)		(here, presents given to bride to impress her)
		yankā v.tr.	'cut'
		yankà sàdākī	'set the brideprice'

COMPREHENSION PRACTICE

Without looking at your books, listen to the passage as your informant reads through it once, pausing to explain in Hausa the meaning of any new words or expressions. Your informant will read through the passage a second time at normal conversational speed and then ask you the questions which follow. Answer in complete sentences.

Mammàn Zâi Yi Aurē

NT Raj Chaudri nè. Inà aikī à Ma'aikatā mài Kùlā dà Gōnā dà Dājī dà Dabbōbī à Kadūna[1]. Jiyà yārōnā, Mammàn, yā zō wurīnā ya cē ìn tàimàkē shì. Na tàmbàyē shì irìn tàimakôn dà ya kè sô ìn yī masà. Sai ya bā nì amsā à kàikàice[2], cēwan tàimakō irìn na tsakānin mài gidā dà yārònsà.

Na cè yà dai faɗā̀ minì irìn tàimakôn mànà. Sā'àn nan ya cè zā̂ shi Kanò gòbe, yā sàmi mātâr dà zâi àurā, àmmā kumā bā̂ shi dà kuɗT.

Na sākè tàmbayàrsà, na cè wànè irìn tàimakō zân yT masà, sai ya maimàità³ cèwan ìn bā shì rancen kuɗin aikìnsà na sātT huɗu. Àmmā à zàtōnā⁴ kuɗìn sun yi yawā̀. Mammàn ya cè ai kyàutā mā yā kàmātà ìn bā shì duk kuɗin aurên. Na kāwō kuɗin sātT biyu na bā shì. Na cè cirèwā zân yi à hankàlT. À ƙàrshē ya kàrɓi kuɗìn, ya cè, "Màdàllā, nā gōdè."

¹Ma'aikatā mài Kùlā dà Gōnā   'Ministry of Animal and Forest
  dà Dājī dà Dabbōbī   Resources'
²à kàikàice   'in a roundabout way'
³maimàità v.intr.   'repeat, say it in another way'
⁴zàtō n.m.   'thinking'
  à zàtōnā   'I thought, in my opinion'

TambayōyT

1. Wànē nè Màlàm Raj Chaudri?

2. Ìnā ya kè aikT?

3. Wà ya zō wurin Màlàm Chaudri jiyà? Mè ya tàmbàyē shì?

4. Dà Màlàm Chaudri ya tàmbàyi Mammàn irìn tàimakôn dà zâi yT masà, wàcè irìn amsà̀ Mammàn ya bā shì?

5. Mammàn, ìnā zā̂ shi gòbe?

6. Don mè zā̂ shi Kanò?

7. Fàɗā̀ manà yawàn ràncen kuɗìn dà Mammàn ya kè sô Màlàm Chaudri yà bā shì.

8. Màlàm Chaudri yā yàrda yà bā Mammàn àbìn dà ya kè sô?

9. Mènē nè zàton Mammàn gà sāmùn kuɗT dàgà wajen mài gidansà?

10. KuɗT nawà Màlàm Chaudri ya bā̂ Mammàn?

11. Màlàm Chaudri zâi cirè kuɗìn dà ya bā Mammàn dàgà àlbāshinsà?

12. Mammàn mè ya cè wà Màlàm Chaudri à ƙàrshē?

GRAMMAR

18.1   "I'm going to", "I'm on my way to"

In the first dialogue of this unit the sentence

        zā̂ ni Kanò gòbe   'I'm going to Kano tomorrow'

is found. The zā̂ with long vowel and falling tone is a special verb-like particle meaning "going to", "be on one's way to". It always indicates movement toward a place and the place is always mentioned in the sentence. The full paradigm, illustrated with cân '(over) there', follows:

Singular		Plural	
zâ ni cân	'I'm going there'	zâ mu cân	'we're going there'
zâ ka cân	'you're(m) going there'	zâ ku cân	'you're going there'
zâ ki cân	'you're(f) going there'		
zâ shi cân	'he's going there'	zâ su cân	'they're going there'
zâ ta cân	'she's going there'		
zâ a cân	'one is going there'		

Some further examples are

ìnā zâ ka?	'where are you going?'
zâ ni gidā	'I'm going home'
zâ shi kàsuwā	'he's going to market'

You have probably noticed that these forms resemble the future aspect pronouns (10.1). They differ in fundamental ways, however.

a) <u>zâ</u> has a falling tone (the future aspect <u>zā</u>, as in <u>zā kà zō</u> 'will you come', has high tone).

b) The pronouns used with <u>zâ</u> have high tone and are identical with the high tone direct object pronouns (11.2). The forms used in the future aspect are low tone and in the first and third person singular, the forms are reduced to <u>zân</u> and <u>zâi</u>.

c) <u>zâ</u> CANNOT BE FOLLOWED BY A VERB since it is a type of verb itself. It can refer to present, past, or future time.

18.2 Auxiliary Verbs

In the first dialogue of this unit, the following sentence is found:

zân rìkà cirèwā à hankàlī   'I'll keep on deducting it gradually'

The verb <u>rìkà</u> 'keep on doing' is one of a number of verbs in Hausa to which we will give the name "auxiliary verbs". They themselves do not indicate any sort of activity. Rather, they say something about how the subject of the verb performs an activity, for example, he kept on doing it, he did it over again, he previously did it, he started doing it, etc. These verbs are followed by the same types of verbal expressions or action nouns that are used after the continuative pronouns (14.2, 11.3).

Some of the most commonly used auxiliary verbs are the following:

dingà	'keep on doing'
fārà	'begin doing'
iyà	'be able to do, can do'
ƙārà	'do again, do some more of'
rìkà	'keep on doing'
sākè	'do over again'
sōmà	'begin doing'

tabà	'have previously done, have ever done'
bà kà fārà girbī ba?	'haven't you begun reaping?'
bàn iyà ɗaukàr bùhun gyàɗā ba	'I can't pick up the sack of peanuts'
shānū sun riƙà shìgā gōnātā	'the cattle kept entering my farm'
zā kà sāke zuwā Kadūna?	'are you going to Kaduna again?'
maƙèrī yā sāke̍ liƙèwā	'the blacksmith patched (it) over again'
kā tabà zuwā Afirkà?	'have you ever gone to Africa?'
bàn tabà zuwā Afirkà ba	'I have never been to Africa'

18.3 The Independent or Absolute Possessive, na/ta

A very common grammatical device in Hausa is to use the linker between nouns to show that the first noun is possessed by the second (shānun Bētì 'Beti's cattle') or that some close relationship holds between them (kuɗin sātī biyu 'money for two weeks'). However, the linker can only be used when the two nouns stand next to each other in the sentence. There are other circumstances where we want to indicate that one noun is a possessor of another or has a similar close relationship, yet for some reason the two do not stand together. In these circumstances the particles na and ta are used before the "possessor". They AGREE IN GENDER WITH THE POSSESSED NOUN. Na is used to refer to masculine or plural nouns, ta to feminine nouns.

a) "Absolute possessive", that is, the possessed noun is not expressed or is grammatically separate from the possessor.

na Mammàn nē	'it's Mamman's'
shānun Bētì sun tsinkè, àmmā na Dembà sunā nân	'Beti's cattle broke loose, but Demba's are here'
wannàn mōtā ta Shēhù cē	'that car is Shehu's'
(cf. wannàn mōtàr Shēhù cē	'that is Shehu's car')

b) When something intervenes between the possessed noun and the possessor such as nan, a relative clause, or a possessive pronoun, the particles na and ta are used.

mōtàr cân ta Garbà	'that car of Garba's'
gidanmù na gàrī	'our house in (of) town'
ràncen kuɗin aikīnā na sātī huɗu	'a loan of my salary for four weeks'
tàimakō irìn na tsàkā- nin mài gidā dà yārònsà	'the kind of help that is between a master and his servant'

(Here it is irī that intervenes between tàimakō and the remainder of the sentence. The linker on irìn is the referential use, that is, 'the kind in question' - see 8.4).

18.4 yā kàmātà

The expression yā kàmātà, which might be translated, 'it is fitting', 'it would be best that', is always followed by a sentence in the subjunctive aspect. The best English rendering of such sentences is usually that the subject of the sentence in the subjunctive "should" or "ought to" do something.

| yā kàmātà kà bā nì duk kuɗin aurên | 'you ought to give me all the marriage money' |
| yā kàmātà yā̀rā sù kòri dabbōbī | 'the children should chase off the animals' |

18.5 Uses of the Word har

The word har in Hausa has no single English equivalent, though you will probably be able to see how its various "meanings" are related. Among European languages, a close equivalent is French jusque as used in jusqu'à and jusque ce qu'à ce que. Following are some of the most common English translations for har, most of which have been illustrated in dialogues in this book. The choice of divisions is somewhat arbitrary and you will see how they blend into each other.

a) "until", "up to" - Har can have the meaning 'until' as a sentence conjunction or before time expressions. When used as a conjunction it can be followed by the completive or subjunctive aspect. It gives a future meaning in the latter case.

kà yī ta tàfiyà har kà jē Fùntuwà	'keep on going until you get to Funtuwa'
yā ajìyè gyàɗā har mōtōcī sun zo	'he stored the peanuts until the trucks came'
nā̀ kai har ƙarfè ukù	'I'll take until three o'clock'

When followed by a noun indicating a place, the best translation for har is often 'up to'. This translation sometimes is best when a time expression follows har as well.

| sāwun shānûn sukà kùwa zō har gidan Bētì | 'the tracks of the cattle went up to Beti's place' |
| har yànzu iyāyen yārinyà bà sù yankà sàdākin ba | 'up till now the parents of the girl haven't set a brideprice' |

The word sai may also be translated by English 'until'. The difference between sai and har with this meaning will be covered in 24.5.

b) "even" - With this meaning, har may be followed by a complete sentence or by a noun. Since 'even' in English is never a conjunction (it can't be used to link two sentences), the English translation of a sentence containing har will have 'even' modifying the verb.

| inà nēman aurē har mā nā kai tōshī | 'I'm seeking marriage and have even given presents' |
| zân bā kà har wannàn | 'I'll even give you this one' |

You may remember that kō had the translation 'even' as well (16.3). There is a very subtle meaning difference between kō and har with this sense.

| har yànzu nā iyà ganinsà | |
| kō yànzu nā iyà ganinsà | 'even now I can see him' |

244

The sentence with har means "even up to this time", the sentence with
kō means "even now, though you would have expected him to be out of
sight". In such sentences, har has the meaning "everything up to and
even including", that is, something over and above what might be expected. Kō has the meaning "all other factors aside", "let alone anything or anyone else", even this is the case.

c) "so much so that", "such a ... that" - The relationship of this meaning of har to the first and second given above is clear, but the best
English renderings of sentences containing har with this meaning will
usually not be literal.

> sunà ta͜sai dà gònàkinsù
> har sunà rasà wurin nōmā

'they have been selling their
farms off so much that they
now lack a place to cultivate'

> yā yi ràunī har yā mutù

'he was so badly injured that
he died'

d) "including", "as well as" - This meaning is clearly related to the
meaning "even" above.

> kàwō wannàn har dà wancàn

'bring this one as well as that
one'

> yā͜ dàuki kāyā dukà har dà
> māsu nauyī

'he took all the loads including
the heavy ones'

One further sentence which occured in dialogue 15A. does not exactly fall under one of these definitions, viz.

> yârankà har nawà nē?

'how many workers do you have?'

Har here gives the sense of 'what is your maximum number of workers?',
though this English rendering may be a little too specific.

GRAMMATICAL DRILLS

Drill 1 - Transform the cue sentences into sentences which contain the
'I am going to', 'I'm on my way' forms as shown in the example.

> Cue: sunà kàsuwā

> Student response: zā͡ su kàsuwā.

1. yanà cân
2. sunà Kanò
3. munà kàsuwā
4. tanà gidā
5. kunà gàrī?
6. anà zaurè
7. kanà gònarkà?
8. Inà fàdàr àlkalī
9. sunà BaucT
10. kinà birnī?
    birnī n.m. 'city'
11. yanà Zāri·yà
12. kanà Lēgàs?
13. inà tashàr͜mōtà
    tashàr mōtà n.m. "lorry park"
    (large lot where trucks "mammy
    wagons", etc. pick up and
    let off passengers and baggage)
14. tanà wajen uwartà
15. munà dājī

Drill 2 - Form sentences containing auliliary verbs. Your cue sentence
will be in the completive aspect. Insert the auxiliary verb indicated
in parentheses and make the necessary adjustments to the original sentence which now becomes the verbal phrase following the auxiliary verb.

8. it rained so much that the road was | an yi ruwā har hanyà̄ tā ɓācì
ruined

Drill 14 - Translate the following sentences into Hausa. They will all
have an occurrence of har in their most idiomatic translations.
1. He buys peanuts in the Kano area and even in the Katsina area.
2. Up to last month they hadn't started planting.
3. There is such a drought this year that all the crops have dried up.
4. Stay in the house (sit in the house) unitl noon.
5. Keep going until you get to Yashi.
6. He even bought her sandals.
7. He was so surprised he couldn't speak (he lacked words).
rasā v.tr. 'lack'
8. I'll tend the cattle until you come back.
9. English people as well as Americans speak English ("hear" English).
10. He has so much money he gives it (away as a) gift.

Drill 15A - 15C - Repeat the initial sentence, then substitute the first
cue into the appropriate place in that sentence. As each cue is given,
substitute it into the sentence formed from the previous cue so that a
new sentence is formed.

15A Initial sentence: inà̄ sôn wannàn

Cues   Student response
1. Mālàm Garbà yà zō   inà̄ sô Mālàm Garbà yà zō
2. yā kàmātà   yā kàmātà Mālàm Garbà yà zō
3. yà nēmi aurē   yā kàmātà Mālàm Garbà yà nēmi aurē
4. yà bâ Mammàn ràncē   yā kàmātà Mālàm Garbà yà bâ Mammàn ràncē
5. ràncen kuɗin aikÎ   yā kàmātà Mālàm Garbà yà bâ Mammàn ràncen kuɗin
                                                              aikÎ
6. na sātÎ huɗu   yā kàmātà Mālàm Garbà yà bâ Mammàn ràncen kuɗin
                                         aikÎ na sātÎ huɗu
7. duk kuɗin aurên   yā kàmātà Mālàm Garbà yà bâ Mammàn duk kuɗin aurên
8. negative perfective   bài kàmātà Mālàm Garbà yà bâ Mammàn duk kuɗin
                                         aurên ba

15B Initial sentence: yanà̄ nēmā
1. Mammàn   Mammàn yanà̄ nēmā
2. nēman tàimakō   Mammàn yanà̄ nēman tàimakō
3. tàimakon mài gidansà   Mammàn yanà̄ nēman tàimakon mài gidansà
4. nēman kuɗÎ   Mammàn yanà̄ nēman kuɗÎ
5. ràncen kuɗÎ   Mammàn yanà̄ nēman ràncen kuɗÎ

252

6. kuɗin aikī	Mamman yanā nēman (rancen) kuɗin aikī
7. na sātī huɗu	Mamman yanā nēman (rancen) kuɗin aikī na sātī huɗu
8. nēman aurē	Mamman yanā nēman aurē
9. har yā kai tōshī	Mamman yanā nēman aurē har yā kai tōshī
10. gaisuwā	Mamman yanā nēman aurē har yā kai gaisuwā
11. gaisuwar iyāyē	Mamman yanā nēman aurē har yā kai gaisuwar iyāyē
12. Mamman yā cē	Mamman yā cē yanā nēman aurē har yā kai gaisuwar iyāyē

15C Initial sentence: yā yi aikī

1. Cirōmà	Cirōmà yā yi aikī
2. kàfin ɓarfè gōmà	Cirōmà yā yi aikī kàfin ɓarfè gōmà
3. dà kwatā	Cirōmà yā yi aikī kàfin ɓarfè gōmà dà kwatā
4. continuative aspect	Cirōmà yanā aikī kàfin ɓarfè gōmà dà kwatā
5. har ɓarfè gōmà dà kwatā	Cirōmà yanā aikī har ɓarfè gōmà dà kwatā
6. yanā tàfiyā	Cirōmà yanā tàfiyā har ɓarfè gōmà dà kwatā
7. tàfiyā dà saurT	Cirōmà yanā tàfiyā dà saurT har ɓarfè gōmà dà kwatā
8. har yā kai Dàurā	Cirōmà yanā tàfiyā dà saurT har yā kai Dàurā
9. Kàtsinà	Cirōmà yanā tàfiyā dà saurT har yā kai Kàtsinà
10. har yā yi haɗarT	Cirōmà yanā tàfiyā da saurT har yā yi haɗarT

GUIDED CONVERSATION

Various situations where marriage is the topic of conversation can be established, for example, conversation between two men about the marriage plans of one of them or conversation between two women on the same subject. Points that might be covered are length of engagement, date and place of marriage ceremony, plans for reception, place they plan to live, things that have been bought for the house, etc. The context may be either Nigerian or American. Since there are great differences between the two cultures, some Hausa vocabulary will have to be adapted to fit American practices.

Vocabulary:

nēman (girl's name) dà aurē   'courting (girl), seeking to marry (girl)'

    baiwā n.f. 'engagement' (in Hausa culture, the ceremony wherein the girl's marriage date is set)
    an yi manà baiwā 'we got engaged'

    ɗaurà aurē 'marriage ceremony'
    an ɗaurà aurē 'the marriage ceremony was performed (one tied the marriage)'

253

bìkī n.m.   festivities surrounding the <u>ɗaurà aurē</u>
(biki can be used for the "wedding reception" for purposes of discussing American marriage, though in Hausa culture it has a much different function, being an
integral part of the marriage itself; for 'wedding
shower' we can use bìkin shāwà)

cōcī n.m.   '(Christian) church'

kyàutā n.f.   'present(s)'

amaryā n.f.   'bride'

angò n.m.   'groom'

Example dialogue: Two girls are discussing one's engagement and marriage
plans.

Student 1:	An cê dà kē dà A., an yi mukù baiwā.	I've heard (one said) that you have gotten engaged to A.
Student 2:	Hakà nē. Watàn jiyà an yi manà.	That's right. It was last month that we got (engaged).
1:	Yàushè zā à ɗaurà aurē?	When will the marriage take place?
2:	Ran àshìrin dà biyu gà watàn gōbe à cōcìn dà kē kusa dà makarantā.	The twenty-second of next month at the church near the school.
1:	Dà kyâu. Zā à yī mukù bìkī?	Good. Will you be given a reception?
2:	Ī, zā à yī à gidan iyàyēnā.	Yes, it will be given at my parents' house.

A similar conversation could take place where one of the participants
has recently gotton married.

2. One student plays the part of a person who needs a loan of money. The
second may play the part of his friend or a professional finance agent.
They may discuss the amount needed, the purpose of the loan, payment of
interest, payment period and means of repayment (regular installments,
repayment in a lump sum, deduction from salary).

Vocabulary:

ràncē n.m.   'loan' (of something, such as money, to be repaid
in kind, as opposed to arō n.m. which is a loan
of something, such as a car, which is to be returned itself)

ruwa(n kuɗī)   'interest'

kashī X cikin   'X percent'
ɗarī

mai dà v.tr.   'repay'

dàbārà n.f.   'plan'

Example conversation: Student 1 is a finance agent and Student 2 is a
person seeking a loan to buy a car.

Student 1: Màlàm, sànnu dà zuwà.   Greetings sir. What brings you
Mè tàfe dà kai?   here (what is going with you)?

Student 2: Inà sô ìn yi wani   I want to take out a loan.
ràncen kudī.

1: Tô, àlkìnmù nè. Ràncen nawà   Well, that's our business. How
ka kè sô?   large a loan do you want?

2: Ai, inà bukàtàr wajen Nairà   Well, I need about ₦500.
dàrī bìyar.

1: Mè zā kà yī dà kudìn?   What do you intend to do with
                                           the money?

2: Inà sô ìn sàyi mōtà. Màtàtā   I want to buy a car. My wife
tā sàmi aikī nīsà dàgà indà   got a job far from where I work.
na kè aikī. Sabò dà hakà, bà   Because of that, we can't use
mù iyà amfānī dà mōtà daya ba.   the same car.

1: Kanà dà dabàrar mai dà kudī?   Do you have a plan for repaying
                                           the money?

2: Ī. Kà iyà cirèwā à hankàlī   Yes. Can you deduct gradually
dàga àlbàshīnā?   from my salary?

1: Ī, in mài gìdankà yā yàrda.   Yes, if your boss agrees. You
Kà san zā kà bā dà ruwan kashī   know you will (have to) pay
gōma cikin dàrī.   interest of ten percent?

2: Ī, nā sanī.   Yes, I know.

255

A. Malam Abdurrahman Wudil has been hired by the Nigerian Tobacco Company
(NTC) to be a sales representative for the Jalingo-Numan area. Before
going to Jalingo, Malam Abdurrahman pays a call on Alhaji Adamu Katsina,
a successful NTC dealer for the Zaria-Funtuwa area. After the usual
pleasantries, Malam Abdurrahman explains his position and says that he
hopes Alhaji can give a few tips on how to start the new business. The
conversation turns to the sale of cigarets.

Àbdùrràhman: Yàyà kàsuwā dai?	How's business?
Àlhajì: Kayya! Kāsuwā kàm, bābù.	Alas! There isn't any business (as for business, there's none).
Àbdùr.: Cikiŋ tābōbîn nan, wàccē ta fi kāsuwā, Mài Bāsùkùr kō Mài Zōbē?	Among these (brands of) cigarets, which one sells better, Bicycle or Three Rings?
Àlhajì: A mânyan garūruwā an fi ṣai dà Mài Bāsùkùr, à Ḳauyukā kùwa sai Mài Zōbē.	In the big cities Bicycle sells better, in the villages it's Three Rings.
Àbdùr.: Kàmar kwālin Mài Bāsùkùr, nawà ka kē sayârwā à watā?	About how many cartons of Bicycle do you sell per month?
Àlhajì: Dâ cạn kwālT dàrT takwàs na kē sayârwạ̀, àmmā yànzu, dàrT bìyar nề.	In the past I used to sell 800 cartons, but now it's (down to) 500.
Àbdùr.: Wànè irìn mùtûm nē kē sàyen Falâis?	What kind of person buys Flight?
Àlhajì: Māsu aikìn ōfìs sun fi sàyentà.	Office workers buy them mostly.
Àbdùr.: À watàn jiyà, kai dà 'yan aikìnkà, Falâis nawà kukà sayar?	Last month how many Flights did you and your workers sell?
Àlhajì: Ai, kwālT mētan kaɗai sukà sayar.	Well, they only sold 200 cartons.
Àbdùr.: Mụtànen EntTsT (NTC)* sun cē mìnì yā kàmātà ìŋ jarràbà tàllàn sauran tābōbìn nan kàmar Gwalìf dà Fai-fài.	The NTC people told me that I should try displaying other (the remainder of) cigarets like Gold Leaf and Five Five Five's.
Àlhajì: Tô, Allàh dai yà bā kà sā'à.	May God give you luck.

---

* Note that English acronyms for companies, official posts, etc. which
have been borrowed into Hausa have, like all other Hausa words, fixed
tone patterns. Some examples are dT'ō 'D.O.' (District Officer),
fTdàburdT 'P.W.D.' (Public Works Department).'

GRAMMAR

19.1 Causative Verbs

"Causative verbs" can be formed from many verb stems. These causitives can usually be roughly translated "cause to do" the action of the basic verb, but normally there is a more idiomatic way to translate them. For example, sayad dà 'sell' is a causative verb based on the verb sàyā 'buy'. There are also a few commonly used causative verbs for which present day Hausa no longer has a corresponding non-causative form, for example mai dà 'replace'. The use of such causative verbs with direct objects, etc. does not differ from causative verbs which do have a corresponding non-causative form.

For many of the more commonly used causative verbs, there are two forms, a short form and a long form. The long form is more productive in the sense that only a few verbs have a short form, while any verb can have a long form if it makes sense semantically.

1) __Formation of the long form__

a) The verb form being made causative is given all high tones;

b) -r is added to the end of the verb (NB: this -r very frequently changes to become the same as the consonant which follows it);

c) dà is used before direct objects of causative verbs (NB: after dà the __independent pronouns__ (4.2) not the direct object pronouns, are used);

d) if the direct object is not expressed or does not follow the verb, the causative verb form is used alone without dà;

e) causative verbs have -wā verbal nouns (14.1); -wā is added to the causative verb formed by a) and b) with the syllable preceding -wā given a falling tone.

Examples:

sayar dà or sayad dà (from sàyā 'buy')	'sell'	yā sayad dà tābā	'he sold cigarets'
		yā sayad dà ita	'he sold them'
		tābā cē ya sayar	'it was cigarets that he sold'
		yā sayar	'he sold (them)'
		yanà sayad dà tābà	'he's selling cigarets'
		yanà sayârwā	'he's selling (them)'
sanar dà or sanad dà (from sanī 'know')	'inform'	nā sanar dà mutànē	'I informed the people'
		nā sanad dà sū	'I informed them'
		sū nè na sanar	'it was they I informed'
		yanà sanârwā	'he's informing (them)'
shayar dà or shayad dà 'cause to drink', 'water' (from shā 'drink')		yā shayad dà dabbōbī	'he watered the animals'
		yā shayad dà sū	'he watered them'

260

yā shayar	'he watered (them)'
yanā shayârwā	'he is watering (them)'

2) The short form of causative verbs - Usually but not always, the short forms are formed by dropping -ar from the long forms. The short form must always have an object (which is preceded by dà, just as with the long forms). If no object follows, the regular causative in -ar is used.

sai dà 'sell' (cf. sayad dà)	nā sai dà tābā	'I sold cigarets'
	nā sai dà ita	'I sold them'
mai dà 'replace' (cf. mayad dà - no corresponding non-causative form)	sai kà mai dà tābā	'you should return the cigarets'
	sai kà mai dà ita	'you should return them'
gai dà 'greet' (cf. gayad dà, causative of gaisā 'exchange greetings')	nā gai dà àbōkīnā	'I greeted my friend'
	nā gai dà shī	'I greeted him'

3) Special form with pronoun direct objects - With a pronoun direct object, there is an alternate form of the causative verbs that can be used. This form, instead of using dà befofe the object, adds -shē to the verb. With the causatives ending in -r, the -r changes to sh with the result being a double -ssh-. Note that with this form, the direct object pronouns (11.2), not the independent pronouns, are used.

sanar dà 'inform'	nā sanad dà mutânē	'I informed the people'
	nā sanasshē shì	'I informed him'
gai dà 'greet'	nā gai dà mài gidā	'I greeted the master of the house'
	nā gaishē shì	'I greeted him'
fid dà 'remove, take off/out' (from fitad dà, causative of fìta 'go out')	nā fid dà rīgā	'I removed the gown'
	nā fisshē tà	'I removed it'

Use of this from varies in frequency of occurence with the verb in question, the dialect, and the speaker. The student should probably restrict his use of this form to verbs he has heard used this way.

19.2 Independent Possessive Pronouns

In 18.4 the use of na/ta with nouns to form the "independent possessive" was described. The independent possessive pronouns are formed in the second and third person singular and all persons of the plural by adding a long vowel, high tone nā- or tā- to the possessive pronouns (8.3). Nā- refers to masculine nouns, tā- to feminine nouns. In the first person singular, the forms are nāwa and tāwa.

261

Referring to Masc. Nouns				Referring to Fem. Nouns			
Singular		Plural		Singular		Plural	
nàwa	'mine'	nāmù	'ours'	tàwa	'mine'	tāmù	'ours'
nākà	'yours(m)'	nākù	'yours'	tākà	'yours(m)'	tākù	'yours'
nākì	'yours(f)'			tākì	'yours(f)'		
nāsà	'his'	nāsù	'theirs'	tāsà	'his'	tāsù	'theirs'
nātà	'hers'			tātà	'hers'		

These forms are used exactly as the independent possessive nouns (18.4).

a) The possessed noun is not expressed or is grammatically separate from the possessor.

nā fi sôn tākà ta dā̀
'I prefer your old brand (yours of (before)'

shānun Bētì sun tsinkè,
àmmā nàwa sunā nàn
'Beti's cattle broke loose, but mine are here'

wannàn gidā nāsù nē
'this house is theirs'

(cf. wannàn gidansù nē
'this is their house')

b) Something intervenes between the possessed noun and the possessor such as nan or a relative clause.

bà nā̀ sôn tābàr nân tākà
'I don't like these cigarets of yours'

wàndon nàn nàwa yā ɓācì
'these pants of mine are ruined'

19.3 "Which one(s)?"

The following words are used as pronouns to mean "which one(s)?":

wànnē   (referring to masculine nouns)
wàccē   (referring to feminine nouns)
wàɗànnē   (referring to plural nouns)

wànnē Àlhajì ya kāwō?
'which one did Alhaji bring?'

wàccē ta fi kàsuwā?
'which one sells better (surpasses at market)?'

wàɗànnē sukà fi tsàdā?
'which ones are more expensive?'

19.4 The Verb fi and Comparison

Hausa forms comparative constructions in a much different way than English. Instead of having comparative adverbs or adjectives like 'better', 'more', 'less', etc. expressions using the verb fi 'surpass, exceed' are usually employed. In this and previous units, we have seen fi used in expressions which can basically be divided into two categories.

a) fi used to compare nouns - To say that 'X is better than Y' or 'there is more of X than Y', fi is simply used to say 'X surpasses Y'. The context will usually determine whether X surpasses Y in quality (is better than) or quantity (is more than).

Mài Zōbè tā fi Mài Bāsùkùr	'Three Rings are better than Bicycle'
tàfiyà tā fi zamā	'traveling is better than staying in one place'
kud'intà sun fi hakà	'it costs more than that' (lit: its money exceeds that way)

b) <u>fi</u> used in verbal expressions - To say 'X does something more' or 'X does something better', <u>fi</u> is used like an auxiliary verb (18.2) and is followed by the verbal expression in which the comparative would occur in English. Often, the most idiomatic English translations are quite different from the structure of the Hausa sentence, but the way the meaning is arrived at is usually clear.

an fi ṣai dà Mài Bāsùkùr à ƙauyukā	'Bicycle (brand cigarets) sells better in the villages (one exceeds (in) selling Bicycle brand in the villages)'
màsu aikìn ōfìs sun fi sàyen Falâis	'office workers buy Flight mostly (office workers exceed (in) buying Flight)'
nā fi sôn tākà ta dâ	'I prefer your old ones (I exceed (in) liking yours of before)'

19.5 "-self"

The expressions 'myself', 'yourself', 'himself', etc. are realized in Hausa as <u>kàinā</u>, <u>kânkà</u>, <u>kânsà</u>, etc. 'my head', 'your head', 'his head', etc. Sometimes for emphasis, an independent pronoun is used at the beginning of a sentence followed by <u>dà kâina</u>, <u>dà kânkà</u>, etc.

nī dà kâina bā nà sôntà	'I don't like them myself'
yī ta kânkà	'be on your guard (do via your head)'
sun yi aikī dà kânsù	'they did the work themselves'
sū dà kânsù sukà yi aikī	'they themselves did the work'

19.6 The Noun <u>kàmā</u> 'similarity'

The noun <u>kàmā</u>, which may be masculine or feminine, when used alone means something like 'similarity', 'equivalent', 'a thing the like of' and can be used in such sentences as

| sun yi kàmā | 'they're similar' |
| kàmarkù bà zā kù yi hakà ba | 'one like you would not do (something) like that' |

In one of its many uses, it is found before nouns to render meanings which are rendered in English by the prepositions 'about' (meaning 'approximately') or 'like' (meaning 'such as'). The meaning 'about' would normally be found where an approximate <u>quantity</u> of the noun with which <u>kàmā</u> occurs is being discussed. The meaning 'like' would be found where the noun is being used as as example.

| kàmar kwālin Mài Bāṣùkùr nawà ka kè sayârwā à watā? | 'about how many cartons of Bicycle do you sell a month?' |

263

```
nā jarràbà tàllàn tābōbT         'I tried displaying cigarets like
kàmar Gwallf dà Fai-fài           Gold Leaf and Five Five Five's'
```

19.7 The Numbers 100 - 1000

100. ɗàrT		600. ɗàrT shidà	
200. mètan/mètin		700. ɗàrT bakwài	
300. ɗàrT ukù		800. ɗàrT takwàs	
400. àrbàminyà		900. ɗàrT tarà	
500. hàmsàminyà		1000. dubū	

The numbers 200, 400, and 500 are also commonly expressed ɗàrT biyu,
ɗàrT huɗu, and ɗàrT bìyar. Use the form preferred by your informant.
The preposition dà is used to connect each part of a number.

765   ɗàrT bakwài dà sìttin dà bìyar

1321   dubū ɗaya dà ɗàrT ukù dà àshìrin dà ɗaya

GRAMMATICAL DRILLS

Drill 1 - Take the subject of each sentence and make it the object of a
causative verb based on the verb of the original sentence. Use nā as
the subject of the new sentence. The English translation of the new sentences is given in parentheses since the idiomatic meaning of the causative verb is not always obvious.

Cue: dabbōbT sun shā

Student response: nā shāyad dà dabbōbT (I watered the animals)

1. mōtà tā tsayà   (I stopped the car) tsayà v.intr. 'stop'

2. kàjT sun ci   (I fed the chickens)

3. dabbōbinsà sun kōmà (I brought back his animals)
                                    kōmà v.intr. 'go back'

4. mutànē sun sanT   (I informed the men)

5. bàƙT sun sàuka   (I lodged the guests) bàƙō n.m. 'guest; stranger'
                                    (bàƙT pl.)

6. sun fìta kōgT   (I ferried them across the river)

7. bàƙō yā ɓatà   (I led the stranger astray)
                                    ɓatà v.intr. 'get lost'

8. awākT sun shìga gidā (I put the goats into the compound)

9. tā gàji   (I tired her)

10. ruwā yā zubè   (I poured the water away)
                                    zubè v.intr. 'flow out'

Drill 2 - Transform the sentences of the pattern wannàn gidansù nē into
sentences which contain independent possessive pronouns as shown in the
examples.

Cue: wannàn gidansù nē   'this is their house'
Student response: wannàn gidā nāsù nē 'this house is theirs'

264

Cue: wannàn hùlarsà cē   'this is his cap'
Student response: wannàn hùlā tāsà cē   'this cap is his'

1. wadànnân buhunànkù nē   7. wancàn ōfìshintà nē
2. waccàn mōtàrsà cē   8. wadànnân shānūnā nè
3. wannàn yārōnā nè   9. wannàn rījìyarkù cē
4. wadànnân wukàkensù nē   10. wannàn littāfìnsà nē
5. wannàn tābàtā cè   11. wannàn rīgàtā cè
6. wannàn kauyènmù nē   12. wannàn àgōgonkà nē

Drill 3 - Replace the noun + possessor following fi by na or ta plus possessor if the possessor is a noun and by the appropriate independent possessive pronoun if the possessor is a pronoun.

Cue: gyàdar Kanō tā fi gyàdar Zāriyà
Student response: gyàdar Kanō tā fi ta Zāriyà
Cue: kèkenkà yā fi kèkēnā   kèkē n.m. 'bicycle'
Student response: kèkenkà yā fi nàwa

1. shānun Bētì sun fi shānun Dembà   7. kìmmānìn Ùmarù yā fi kìmmānìn
2. jàwābìnkà yā fi jàwābìn Ùmarù   Àli
3. gōnarkà tā fi gōnātā   8. yàran Àli sun fi yàransà
4. hankàlin kàrē yā fi hankàlin tunkìyā 9. bārikin BaucT yā fi bārikìn
   kàrē n.m. 'dog'   Dàurā
5. tuwon dàwà yā fi tuwon masàrā   10. àbincinmù yā fi àbincinsà
6. tābàrkà ta dà tā fi tābàrkà ta   11. tābarmarsà tā fi tābarmartà
   yànzu   12. tābàr wannàn dan tēbùr tā fi
                                           tābàr wancàn

Drill 4 - Form questions on the pattern cikin tābōbin nàn, wàccē ta fi
kàsuwā?

Cue: fensirōrī
Student response: cikin fensìrōrin nàn, wànnē ya fi kàsuwā?

1. wukàkē   3. littàttàfai   5. tēburōrī   7. hūlunà   9. alkalumà
2. mōtōcī   4. tàkàrdū   6. tābàrmī   8. agōgunā 10. màdūbai
                                                          (madūbī n.m.
                                                           'glasses')

Drill 5 - Using pairs of items below, construct sentences on the pattern
Mài Zōbè yā fi Mài Bāsùkùr as shown in the example.
Cues: tàfiyà - zamā
Student response: tàfiyà tā fi zamā

1. aikī - ragwancī n.m. 'laziness'   4. bīrō - fensìr
2. mōtà - kèkē   5. Hausa - Tūrancī
3. Fai-fài - Mài Zōbè   6. àlkalàmī - bīrō

265

7. jirgin samã - jirgin ƙasà

8. zaman gàrⲦ - zaman ƙauyè

9. mùtûm mài hankàlⲦ - mùtûm maràs
   hankàlⲦ

10. ilìmⲦ (n.m. 'knowledge') -
    jãhilcⲦ (n.m. 'ignorance')

<u>Drill 6A - 6B</u> - Make the changes described in 6A and 6B so that the sentences contain the "-self" construction.

6A Add the "-self" construction corresponding to the subject to the end the sentence.

      Cue: tã dafà àbincin nàn

      Student response: tã dafà àbincin nàn dà kântà

6B Put the "-self" construction at the beginning of the sentence by putting first the appropriate independent pronoun or noun followed by <u>dà kâi-</u>.

      Cue: tã dafà àbincin nàn

      Student response: ita dà kântà ta dafà àbincin nàn

1. yã gyàrà mõtàrsà

2. sun jãwō hankàlin màsu gyàɗã

3. kun saukè kãyã dàgà mõtà?

4. mun ƙōri dabbōbⲦ

5. nã kai bùhū kusa dà tashàr
   jirgin ƙasà

6. tã ɗinkà rīgar nàn

7. muhùtⲦ yã kimmà.tà ɓàrnâr

8. sun hùɗà dōyà

9. kun kãwō masàrà dàgà kàsuwã?

10. Ùmarù yã bi sãwun shãnûn

<u>Drill 7</u> - Perform the calculations indicated below.

      Cue: ɗarⲦ ukù à ɗēbè ɗàrⲦ dà hàmsin, nawà kè̃ nan?
                          (300 - 150 = ?)

      Student response: ɗàrⲦ ukù à ɗēbè ɗàrⲦ dà hàmsin, ɗàrⲦ dà hàmsin kè̃
                                              nan
                          (300 - 150 = 150)

      Cue: ɗàrⲦ ukù dà ɗàrⲦ huɗu, nawà kè̃ nan?
                          (300 + 400 = ?)

      Student response: ɗàrⲦ ukù dà ɗàrⲦ huɗu, ɗàrⲦ bakwài kè̃ nan
                          (300 + 400 = 700)

1. 250 + 250 = ?

2. 450 - 150 = ?

3. 500 + 500 = ?

4. 400 + 400 = ?

5. 100 - 50 = ?

6. 900 - 450 = ?

7. 1000 - 600 = ?

8. 600 + 220 = ?

9. 750 + 150 = ?

10. 200 + 400 = ?

<u>Drill 8A - 8B</u>

8A Change the causative verbs to their short forms.

      Cue: mun gayad dà Mūsã

      Student response: mun gai dà Mūsã

8B Insert the appropriate direct object pronoun for each object noun and transform the verbs to their -she forms.

Cue: mun gayad dà Mūsā

Student response: mun gaishē shì

1. zân sayad dà kāyanmù
2. sun ciyad dà awākT
3. Mammàn yā fitad dà hùlarsà
4. kun gayad dà su Sālè?
5. nā mayad dà tābà̃

6. HàlTmà tā ciyad dà zâbT
7. zā kì sayad dà gōrò?
8. mun gayad dà àbōkanmù
9. kun fitad dà tākalmànkù?
10. kā mayad dà bTrò?

Drill 9A - 9C

9A Delete the dative pronoun from the sentence and change the verb to the short form of the causative whenever possible.

Cue: Shēhù yanà̃ fitar minì dà bùhū

Student response: Shēhù yanà̃ fid dà bùhū

9B Delete all objects. This will make it necessary to replace the plain verb with the verbal noun.

Cue: Shēhù yanà̃ fitar minì dà bùhū

Student response: Shēhù yanà̃ fitârwā

9C Delete the objects and change the sentence to the completive aspect.

Cue: Shēhù yanà̃ fitar minì dà bùhū

Student response: Shēhù yā fitar

1. Mammàn yanà̃ tafiyar masà dà cìnikin gyàɗarsà
2. su Audù sunà̃ ciyar minì dà kājT
3. HàlTmà tanà̃ sayar musù dà kwandunà̃
4. inà̃ ɓatar mikì dà kuɗinkì   ɓatar dà v.caus. 'spend'
5. anà̃ tsayar masà dà mōtà̃   tsayar dà v.caus. 'stop'
6. tanà̃ zubar manà dà ruwā   zubar dà v.caus. 'pour'
7. ɗan tēbùr yanà̃ mayar makà dà tābà̃
8. yârā sunà̃ fitar matà dà kāyā
9. Sulè yanà̃ ciyar masà dà dabbōbT
10. yanà̃ sayar minì dà rTgunà̃

Drill 10 - In each of the sentences is a phrase of the form demonstrative - noun - possessive pronoun, for example wannàn mōtàrsà 'this car of his'. Change the sentences by replacing the demonstrative preceding the noun by nân/nàn or cân/càn following the noun. In doing this you will also have to use the independent possessive pronoun corresponding to the possessive pronoun, giving mōtàr nân tàsà.

Cue: wannàn rTgarsà tanà̃ dà kyâu

Student response: rTgar nàn tàsà tanà̃ dà kyâu

267

1. bā nã̀ sôn wannàn tābàrsà
2. yāyā̀ wannàn kā̀suwarkù?
3. mù ci wannàn àbincintà
4. wannàn hatsīnā yā yi àlbarkā̀
5. sài à kāmà wadàncân shānunsà

6. kā ga wannàn bùdurwāta?
7. mēnē nè̀ cikin waccàn rùmfarsà?
8. wannàn kàmashònkà yā yi yawā̀
9. bà zân sàyi wannàn tābàrkà ba
10. yā yi àmfānī dà wadànnân mōtōcinsà

Drill 11 - Substitute the appropriate independent possessive pronoun for the object noun + possessive pronoun in the sentences below as shown in the examples.

Cue: nā fi sôn kè̀kensà na dâ
Student response: nā fi sôn nā̀sà na dâ
Cue: sun fi sôn rīgātā ta dâ
Student response: sun fi sôn tā̀wa ta dâ

1. nā fi sôn hūlunànkù na dâ
2. nā fi sôn àbincintà na dâ
3. nā fi sôn mōtàrmù ta dâ
4. nā fi sôn littāfìnsà na dâ
5. sun fi sôn gidānā dâ

6. nā fi sôn ōfìshinsù na dâ
7. nā fi sôn kāyankù na dâ
8. nā fi sôn tābàrtà ta dâ
9. nā fi sôn ƙauyènmù na dâ
10. tā fi sôn rīgātā ta dâ

Drill 12A - 12B

12A Take the direct object and question it with wànè/wàcè/wàdànnè.

Cue: sun ga yārò̄
Student response: wànè yārò̄ sukà ganī?
Cue: tā sàyi wuƙā
Student response: wàcè wuƙā ta sàyā?

12B Instead of modifying the direct object with wànè/wàcè/wàdànnè to question it, replace it by wànnē/wàccē/wàdànnē 'which one(s)?'.

Cue: sun ga yārò̄
Student response: wànnē sukà ganī?
Cue: tā sàyi wuƙā
Student response: wàccē ta sàyā?

1. inà̀ sôn wannàn àkwàtì
2. shānū sun ɓāta gōnā
3. mà̀su gyàɗā̀ sun ga rùmfātā
4. Filànī sunā̀ kīwòn shānū
5. yanà̀ sôn bùdurwā

6. yā kàmàtà mù jarràbà wàdànnan tabōbī
7. mun ga kōgī
8. matàfìyā sun bi wannàn hanyà̀
9. sun bar ƙauyè jiyà
10. yā àuri bàzawàrā̀

Drill 13 - You will be given a sentence in the continuative or completive followed by a noun cue. Construct compound sentences as illustrated.

268

Cues:	mutằnē sunằ sàyen Falâis (Mài Zōbḕ)
Student response:	mutằnē sunằ sàyen Falâis ˏàmmā sun fi sàyen Mài Zōbḕ
	'the people buy Flight but they buy more 3 Rings'
Cues:	anằ tàllàn cingàm (gōrò̀) cingàm n.m. 'chewing gum'
Student response:	anằ tàllàn cingàm àmmā an fi tàllàn gōrò̀
	'chewing gum is displayed, but more kola is displayed'

1. inằ sôn wannàn tābằ (tākà ta dâ)
2. sunằ sằ wàndō dà taguꞋwā (rĩgā)
3. mutằnē sun shā ruwằ (glyằ)
4. anằ sàyen gwēbằ (lềmō)
5. 'yan tēbùr sunằ tàllàn Mài Bāsùkùr (Falâis)
6. matàfìyā sunằ bĩn hanyàr Dàurā (Kàtsinằ)
7. Mammàn yanằ sôn Kànde (Hàdĩzà)
8. mun ga birĩ (dilā n.m. 'jackal')
9. munằ sai dà tābàr nân (waccàn)
10. sun ci masàrā (dāwằ) masàrā n.f. 'corn'

Drill 14 - Answer the question wàcè shēkarằ akà hàifē kà/kì? with the years listed below. Alĩf is the word for 'thousand' in dates.

Cue:	wàcè shēkarằ akà hàifē kà? (1936)
Student response:	an hàifē nĩ alĩf ɗàiĩ ɗarà dà talằtin dà shidà

1. wàcè shēkarằ akà hàifē kà? (1942) 6. wàcè shēkarằ akà hàifē kà? (1948)
2. wàcè shēkarằ akà hàifē kà? (1951) 7. wàcè shēkarằ akà hàifē kà? (1932)
3. wàcè shēkarằ akà hàifē kà? (1906) 8. wàcè shēkarằ akà hàifē kà? (1918)
4. wàcè shēkarằ akà hàifē kà? (1922) 9. wàcè shēkarằ akà hàifē kà? (1963)
5. wàcè shēkarằ akà hàifē kà? (1876) 10. wàcè shēkarằ akà hàifē kà? (1910)

Drill 15A - 15C - Repeat the initial sentence, then substitute the first cue into the appropriate place in that sentence. As each cue is given, substitute it into the sentence formed from the previous cue so that a new sentence is formed.

15A Initial sentence: wannàn yā fi

Cues	Student response
1. wànè tằkàlmĩ	wànè tằlàkmĩ ya fi?
2. tàbarmā	wàcè tàbarmā ta fi?
3. tābằ	wàcè tābằ ta fi?
4. fi kằsuwā	wàcè tābằ ta fi kằsuwā?
5. wàccē	wàccē ta fi kằsuwā?

6. wànnē   wànnē ya fi kàsuwā?

7. cikin tākalmàn nân   wànnē cikin tākalmàn nân ya fi kàsuwā?

8. tābōbin nàn   wàccē cikin tābōbin nàn ta fi kàsuwā?

9. wannàn kō waccàn   wàccē cikin tābōbin nàn ta fi kàsuwā, wannàn ko
                                        waccàn

10. Mài Bāsùkùr kō   wàccē cikin tābōbin nàn ta fi kàsuwā, Mài Bāsùkùr
     Mài Zōbè   kō Mài Zōbè

15B **Initial sentence:** nā jarràbà mōtàtā

1. future aspect   zân jarràbà mōtàtā

2. tàllàn gōrò   zân jarràbà tàllàn gōrò

3. tābōbᴛ   zân jarràbà tàllàn tābōbᴛ

4. sauran tābōbᴛ   zân jarràbà tàllàn sauran tābōbᴛ

5. zā kà jarràbà   zā kà jarràbà tàllàn sauran tābōbᴛ

6. yā kàmātà   yā kàmātà kà jarràbà tàllàn sauran tābōbᴛ

7. kàmar su Mài Zōbè   yā kàmātà kà jarràbà tàllàn sauran tābōbᴛ kàmar
     dà Fàlâis   su Mài Zōbè dà Fàlâis

8. kàmar wadànnân   yā kàmātà kà jarràbà tàllàn sauran tābōbᴛ kàmar
                                     wadànnân

9. sun cê yā kàmātà   sun cê yā kàmātà kà jarràbà tàllàn sauran tābōbᴛ
                               kàmar wadànnân

10. sun cê minì   sun cê minì yā kàmātà kà jarràbà tàllàn sauran
                              tābōbᴛ kàmar wadànnân

15C **Initial sentence:** nā sayad dà Mài Zōbè

1. Mài Bāsùkùr   nā sayad dà Mài Bāsùkùr

2. tābā   nā sayad dà tābā

3. nā kārè ...   nā kārè sayad dà tābā

4. future aspect   zân kārè sayad dà tābā

5. dōlè   dōlè ìn kārè sayad dà tābā

6. wannàn tābā   dōlè ìn kārè sayad dà wannàn tābā

7. kàfin ìn tàfi gidā   dōlè ìn kārè sayad dà wannàn tābā kàfin in tàfi gidā

8. kàfin à bā nì wata   dōlè ìn kārè sayad dà wannàn tābā kàfin à bā nì wata

9. waccàn   dōlè ìn kārè sayad dà wannàn tābā kàfin à bā nì
                      or   waccàn
                   dōlè ìn kārè sayad dà waccàn tābā kàfin à bā nì wata

10. wâddà ka kè nufᴛ   dōlè ìn kārè sayad dà wannàn tābā kàfin à bā nì
                    or   wâddà ka kè nufᴛ
                   dōlè ìn kārè sayad dà waccàn tābā kàfin à bā nì
                    or   wâddà ka kè nufᴛ
                   dōlè ìn kārè sayad dà wâddà ka kè nufᴛ kàfin à
                            bā nì wata

GUIDED CONVERSATION

1. Various situations can be imagined where one student takes the part of a salesman and the second a person discussing his business with him. You may want to take up the situations given for conversation 1 of Unit XIV since you now have more command of relevant expressions and vocabulary. A second, related suggestion is for one person to take the part of a used car salesman and the second the part of a buyer. You might discuss the age of the car (use the expressions for dates in <u>Drill 14</u>), the condition of the car (using the various quality expressions we have learned), the previous owner, a test drive, use of the car (and as a related area, its size, power, etc.), and, of course, price.

Example conversation:

Seller:	Bark̀ā dà zuwà, Màlàm. Mōtà zā kà sàyà?	Welcome, sir. Are you going to buy a car?
Buyer:	Hakà nē. Inà bukàtàr̃ mōtà dà na iyà tūk̀àwā zuwà aikī.	That's right. I need a car that I can drive to work.
Seller:	Gà mōtàrkà à nân, tanà aikī sōsai kumà bā tsàdā.	Here's your car, it runs great and is cheap besides.
Buyer:	Shèkar̃àrtà nawà?	How old is it?
Seller:	Ta allf d̀àrĪ tarà dà sìttin cè. Dūbi tāyà, sai kà cè sàbuwā.	It's a 1960. Look at the tires, you'd say they're new.
Buyer:	Mîl d'intà nawà nē?	How many miles on it?
Seller:	Wàllàhì! Tanà aikī sōsai! Sai kà jarràbà tūk̀àwā.	I swear! It runs beautifully! You should take it out for a test drive (try driving it).
Buyer:	Wànē nè kè dà ita kàfin kà sàmē tà?	Who owned it before you got it?
Seller:	K̀âi! Wani tsōhō nè wàndà kè zuwà cōcĪ cikintà kawài.	Oh! An old man who only went to church in it.
Buyer:	Nawà nē kud'intà?	How much is it?
Seller:	Ai kud'intà ta gàskiyà dālàr̃ d̀àrĪ blyar, àmmā sabō dà, yàu Lìttlnĭn nè kuma sabō dà kai nē, zàn bā kà kàmar kyàutā. Dālàr̃ d̀àrĪ ukù dà hàmsin.	Well, its true price (money of truth) is $500, but because today is Monday and because it's you as well, I'll give it to you as a gift. $350.

Vocabulary: tāyà n.f. 'tire'
(tāyōyĪ pl.)

2. One student takes the part of a person returning some defective product to a store and a second student takes the part of the person to whom it is returned. Things that might be taken back are defective clothing, spoiled or insect infested food, an appliance such as a radio which doesn't work, a defective book (pages missing, unclear printing, etc.). The two discussants can decide on what kind of adjustment can be made (return of money, new item, partial return of money), when the item was bought, problems had in the store previously. See conversation 2 of Unit XVI for some terms that indicate various kinds of damage that products might have.

Vocabulary: kwancè v.tr. or intr. 'untie, undo; come untied, come un-
sewed'

rahusā̀ n.f. 'sale'

sàu n.m. 'time' (in the sense of 'two times',
etc. - French fois)

Example conversation:

Buyer:	Gā̀ wàndôn dà na sàyā à ̯nâñ. Kin ganT, duk ya kwancè.	Here's a pair of pants that I bought here. You see, it's come unsewed.
Sales-woman:	Yàushè ka sàyā?	When did you buy (them)?
Buyer:	Mākòn jiyà. ̯Sàu ɗaya na ̯sā̂ shi yā kwancè hakà à ƙafā.	Last week. One time I put them on and the sewing came undone like that in the leg.
S.W.:	Bā mā̂ rahusā̀ à lōkàcîn?	Weren't we having a sale at the time?
Buyer:	Àkwai rahusā̀.	There was a sale.
S.W.:	Tō̂, bā mā̂ iyā̀ mai dà kuɗìn kāyā dà mu̯ kè ̯sayârwā à lōkàcin rahusā̀.	Well, we can't return money on goods sold during a sale.
Buyer:	Wàllāhi! ̯Wannàn kàntin banzā nè̂! Kunā sayad ̯dà ƙàyā̂ marā̀-sā kyâu kuma̯ kunā bā māsu sà-yeñ̯su̯ wàhalā̂! Bà zân ƙàrà zuwā̂ nân ba!	By God this is a worthless store! You sell inferior quality goods and then you give customers trouble! I'm not coming back here!

3. Discuss the various aspects of smoking. One student might ask another if he smokes, has ever smoked, or has thought about smoking. If he has stopped smoking, you might ask him why he stopped.

Vocabulary: shân tābā̂ 'smoking cigarets (or other tobacco products)'

cīwò n.m. 'illness'

tārī n.m. 'coughing'

Example conversation:

Student 1:	Kā tābà̀ shân tābā?	Have you ever smoked?
Student 2:	Dā̂ mā inà shā̀, àmmā nā barī.	I used to smoke, but I quit.
1:	Mè̀ ya sā̂?	What caused (it)? (i.e. stopping smoking)
2:	Don kullum ni kè̀ tārī̯ kumā inà̀ ɓatad dà kuɗī dà yawā̂.	Because I was always coughing and I was spending a lot of money (on it).
1:	Mènē nè màgànin tārī?	What was the cure for the cough-ing?
2:	Barìn tābā̂.	Leaving off cigarets.

UNIT XX

DIALOGUES

A. Mamman brings his bride, Kande, back to a small house he has rented on the edge of the old city of Zaria. About three weeks after her arrival Kande is awakened at about one o'clock in the morning by a strange noise in the room.

Kande: Af! Wānē nē? Kâi! Mammàŋ, Mammàŋ! Tằshi! Tāshi!ˌ Gā ɓàrāwŏ yanā fìtā ta tāgà!

Oh! Who's that? Hey! Mamman, Mamman! Get up! Get up! There's a thief going out the window!

Mammàn: Kâi! Tʂàyā! Tsàyā! Ai, gā shi yanā tsallàkằ katangā rìƙe dà kāyanmù!

Hey! Stop! Stop! Look he's jumping over the wall holding our goods!

Kande: Àshē?! Bài yìwu ba! Àkwai fasàssun kwalàbē à kâŋ katạngā. Bī shi dà gudù! Kằmā shi!

Really?! That's not possible! There are broken bottles on top of the wall. Run after him! Catch him!

Mammàn: Kē,ˌkinā dà wâutā. ʼBàrāyī sunà tằfe dà wuƙà kōyàushē. Kinā sŏ yà kashē ni?

You don't have good sense. Thieves always carry knives. Do you want him to kill me?

Kande: Mè zā mù yi? Mè zā mù yi?

What will we do? What will we do?

Mammàn: Kē, hūce dai! Ìdan akà yi sātằ sai à kirāwō 'yan sandā.

Calm down! In case of theft one should call the police.

Kande: Kadà kà bar nì à ɗằkīˌ nī kaɗai! Kīlà ɓàrāwō yằ kōmō.

Don't you dare leave me in this room alone! Maybe the thief will come back.

Mammàn: Bà zâi kōmō ba. Watàƙīlà yàŋzu yā çi rabìn hanyā. Inā tàfiyā cājì ōfìs. Zân dāwō dà 'yan sandā.

He won't come back. He's probably far away by now (he has "eaten" half of the road). I'm going to the Charge Office. I'll come back with the police.

Kande: Tŏ, yi saurī!

OK, but hurry up!

Vocabulary

ɓàrāwŏ n.m. (ɓàrāyī pl.)	'thief'		(watà)ƙīlà	'maybe'
cājì ōfìs n.m.	'Charge Office'		kirāwō v.tr.	'call (here)'
dāwō v.intr.	'come back'		kōmō v.intr.	'come back'
fasàssū adj.pl.	'broken'		kwalabā n.f. (kwalàbē pl.)	'bottle'
gudù n.m.	'running'		rabī n.m.	'half'
hūce v.intr.	'cool off, calm down'		sātằ n.f.	'theft'
kằmā v.tr.	'catch, seize'		tàfe (see 20.3)	'going along'
kashē v.tr.	'kill'		tsallàkā v.tr.	'jump over'
katangā̄ n.f. (kàtàngū pl.)	'wall of a compound'		ɗan sàndā n.m. ('yan sàndā pl.)	'policeman' (son of the stick)

yìwu v.intr. 'be possible' | wâutā n.f. 'senselessness'

B. Forty-five minutes later Mamman returns with a policeman, who promptly begins his investigation.

Ɗan Sàndā: Ɓàrāwò yā shigō ta tāgà, kō? Bà kù rufè ba?
The thief came in through the window, huh? Didn't you close it?

Kànde: T, bà mù rufè ba. Àkwai zāfT dà yawà à ɗākT.
No, we didn't. It was awfully hot in the room.

Ɗan S.: Ìdan bà kù rufè ba, sai kù sā wani àbù wândà zâi yi ƙārā in ɓàrāwò yā lallaɓō.
If you don't lock up, you should put something that will make a noise if a thief (tries to) sneak in.

Mammàn: Abìn dà ya sā na yi màmākī shī nḕ yaddà ya tsallàkà katangā. Gà fàsàssun kwalàbē à kântà.
The thing that surprised me was the way he jumped over the wall. There are broken bottles on top of it.

Ɗan S.: Wannàn bà dabò ba nè. Yā bazà bàrgō à kân kwalàbên. Sabò dà hakà bà sù yT masà ràunT ba.
That's no trick. He spread a blanket on top of the bottles. Because of that they didn't cut him.

Kànde: Wàyyô! An kwāshè manà kāyā dukà.
Alas! All our possessions have been stolen.

Ɗan S.: Yi haƙurT, mwâ kāmà shi. Yànzu mù tàfi cājì ōfìs kù faɗi àbîn dà akà sātà.
Have patience, we will catch him. Now let's go to the Charge Office and you state what has been stolen.

Vocabulary

bàrgō n.m. (bargunà pl.)	'blanket'	sā v.tr.	'put, put on; cause
bazà v.tr.	'spread, drape'	sātā (i/ē) v.tr. (sātā v.n.f.)	'steal'
dabò n.m.	'trick'	shigō v.intr.	'come in'
haƙurT n.m.	'patience'	rufè v.tr.	'close'
ƙārā n.m.	'noise'	wàyyô	'alas!'
kwāshè v.tr.	'collect and remove'	zāfT n.m.	'heat'
lallaɓō v.intr.	'sneak in, poke one's head in'		

COMPREHENSION PRACTICE

Without looking at your books, listen to the passage as your informant reads through it once, pausing to explain in Hausa the meaning of any new words or expressions. Your informant will read the passage a second time at normal conversational speed and then ask you the questions which follow. Answer in complete sentences.

Shìgar Ɓàrāwò Gidan Mammàn

Jiyà dà dare, wani mài sūnā[1] Mammàn ya kirāwō nì wai ɓàrāwò yā shìga ɗākìnsà. Dà na yi bìncìkē,[2] gà àbîn dà na ganT:

274

Mammàn dà màtarsà sunà barcī à ɗàkī, bà sù rufè tāgà ba don gùmī.

Tô, kā san in Ɓàrāwō yā ga tāgà à bùɗe hakà, lallē sai yà shigō. Kànde,

màtar Mammàn, ta ji wata irìn ƙārā à ɗàkī. Dà ta tāshì, sai ta ga wani

yanà fìtā ta tāgà. Ta kirā Mammàn, shī mā, ya tāshì, sai ya ga Ɓàrāwō

yanà tsallàkà katangā rìRe dà kàyansù. Mammàn dà màtarsà sukà yi màmā-

kī don fàsàssun kwalàbē dà kè kàn katangā bà sù hanà[3] Ɓàrāwō yà tsallàkà

ta ba. Ai, Ɓàrāyi sunà dà wàyō[4]... sunà bazà bàrgō à kàn kwalàbēn. Sabò

dà hakà bā sà yìn ràunī.

Tô, Kànde tanà sô mijìntà[5] yà bi Ɓàrāwō yà kāmà shi, àmma Mammàn

ya ƙi[6] don yanà tsòron[7] kadà Ɓàrāwō yà kashè shi. Hankàlī gàrē shì.

Kā san Ɓàrāyī sunà tàfe dà wuƙā kōyàushē. Mammàn ya ga dai yā fi yà

kirāwō mù. Gàskiyarsà. Mwà kāmà Ɓàrāwòn bà dadèwā.[8]

[1] sūnā n.m.	'name'	[5] mijì n.m.	'husband'
[2] bìncìkē n.m.	'investigation'	[6] ƙi v.tr.	'refuse'
[3] hanà v.tr.	'prevent'	[7] tsòrō n.m.	'fear'
[4] wàyō n.m.	'cleverness'	[8] bà dadèwā	'before long'
		[9] dàbārā n.m.	'plan, scheme'

Tambayōyī

1. Wànē nē ya kè bā dà wànnan làbārī?

2. Don mè Mammàn ya kirāwō 'yan sàndā?

3. Dà wà dà wà su kè barcī à ɗàkī?

4. Don mè tāgōgin ɗàkī su kè bùɗe?

5. In Ɓàrāwō yā ga tāgà à bùɗe, mè zâi yi?

6. Dà farkō, wà ya tāshì, Mammàn kō Kànde?

7. Mè ya sâ Kànde ta tāshì?

8. Kō tā ga wani yanà shigòwā ta ƙofà?

9. Dà Mammàn ya tāshì, mè ya ganī?

10. Mè Ɓàrāwō ya kè rìRe dà shī?

11. Mè ya sâ Mammàn dà Kànde sukà yi màmākī?

12. Mēnē nē dàbāràr[9] Ɓàrāyī?

13. Dà Kànde ta ga Ɓàrāwō, mè ta kè sô mijìntà yà yi?

14. Don mè Mammàn ya kè tsòron Ɓàrāwòn?

15. 'Yan sàndā zā sù kāmà Ɓàrāwòn?

275

20.1 The Indefinite Future Aspect

Following is the paradigm of subject pronouns which indicate the aspect which we will refer to as the "indefinite future" (the forms preferred in Kano are to the left):

Singular		Plural	
nâ zō	'I will (probably) come'	mwâ/mâ/mûn zō	'we will (prob-ably) come'
kâ zō	'you(m) " " " '		
kyâ/kîn zō	'you(f) " " " '	kwâ/kûn zō	'you " " " '
yâ zō	'he " " " '	swâ/sâ/sûn zō	'they " " " '
tâ zō	'she " " " '		
â/ân zō	'one " " " '		

As has been suggested in other cases, the student should find out which forms his informant prefers and make a habit of using these forms.

The meaning of the indefinite future may be thought of as a future aspect with a phrase like "the Lord willing", "circumstances permitting", "circumstances dictating", etc. understood.

Some examples of this aspect in use are:

ƙīlà ɓàrāwò yâ kōmō	'maybe the thief will come back'
yi haƙurī, mwâ kāmà shi	'be patient, we'll catch him'
nâ kai har ƙarfè ukù kàfin ìn gamà	'I may take till 3 o'clock before I finish'

The negative of the indefinite future is formed exactly as the regular future aspect, that is, by prefixing a short, low tone bà before the indefinite future pronouns and a short high tone ba at the end of the sentence (see 11.1 and 12.2).

20.2 The kō- plus interrogative word formations

We have already seen kōwànè/kōwàcè/kōwàdànnè used as adjectives to mean 'each', 'any', 'every' in 16.3. We will now examine the more general question of how kō- plus an interrogative word functions in Hausa.

The equivalent of the English generic indefinite words 'anyone', 'everyone', 'whoever'; 'anytime', 'whenever', etc. are formed by adding kō- to an interrogative word.

Interrogative Word		Indefinite	
wà	'who'	kōwā	'anyone' 'everyone' 'whoever'
mè	'what'	kōmè	'anything' 'everything' 'whatever'
ìnā	'where'	kō'ìnā	'anywhere' 'everywhere' 'wherever'
yaushè	'when'	kōyaushè	'anytime' 'at all times' 'every time' 'whenever'
wànnē	'which one(m)'	kōwànnē	'each one' 'every one' 'whichever one(s)'
wàccē	'which one(f)'	kōwàccē	
wàdànnē	'which ones'	kōwàdànnē	

mḛnē nḛ̀ 'what is it'   kō mḛnē nḛ̀ 'whatever it is'
wǎnē nḛ̀ 'who is it(m)'   kō wǎnē nḛ̀ 'whoever it is'
wǎcē cḛ̀ 'who is it(f)'   kō wǎcē cḛ̀ 'whoever it is'

Note that the one-word forms end on high tone even if the interrogative forms have all low tones. (This does not apply to the adjectives
kōwànè/kōwàcè/kōwàdànnè).
These words are being called <u>generic indefinites</u> as opposed to the
plain indefinites <u>wani/wata/wasu</u> (12.5) because the words in the present
section refer to any individuals whatever of a group, without exception,
whereas <u>wani/wata/wasu</u> refer to a single individual. The latter are indefinite in that they are unknown or unfamiliar to the hearer. This
difference between "generic" indefinites and plain indefinites will help
to explain some differences between declarative sentences and negative
and interrogative sentences.

a) <u>kōwā</u> 'everyone', <u>kōmē</u> 'everything'

    kōwā yanà sāmùn àlbâshin Nairà   'everyone gets a salary of five
    bìyar   Naira'
    nā bâ kōwā àlbâshinsà   'I gave everyone his salary'
    kōmē yā yi daidai   'everything is all right'
    an gyārà kōmē   'everything has been repaired'

In the negative, <u>kōwā</u> and <u>kōmē</u> as objects following the verb mean
'anyone' and 'anything'. They cannot be used as subjects of negative sentences (note that 'anyone' and 'anything' cannot be used
as subjects of negative sentences in English, either). The <u>nega-
tive</u> generic indefinites used as the subjects are bâ wândà 'no one
(there is not one who)' and bâ àbin dà 'nothing (there is not a
thing which)'. These latter forms must also be used if the direct
object is put at the beginning of the sentence for emphasis.

<u>Object following verb</u>:
    bàn ga kōwā ba   'I didn't see anyone'
    kadà kà gayà wà kōwā   'don't tell anyone'
    bàn ga kōmē ba   'I didn't see anything'
    kadà kà bā sù kōmē   'don't give them anything'

<u>Subject, or object, placed at beginning of sentence</u>:
    bâ wândà ya zō   'no one came'
    bâ wândà na ganī   'I saw <u>no one</u> (there was no one I saw)'
    bâ àbin dà ya fàru   'nothing happened'
    bâ àbin dà na ganī   'I saw <u>nothing</u> (there is nothing
                                          I saw)'

In interrogative sentences, <u>kōwā</u> and <u>kōmē</u> always mean 'everyone' and
'everything' just as in declarative sentences. However, 'anyone' and
'anything' (which were just expressed by <u>kōwā</u> and <u>kōmē</u> in negative
sentences) are expressed by <u>wani/wata/wasu</u>, or alternatively, when
used as the subject of the verb or an object moved to the beginning
of a sentence, by àkwai wândà 'there is one who' and àkwai àbin dà

277

'there is a thing that'.*

wani yā zō?

àkwai wândà ya zō?

'did {anyone / someone} come,'

wani àbù yā fāru?

àkwai àbîn dà ya fāru?

'did {anything / something} happen?'

but

kōwā yā zo?   'did everyone come?'

kā ga kōwā à cân?   'did you see everyone there?'

kōmē yā yi kyâu?   'is everything all right?'

yā ci kōmē?   'did he eat everything?'

b) kō'ìnā 'everywhere, wherever'; kōyàushē 'anytime, always, whenever'

These words are parallel grammatically to kōwā and kōmē in declarative, negative, and interrogative sentences.

kō'ìnā mukà jē, sai   'everywhere he went, we
mun gan shì   saw him'

ɓarāyī sunà tàfe dà wuƙā   'thieves always carry knives'
kōyàushē   (thieves go around with knives
                           at all times/anytime)

Negative sentences: Following the verb, kō'ìnā and kōyàushē can be used to mean 'anywhere', 'anytime, never'. When coming at the beginning of a sentence, the forms bâ indà 'nowhere (there is no place that)', bâ lokàcin dà 'at no time (there is no time that)' are used.

bàn gan shì kō'ìnā ba   'I didn't see him anywhere'

bâ shì dà àmfānī kōyàushē   'it's never any use (it doesn't
                            have use (at) anytime)'

bâ indà na gan shì   'nowhere did I see him'

bâ lōkàcîn dà na gan shì   'at no time did I see him'

Interrogative sentences: kō'ìnā and kōyàushē always mean 'everywhere' and 'always, everytime' in interrogative sentences. For the meanings 'anyplace' or 'someplace' and 'anytime' or 'sometime', wani wurī and wani lōkàcī must be used, or at the beginning of a question, àkwai indà and àkwai lōkàcìn dà.

kā gan shì wani wurī?   'did you see him someplace?'

zân gan kà wani lōkàcī kumā? 'will I see you sometime again?'

àkwai indà na iyà ɓōyèwā?   'is there someplace I can hide?'

àkwai lōkàcîn dà zân iyà   'is there sometime when I can
ganinkà?   see you?'

*There is undoubtedly a subtle dinstinction in meaning between sentences having wani as subject and those having àkwai wândà as subject, just as there is between the English sentences 'did someone come?' and 'did anyone come?'. The main point of this grammar section is to show proper use of kōwā, kōmē, etc., so such subtle distinctions will not be belabored.

278

c) kōwànnē(m), kōwàccē(f) 'whichever one', 'anyone who'

    kōwànnē ka kè sō, zân yàrda   'whichever one you want, I'll
                                       agree (to it)'

    kōwàccē ta yi cikī, tâ   'any (woman) who becomes preg-
    haifù   nant will give birth'

These two words can be used with the -n linker and a plural possessive
pronoun (mù, kù, sù) to mean 'each/any one of us/you/them'

    nā bâ kōwànnensù Nairā ukù   'I gave each of them three Naira'

    kōwànnenmù yā sāmi àbîn da   'each one of us got what he
    ya kè sō   wanted'

    kōwàccenkù tanā iyà tàfiyā   'anyone of you women can go'

d) kō wānē nè(m), kō wàcē cè(f) 'no matter who it is', 'whoever it is';
   kō mēnē nē 'no matter what it is', 'whatever it is'

    kō wānē nè ya zō, kà cê   'whoever it is that has come,
    masà bā nā nân   tell him I'm not here'

    kō wàcē cè ta tàmbayā, kà   'whoever it was that asked,
    bā ta amsā   give her the answer'

    kō mēnē nè ya bā kà, kà   'whatever he gave you, put it
    ajìyē shi à tēbùr   on the table'

20.3 Adverbial Nouns of State

By changing all tones of a verb to low except the last syllable and
substituting short -e for the final vowel, forms that have been called
"adverbial nouns of state" can be formed. These forms indicate that the
subject of the sentence is in the state indicated by the verb (as opposed
to the subject's actually performing the action). They can usually be
translated as a past or present participle in English. Note that in the
first and third examples, the noun which would normally be the direct object of the verb is used with the preposition dà. Examples:

    gā shi, yanā tsallàkà katangā   'there he is, he's jumping over
    riƙe dà kāyanmù   the wall holding our goods'
                                       (riƙe form riƙē 'hold')

    ɓàrāyī sunā tàfe dà wuƙā   'thieves go around with knives'
                                       (tàfe from tàfi 'go')

    yanā ɗauke dà buhun gyàɗā   'he's "loaded up" with a peanut
                                       sack'
                                       (ɗauke from ɗaukā 'take')

These adverbial nouns of state are commonly used after continuative
pronouns as in the second and third examples, but they may also be used
separately to modify a noun. In the latter case they are usually used
with the preposition à. They must also be used with à if they are placed
before the continuative pronouns for emphasis.

    yanā zàune   'he is seated'
                                 (zàune from zaunā 'sit down')

    gā shi cân à zàune
          or   'there he is over there, seated'
    gā shi cân zàune

nā ga mùtûm à zàune   'I saw a man seated'

à zàune ya kè   'he was <u>seated</u>'

20.4 <u>-o</u> Verbs: "Action Toward the Speaker"

The verbal type which we will call the "<u>-o</u> verb" is formed from another verb by changing all tones of the original verb to high tone and substituting <u>-o</u> for the final vowel of the original verb. Monosyllabic verbs and a few other verbs add the syllble -wo or -yo to the root verb, giving verbs like <u>biyō</u> 'follow (here)' and <u>kirāwō</u> 'call (here)' from <u>kirā</u> 'call'.

This verb form is usually said to mean "action toward the speaker", and this is in large part true. More generally, it indicates movement toward the place of reference (often, toward the speaker) or action whose effects are directed toward the place of reference. The differences between <u>-o</u> verbs and the related non <u>-o</u> verbs can be clearly illustrated with the verbs <u>fìta</u> 'go out' and <u>shìga</u> 'go in'.

yā fìta	'he went out'	(said from inside the house)
yā fitō	'he came out'	(said from outside the house)
yā shìga	'he went in'	(said from outside the house)
yā shigō	'he came in'	(said from inside the house)

Further examples are:

makèrī yā sayō gawàyī	'the blacksmith bought (and brought here) some charcoal'
sai à kirāwō 'yan sàndā	'the police should be called'
nā ganō shì dàgà nīsā	'I saw him (coming toward me) from far off'
kù kāwō minì kujèrā	'bring me a chair'
sun zō gidā	'they came home'
ɓàrāwō yā lallaɓō	'the thief sneaked in'
yànzu ya kè kōmôwā	'now he is coming back'

<u>-o</u> verbs have a short final vowel when at the very end of a sentence, but a long final vowel everywhere else. They always have <u>-wā</u> verbal nouns with a falling tone on the syllable preceding -wā, for example, kāwôwā from kāwō 'bring'.

In the imperative, these verbs always have the tone pattern low-high (low-low-high for three syllable <u>-o</u> verbs), even before noun objects.

kàwō ruwā	'bring water'
kàwō shì	'bring it'
kàwō	'bring (it)'

20.5 Past Passive Participles

"Past passive participles" can be formed from any verb by

a) dropping the final vowel of the verb;

b) adding a syllable -aCC- (where C is the last consonant of the verb);

280

c) adding the suffix -ē for masculine singular, -iyā for feminine singular, -ū for plural (some dialects add -ā for feminine singular, -ī for plural).

In the singular the tones are low on the verb stem and high on the syllable -aCC- and the ending -ē or -iyā. In the plural the tones are all low except the final -ū.
When used as a noun, these past passive particles mean 'the person(s) or thing(s) which have undergone the action of the verb'. Note in the following examples the palatalization described in 8.3 takes before the endings -ē and -iyā.

Verb	Masculine	Feminine	Plural	
fasà 'break'	fàsasshē	fàsasshiyā	fàsàssū	'broken one(s)'
dafà 'cook'	dàfaffē	dàfaffiyā	dàfaffū	'cooked one(s)'
sàrā 'cut down'	sàrarrē	sàrarriyā	sàràrrū	'one(s) that is/are cut down'
ɓatà 'get lost'	ɓàtaccē	ɓàtacciyā	ɓàtàttū	'lost one(s)'

etc.

fàrarrē, k̃àrarrē	"no sooner said that done" (one begun (fārā) (is) one finished (k̃àrē)')
kù tattàrà kwalàɓê,,kù sâ fàsàssū cikin àkwàtin nàn	'gather the bottles and put the broken ones in this box'

These forms can also be used to modify nouns. They are placed before the noun and the appropriate linker is used.

fàsasshiyar kwalabā	'broken bottle'
fàsàssun kwalàɓē	'broken bottles'
sàrarren dājī	'cleared (area of) bush'

20.6 Uses of ɗā 'son', 'yā 'daughter', 'yā'yā 'children'

Used alone, the words ɗā, 'yā, and 'yā'yā (shortened to 'yā in the constructions discussed below) mean 'son', 'daughter', and 'children' respectively. However, they have a number of other uses when put before other nouns. Some of these uses are:

a) Profession - ɗā, 'yā(f) or 'yā(pl) is used with a noun indicating some place or thing characteristic of a profession.

ɗan sàndā	'yan sàndā	'policeman/men' (son(s) of the stick)
ɗan tēbùr	'yan tēbùr	'small trader(s)' (son(s) of the table)
ɗan/'yar kàsuwā		'market trader' (son/daughter of the market)

b) Native of a place - ɗā(m), 'yā(f), or 'yā(pl) is used before a place name.

ɗan/'yar/'yan Kanǒ	'native(s) of Kano' (son/daughter/ children of Kano)

281

c) <u>Diminuatives</u> - used before a noun, ɗa̅, 'ya̅(f), and 'ya̅(pl) form diminua-
tives of the noun. In this usage, ɗa̅, 'ya̅(f), and 'ya̅(pl) must agree
in number and gender with the noun.

ɗan ya̅ro̅	'little boy'
'yar ka̅suwa̅	'a little market'
'yan kwala̅be̅	'little bottles'
ɗan kuɗi̅	'a little money'

GRAMMATICAL DRILLS

<u>Drill 1</u> - The sentences below are in the future aspect. Transform them
into the indefinite future aspect.

Cue: yi ha̍ƙurT, za̅ mu̍ ka̅ma̍ ɓa̍ra̅won

Student response: yi ha̍ƙurT, mwa̅̂ ka̅ma̍ ɓa̍ra̅won

1. ƙT̅la̍ ɓa̍ra̅won za̍i ko̅mo̅

2. za̍n da̅wo̅ da̍ 'yan sa̍nda̅

3. wa̍taƙT̅la̍ za̅ su̍ ci rabi̍n hanya̅̂

4. za̅ a̍ kwa̅she̍̀ musu̍ ka̅ya̅

5. za̅ ta̍ baza̍ ba̍rgo̅ a̍ ƙasa̍

6. za̅ ku̍ ta̍fi ca̅ji̍ o̅fi̍s

7. za̅ ki̍ fa̍ɗi a̍bin da̍ aka̍ sa̅ta̅

8. za̅ mu̍ sa̅̂ fa̍sa̍ssun kwala̅be̅ a̍ kân
    katanga̅

9. za̅ ka̍ ko̅mo̅ gida̅ wajen ƙarfe̍̀ huɗu

10. 'yan sa̅nda̅ za̅ su̍ sa̅mi ka̅ya̅

<u>Drill 2</u> - Answer each of the questions by replacing the interrogative
word with the corresponding <u>ko̅-</u> + interrogative word form. Sometimes this
will entail moving the <u>ko̅-</u> word to some other position in the sentence,
since the interrogative word normally comes at the beginning no matter
what its function (direct object, etc.). Give the English translations
of your responses.

Cue: me̍̀ ɓa̍ra̅wo̍̀ ya sa̍̀ta̅?

Student response: ɓa̍ra̅wo̍̀ ya̅ sa̍̀ci ko̅me̅
                   'the thief stole everything'

Cue: wa̍ce̍̀ iri̍n giya̍̀ ka ke̍̀ so̅̂?

Student response: ina̅ so̍n ko̅wa̍ce̍̀ iri̍n giya̍̀
                   'I like any kind of alcoholic beverage'

1. wa̍ce̍̀ ya̅rinya̍̀ ta yi kyâu?

2. wa̅ ya ke̍̀ sa̍yen Ma̍i Zo̅be̍̀?

3. wa̍nne̅ na iya̍̀ ɗauka̍̀?

4. ìna̅ ka gan shi̍̀?

5. me̍̀ suka̍̀ sa̍ya̅?

6. ya̍ushe̍̀ ɓa̍ra̍̀yT̅ su ke̍̀ ta̍fe
    da̍̀ wuƙa̍̀?

7. wa̍ne̍̀ iri̍n mu̍tûm ya ke̍̀ so̍n ta̅ba̍r
    na̍̂n?

8. wa̍cce̅ ka ba̅ sule̍̀ biyu?

9. me̍̀ ya gya̅ra̍̂?

10. ya̍ushe̍̀ ka ke̍̀ amfa̅nT̅ da̍̀ wanna̍̀n?

11. wa̅ ya ke̍̀ a̍mfa̅nT̅ da̍̀ wanna̍̀n?

12. ìna̅ ɓa̍ra̍̀yT̅ su ke̍̀ cikin ga̍̀rin na̍̀n?

<u>Drill 3</u> - Supply the adverbial noun of state based on the verb in the
first sentence in the blank of the second sentence.

Cue: Uwargidā tā dafà àbinci.   Àbinci yanā ____.

Student response: Àbinci yanā dàfe.

1. Uwargidā₎tā rufè tāgà.
   Tāgà tanā ____.
2. BjrT yā gudù.
   Gā shi cân à ____.
3. Sun zaunā wajen ƙarfè biyu.
   Har yànzu sunā ____.
4. Nā ɗaure tuŋkìyā.
   Tunkìyā tanā ____.
5. An rufè ƙantT don yâu Lahàdì nē.
   ƙantT yanā ____.

6. Mammàn yā būɗè ƙōfà.
   Ƙōfà tanā ____.
7. Jirgin ƙaşà yā tsayà.
   Yànzu yanā ____.
8. Yā rikè kāyanmù.
   Gā shi nân ____ dà kāyanmù.
9. Gā şhi yanā ɗaukàr bùhun gyàɗà.
   Yanā ____ dà bùhun gyàɗà.
10. ßàràyT sunā tàfiyà dà wuƙā.
   Sunā ____ dà wuƙā kōyàushē.

Drill 4 - Change the verbs in the sentences below to -o verbs and make any other changes that may be necessary. After you have substituted the appropriate -o verb you should translate the sentence so that the instructor can check whether you understand the change in meaning that has been effected by the substitution of the -o verb. (Note that f becomes h before o and u, hence tàfi becomes tahò.)

Cue: yâransà zā sù àikē shì cân

Student response: yâransà zā sù aikō shì nân
                             'his children will send him here'

Cue: zā tà tàfi gòbe

Student response: zā tà tahō gòbe 'she will come tomorrow'

1. zà sù kai sù cân
2. zân tàmbàyē tà
3. Kànde zā tà sàyi kāyan làmbū
4. zā à kirā mukù ɗan sàndā
5. zài shìga ta tāgà̃
6. 'yan sàndā zā sù kāmà ßàràwō

7. zàn bT sù cân
8. zā sù fìta dàgà nân
9. zā kì ɗìbà minì ruwan shā̃
10. zā mù àiki Mammàn cân
11. ßàrāwō yā kōmà gidân
12. zā mù tàfi waccàn ƙauyè

Drill 5 - Construct sentences on the pattern waŋnàn/waɗànnân (past passive participle)(noun) nē/cē based on the cue sentences.

Cue: wannàn làbārī yā tàbbatà
                     tàbbatà v.intr. 'be confirmed'

Student response: wannàn tàbbàtaccen làbārī nē

Cue: an sāmi wannàn sàƙō   sàƙō n.m. 'message'

Student response: wannàn sàmmammen sàƙō nē

1. an gyārà waɗannân tākalmā̃
2. an dafà wannàn shìnkāfā̃
3. an sāri wannàn itàcē̄
4. an ajìyè wannàn gyàɗà
5. an fasà waɗannân kwalàbē

6. an nēmi wannàn yārinyà̃
7. an sàci waɗànnân kāyā
8. an sàyi wannàn fartanyà̃
9. wannàn yārō̄ yanā̃ làfiyà̃
10. an fārà wannàn aikT

283

Drill 6A - 6B

6A Translate each of the sentences on the left, covering the answers on the right. Each Hausa sentence will have the form shī ... nē, ita ... cē, sū ... nē with a ɗan/'yar/'yan construction meaning "native of" inserted in the blank.

1. he's a native of Kano   shī ɗan Kanò nē

2. they're natives of Nigeria   sū 'yan Nìjēriyà nē

3. he's a city boy   birnī n.m. 'city'   shī ɗan birnī nē

4. she's a native of Katsina   ita 'yar Kàtsinà cē

5. they're men of the world   dūniyà n.f. 'world'   sū 'yan dūniyà nē

6. he's a countryman   shī ɗan ƙasā nē

7. she's a native of America   ita 'yar Amìrkà cē

8. he's a man of the world   shī ɗan dūniyà nē

6B Substitute the noun cues into the frame sentence mun ga ɗan/'yar/'yan ... 'we saw a/some little ...'.

Cue: yārò

Student response: mun ga ɗan yārò

Cue: kàsuwā

Student response: mun ga ɗan kàsuwā

1. yārinyà   3. kwalabā   5. ƙauyè   7. tunkìyā   9. ƙwankì ukù

2. ɗakī   4. kāyā   6. mòtsī   8. wannàn   10. tsuntsàyē
                                n.m. 'movement'

Drill 7 - In answer to questions concerning how, when, where someone will do something, give an answer in the indefinite future. For each question a cue will be given which should be inserted into your answer. In the light of the explanation of the meaning of the indefinite future in 20.1, try to picture the reason in each sentence for using this aspect rather than some other.

Cue: yàushè zā kà gamà aikī? (kāfin kà dāwō)

Student response: nā gamà kāfin kà dāwō

Cue: yàyà zā sù iyà shìgā? (ta tāgà)

Student response: sā iyà shìgā ta tāgà

1. ìnā zā kù kāmà Bàrāwō? (cikin ùnguwar nàn)

2. yàushè zâi dāwō? (wajen ƙarfè biyu)

3. yàushè Bàrāwō zâi kōmō? (bāyan kā tàfi)

4. yàushè zân iyà? (yâu dà gòbe)

5. kā iyà sai dà tābàr nân dukà? (in bā̂ ta dà tsādā)

6. wà zâi tàimàkē mù? (Sà'īdù)

7. mutànē zā sù sàyi wannàn tābà? (in nā yi tàllàntà)

8. ìnā zā mù gan shì? (dàgà dūtsèn nàn)

9. yàushè zā tà mai dà kuɗī? (watàn gòbe)

10. yàushè zā kù kāmà Ɓàrāwòʔ? (kàfin yà fìta gàrī)

<u>Drill 8A - 8C</u> - Cover up the answers on the right and as each English
sentence is given, give the Hausa translation.

1. they get a commission on every box | sunā sāmùn kàmashō gà kōwànè àkwàtì
2. they get a commission on every car | sunā sāmùn kàmashō gà kōwàcè mōtā
3. they get a commission on all bags | sunā sāmùn kàmashō gà kōwàɗànnè buhunā
4. they get a commission on every gown | sunā sāmùn kàmashō gà kōwàcè rīgā
5. the price of each bundle is ₦1 | kuɗin kōwànè damī Nairā ɗaya nè
6. the price of each goat is ₦1 | kuɗin kōwànè àkwiyā Nairā ɗaya nè
7. the price of each bag is ₦1 | kuɗin kōwànè buhū Nairā ɗaya nè
8. all children came | kōwàɗànnè yârā sun zo
9. every boy came | kōwànè yārō yā zo
10. every girl came | kōwàcè yàrinyà tā zo

1. each one of you will get a salary | kōwànnenkù zâi sàmi àlbâshī
2. each one of them will get a salary | kōwànnensù zâi sàmi àlbâshī
3. each one of us will get a salary | kōwànnenmù zâi sàmi àlbâshī
4. each one of the women brought kolas | kōwàccē dàgà cikin mātā tā kāwō gōrò
5. each one of the traders brought a blanket | kōwànnē dàgà cikin 'yan kàsuwā yā kāwō bàrgō
6. all of the farmers brought their hoes | kōwàɗànnē dàgà cikin manōmā sun kāwō fartanyōyinsù
7. I asked each one of them | nā tàmbàyi kōwànnensù
8. they asked each one of us | sun tàmbàyi kōwànnenmù
9. we asked each one of the teachers | mun tàmbàyi kōwànnē dàgà cikin màlàmai
10. we asked each one of the girls | mun tàmbàyi kōwàccē dàgà cikin 'yam mātā

1. whoever it is that asks me, I can help him | kō wànē nè ya tàmbàyē nì, nā iyà tàimakonsà
2. whoever it is that asks me, I can help her | kō wàcē cè ta tàmbàyē nì, nā iyà tàimakontà
3. whatever it is that is damaged, I can repair it | kō mēnē nè ya Ɓàcì, nā iyà gyāransà
4. no matter who she is that said that, it's a lie | kō wàcē cè ta cè hakà, ƙaryā nè
5. no matter who he is that said that, it's a lie | kō wànē nè ya cè hakà, ƙaryā nè
6. no matter what it is that he said, it's a lie | kō mēnē nè ya cè, ƙaryā nè

285

8. mun sǎmi wata ɓǎtacciyar hǔlā (àgōgo)

9. ƙƚ1à HàlƚMà zā tà bā mù sōyayyen nāmā̀ (kǎzā)   sōyā̀ v.tr. 'roast'

10. mun ga wani màtaccen dōkƚ à hanyā̀ (zǎbƚ)   màtaccē from mutù 'die'
    dōkƚ n.m. 'horse'

Drill 13 - Substitute the questions below into the pattern sentence abîn
dà ya sā̂ na yi mǎmākƚ shƚ nè̂ ... making whatever changes may be necessary.

Cue: yāyā̀ ya kè̂ tsallàkà katangā?

Student response: abîn dà ya sā̂ na yi mǎmākƚ shƚ nè̂ yaddà
                   ya kè̂ tsallàkà katangā

Cue: yàushè kikà dāwō dàgà kàsuwā?

Student response: abîn dà ya sā̂ na yi mǎmākƚ shƚ nè̂ lōkàcîn
                   dà kikà dāwō dàgà kàsuwā

Cue: ìnā macƚjƚ ya shìga   macƚjƚ n.m. 'snake'

Student response: abîn dà ya sā̂ na yi mǎmākƚ shƚ nè̂ indà
                   macƚjƚ ya shìga

1. yāyā̀ kikà kwāshè dukàn kāyā?

2. ìnā ya mutù?

3. yàushè kukà zō ōfìshinkù?

4. yāyā̀ ta kè̂ yînsà?

5. yàushè ya kè̂ shân giyā?
   giyā n.f. any alcoholic
   beverage

6. ìnā ka kè̂ sāmùnsù?

7. yāyā̀ su kè̂ tàimakōnā?

8. ìnā mōtà ta ɓàcì?

9. yàushè ma'àjkatā sukà tāshì dàgà
   aikƚ?

10. yāyā̀ ki kè̂ sàyen wadànnân kāyā?

Drill 14 - Translate the English sentences below in Hausa. If two translations are possible, supply both.

1. Whichever one you like, I'll buy it.

2. Is there sometime when he came?

3. Did someone go out?

4. Did she see someone there?

5. Did she see everyone there?

6. Is everything stored?

7. She saw no one.

8. We didn't see her anywhere.

9. At no time did we sell them.

10. He paid everyone five shillings.

11. Did everyone arrive safely?

12. No one went out.

13. Will she do it sometime?

14. Each one of us will go to the
    market tomorrow.

15. Whatever they bought, store
    it in the box.

Drill 15A - 15C - Repeat the initial sentence, then substitute the first
cue into the appropriate place in that sentence. As each cue is given,
substitute it into the sentence formed from the previous cue so that a
new sentence is formed.

15A Initial sentence: tā bazà rīgā

Cues   Student response

1. zanè̀   tā bazà zanè̀

288

2. bàrgō   tā bazà bàrgō

3. Ɓàrāwō   Ɓàrāwǒ yā bazà bàrgō

4. à kân katangā   Ɓàrāwǒ yā bazà bàrgō à kân katangā

5. kwalàbē   Ɓàrāwǒ yā bazà bàrgō à kân kwalàbē

6. fàsàssū   Ɓàrāwǒ yā bazà bàrgō à kân fàsàssun kwalàbē

7. Ɓàrāwòn dà ya   Ɓàrāwòn dà ya lallaɓō yā bazà bàrgō à kân
    lallaɓō   fàsàssun kwalàbē

8. dà ya kwāshè kāyā   Ɓàrāwòn dà ya kwāshè kāyā yā bazà bàrgō à kân
                          fàsàssun kwalàbē

9. dà ya tsallàkà   Ɓàrāwòn dà ya tsallàkà katangā yā bazà bàrgō
    katangā   à kân fàsàssun kwalàbē

10. rìke dà kāyanmù   Ɓàrāwòn dà ya tsallàkà katangā rìke dà kāyanmù
                         yā bazà bàrgō à kân fàsàssun kwalàbē

15B Initial sentence: yā tàfi cājì ōfìs

1. nā   nā tàfi cājì ōfìs

2. continuative aspect   inā tàfiyà cājì ōfìs

3. munà   munà tàfiyà cājì ōfìs

4. subjunctive aspect   mù tàfi cājì ōfìs

5. yànzu mù tàfi   yànzu mù tàfi cājì ōfìs

6. don mù kirāwō ɗan   yànzu mù tàfi cājì ōfìs don mù kirāwō ɗan
    sàndā   sàndā

7. 'yan sàndā   yànzu mù tàfi cājì ōfìs don mù kirāwō 'yan
                        sàndā

8. don mù fadà musù   yànzu mù tàfi cājì ōfìs don mù fadà musù

9. fadà musù hakà   yànzu mù tàfi cājì ōfìs don mù fadà musù hakà

10. fadà musù àbin dà   yànzu mù tàfi cājì ōfìs don mù fadà musù àbin
    akà sātā   dà akà sātā

15C Initial sentence: ɗan sàndā yā kōmà

1. kōmō   ɗan sàndā yā kōmō

2. 'yan sàndā   'yan sàndā sun kōmō

3. Ɓàrāwō   Ɓàrāwǒ yā kōmō

4. indefinite future   Ɓàrāwō yâ kōmō

5. ƙīlà   ƙīlà Ɓàrāwǒ yâ kōmō

6. don yà kashè ni   ƙīlà Ɓàrāwǒ yâ kōmō don yà kashè ni

7. kashè mu   ƙīlà Ɓàrāwǒ yâ kōmō don yà kashè mu

8. kwāshè kāyā   ƙīlà Ɓàrāwǒ yâ kōmō don yà kwāshè kāyā

9. sauran kāyā   ƙīlà Ɓàrāwǒ yâ kōmō don yà kwāshè sauran kāyā

10. manà   ƙīlà Ɓàrāwǒ yâ kōmō don yà kwāshè manà sauran
                         kāyā

GUIDED CONVERSATION

1. Use as the basis of a conversation the circumstances that surrounded a theft (real or imaginary) of which one of the class members was a victim. Such a theft might involve money, a car, a bicycle, books, a purse or briefcase, a coat, etc. The discussion might cover such aspects of the theft as the place (town and specific location), time of theft, relative position of the victim with respect to the theft, whether or not the stolen goods were retrieved or insured, value of goods, etc.

Useful vocabulary: kūbà   n.m.   'lock (on a door)'

                 kullè   v.tr.   'lock'

                 kwàdō   n.m.   'padlock'

                 ìnshōrà   n.f.   'insurance'

Example conversation:

Student 1:	Nā ji an sàci kèkenkà.	I heard your bicycle was stolen.
Student 2:	Hakà ṇē. Jiyà dà dare akà sātā.	That's right. Yesterday evening it was stolen.
1:	Inā ka kè lōkàcin sātā?	Where were you at the time of the theft?
2:	Inà ōfìshīnā inà aikī. Nā fitō ìn tàfi gidā, àshē! kèkē bābù!	I was in my office working. I came out to go home, and lo and behold! no bicycle!
1:	Bà kà kullè ba.	Didn't you lock it?
2:	Ā'à. Àkwai kwàdō gàrē shì. Inà tsàmmānī ɓàrāwò yā ɗauki kèkē ya sā shi à mōtā don ̗yà kaị shì wani wurī yà yanke kwàdōn.	Yes (I did lock it). There was a padlock on it. I think the thief took it and put it in a car so that he could take it someplace else and cut the lock off.
1:	Kā faɗà wà 'yan sàndā?	Did you tell the police?
2:	Ī, àmmā nēman sàtaccen kèkē dà wùyā ya kè. Nā ̗gōdè wà Allāh àkwai ìnshōrà gàrē nì.	Yes, but looking for a stolen bicycle is hard. I thank God I have insurance.

2. In Unit XVI, a number of expressions that could be used in a court room were learned. There, in the Guided Conversation, we concentrated on traffic court and settlement of damage claims. With the vocabulary in that unit and a few further expressions, a criminal court scene will provide interesting material for further conversations. Some possible cases that might be brought before the judge are

assault and battery - yā yī masà dūkā dà sàndā	'he beat him with a stick (he did to him beating...)'
swindling; embezzlement - yā ci amānàrsà	'he swindled/betrayed him' (he "ate" his trust)
gambling - sun ̗yi cāca sunā̀ cāca ɗan cāca	'they gambled' 'they are/were gambling' 'gambler'

theft - yā ɣī musù sātàr X	'he stole X from them'
yanā sātàr X	'he's stealing x'

possession of drugs - yanà da $\begin{cases} \text{ganyē} \\ \text{wīwī} \end{cases}$ 'he has/had marijuana (in his) possession'

yanà shân $\begin{cases} \text{ganyē} \\ \text{wīwī} \end{cases}$ 'he is/was smoking marijuana'

Other vocabulary and expressions:

bincìkā v.tr.	'investigate'
(bìncìkē v.n.m.)	
kasŏ n.m.	'prison'
yā taɓà kasŏ	'he's been in prison before'
lauyà n.m.	'lawyer'
sâ wà mùtûm lâifin X	'charge a person with the crime of X'
kā amsà lâifinkà, kō bà . kà amşâ ba?	'do you plead guilty or innocent?'
bàn amsâ ba	'not guilty'
nā amsà lâifīna	'guilty'
an ɗaurè shi watā shidà	'he was imprisoned (one tied him) for six months'
sàllamâ (i/ē) v.tr.	'acquit (of a crime)'

Various things that could be covered are description of the crime, circumstances of arrest and evidence that led to arrest, alibis or excuse or defendant, testimony of witnesses (màsu shaidà), lawyer's arguments, judgement (prison term, fine, repayment of money or goods, acquittal).

Example conversation (sequel to dialogues of Unit XX):

Akàwu:	An sâ wà Ùsmân Hārūnà lâifin sātàr kāyan gidā.	Usman Haruna has been charged with stealing household goods.
Àlkālī:	Tô, ɗan şàndā, mēnē nè shaidā cēwā mùtumìn nân ya yi sātàr?	All right, officer, what is the evidence that this man committed the theft?
Ɗan Sànda:	Wani mài sūnan Mammàn yā yi kārā à cājì ǫ̀fìs wai,an yī maşà,sātā. Munā tsàmmānī Usmân yā yi sātàr.	A person by the name of Mamman registered a complaint at the Charge Office that he has been robbed. We think that Usman committed the theft.
Àlkālī:	Mē ya sâ ku kè tsàmmānī Ùsmân kè nan?	What makes you think it was Usman?
ƊS:	Munā bìncìkē à kàsuwā sai mukà yi sā̀'ā. Mun kāmà Ùsmân yanā sai dà rēdiyòn Mammàn.	We were investigating at the market and were lucky. We caught Usman selling Mamman's radio.
Àlkālī:	Yàyà ka san rēdiyòn Mammàn kē nan?	How do you know it was Mamman's radio?

DS:	Mammàn yā rubūtā lambàr rēdiyònsà. Kumā lambàr rēdiyòn dà Ùsmân ya kè sayârwā dà lambàr dà Mammàn ya rubūtā ɗaya nè.	Mamman had written down the (serial) number of his radio, and the number of the radio that Usman was selling and the number that Mamman had written were the same.
ÀlƘàlT:	Tò Ùsmân, kā amsà lâifinkà kō bà kà amsà ba.	All right Usman, do you plead guilty or innocent.
Ùsmân:	Bàn amsà ba. Nā iskè rēdiyòn à gēfèn hanyà.	Innocent. I found the radio alongside the road.
ÀlƘàlT:	Àmmā bà kà kai shì cājì òfìs ba. Dà sātā dà sai dà sātàttun ƙāyā duk lâifī nè. Nā ɗaurè ka watà shidà dà biyàn Nairā ɗàrT tàrā.	But you didn't take it to the Charge Office. Theft and selling stolen goods are both crimes. I sentence you to six months and payment of a fine of ₦100.

UNIT XXI

DIALOGUES

A. The earliest schools in Africa were the Koranic schools (makarantar Muhàmmàdiyyā) where Muslim boys were taught to read, write, and recite the Koran. The last century has seen the establishment of European-type schools throughout Africa. Since the first of these were set up by Christian missionaries, both public and mission schools are called "Christian Schools" (makarantar nàsàriyyā) today. Teachers in the Koranic schools see these "Christian" schools to be in direct opposition to their teachings and hence are somewhat reluctant to accept them.

In the following dialogue Malam Abubakar wants to enroll his son, Isa, in Koranic school so that he will have proper instruction in his religion. At the same time he wants Isa to attend public school because he realizes the necessity of learning the "three R's" for life in the modern world. As he expects, he meets with some opposition to his plan from the head of the Koranic school.

Àbūbakàr:	Allāh yà gāfàrtà Mālàm! Nā kàwō Isa makarantā nè.	Greetings Malam! I have brought Isa to school.
Mālàm:	Mādàllā. Hakà a kè̂ sô̂.	Praise be to God. That is as it should be (as one wants).
Àbūbakàr:	Zâi fārà yâu?	Should (will) he begin today?
Mālàm:	Ā'à, ran Làràbā.	No, on Wednesday.
Àbūbakàr:	Mè̂ zā à kàwō ran Làràbā?	What should be brought on Wednesday?
Mālàm:	Kuɗin Làràbā zâi kàwō.	He should bring Wednesday's money. (School fees are paid every Wednesday.)
Àbūbakàr:	Bāyan hakà Mālàm, inà sô̂ yà ɗingà zuwà makarantar nasàriyyà.	By the way Malam, I want him to keep going to public (Christian) school.
Mālàm:	Makarantā? Makarantā? Wànnàn ita cè̂ makarantā sôsai; wàccan makarkatā cè̂.	School? School? This is the real school; that (i.e. Christian school) is a place of deviation (from the true road).
Àbūbakàr:	Yā kàmàtà yàranmù sù sàmi illmin zāmànī. A makarantar zāmànī zâi kōyō kàràtū dà rubūtū dà kuma màganā dà Tūrancī.	Our children must receive a modern education. At a modern school he will learn to read and write and also to speak English.
Mālàm:	Tô̂, Allāh yà sā̂ kadà yà mântā dà àl'àdàrmù.	So be it (but) may God grant that he not forget our customs.

Vocabulary

àl'àdà n.f. (àl'àdū pl.)	'custom'		kàràtū n.m.	'reading'
			kōyō v.tr.	'learn'
ɗingà v.aux.	'continue doing'		makarkatā n.m.	'place of devia-
illmī n.m.	'wisdom, knowledge'		(màkàrkàtai pl.)	tion'

293

màganā̀ n.f.	'speech, words'	rùbūtū n.m.	'writing'
yi màganā̀ dà X	'talk to X; talk in X'	Tūrancī̄ n.m.	'English (lan-
yi màganā̀ à kân X	'talk about X'		guage)'
mântā̄ (dà X) v.intr.		zāmànī̄ n.m.	'modern times,
	'forget (X)'		the modern
nàsārìyyā̀ n.f.	'Christianity,		world'
	Christian affairs'		

B. Like all fathers, Malam Abubakar is mildly curious as to how his son is
getting along at school. Late one afternoon he comes into the house and
sees Isa reading in one corner of the room. On the table next to him
there is a notebook filled with writing. Malam Abubakar interrupts
Isa's activities.

Abūbakàr: Īsa, kanà̀ yîn nazàrī̄.   Isa, you are really studying.
Mề ka rubūtā cikin ɗan   What did you write in that
littāfìn nân?   notebook (little book)?

Īsa: Nā rubù̀tà àbîn dà zân yi   I wrote my assignment (the thing
nazàrī̄ à kâi. Yànzu zân   that I will study on). Now I
karàntà shāfī̄ biyu dàgà   am going to read two pages from
wannàn littāfī̄.   this book.

Abūbakàr: Nazàrin makarantar   Are you doing Koranic studies
Muhàmmàdiyyà kạ kề yî   or for the regular school?
kō na nàsārìyyā̀?   (Are you doing studies of the
Koranic school or of the Christian
school?)

Īsa: Inà̀ nazàrin makarantar   I'm (doing) study for "Christian"
nàsārìyyā̀. Yànzu ạ̀ ma-   school. Now I am in "slate"
karantar àllō na kề. Bābù   school (the stage of Koranic
aikī̄ dà yawà à makarantâr   school where students have begun
nan.   to copy passages of the Koran on
slates). There isn't a lot of
work in that school.

Abūbakàr: Kanà̀ sôn makarantar àllō?   Do you like "slate" school?

Īsa: Bā̀ kạmar makarantar nàsā-   Not as much as the "Christian"
riyyā̀ ba, sạbō dà ạ̀ ma-   school, because at the "Christian"
karantar nàsārìyyā̀ munā̀   school we do all kinds of fun
yîn abūbuwā̀ irī̄-irī̄ na   things.
ban shà'awā̀.

Abūbakàr: Kàmar mề?   Like what?

Īsa: Kàmar wàkẹ-wàkề dà mồtsin   Like singing and exercise and
jìkī̄ dà wāsan ɓōyō. À   hide and seek (game of hiding).
makarantar àllō munā̀   At "slate" school we just sit.
zàune kawài.

Abūbakàr: Kà̀ bā̄ dà kọ̀karī̄ à makaran-   Work hard (give effort) at Koranic
tar àllō dòmin zâi tàimàkē   school because it will help you
kà̀ dūniyā̀ dà lāhirà.   in this world and the next.

294

Vocabulary

àllō ŋ.m.	'slate, blackboard'	nazàrT n.m.	'studying, reading to oneself'
(allunā pl.)			
ɓōyō n.m.	'hiding'	rubùt̃ā v.tr.	'write'
irT̃-irT̃	'all kinds, various kinds'	(rùbùtū v.n.m.)	
		shà'awā n.f.	'pleasure'
jìkT ŋ.m.	'body'	àbîn ban shà'awā	
(jikunā pl.)			'delightful things (something giving pleasure)'
karàŋtā v.tr.	'read'		
(kàrātū v.n.m.)		wāk̃ā n.f.	'singing, song'
k̃ōk̃arT n.m.	'effort'	(wāk̃e-wāk̃ē pl.)	
làhirā n.f.	'the next world'	wās̃ā n.m.	'playing, game'
mōtsT n.m.	'movement'	(wāsànnT pl.)	
Mùhàmmadiyyā n.f.		zaunā v.intr.	'sit down'
	'Islam, Muslim affairs'		

COMPREHENSION PRACTICE

Without looking at your books, listen to the passage as your informant reads through it once, pausing to explain in Hausa the meaning of any
new words or expressions. Your informant will read the passage through
a second time at normal conversational speed and then ask you the oral
questions that follow. Answer them in complete sentences.

Tàfiyà Makarantar Mùhàmmàdiyyā

Sūnānā Īsa. A màkòn jìyà ùbānā ya kai nì makarantar Mùhàmmàdiyyā.

Ya yi màganà dà mālàm, ya gayā masà yanā sô ìn tàfi makarantar Mùhàmmàdiyyā àmmā yanā sô ìn dingà tàfiyā makarantar nàsàriyyā dōmin ìn kōyō
kàrātū dà rùbùtū dà TūrancT. Mālàm bài yi maràbā dà[1] wànnan àl'amàrT[2]
ba àmmā ya yàrda. Sukà yàrda ìn dingà tàfiyā makarantar Mùhàmmadiyyā dà
k̃arfè takwàs zuwā k̃arfè tarà. Dà k̃arfè tarà zân tàfi makarantar nàsàriyyà.

Māk̃ō na farkō à makarantar Mùhàmmàdiyyā, Mālàm ya kàràntà r̃ātihā[3],
inā bînsà. Bāyan hakà, ya bā nì àllō dà àlk̃alàmT dà tàwadā[4]. Na yi
rùbùtū à àllōnā. A makarantar Mùhàmmàdiyyā àkwai wani mùtûm sūnansà
Mālàm Rābi'ù wāndà ya k̃è bā dà kàrātū. Yanà dà būlàlà[5] waccè ya k̃è dukàn[6]
wadànda su k̃è barcT kō wāsā. Yā kàmātā duk wàndà[7] ya k̃è makarantā yà mai
dà hankàlinsà[8] à kàrātū.

Nā fi sôn makarantar nàsàriyyā sabò dà munà yîn abūbuwà irT̃-irT̃ na
ban shà'awā. A makarantar àllō munà zàune kawài, àmmā ùbānā yanā sô ìn
bā dà k̃ōk̃arT à makarantar àllō don zā tà tàimàk̃è nì dūniyà dà làhirā.

[1]maràbā	'welcome'	[2]àl'amàrT n.m.	'plan, affair'
bài yi maràbā	'he didn't welcome		
... ba	that plan'		

295

³Fātihā̀ n.m. prayer consisting of the first verse of the Koran

⁴tàwadà̄ n.f. 'ink'

⁵būlā̀lā̀ n.m. 'long switch made of hide'

⁶dūkà̄ n.m. 'thrashing'

⁷duk wàndà̀ 'all those who ..

⁸bā̄ dà̀ hankàli 'put one's mind to'

Tambayōyī

1. Ìnā̄ ùban Īsa ya kai shì mākòn jiyà̀?
2. Wā̀ ya yi màganà̀ dà shT̄?
3. Mēnē̄ nè̄ d̀alTlìn dà ùban Īsa ya kè̄ sô dànsà yà dingà̀ tàfiyā̀ makarantar nàsā̀riyyā̀?
4. Mā̀làm yanà̄ farin cikT̄ dà jîn d̀abā̀rà̀r ùban Īsa?
5. Yàushè Īsa zâi tàfi makarantar Muhàmmàdiyyā̀?
6. Mākòn na farkō mè̄ Īsa ya yi à Makarantar Muhàmmàdiyyā̀?
7. Dà mè̄ dà mè̄ ya yi àmfānī dà sū don yîn rùbùtū?
8. Wā̀nē̄ nè̄ Mā̀làm Rābi'ù? Mēnē̄ nè̄ aikìnsà?
9. Ìdan wani d̀an makarantā yā̀ yi barcī, mè̄ zâi fàru?
10. Kō yā̀ kàmàtà duk wàndà̀ ya kè̄ makarantā yà̀ yi wā̀sā̀?
11. Don mè̄ Īsa ya fi sôn makarantar nàsā̀riyyà̀?
12. Mè̄ ùban Īsa ya kè̄ sôn d̀ansà yà yi à makarantar àllō?
13. Mēnē̄ nè̄ àmfā̀nin makarantar àllō?
14. À̀kwai màkàràntū kàmar makarantar Muhàmmàdiyyā̀ à Amìrkà?
15. Anà̀ kōyon Hausa à makarantar Muhàmmàdiyyā̀?

GRAMMAR

21.1 Three-Syllable Verbs

There are a large number of three-syllable verbs beginning on a high tone (unlike variable vowel verbs, which begin on low tone) and which end in -ā or -ē. These verbs undergo very regular changes before objects (the same rules also apply to two-syllable verbs with a falling tone on the first syllable and a high tone on the second):

a) The tone pattern is high-low-high before pronoun objects, all indirect objects, or when no object follows the verb. The final vowel is long in all these cases.

bàn karàntā ba	'I didn't read'
Īsa yā̄ rubùtā wà ùbansà	'Isa wrote to his father'
mè̄ ka rubùtā cikin d̀an littā̀fìn nân?	'what have you written in this little book?'
Allā̀h yà sā̂ kadà yà màntā dà àl'ādàrmù	'may God grant that he not forget our customs'

296

PRONOUN DIRECT OBJECTS HAVE HIGH TONE. This is counter to the statement in 11.2 that pronoun objects have tone opposite that of the preceding syllable. The explanation for this is that the basic tone pattern of the verb is high-low-low. The tone of the pronoun is opposite this basic tone. However, no word in Hausa ending in a long vowel can also end in two low tones, so the final low tone is raised.

nā karàntā shi   'I read it'

Īsa yā rubūtā ta   'Isa wrote it'

ɓàrāwŏ yā tsallàkā ta   'the thief leapt over it'

b) Before noun direct objects the final syllable is low, that is, the verb has tone pattern high-low-low, and the last vowel is short.

yànzu zân karàntà shāfī̀   'now I'm going to read two pages'
biyu

nā jarràbà tàllàn sauran   'I tried displaying these other
tābōbîn nan   (brands) of cigarets'

nā rubūtà àbîn dà zân yi   'I've written what I am going to
nazàrī̄ à kâi   study over'

All the verbs described in this section have -wā verbal nouns, though some of them also have a second 'non -wā'' verbal noun, for example, karàntā 'read', kàrātū 'reading'; rubūtā 'write', rubūtū 'writing'. The final syllable of the verb takes a falling tone when -wā is added.

sunà jarràbāwā   'they're having a test'

ɓàrāwŏ yanà tsallàkāwā   'the thief is leaping over'

21.2 Two-Syllable Verbs Before Objects

In 10.3, it was mentioned that final vowels of verbs vary according to what follows the verbs, but a full explanation has been deferred until now.

Variable vowel verbs of both two and three syllables were described fully in 13.1; verb ending in -o were described in 20.4 where it was pointed out that the final -o is long everywhere except when the verb is the last word in the sentence; three-syllable verbs have just been described in 21.1.

This leaves us with two-syllable verbs having the tone pattern high-low and ending in -a or -e. These verbs have the following forms:

a) The final vowel is short when the verb is followed by a noun direct object.

yā bazà bàrgō à kân   'he draped a blanket over the
kwalàbē   (broken) bottles'

bà kù rufè tāgà ba?   'didn't you close the window?'

mwâ kàmà ɓàrāwòn   'we'll catch the thief'

b) The final vowel is long everywhere else, that is, when followed by a pronoun direct object, an indirect object, or no object at all.

bà kù rufè ta ba?   'didn't you close it?'

mwâ kàmà shi   'we'll catch him'

297

an kwāshḕ manà kāyā dukà   'all our possessions have been stolen'

zâi fārā̀ yâu?   'will he start today?'

c) In the imperative, two-syllable transitive verbs which normally begin in high tone and end in -a or -e have the tone pattern low-low before noun direct objects and the final vowel is short. Everywhere else (before pronoun direct objects, all indirect objects, or when no object directly follows) they have the tone pattern low-high and the final vowel is long. PRONOUN DIRECT OBJECTS HAVE HIGH TONE. This is for the same reason that was given for the high tone of pronoun direct objects after three-syllable high tone verbs, that is, the basic tones are low-low, which causes the pronoun to take high tone. But since a Hausa word can't end in the tone pattern low-low if the word ends in a long vowel, the final syllable of the verb is raised.

    kḗ, hǔcḗ dai!   'hey, calm down!'

    kàmá ɓàrāwò!   'catch the theif!'

    kàmā̀ shi!   'catch him!'

21.3 Demonstrative Meaning "this/that thing in question"

Besides the differences of meaning between "this" and "that" in English or wannàn and wancàn in Hausa, there is a second way to divide demonstratives into two groups according to meaning: (1) demonstratives referring to things in sight which one can point to and (2) demonstratives referring to something mentioned or understood in a conversation or narrative. This difference is quite important in Hausa because the form of the demonstrative itself depends on which of these two meanings is indicated. Demonstratives of type (1) have already been described, so we will describe type (2) by showing how it differs from type (1).

a) wànnan, wàncan/wàccan, wàdànnan, wàdàncan

In 5.2 and 7.3 we described how wannàn, etc. with tones high-low (high-low-falling in the plural) could be used to mean 'this' or 'that' thing being indicated. The same forms with the tone patterns just reversed (low-low-high in the plural) mean 'this/that one in question', 'this/that one to which we have reference'.

    wànnan ɓàrāwò yā kwāshḕ   'that thief stole our goods'
    manà kāyā

    wannàn iṭa cḕ makarantā   'this (school where we are now
    sōsai; wàccan makarkatā   located) is the real school;
    cḕ   that (school that you have just
                               mentioned) is a place of deviation'

b) Noun plus nan or can

In 13.2, it was shown how nàn/nân and càn/cân (low tone after a noun ending in high tone, falling tone after a noun ending in low tone) can be attached to a noun by use of the linker to give the meaning 'this' or 'that thing' (being indicated). Nan or can with high tone can be attached by means of the linker to a noun to mean 'this/that one in question', etc. A noun normally ending in high tone has falling tone; a noun ending in low tone remains unchanged.

cikin t̄b̄ob̄în nan wàccē
ta fi k̄asuwā?

'among these (brands of) cigarets
(that we are talking about) which
sells better?'

b̄ab̀u aik̄T dà yawā à
makarantâr nan

'there's not a lot of work at that
school (that was just mentioned)'

à cikin sh̄ekar̀ar çan
an yi ruwā dà yawā

'in that year it rained a lot'

c) nan and can meaning 'here' and 'there'

The same tone changes apply to nan and can meaning 'here' and 'there'.
With a falling tone, the place indicated is in sight; with a high tone
it is a place referred to, but not being physically indicated by some
gesture.

Question: ìnā tak̀ardark̀a? 'where is your paper?'

Answer 1: gā ta nân çikin   'here it is in my book (the student
          littāfī   shows it to the teacher)'

Answer 2: tanā can à gidā   'it's there at home (the student
                               didn't bring it to school)'

21.4 The ma- Place Nouns and Instrument Nouns

Nouns meaning "place where such and such an activity takes place"
can be formed by adding the prefix ma- to the verb denoting the activity and replacing the final vowel of the verb with -ā. These nouns always have all high tone. The plurals nearly always end in -ai and have
all low tone except the last syllable.

Verb		Place noun	Plural	
kar̀antā	'read'	makarantā	màkàràntai/màkàràntū	'school'
kark̀atā	'swerve'	makarkatā	màkàrkàtū	'place of deviation (from the correct path)'
aunā	'weigh'	ma'aunā	mà'àunai	'place where grain is sold by measure ("weighing place")'
kash̄e	'kill'	makasā	màkàsai	'vital spot on the body'
k̄erā	'forge'	mak̄erā	màk̄èrai	'forge, smithy'

A few place nouns add -T instead of -ā, in which case they are masculine.

| sallà | 'prayers' | masallācT | màsàllàtai | 'place for praying, mosque' |

Nouns meaning "instrument with which an action is done" are formed
in the same way as place nouns except that instrument nouns always have
the suffix -T in the singular instead of -ā and are masculine. They
have the same type of plural as the place nouns.

bud̄e	'open'	mabud̄T	màbūdai	'key'
dūb̀a	'look at'	madūbT	màdūbai	'mirror'
gwadā	'measure, test'	magwajT	màgwàdai	'measuring stick'

299

21.5 n̄e̱ as a Sentence Emphasizer

By this time you are quite familiar with n̄e̱ and c̱e̱ used with nouns to mean 'it is ...'. The word n̄e̱ (not c̱e̱, since it is only used with feminine nouns) can also be used for what we will call a "sentence emphasizer" for want of a better term. This is probably not really an accurate term for this use of n̄e̱ since it can be placed at the end of almost any sentence with little if any change in meaning. In fact, its frequency of use is probably just a part of the speech patterns of individual speakers and as such would be used very frequently by some speakers and almost never by others. We have seen one example of this usage in dialogue A of this unit.

nā kāwō Īsa makarantā nè̱   'I have brought Isa to school'

N̄e̱ can also be used at the end of a question, again with no basic meaning change from the question without n̄e̱, though the addtion of n̄e̱ may indicate surprise. Question intonation must be used even with n̄e̱ added.

zâi fārā̀ yâu ne̱?   'is he going to start today?'

kanā̀ nazàrī nè̱?   'are you studying?'

As in its other uses, n̄e̱ must have tone opposite the preceding syllable.

GRAMMATICAL DRILLS

Drill 1A - 1B - In drills 1A and 1B there are two columns of cues: on the left is a set of sentences containing two and three syllable verbs beginning in high tone. On the right is a set of nouns and pronouns. Take each of the sentences on the left of each drill and insert all the nouns and pronouns on the right into it in turn as direct objects. The pronoun cues are independent pronouns, so you will have to use the corresponding direct object pronoun. Pay careful attention to tones and vowel lengths of the verbs.

Example: 1. nā jarràbā   a. mōtà̱

            2. Àli zâi tūƙā̀   b. shī
               tūƙā̀ v.tr. 'drive'

First sentence 1 is repeated, then as the cues are given, the following responses should be given.

Cues	Student response
1. nā jarràbā	nā jarràbā
mōtà̱	nā jarràbà mōtà̱
shī	nā jarràbā shi
2. Àli zâi tūƙā̀	Àli zâi tūƙā̀
mōtà̱	Àli zâi tūƙà mōtà̱
shī	Àli zâi tūƙā̀ shi

IA 1. mālàm zâi rubūtā
2. ruwā yā ɓātā̀
3. nā ajìyē
4. dà̀lìbai zā sù karàntā
5. kù kāmā̀

a. takàrdā
b. shī̄
c. littāfī̀
d. ita

IB 1. matàfìyā sun ƙètàrē
   ƙētàrē v.tr. 'cross'
2. gòbe zā sù wucè
3. 'yan sàndā sun 1ī̄ƙè
4. bàn iyà tsallàkā ... ba
5. ƙàzântā tā ɓātā̀
   ƙàzântā n.f. 'filth'

a. hanyā̀
b. shī̄
c. kōgī̄
d. ita

(1ī̄ƙè in 3 means
block, as a road
block)

Drill 2 - Replace the direct object nouns by pronoun direct objects or
drop the object, whichever is more appropriate. Watch tones and vowel
lengths.

Cue: muhùtī̄ yā kimmàntà ɓàrnâr
Student response: muhùtī̄ yā kimmàntā̄

1. kanā̀ sôn kà jarràbà kêkên?
2. àkāwu yā karàntà ƙārā
3. kù ajìyè buhunàn nân
4. kun iyà tsallàkà dūtsèn nân?
5. bàri mù ƙètàrè hanyā̀

6. Īsa yā rubùtà sūnansà
   sūnā̀ n.m. 'name'
7. sai yà kimmàntà kudìnsà
8. sun ƙètàrè kōgī̄ dà sāfe
9. dà̀lìbai zā sù karàntà lìttàttà̀fansù
10. bàri ìn jarràbà sābuwar mōtātā

Drill 3 - Replace the direct object noun by the appropriate direct object pronoun or drop the object. Watch tones and vowel lengths.

Cue: 'yan sàndā sun kāmà̀ ɓàrāyī̄
Student response: 'yan sàndā sun kāmā̀ su

1. kun bazà làbārìn nan?
2. Īsa yā rufè littāfìnsà
3. wà̄ ya kashè ƙwàrin nàn?
4. mun kwāshè ruwân dàgà jirgī̄
5. kun aunà gyàdā̀ dukà?

6. mun wucè matàfìyā à hanyā̀
7. dūbā, kā ɓàtà rīgātā̀
8. 'yan sàndā sun 1ī̄ƙè hanyā̀
9. kun shūkà hatsī̄ dukà?
10. kù rufè tāgōgī̄

Drill 4A - 4B

4A Modify the noun in each sentence by wànnan or wàdànnan 'that/those
(being referred to)'.

Cue: makarantâr bā̀ ta dà kyâu
Student response: wànnan makarantā bā̀ ta dà kyâu

301

4B Modify the noun in each sentence by <u>nan</u> 'that/those (being referred to)'. Pay careful attention to the tone on the final syllable of the noun.

                Cue: makarantâr bâ ta dà kyâu

             Student response: makarantâr nan bâ ta dà kyâu

1. kō an bar àl'àdàr?   6. wà ya kè sàyen tābàr?

2. abūbuwà sun bā nì màmākì   7. kā san wani à ƙauyèn?

3. wàsân na ban shà'awà nē   8. sàdākìn yā yi yawà

4. kadà kù mântā dà màganàr   9. mun karàntà littāfìn

5. Hārūnà zâi àuri bàzawàrâr   10. kanà sô kà àuri yārinyàr?

Drill 5 - Form <u>ma-</u> "place nouns" (21.4) from the cues below.

                Cue: ìnā wurîn dà a kè dìnkìn tufāfî?

             Student response: wannàn madìnkar tufāfî cē

1. ìnā wurîn dà a kè kāmà kīfī?   kīfī n.m. 'fish'

2. ìnā wurîn dà a kè aunà shìnkāfā? shìnkāfā n.f. 'rice'

3. ìnā wurîn dà a kè ajìyè kuɗī?

4. ìnā wurîn dà akà hàifē kà?

5. ìnā wurîn dà a kè sāƙà tàbarmā?   sāƙà v.tr. 'weave'

6. ìnā wurîn dà ɓàrāyī su kè fìtā?

7. ìnā wurîn dà jirgī kè shân ruwā?
   'where does the train take on (drink) water?'

8. ìnā wurîn dà a kè rinà tufāfî?   rinà v,tr, 'dye'

9. ìnā wurîn dà a kè ɓōyè kāyā?   ɓōyè v.tr. 'hide'

10. ìnā wurîn dà a kè rēgà hatsī?   rēgà v.tr. 'sift, shake to
                                         remove sand, etc.'

Drill 6 - In response to a sentence anà ... dà wannàn 'one does ... with this', give a sentence wannàn ma- ... nē 'this is a ...', supplying the ma- instrument noun based on the verb or action noun of the cue sentence (see end of 21.4). If the verb or action noun is followed by a noun in the cue, do not include this latter noun in the response. Where the instrument noun will have an idiomatic translation, it is given in parentheses.

                Cue: anà awòn gyàdā dà wannàn (scales)
                                (awō = verbal noun of aunà 'weigh')

             Student response: wannàn ma'aunī nē 'this is (a set of) scales'

1. anà girbī dà wannàn   5. anà būdè ƙōfà dà wannàn (key)

2. anà kāmà dabbōbī dà wannàn 6. anà ɗaukàr kāyā dà wannàn (handle)
   (weapon)

3. anà kòrar tsuntsàyē dà wannàn 7. anà rēgà hatsī dà wannàn (sieve)

4. anà dūban fuskà dà wannàn   8. anà ɗaurè kāyā dà wannàn
   (mirror) dūbà v.n.m. of   ɗaurè v.tr. 'tie up'
      dūbà 'look at'

Drill 7 - Place the direct object at the beginning of the sentence for emphasis.

Cue: yanà kāmà kTfT

Student response: kTfT ya kē kāmàwā

1. munà kōyō Hausa
2. uwargidā tanà bazà zanè
3. Kànde tanà kirāwō d̀an sàndā
4. kàjT sunà k̀etàrè hanyà
5. yârā sunà rufè tāgōgT
6. munà kashè k̀wàrT
7. anà d̀aukō kāyanmù
8. mài gidā yanà cirè kud̀T dà hankàlT

9. nā iyà tsallàkà katangar nàn
10. Īsa, kanà kāwō littāfìnkà?
11. aikìn nan yanà jāwō wàhalà
12. yanà jarràbà sābuwar mōtàrsà
13. anà būd̀è k̀ōfàr gàrT
14. Ùmarù yanà biyō sāwun shānū
15. muhùtT yanà kimmàntà 6àrnâr

Drill 8A - 8B

8A Delete the phrase yā kàmàtà and the subjunctive pronouns from the sentences below and change the verb to the imperative.

Cue: yā kàmàtà kà kāwō littāfìnkà

Student response: kāwō littāfìnkà

8B Follow the instructions for 8A, but replace the direct object with the appropriate direct object pronoun or drop the object.

Cue: yā kàmàtà kà kāwō littāfìnkà

Student response: kāwō shì

1. yā kàmàtà kà bazà rīgunà
2. yā kàmàtà kà gyàrà fartanyà
3. yā kàmàtà kì rufe tāgà
4. yā kàmàtà kà sàri itàtuwà
5. yā kàmàtà kì dafà àbinci
6. yā kàmàtà kà gamà aikìn

7. yā kàmàtà kà k̀ori birōrT
8. yā kàmàtà kà kāwō gyàd̀à
9. yā kàmàtà kà d̀auki kāyà
10. yā kàmàtà kà hanà dabbōbT

    hanà v.tr.   'prevent, stop'

11. yā kàmàtà kà biyà tàrâr
12. yā kàmàtà kà kāmà 6àrāwō

Drill 9 - Change wannàn/wancàn, etc. meaning 'this/that one' (that we can see) to wànnan/wàncan etc. 'that one' (in question). Change nàn/nân or càn/cân 'this/that one' (that we can see) to nan or can 'this/ that one' (in question). If this drill is done with an informant, he might also want to repeat the sentences using the tone pattern meaning 'that one' (in question), etc. and have the student change it to the demonstrative meaning 'this/that one' (that we can see).

Cue: wannàn hanyà bâ ta dà kyâu

Student response: wànnan hanyà bâ ta dà kyâu

Cue: hanyàr nân bâ ta dà kyâu

Student response: hanyàr nan bâ ta dà kyâu

1. wannàn makarantā makarkatā cè
2. wannàn kàràtū yanà dà wùyā
3. kadà kà mântā dà wannàn màganà
4. wà ya ɓàtà wannàn àllõ?
5. 'yan sàndā sun kāmà wannàn ɓàrāwõ?
6. wadànnân abūbuwà sun bā kà màmākī?
7. wannàn rīji̇yā tanà dà zurfī
   zurfī n.m. 'depth'
8. yârā sun fasà wadànnân kwalàbē

1. makarantar nàn makarkatā cè
2. kàràtun nàn yanà dà wùyā
3. kadà kà mântā dà màganàr nân
4. wà ya ɓàtà àllon nàn?
5. 'yan sàndā sun kāmà ɓàrāwòn nân?
6. abūbuwàn nân sun bā kà màmākī?
7. rīji̇yar nàn tanà dà zurfī
8. yârā sun fasà kwalàben nàn

Drill 10 - You will be given a sentence of the form mè zā à yī à ...?
'what would one do at ...?' with a ma- "place noun" in the blank or
mè zā à yī dà ...? 'what would one do with a ...?' with a ma- "instrument noun" in the blank. Some of the place nouns in this drill end in
-ī, not -ā, so your cue in these cases must be whether the preposition
à 'at' or dà 'with' has been used. Respond to the cues with a sentence
sai à ... ī one should ...' with the verb from the place or instrument
noun in the blank. Some of the cue sentences will be followed by a noun
in parentheses. This noun should be inserted into the response as in
the examples. Otherwise, simply supply the proper verb.

Cue: mè zā à yi à matsayī

Student response: sai à tsayā

Cue: mè zā à yi dà ma'aunī? (gyàɗà)

Student response: sai à aunà gyàɗà

1. mè zā à yi à mazaunī?
2. mè zā à yi dà maɗaukī? (jàkā)
3. mè zā à yi dà makõrī? (awākī)
4. mè zā à yi à masaukī?
5. mè zā à yi dà maɗaurī? (kāyā)
6. mè zā à yi à mashigī? (ruwā)

7. mè zā à yi à mafitā?
8. mè zā à yi dà mabūdī? (kõfà)
9. mè zā à yi à ma'aunā? (gyàɗà)
10. mè zā à yi à madafā? (àbinci)
11. mè zā à yi dà masārī? (dājī)
12. mè zā à yi dà marufī? (kwaryā)
    kwaryā n.f. 'calabash'

Drill 11 - Substitute the appropriate direct object pronoun or delete
the object. Make necessary changes in the verbs.

Cue: yā bazā̀ bàrgō à kân kwalàbē

Student response: yā bazà shi à kân kwalàbē

1. mwâ kāmà ɓàrāyī
2. Īsa yā kõyō kàràtū dà rubùtū
3. zâi dūbà makarantar nàsàriyyà
4. tā biyā yârā
5. mun ɗauki dūtsē
6. zâi kàrà fāɗintà

7. nā gyārà mõtàtā
8. sun cìri clyāwà
9. kun bazà bàrgō
10. tâ sàyi kwandunā
11. uwargidā tā rufè kõfà
12. ɓàrāwõ yā sàci kudī

304

Drill 12 - Replace the object nouns in the sentences below with the appropriate direct object pronouns or drop the objects.

Cue: Mūsā yā karàntà shāfī biyu

Student response: Mūsā yā karàntā su

1. mun kirāwō ɗan sàndā
2. su Mammàn zā sù tàimàki yârā
3. muhùtⓣ yā kimmàntà ɓàrnâr
4. mun zìyàrci àbòkanmù
5. ɓàrāwō yā tsallàkà katangā
6. kin rubùtà ɗan littāfī

7. nā tambayō làbārī
8. nā karàntà takàrdā
9. tā tàmbàyi Sulè
10. Màlàm Shēhù yā tàimàki ma'àikàta
11. Àbūbakàr yā jarràbà mōtà
12. matàfìyā sun ƙētàrè kōgⓣ

Drill 13 - Place the phrase following the continuative pronouns before them as illustrated.

Cue: yànzu yanà makarantar Mùhàmmàdiyyà

Student response: yànzu à makarantar Mùhàmmàdiyyà ya kè

1. yànzu munà gidā
2. yànzu kinà gidan Aishà
3. yànzu yanà ōfìshīnā
4. yànzu kanà wurin maƙērⓣ
5. yànzu inà kàntin Kinsùwài
   Kinsùwài Kingsway stores
   (largest chain store in Nigeria)

6. yànzu tanà kàsuwā
7. yànzu kunà makarantar nàsàriyyà
8. yànzu sunà wajen STdi
9. yànzu tanà Zāriyà
10. yànzu yanà tashàr jirgin ƙasà

Drill 14 - Change sentences of the pattern kanà yìn nazàrin makarantar Mùhàmmàdiyyà kō nazàrin makarantar nàsàriyyà? to fit the pattern nazàrin makarantar Mùhàmmàdiyyà ka kè yī kō na nàsàriyyà?

Cue: sun būɗè ƙòfàr ɗàkìn Shēhù kō ƙòfàr ɗàkìn Mūsā?

Student response: ƙòfàr ɗàkìn Shēhù sukà būɗè kō ta Mūsā?

1. kanà sôn aikìn maƙērⓣ kō aikìn lēbùrà? lēbùrà n.m. 'laborer'
2. ɓàrāwō yā tsallàkà katangar gidan Shēhù kō katangar gidan Mammàn?
3. sunà ɗaukàr bùhun gyàɗà kō bùhun hatsī?
4. kunà sà rìgar Hàusàwā kō rìgar Yarabāwā?
5. tanà dafà àbincin Hàusàwā kō àbincin Tùràwā?
6. kunà yìn màganà à kân gōnar Shēhù kō à kân gōnar Mùhammadù?
7. yanà sàyen mōtàr Ingìlà kō mōtàr Amìrkà?
8. sunà karàntà lìttàttàfan Nījēriyà kō lìttàttàfan Rashà?
9. kunà tàfiyà makarantar Mùhàmmàdiyyà kō makarantar nàsàriyyà?
10. anà kōyà musù màganàr Tùrancī kō màganàr Hausa? kōyà v.tr. 'teach'

305

Drill 15A - 15C - Repeat the initial sentence, then substitute the first cue into the appropriate place in that sentence. As each cue is given, substitute it into the sentence formed from the previous cue so that a new sentence is formed.

15A Initial sentence: zâi rubùtà littāfī

Cues	Student response
1. karàntà	zâi karàntà littāfī
2. kōyō kàràtū dà rubùtū	zâi kōyō kàràtū dà rubùtū
3. à makarantar Mùhàmmàdiyyā	zâi kōyō kàràtū dà rubùtū à makarantar Mùhàmmàdiyyā
4. nàsàriyyà	zâi kōyō kàràtū dà rubùtū à makarantar nàsàriyyà
5. zāmànT	zâi kōyō kàràtū dà rubùtū à makarantar zāmànT
6. yi	zâi yi kàràtū dà rubùtū à makarantar zāmànT
7. continuative aspect	yanà (yîn) kàràtū dà rubùtū à makarantar zāmànT
8. wàk̃e-wàk̃e	yanà wàk̃e-wàk̃e à makarantar zāmànT
9. mōtsin jìkT	yanà mōtsin jìkT à makarantar zāmànT
10. wàsan ɓōyō	yanà wàsan ɓōyō à makarantar zāmànT

15B Initial sentence: yā karàntà littāfī

1. littāfìn nân	yā karàntà littāfìn nân
2. littāfìn nan	yā karàntà littāfìn nan
3. yàrā	yàrā sun karàntà littāfìn nan
4. ɗàlìbai	ɗàlìbai sun karàntà littāfìn nan
5. subjunctive aspect	ɗàlìbai sù karàntà littāfìn nan
6. mālàm yanà sô	mālàm yanà sô ɗàlìbai sù karàntà littāfìn nan
7. shāfī biyu	mālàm yanà sô ɗàlìbai sù karàntà shāfī biyu
8. ɗarT	mālàm yanà sô ɗàlìbai sù karàntà shāfī ɗarT
9. dàgà lìttàttàfansù	mālàm yanà sô ɗàlìbai sù karàntà shāfī ɗarT dàgà lìttàttàfansù
10. dàgà littāfìn nan	mālàm yanà sô ɗàlìbai sù karàntà shāfī ɗarT dàgà littāfìn nan

15C Initial sentence: yā yi aikī

1. k̃ōk̃arT	yā yi k̃ōk̃arT
2. continuative aspect	yanà k̃ōk̃arT
3. bā dà	yanà bā dà k̃ōk̃arT
4. kanà	kanà bā dà k̃ōk̃arT
5. subjunctive aspect	kà bā dà k̃ōk̃arT
6. yā kàmàtà	yā kàmàtà kà bā dà k̃ōk̃arT

7. à m̧akaṇtar   yā kàmātà kà bā dà k̓ók̓arī à makarantar nàsāriyyà
    nasāriyyà
8. Mùhàmmàdiyyā̧   yā kàmātà‸kà bā dà k̓ók̓arī à makarantar Mùhàmmà-
                          diyyā
9. don kà kōyō kàrātū   yā kàmātà‸kà bā dà k̓ók̓arī à makarantar Mùhàmmà-
                          diyyā̧ don kà kōyō kàrātū
10. zâi ţàimàkē kà ‸   yā kàmātà‸kà bā dà k̓ók̓arī à makarantar Mùhàmmà̧-
    dūniyā̧ dà lāhirā   diyyā̧ don zâi ţàimàkē kà dūniyā̧ dà lāhirā

GUIDED CONVERSATION

1) Numerous topics about school or schools can serve as a basis for conversations. Some suggestions are a comparison of two universities and what
is better or worse about one than the other; discussion of a student's
program (course requirements for his degree, type of degree, future
plans, why he is taking Hausa); reminiscences about earlier school years
(that old witch of a teacher in the fourth grade, how arithmetic was so
hard, how you were spanked for not getting all A's, how you liked to
sing in the school chorus, etc.); a topic that suggests itself in the
dialogues of this unit is a discussion of how the programs of parochial
schools and public schools in America differ. Note that the entire
thrust of the Koranic school differs from that of the public schools,
but this is not true of American parochial schools. Some additional vocabulary that might be useful is given below.

jāmi'ā̧ n.f.	'university'	àddīnī̧ n.m.	'religion, a
ajī̧ n.m̧.	'school class; grade	(àddīnai pl.)	religion'
(azūzuwā̧ pl.)	(level) in school'	harshē ‸n.m.	'language; tongue'
kwâs n.m.	'course (in school)'	(harsunā̧ pl.)	
(kwasōshī̈ pl.)		lābārìn k̓asā̧	'geography'
jarràbāwā n.m.	'test, examination'	lissāfī̧ n.m.	'mathematics'
takàrdar		lìţţaţţàfai n.pl.	
makarantā̧	'diploma'		'literature'
jarràb̧àwar	'(university) degree'	tārīhī̧ n.m.	'history'
jāmi'ā̧	(test of university)	Tūrancī̧ n.m.	'English (language)'

Example conversation between an American and a Hausa student in an American university:

Bill: Yàyā̧ ka k̓è jī̧ dà aikìn   How are you doing (feeling)
        makarantā̧?   with your school work?

Hasàn: Aikìn makarantā̧ à Amìrkà,   School work in America is tough!
        àkwai wùyā̧!

Bill: Àkwai bambancī̧‸¹ dà na   Is there a difference with
        Nījēriyā̧?   Nigeria's (type of work)?

Hasàn: Ī, àkwai. À Nījēriyā̧, in   Yes, there is. In Nigeria, when
        kā‸d̓auki jarràbāwā‸kàmar   you take examinations of about
        irī ukù wàtō tārīhī̧,   three kinds, that is, history,
        Tūrancī̧, dà lissāfī̧, sun   English, and mathematics, they
        ìsa.²   suffice.

307

Bill:	Mēnē nè dàlⁱlin³ wùyar aikìn makarantā à Amìrkà?	What is the reason for the hardness of American school work?
Hasàn:	Saβō dà sai kā san abūbuwā irī dàban-dàban,⁴ bā sai kwâs gùdā ba.	Because you have to know all different kinds of things, not just one course (area).
Bill:	Bābù kōmē in kā yi nazàrī dà kyâu.	In makes no difference if you study well.
Hasàn:	Inā iyàkar kōkarīnā.	I'm doing my best (limit of my effort).

[1] bambancì n.m.   'difference'

[2] ìsa v.intr.   'suffice, be sufficient'

[3] dàlīlī n.m.   'reason, cause'

[4] dàban-dàban (following a plural noun) 'different'

[5] iyàkā n.m.   'limit'

2) Discuss a test or other school work, including preparations made for it, what it covers or covered, and how well you did on it if it has already been completed and graded.

Further useful vocabulary:

aikìn gidā   'homework'

aikìn bìncìkē   'research paper'

yā ci jarrà- bāwā   'he passed the test'

yā fādì   'he flunked (he fell)'

matsayī n.m.   'grade (on a paper, test, etc.)'

Example conversation between Isa and one of his younger classmates. Isa has just taken one of the General Certificate of Education (GCE) exams which must be passed in the British (and Nigerian) educational system in order to advance.

Bellò:	Īsa, yāyā jarràbāwarkà ta jiyà?	Isa, how was your exam yesterday?
Īsa:	Àkwai wùyā! Àmmā inā fātā bà zān fādì ba.	It was tough! But I hope I won't flunk.
Bellò:	Dà mè dà mēnē nè cikin jarràbāwā tākù?	What all was on your test?
Īsa:	Kâi! Bâ àbin dà bābù! Wātō dà akà bā mù tambayōyī, sai gùmī ya karyō minì.	Wow! There wasn't anything that wasn't (on it)! You know when they gave us the questions, I broke out in a sweat (sweat "broke" to me).
Bellò:	Kū nawà kukà ɗauki jarràbāwār?	How many of you took the exam?
Īsa:	Wajen mū hàmsin nè. Àkwai mātā kàmar àshìrin.	There were about fifty of us. There were about twenty girls.
Bellò:	Inā fātā kà ci jarràbāwār.	I hope you pass the test.
Īsa:	In Allàh yā yàrda, zân ci.	If God wills it, I'll pass.

308

UNIT XXII

DIALOGUES

A. The traditional rulers of Hausa speaking territory were the emirs.
Elected by the provincial chiefs, the emirs served in perpetuity or
until they so displeased the chiefs that they were deposed. When the
British, under Lord Luggard, conquered Northern Nigeria, they chose
to construct their governmental machine around the emirs and the
chiefs. Today the emirs' powers have diminished considerably. The
actual administration of governmental services in their emirates is
conducted by a corps of professionally trained civil servats who
answer to the Permanent Secretaries of their respective ministries
rather than to the emirs. Nevertheless, the word of an emir carries
considerable weight with the rural population of his emirate, and the
emirs still have sources of funds with which they maintain palaces
and large staffs of retainers.
In the following dialogue, George Stathes, a Ford Foundation consultant attached to the Ministry of Trade and Industry in Kaduna, pays
a call on an emir. Stathes wants to initiate a credit system in the
emirate to encourage the expansion of small businesses which he be-
lieves have potential. He knows that if the emir approves of the plan,
it will catch on quickly. When he arrives, the emir is too busy to
see him immediately.

Sallamà:	Rân Sarki yà dadê. Gà wani dōgon Bàtūrē yā zō wurinkà.	May the life of the Emir be pro- longed. There is a certain tall European who has come to see you (has come to your place).
SarkT:	Dàgà ìnā ya kē?	Where is he from?
Sallamà:	Yā zō nē dàgà Ma'aikatar Cìnikī dà Sana'ō'T ta Kadūna.	He has come from the Ministry of Trade and Industry at Kaduna.
SarkT:	Sai yà dākàt̃ā kàɗan. Jàkādìyâ, kāwō miṇì àlkyabbà dà tākalmā.	Have him wait a bit. Jakadiya, bring me a burnous and sandals.
Jàkādìyā:	Rân SarkT yà dadê. Wàcè irī̀?	May the life of the Emir be prolonged. What kind?
SarkT:	Kāwō baꝅâr ... Sarkin Zagī, yāyà sābon ìnqar- màn nan?	Bring the black one ... Sarkin Zagi, how is that new stallion?
Sarkin Zagi:	Rân SaꝅkT yà dadê. Yanā̀ dà hàlāmun zâi yi ɡudù.	May the life of the Emir be pro- longed. He has signs of being swift (he will do running).
SarkT:	Jē ka kà gwadā̀ shi.	Go and test him.
(Jàkādìyā tā shìga dāꝅke dà baꝅar àlkyabbà; SarkT ya sâ.)		(Jakadiya enters carrying a black burnous; the Emir puts it on.)
SarkT:	Tô, Sallamà, bàri Bàtūrē yà shigō.	All right, Sallama, have the European come in.

àlkyabbā n.f. (àlkyàbbū pl.)	'burnous' (a large, heavy robe)		jè ka	'go!' (see 22.5)

àlkyabbā   n.f.   'burnous' (a large,
(àlkyàbbū pl.)   heavy robe)

baƙT adj.m.   'black'
(baƙā f.; bakāƙē pl.)

dākàtā   v.intr.   'wait'

dōgō adj.m.   'tall'
(dōguwā f.; dōgāyē pl.)

gwadā   v.tr.   'measure, test'

hàlāmā   n.f.   'sign, indication'
(hàlāmū pl.)

ìngarmā   n.m.   'large stallion'
(ìngàrmū pl.)

jàkādìyā   n.f.   'female attendant
                        at the emir's
                        palace'

jè ka   'go!' (see 22.5)

ma'aikatā n.f. 'work-place, bu-
(mà'àikàtai pl.)   reau, ministry'

sābō adj.m.   'new'
(sābuwā f.; sàbàbbT pl.)

Sallamà   n.m.   'court messenger'

sàna'ā   n.f.   'trade, occupation'
(sana'ō'T pl.)

sarkī n̨.m.   'emir'
(sarākunā pl.)

wurT n.m.   'place'
(wurārē pl.)

zagT n.m.   'runner in front of
                      horsemen'

Sarkin ZagT   'stable-master'

B. Stathes is ushered before the Emir.

Stathes: SarkT, yàyà akà jT dà
          jàma'ā?

Emir, how fare your people (what
is heard from the people)?

SarkT: Mun̨ gōdę̀ Allāh! Sànnu dà
          zuwà! Dā mā an rigā an
          sanad dà nT zā kà zō.

Thanks be to God! Welcome! I
had already been informed that
you would come.

Stathes: Nā zō nè̄ don ìn bayyànā
          makà shirìn bā dà rancē
          don kyautàtà ƙanānàn
          sana'ō'T.

I came in order to inform you of
the plan for giving loans for
the improvement of small businesses.

SarkT: Mādàllā, mutànēnā kùwā zā
          sù ƙàru ƙwarai ìdan sukà
          sāmi wànnan tàimakō.

Fine. My people will gain (pros-
per) much if they get this help.

Stathes: Ammā fa wândā duk zā à bā
          rancên sai yā iyà ƙiyàyè
          littàttāfan lissāfT dà a
          kē bukātà.

But whoever is to be given a
loan must be able to keep the
account books which are required.

SarkT: Inā fātā mutànēna zā sù iyà.

I hope my people will be able
(to do so).

Stathes: Zā sù iyà mànà, tun dà ya
          kē zā à kōyà musù.

They will be able to since they
are going to be taught (how to).

SarkT: Har nawà a kē iyà bā mài
          sàna'ā rancē?

Up to how much of a loan can be
given to a business owner.

Stathes: Aną̄ iyà bayârwą̄ kàɗan dà dą̀
          yawà, ammā bā yā wucè Nairā
          dubū bìyar.

Small or large (amounts) can be
given, but it (the total amount)
can't be more that ₦5000.

SarkT: Ta yàyà mùtûm zâi̧ iyà
          dàcēwā dà sāmùn rancên?

How does a person qualify (he can
be able to be suited) to get a loan?

Stathes: Ìdan nā ga sàna'àr, kuma mài If I see the business and the
ita yā yàrda zâi̱ ajìyè̱ lìt- owner agrees to keep the account
tàttāfan lissāfī, sai a bā books, he will be given a loan
shì ràncē gwàrgwadō. accordingly (to the size and
  type of business).

SarkT: Ī, a̱i kùwā wànnan shirī̀ Yes, that arrangement makes
yanā dà mà'ànā. sense.

Vocabulary

bayyànā v.tr.	'explain'	kyautàtā v.tr.	'improve'
bùkàtā n.f.	'need, requirement'	ƙàru v.intr.	'make progress,
dàcè (dà X) v.intr.			benefit'
	'be suited, suita-	ƙwarai adv.	'a lot, much'
	ble (for X)'	lissāfī n.m.	'arithmetic,
fātā n.m.	'hoping'		accounting'
dubū n.m.	'1000'	mà'ànā n.f.	'sense, meaning'
gwàrgwadō n.m.	'a proportionate	rigā v.aux.	'to have previous-
	amount'	(see 22.3)	ly done, already
jàma'à n.f.	'the people'		done'
ƙàramT adj.m.	'small'	sanad dà v.caus.	'inform'
(ƙàramā f.; ƙanānà pl.)		shirī̀ n.m.	'plan, prepara-
kiyàyē v.tr.	'take care of'		tion'
		tun (dà ya kè)	'since'

COMPREHENSION PRACTICE

Without looking at your books, listen to the passage as your informant reads through it once, pausing to explain in Hausa the meaning of
any new words or expressions. Your informant will read the passage a
second time at normal conversational speed and then ask you the questions
which follow. Answer in complete sentences.

Zìyāràr Fādàr SarkT

LōkàcT lōkàcT[1] inā zìyāràr sarākunàn NTjērìyā ta arēwa don ìn yi
musù bàyānT gàme dà àbìn dà GwamnatT kè yî don kyautàtà zaman mutānē.
Gā mō wani mìsālT na yaddà na sàdu[2] dà wani sarkT.
Dà na Ìsa[3] fādàrsà, na fadā̀ wà Sallamà, "Gà ni nā zo." ShT Sallamà
ya shìga fādàr yà sanad dà sarkT. Na dākàtā kàɗan har Sallamà ya dāwō
ya yT minì isō.[4] Dà na shìga fādàr, sai na ga sarkT à zàune yanā̀ sànye[5]
dà baƙar àlkyabbā̀.
Na yT masà gaisuwā ta ladàbT,[6] shT mā ya cè an rigā an sanad dà shT
zân zo. Bāyan gaisuwâr, na gayā masà dàlTlìn zuwànā, wàtō, ìn bayyànā
masà shirìn bā dà ràncē don kyautàtà ƙanānàn sana'ō'T. Dà na fàɗì wannàn,
sarkT ya yi murnā don yā ga mutānensà zā sù ƙàru ƙwarai ìdan sukà sāmi

311

tàimakôn nan. Àmmā fuskàrsà ta sauyà⁷ kàɗan dà na cè duk wàndà zā à bā
ràncên, sai yā iyà kiyàyè lìttàttàfan lissāfì. Kā san bà mutànē dukà
sukà iyà lissāfì ba. Tò bā kōmē, màsu sana'ō'T zā sù iyà tun dà ya kè
zā à kōyā musù.

Dà sarkT ya ji wannàn, yanà sô ìn ci gàba dà bàyānT. Na cè mài
sàna'à yanà iyà sāmùn kàɗan kō dà yawà ìdan àbîn dà ya kè sô bà zâi
wucè Nairā 5000 ba. Mài sàna'à yâ iyà dācèwā dà sāmùn ràncên ìdan na
dūbà sàna'àrsà kumā ya yàrda zâi ajìyè lìttàttàfan lissāfì. SarkT dai,
ya ga shirìn nan na bā dà ràncē yanà dà mà'ànā.

[1] lōkàcT lōkàcT 'from time to time' [5] sànye   adverbial noun of state
[2] sàdu v.intr. 'meet'   for sà 'put on (clothes)'
[3] ìsa n.intr. 'arrive'   [6] ladàbT n.m. 'politeness'
[4] yi ... isô 'be shown in'   [7] fuskà tā sauyà 'his expression changed'
                                       [8] nan dà nan 'immediately'

Tambayōyī

1. Don mè Mālàm Stathes ya kè zìyāràr sarākunàn NTjēriyà ta arèwa?
2. Wànē nè Sallamà? Mènē nè aikìnsà?
3. Bāyan Mālàm Stathes yā ìsa fādàr sarkT, mè Sallamà ya yi?
4. Mālàm Stathes yā shìga fādàr nan dà nan?[8]
5. Yāyà ya sàmi sarkT?
6. Mè ya yi bāyan an yT masā isô?
7. Mè sarkT ya cè gàme dà zuwàn Mālàm Stathes?
8. Gàme dà mè Mālàm Stathes ya bâ sarkT bàyānT?
9. Dà sarkT ya ji bàyānìn nan, don mè ya yi murnà?
10. Duk wàndà zā à bā ràncên, mè zâi iyà kiyàyèwā?
11. SarkT yā yi shakkàr mutànensà zā sù iyà kiyàyè lìttàttàfan lissāfì?
12. Mè zâi sā màsu sana'ō'T zā sù iyà kiyàyè lìttàttàfan nan?
13. Màsu sana'ō'T zā sù iyà sāmùn ƙàramin ràncên kurùm?
14. Har nawà a kè iyà bâ mài sàna'à ràncē?
15. Ta yàyà mùtûm zâi iyà dācèwā dà sāmùn ràncên?
16. SarkT yanà tsàmmānT wànnan shirìn àbîn banzā nè?

GRAMMAR

22.1 Adjectives

We have noted that Hausa very frequently uses nouns of quality, such
as zāfT 'heat' or kyâu 'beauty, goodness', in various ways to express
what we normally express in English by use of adjectives. Hausa does
have a limited class of words which we will call "adjectives" which can
be used to modify nouns. Typically, they have three forms: masculine

singular, feminine singular, and plural.
The most commonly used adjectives are:

Masculine	Feminine	Plural	
baƙT	bakā	baƙàƙē	'black'
farT	farā	farãrē	'white'
jā	jā	jàjàyē	'red'
sābō	sābuwā	sàbàbbT	'new'
tsōhō	tsōhuwā	tsòfàffT	'old'
bàbba	bàbba	mânyā	'big; important'
ƙàramT	ƙàramā	ƙanānà	'small'
dōgō	dōguwā	dōgàyē	'tall'
gàjērē	gàjērìyā	gàjèrū	'short'
ƙàtò	ƙàtuwā	ƙattT	'huge'

All past passive participles (20.5) are adjectives as well and follow the rules below. Adjectives can be used in either of two ways to modify nouns directly:

a) Most frequently the adjective directly precedes the noun and is attached to it by the appropriate linker, that is, -n used with masculine and plural nouns, -r with feminine nouns.

gà wani dōgon Bàtūrè	'there's a certain tall European'
yàyà sābon ìngarmàn nan?	'how's that new stallion?'
tā shìga ɗauke dà baƙar àlkyabbà	'she entered carrying a black burnous'
mânyan mōtōcT sun zō dàgà Jàs	'trucks (big cars) came from Jos'
àkwai fàsàssun kwalàbē à ƙân katangā	'there are broken bottles on the wall'

b) Adjectives can directly follow the noun they modify in which case no linker is used.

ìngarmà sābō yanà dà àlàmun gudù	'the new stallion shows signs of being a runner'
kàwō àlkyabbà baƙā	'bring the black burnous'
kâr à bā yàrā ƙanānà tābà	'one shouldn't give small children tobacco'

They can also be used with nē/cē just like predicate adjectives in English.

ìngarmàn nân sābō nè	'this stallion is new'
àlkyabbàtā baƙā cè	'my burnous is black'
tàkalmà tsòfàffT nè	'the sandals are old'

Hausa adjectives can be used as nouns to mean 'black one', 'old one', 'tall one', etc.

kằwō baƙâr	'bring the black one'
sābuwā cḕ à nân gàrîn	'it's a new one in (for) this town'
tsōhō yā sâ àlkyabbằ	'the old man put on a burnous'
mânyā bā sā hawā jằkī	'important people don't ride donkeys'

22.2 -u Verbs

Verbs which we will call "-u verbs" can be formed by replacing the final vowel of a verb by high tone, short -u and giving the preceding syllable(s) of the verb low tone. With monosyllabic verbs, the syllable -wu or -yu (depending on the verb) is added to the verb and low tone given to the verb root.

All -u verbs are intransitive. Usually, the noun that would be the object of a transitive verb is the subject of the corresponding -u verb.

(intransitive)	mutằnē sun tằru	'the people assembled'
(transitive)	an tārà lìttàttằfai	'the books were gathered'
(intransitive)	nā rằbu dà ita	'I've left her' (I separated from her)
(transitive)	yā rabā́ su	'he separated them'
(intransitive)	gyàdằ tā sằmu sōsai	'there have been plenty of peanuts' (the peanuts have obtained well)
(transitive)	mài gyàdằ yā sằmi gyàdằ dà yawằ	'the peanut buyer has gotten a lot of peanuts'

Some -u verbs may also mean that (a) the subject has completely undergone the action or change of state indicated by the verb or (b) that the subject's undergoing the action is within the realm of possibility.

a) mutằnēnā zā sù ƙàru ƙwarai   'my people will profit greatly'
   (ƙàru from ƙàrā 'increase')

   àbinci yā dằfu   'the food is thoroughly cooked'
   (dàfu from dafằ 'cook')

b) bài yìwu ba   'it's impossible (to do)'
   (yìwu from yi 'do')

   hanyàr nân tā bìyu   'this road is usable (followable)'
   (bìyu from bi 'follow')

-u verbs have -wā verbal nouns and unlike other verbs that end in high tone, the final syllable of the verb before -wā does not become falling tone: ƙàruwā from ƙàru 'benefit', kàràntuwā from kàràntu 'be well read'. Often, the "possibility" meaning is expressed using the continuative aspect rather than the completive.

bā yằ yìwuwā	'it's impossible'
hanyằ tanằ bìyuwā	'the road can be followed'

22.3 rigā 'to have already done'

The adverb "already" in English has no one-word translation in Hausa. Instead, the auxiliary verb rigā 'to have done already' must be used. Rigā is unlike other auxiliary verbs in that it is not followed by a verbal construction alone, but by a full sentence. Rigā is rarely used in any aspect but the completive; if rigā is completive affirmative or negative, the verb following it will be in the completive affirmative, but if rigā is relative completive, the following verb will be too. If rigā is in the future or subjunctive, the verb following rigā will be in the subjunctive.

an rigā an sanad dà nī zā kà zō	'I had already been informed that you would come'
mè sukà rigā sukà yi?	'what have they already done?'
bà sù rigā sun zō ba	'they haven't already come/yet come'
zân rigā ìn zō	'I will have already come'

There is some dialectal difference, for example, for some speakers the second example might be mè sukà rigā sun yi? and the third bà sù rigā bà sù zō ba. Follow the usage pattern of your informant.

22.4 Indefinites Using duk/dukà

A rather long exposition was given in Unit XX of a group of words formed with kō- plus an interrogative pronoun or adjective. These words had meanings such as 'everyone', 'everywhere', 'always', 'everytime', etc. They cannot be modified by relative clauses to give phrases like 'everyone/anyone who came', 'everywhere we went', or 'everytime that I see him', To form such phrases in Hausa, the word duk or dukà is used in conjunction with a noun modified by a relative clause (or by a relative clause alone if the relative pronouns wândà/wâddà/wadàndà meaning 'the one(s) who' are used). Most commonly, duk(à) comes at the very beginning of the relative construction, or at the very end, but as can be seen from the sentence in dialogue B of this unit, it can be found within the relative clause as well.

wândà duk zā à bā ràncên, sai yā iyà kiyāyè lìttàttàfan lissāfī	'whoever/anyone who is to be given a loan must be able to keep the account books'

Some further examples are

kà bā nì làbārìn duk àbîn dà ka ganī	'give me the news (i.e. tell me about) everything you saw'
hanyàr dà mukà bī dukà, sai mukà gàji	'whatever road we followed, we got tired'
duk indà mukà jē, sai mukà gan shī	'wherever we went, we saw him'

Note that duk(à) can be used to modify nouns just as kōwànè/kōwàcè/kōwàdànnè can. The difference between these two is the same as English 'all' and 'every' where 'every' puts emphasis on the individual items of an entire group, and 'all' puts emphasis on the group itself. Dukà can precede the noun it modifies in which case it is attached with the

315

masculine linker -n, or it can follow the noun.

> dukàn mātā or mātā dukà   'all women'
>
> kōwàcè mātā   'every woman'

22.5 jḕ ka 'go!'

In the second person singular or plural, the following forms can be used with the imperative meaning 'go (in a direction away from the speaker)!'

> jḕ ka   'go!' (to a single male person)
>
> jḕ ki   'go!' (to a single female person)
>
> jḕ ku   'go!' (to several people)

These forms are somewhat special in that the subject pronouns follow the verb. As with any imperative verb, these forms can be abrupt in meaning, as 'beat it!', but they are not necessarily so as seen in dialogue A of this unit. The goal of the motion may or may not be expressed.

> jḕ ka kà gwadā shi   'go and try him out'
>
> jḕ ki/jḕ ka/jḕ ku kàsuwā 'go to market'

22.6 in/ìdan 'when', 'if'

Hausa has a single word (with two interchangeable forms, in or ìdan) to express the senses of both 'when' and 'if' in sentences like 'when it rains' and 'if it rains'. Note that the only difference between these phrases in English is the degree of certainty on whether or not it will rain. In Hausa, the degree of certainty must be gleaned from context.

The aspect used in in/ìdan clauses is normally the completive (relative or regular form) even though the meaning is usually future (note that in English, we usually use the simple present, even though the meaning is also future).

> mutànēnā kùwā zā sù ƙàru   'my people will profit much if
> ƙwarai ìdan sukà sāmi   they get this help'
> wannàn tàimakō
>
> ìdan mài sàna'à yā yàrda,   'if the business owner agrees,
> zâi ajìyè lìttàttāfan   he will keep the account books'
> lissāfī

When the first clause is the "if" clause, the second clause may be in the future, the indefinite future, or the subjunctive with or without sai preceding. These three aspects all give virtually the same meaning in this context.

> in yā tàimàkē nì, zân gamà aikī   ⎫
> in yā tàimàkē nì, nā̂ gamà aikī   ⎬ 'if he helps me,
> in yā tàimàkē nì, sai ìn gamà aikī ⎪   I'll finish the
> in yā tàimàkē nì, ìn gamà aikī   ⎭   work'

NB: In English, it is possible to have a sentence such as

if he sees an open window, a thief will come in

where 'he' in the first clause refers to 'thief' in the second. This is not possible in Hausa, that is, in the sentence

in yā ga tāgà à būɗe,   'if he sees an open window,
ɓàrāwō zâi shigō   a thief will come in'

the yā in the first clause must refer to someone other than ɓàrāwō in the second clause. This sentence would have to be rephrased to get the meaning that ɓàrāwō and yā refer to the same person:

in ɓàrāwō yā ga tāgà   'if a thief sees an open window,
à būɗe, zâi shigō   he'll come in'

That is, the antecedent of a pronoun in Hausa must always come somewhere in the sentence before the pronoun. This comment applies to any complex sentence, not just sentences using in/ìdan.

GRAMMATICAL DRILLS

Drill 1 - Change the sentences below, which have adjectives in the nē/cē construction, for example ìngarmàn nàn sābō nē, so that they fit the pattern wannàn sābon ìngarmā nē.

Cue: Bàtūrèn nàn dōgō nè

Student response: wannàn dōgon Bàtūrè nē

1. àlkyabbàr nân baƙā cē   7. kujèrar nàn gàjērìyā cè

2. tākalmàn nân jàjāyè nè   8. àbincin nàn dàfaffē nè

3. ìngarmàn nân farT nè   9. rìgar nàn farā cè

4. ōfìsōshin nàn sàbabbī nè   10. dūtsèn nân dōgō nè

5. kwalabar nàn fàsasshiyā cē   11. mōtàr nân sābuwā cē

6. itātuwàn nàn mânyā nè   12. màcèn nàn tsōhuwā cè

Drill 2 - Substitute the nouns in parentheses for the nouns preceded by adjectives in the sentences below and make any other changes that may be required.

Cue: SarkT yā cē wà Jàkādìyā tà kāwō masà
                        jar àlkyabbā (tākalmā)

Student response: SarkT yā cē wà Jàkādìyā tà kāwō masà
                        jàjāyen tākalmā

1. HàlTmà tā cē minì tanà sôn wani ƙàtòn bùhū (tukunyā)

2. à kāsuwā a kē sayad dà wasu ƙanānàn kwandunā (tagùwā)

3. sàrarren dājī yā ƙōnè (itātuwà)   ƙōnè v.intr. 'burn up'

4. yầyā sābon ìngarmā? (gōdìyā n.f. 'mare')

5. yā sā wata tsōhuwar rìgā (wàndō)

6. jiyà nā sàyi wata ƙàramar kàzā à kàsuwā (kàjī)

7. yā bayyànā manà sābon sābon làbārìn nāsà (dàbārā n.f. 'plan')

317

Cue: Sarkī bà zâi yàrda ba. Sabō dà hakà
ma'àikàcin Ma'aikatar Cìnikī dà Sana'ō'Ī
bà zâi iyà fārà shirìn bā dà ràncē ba.

Student response: In SarkĪ yā yàrda, ma'àikàcin Ma'aikatar
Cìnikī dà Sana'ō'Ī zâi iyà fārà shirìn bā
dà ràncē.

1. Ma'àikàcī bà zâi bayyànā wà SarkĪ shirìn bā dà ràncē ba. Sabō dà
hakà bà zâi iyà gànēwā ba. gànē v.intr./tr. 'understand'

2. Ma'àikàcī bà zâi bā nì ràncē ba. Sabō dà hakà bà zân k̃aru ba.

3. Mài sàna'àr bà zâi ajìyè lìttàttàfan lissāfī ba. Sabō dà hakà bà
zā mù iyà bā shì ràncē ba.

4. Makèrī bà zâi tàfi yà sàyi gawàyī ba. Sabō dà hakà bà zâi gamà
gyāran mōtàrmù kàfin k̃arfè ukù ba.

5. Àlk̃àlī bà zâi yardam mìnì ìn jē gidā ìn d̃aukō kud̃ìnā ba. Sabō dà
hakà bà zân iyà biyā tàrātā ba.

6. Bàtūrè bà zâi gayà wà Sallamà kō dàgà ìnā ya kè ba. Sabō dà hakà
bà zâi iyà ganin SarkĪ ba.

7. Bà zā sù karàntà jàrĪdà ba. Sabō dà hakà bà sù sàmi làbārìn ba.

8. 'Yan makarantā bà zā sù yi nazàrī ba. Sabō dà hakà bà sù ci
jarràbàwā ba. ci jarràbàwā 'pass an examination'

9. Bà tà rufè tāgà ba. Sabō dà hakà k̃àrāwō yā shìga d̃àkì.

10. Mūsā dà Kànde bà zā sù bayyànā wà 'yan sàndā yaddà k̃àrāwō ya shiga
d̃àkìnsù ba. Sabō dà hakà 'yan sàndā bà zā su iyà kàmā k̃àrāwō ba.

Drill 7 - Answer the questions with the Hausa adjective equivalent of
the English cues as shown in the examples by replacing 'no, he/she/they
is/are ...' with the cue adjective in the blank.

Cue: rēdiyònkà sābō nè? (reconditioned = repaired)
'is your radio new?'

Student response: à'à, gyàrarrē nè 'no, it's a reconditioned one'

Cue: kā sàyi jàjàyen tàkalmā? (black)
'did you buy red sandals?'

Student response: à'à, bak̃àk̃ē nè 'no, they're black'

1. àkwai k̃anānàn duwàtsū à hanyà? 6. mōtàrsà sàtacciyā cè? (bought)
(big)
7. yàransà gàjèrū nè? (tall)
2. Bàtūrè dōgō nè? (short)
8. inà tsàmmānī buhunàn nan k̃àttĪ
3. àlkyabbàrkà farā cè? (black) nè? (small)
4. gidankà sābō nè? (old)
9. tàkalmànkà bak̃àk̃ē nè? (red)
5. fìrijìŋkà k̃aramĪ nè? (huge) 10. wannàn lìttāfī sābō nè? (well
fìrijĪ n.m. 'refrigerator' known ≡ known, past participle
of sanĪ)

320

Drill 8 - Answer the question har nawà a kè iyà bā dà rànce? by inserting the number below into the pattern sentence anā iyà bayârwā kadan dà dà yawā, àmmā bā yā wuce (number).

Cue: har nawà a kè iyà bayârwā? (₦3000)

Student response: anā iyà bayârwā kadan dà dà yawā,
                        àmmā bā yā wuce Nairà dubū ukù

1. ₦2000   3. ₦3500   5. ₦4600   7. ₦7000   9. ₦1000
2. ₦6000   4. ₦8200   6. ₦9100   8. ₦2400   10. ₦1500

Drill 9 - Join the pairs of sentences below into one complex sentence that joins the two clauses (formerly sentences) with tun dà as shown in the example.

Cue: Mutànen SarkT zā sù iyà kiyâyè lìttàttàfan
                  lissāfī. Ma'àikàcin Ma'aikatar CìnikT dà
                  Sana'ō'T zâi kōyā musù.

Student response: Mutànen SarkT zā sù iyà kiyâyè lìttàttàfan
                  lissāfī tun dà ma'àikàcin Ma'aikatar CìnikT
                  dà Sana'ō'T zâi kōyā musù.

1. Tūrāwā zā sù iyà màganā dà Hausa. Mālàm Isa zâi kōyā musù.

2. Zā tà iyà ganinkà. Zā mù kai tà wurinkà gòbe.

3. Zā mù iyà tàfiyā Kanò gòbe. MàkānTkT yā gyàrà mōtàrmù yâu.

4. Zân iyà tafiyad dà sàna'àtā. Ùbānā yā nūnā minì yaddà a kè yî.

5. Ùmarù zâi iyà biyàn tàrarsà. AlkalT yā yardam masà yà jē gidansà yà dauko.

6. Isa zâi iyà kàràtū dà rùbùtū. Zā à kōyā masà à makarantar nàsàriyyà.

7. Yâranmù bà zā sù mântā dà àl'àdàrmù ba. Zā mù àikē sù makarantar Muhàmmàdiyyà.

8. Isa yanà sôn makarantar Nàsàriyyà. Yanā yîn abūbuwā irī-irī à makarantàr nan.

9. Isa zâi dingà zuwā makarantar Muhàmmadiyyà. Àbîn dà ya kōyō zâi tàimàkē shì dūniyā dà làhirà.

10. Uwargidā zā tà shiryà àbinci. HàlImà tā sàyi àbincîn dà uwargidā ta cè ta kè sô.

Drill 10A - 10B - Cover up the answers on the right and as each English sentence is given, give the Hausa translation.

10A 1. I have already read that book | nā rigā nā karàntà littāfìn nan

2. I have already started reading | nā rigā nā fàrà kàràtū

3. Jakadiya has already brought the burnous | Jakàdìyā tā rigà tā kāwō àlkyabbà

4. Isa has already gone to school | Isa yā rigà yā tàfi makarantā

5. we have already started slate school | mun rigā mun fàrà makarantar àllō

321

6. when he comes, we will have
   already eaten dinner

   in yā zō, zā mù rigā mù ci àbinci

7. when he comes, Isa will have
   already finished studying

   in yā zō, Īsa zâi rigā yà gamà nazàrī

8. when he comes, the Emir will
   have already put on a burnous

   in yā zǫ, Sarkī zâi rigā yà sâ àlkyabbā

9. I should have already
   finished studying

   yā kàmātà ìn rigā ìn gamà nazàrī

10. he should have already fixed
    the car

    yā kàmātà yà rigā yà gyārà mōtā

10B If your informant prefers to repeat the negative after <u>rigā</u>, change the
Hausa sentences accordingly.

1. I haven't read the book yet

   bàn rigā nā karàntà littāfìn nan ba

2. I haven't started reading yet

   bàn rigā nā fārà kàrātū ba

3. Jakadiya hasn't brought the
   burnous yet

   Jàkādìyā bà tà rigā tā kāwō àlkyabbā ba

4. Isa hasn't yet gone to school

   Isa bài rigā yā tàfi makarantā ba

5. we haven't yet started slate
   school

   bà mù rigā mun fārà makarantar àllō ba

<u>Drill 11A - 11B</u> - Cover up the answers on the right and as each English
sentence is given, give the Hausa translation. <u>In</u> and <u>ìdan</u> are interchangeable in all the Hausa sentences.

11A 1. if you want, I'll help you

    in kanā sô, zân tàimàkē kà

2. if it's expensive, don't buy it

   in yanā dà tsàdā, kadà kà sàyā

3. if it rains, we can't go

   in an yi ruwā, bà zā mù iyà zuwā ba

4. if the plan makes sense, I'll
   agree

   in shirī yanā dà mà'ànā, zân yàrda

5. what will I do if he doesn't come

   mè zân yi in bài zō ba

6. I'll put on the black burnous
   if the European comes

   zân sâ baƙar àlkyabbā in Bàtūrè
   yā zo

7. he'll forget our customs if he
   goes to the Christian school

   zâi mântā dà àl'àdàrmù in yā tàfi
   makarantar nàsàriyyā

8. call the police if you have
   been robbed

   kù kirāwǫ 'yan sàndā in an yī
   mukù sātā

11B 1. when I get back I'll see him

    in nā dāwō, zân gan shì

2. when Jakadiya brings the burnous,
   call the European

   in Jàkādìyā tā kāwō àlkyabbā, kà
   kirāwō Bàtūrè

3. when Isa goes to school, he'll
   take his money

   in Īsa yā tàfi makarantā, zâi
   kai kuɗinsà

4. when a thief robs you, call
   the police

   in ɓàrāwǒ yā yi makà sātā, kà
   kirāwō 'yan sàndā

322

5. I'll help them when I'm informed	zân tàimàkē sù in an sanad dà nī
6. I'll start selling another cigaret when I finish selling these	zân fārà sai dà wata tābà in nā ƙārè sai dà wannàn
7. Mamman will take the parents' "greetings" when his boss gives him the money	Mamman zâi kai gaisuwar iyàyē in mài gidansà yā bā shì kuɗī
8. the thief will bring a knife when he returns	ɓàrāwò zâi kāwō wuƙā in yā kōmō

Drill 12A - 12B - Cover up the answers on the right and as each English sentence is given, give the Hausa translation. The word <u>tun</u> alone followed by a noun cue can be used in the same way as English 'since' in time expressions. <u>Tun dà</u> or <u>tun dà ya kè</u> (with virtually identical meanings) is used as a conjunction meaning 'since'. Note that in 12B, whereas the "since" clause in English preferably comes at the end, it preferably comes at the beginning in Hausa, though <u>tun</u> used as a preposition in time expressions commonly comes at the end as in 12A.

12A	1. he's been working since yesterday	yanà aikī tun jiyà
	2. since that time I haven't seen him	tun lōkàcîn nan bàn gan shì ba
	3. since when have you known this?	tun yàushè ka san wannàn?
	4. he hasn't come to the chief's palace since Monday	bài zō fādàr SarkT tun ran Littìnîn ba
	5. has it rained since last month?	an yi ruwā tun watàn jiyà?
	6. it's been raining since last month	anà ruwā tun watàn jiyà
	7. there's been a drought since last month	anà farī tun watàn jiyà
	8. he's spoken Hausa since 1950	yā iyà Hausa tun alīf ɗarī tarà dà hàmsin
12B	1. they went to Kàtsinà since they got work	tun dà sukà sàmi aikī, sun tàfi Kàtsinà
	2. they came to the chief's palace since they were called	tun dà akà kirā sù sun zō fādàr SarkT
	3. we haven't seen him since we started work	tun dà mukà fārà aikī bà mù gan shì ba
	4. he can't start today since he didn't bring his money	tun dà bài kāwō kuɗinsà ba, bài iyà fārāwā yâu ba
	5. he can start today since he brought his money	tun dà ya kāwō kuɗinsà, yā iyà fārāwā yâu
	6. the thief wasn't hurt since he spread a blanket over the bottles	tun dà ɓàrāwò ya bazà bàrgō à kàn kwalàbên, bài yi ràunī ba
	7. since I didn't know anyone there I went home	tun dà bàn san kōwā à can ba, nā tàfi gidā
	8. since I don't smoke, I don't cough	tun dà bā nà shàn tābà, bā nà tàrī

323

Drill 13 - This drill is meant to reinforce the way the kō- forms of 20.2 and the duk(à) forms of 22.4 are related. Link the two cue sentences by making the kō- form the antecedent of a relative clause. However, remember that kō- forms themselves cannot be modified by relative clauses and must be replaced by a relative clause containing duk(à). As was pointed out in 22.4, the position of duk(à) in the clause is fairly free. For uniformity, in this drill use duk at the beginning of the clause in each case.

Cue:	Nā ji kōmē. Sun fàɗi kōmē. 'I heard everything. They told everything.'
Student response:	Nā ji duk àbîn dà sukà fàɗā. 'I heard everything that they told.'
Cue:	Nā gan shì kō'ìnā. Nā jē kō'ìnā. 'I saw him everywhere. I went everywhere.'
Student response:	Nā gan shì duk indà na jē. 'I saw him everywhere that I went.'
Cue:	Kōwā yā dākàtā. Kōwā yā zō wurin SarkĪ. 'Everyone waited. Everyone came to the Emir's place.'
Student response:	Duk wândà ya zō wurin SarkĪ yā dākàtā. 'Everyone who came to the Emir's place waited.'

1. Munā̀ zuwā̀ kōyàushē. Kōyàushē mu kè̀ ganinsà.

2. Kin sàyi kōmē? Kōmē yanā̀ kàntĪ.

3. Wànnan shirĪ zâi kyautàtà kōwàcè sàna'ā̀. Kōwàcè sàna'ā̀ tanā̀ sôn tàimakō.

4. Zā à bā dà tàimakôn kō'ìnā. Anā̀ bùkatàrsà kō'ìnā.

5. Kà gwadà kōwànè ìngarmā̀. Kōwànè ìngarmā̀ yanā̀ dà hàlā̀mun gudū̀.

6. 'Yan sàndā sun tàmbàyi kōwā. Kōwā yanā̀ wurin sātā̀.

7. Yā kàmàtā ìn dākàtā kōyàushē. Inā̀ zuwā̀ fàdàr SarkĪ kōyàushē.

8. Ɓàrāwò yā sàci kōmē. Kōmē yanā̀ cikin àkwàtì.

9. Īsa yā kàwō kuɗĪ kōwàcè Lārabā̀. Yā zō makarantā kōwàcè Lārabā̀.

10. An bā kōwā ràncē. Kōwā yā iyà ajìyè littāfìn lissāfĪ.

11. Àkwai 'yan sàndā kō'ìnā. Munā̀ sô mù ɓuya kō'ìnā. Ɓuya v.intr. 'hide'

12. Kā sai dà kōmē. An bā kà kōmē.

Drill 14A - 14C - Repeat the initial sentence, then substitute the first cue into the appropriate place in that sentence. As each cue is given, substitute it into the sentence formed from the previous cue so that a new sentence is formed.

14A Initial sentence: yā shìga

Cues	Student response
1. Sallamà	Sallamà yā shìga
2. rìke dà takàrdā	Sallamà yā shìga rìke dà takàrdā

3. sáƙō n.m. 'message'   Sallamà yā shìga rìƙe dà sáƙō
4. tākalmà   Sallamà yā shìga rìƙe dà tākalmà
5. Jàkādìyā   Jàkādìyā tā shìga rìƙe dà tākalmà
6. jājàyē   Jàkādìyā tā shìga rìƙe dà jājàyen tākalmà
7. sábàbbī   Jàkādìyā tā shìga rìƙe dà sábàbbin tākalmà
8. ɗauke dà   Jàkādìyā tā shìga ɗauke dà sábàbbin tākalmà
9. àlkyabbà   Jàkādìyā tā shìga ɗauke dà (sābuwar) àlkyabbà
10. baƙā   Jàkādìyā tā shìga ɗauke dà baƙar àklyabbà

14B Initial sentence: bà à gayà wà Sarkī ba
1. masà   bà à gayà masà ba
2. minì   bà à gayà minì ba
3. bayyànā   bà à bayyànā minì ba
4. sanad dà   bà à sanad dà nī ba

5. completive
   affirmative   an sanad dà nī
6. an sākè   an sākè sanad dà nī
7. an riƙà   an riƙà sanad dà nī
8. an rigā   an rigā an sanad dà nī
9. jiyà mā   jiyà mā an rigā an sanad dà nī
10. dâ mā   dâ mā an rigā an sanad dà nī

14C Initial sentence: sun ƙàru
1. mutānē   mutānē sun ƙàru
2. mãsu sàna'à   mãsu sàna'à sun ƙàru
3. sāmi kuɗī   mãsu sàna'à sun sāmi kuɗī
4. kyàutā   mãsu sàna'à sun sāmi kyàutā
5. ràncē   mãsu sàna'à sun sāmi ràncē
6. future aspect   mãsu sàna'à zā sù sāmi ràncē
7. in sun tàmbàyē mù   mãsu sàna'à zā sù sāmi ràncē in sun tàmbàyē mù
8. in sun kiyàyè   mãsu sàna'à zā sù sāmi ràncē in sun kiyàyè
   lìttàttàfan lissāfī   lìttàttàfan lissāfī
9. iyà kiyàyè   mãsu sàna'à zā sù sāmi ràncē in sun iyà kiyàyè
                             lìttàttàfan lissāfī
10. dà a kē bukātà   mãsu sàna'à zā sù sāmi ràncē in sun iyà kiyàyè
                             lìttàttàfan lissāfìn dà a kē bukātà

325

GUIDED CONVERSATION

1) Discuss some aspect of having to wait somewhere for something. Suggestions are waiting in a line for school registration, at the Post Office, at the movies (sìnìmā), etc.; being caught in a traffic jam or being delayed by heavy traffic; waiting in an office to see a doctor, a dentist, an important official of some kind. You might wish to discuss reasons for the delay and inconveniences it caused you.

Vocabulary: jērī m.sg./pl.   'line (of people)'
sun yi jērī   'they formed a line'

tàflye-tàflyē, 'traffic'
mōtōcī dà yawà sukà wucè à hanyà
'the traffic on the road was heavy'

Example dialogue:

Student 1: Jiyà nā jē wajen likità.   Yesterday I went to the doctor's.

Student 2: Ap! Mè ya sàmē kà.   Oh? What was the matter?

1: Nā jē à dūbà lāfiyàtā kurùm.   I just went for a check up (that
Duk dà hakà, bā lābārī mài dādī.   one might examine my health).
                                         Nevertheless, it was unpleasant
                                         (there was no news of pleasant-
                                         ness).

Ai dà na ìsa can, an cê ìn   Well when I got there, I was
dākàtā kàɗan. Nā dākàtā, nā   told to wait a little. I
dākàtā, bà à kirā nì ba.   waited and waited and wasn't
                                         called.

2: Kā sàmi shìgā?   Did you ever get in (gain entrance)?

1: Ī, àmmā sai dà na dākàtā mintī   Yes, but (not) until I had waited
àrbà'in dà bìyar.   45 minutes.

2: Ai hàƙurī shī nē biyàn bùkàtā.   Well, patience will take care of
                                         one's needs (patience is "paying"
                                         of needs).

2) Have one student play the role of someone interviewing an official in business or government, or alternatively, have two or more students discuss such an interview that may have taken place. Some possibilities are discussion of wage increases or other benefits with a company official; carrying a complaint to a business official about the conduct of his business; carrying a petition to the Governor or other government official covering some issue of current interest.

Vocabulary: gwamnà n.m.   'governor'

mài gidā   "the boss"

sakatarè n.m./f.'secretary' (either government official
                                 or typist)

shugàbā n.m.   'leader, director, head'
(shùgàbànnī pl.)

In the following example, Malam Tanko, a civil servant in Agadez, Niger, enters the Post Master's office of get an explanation of a mysterious charge on a package he has just picked up.

326

Tankò:	Inā kwānā.	Good morning.
Shùgàban Gidan Wayà:	Lāfiyā lau. Àkwai tàimakō dà zân yī makà nē?	Good morning. Is there some way I can help you?
Tankò:	Inā sô kà yī minì bàyānī à kân wannàn kuɗī dalā sìttin[1] dà zân biyā kāfin ìn kàrɓi ɗan ƙunshìn nân.	I want you to explain to me this charge of 300 francs that I have to pay before receiving this little package.
SGW:	Bàri ìn ga rìsītìnkà.[2]	Let me see your receipt.
Tankò:	Gā shi nân.	Here it is.
SGW:	Kā gānè cêwaɲ ƙunshìn nân yā yi wajen mākò bìyar à nân. Wàtồ, bāyan ƙunshī yā yi mākò biyu, zā à biyā dalā àshìrin à mākò.	You understand that this package has been here about five weeks. That is, after a package is here two weeks, one pays 100 francs a week.
Tankò:	Sai jiyà akà sanar dà nī cêwan inā dà ƙunshī à nân!	Only yesterday was I informed that I had a package here!
SGW:	Zā mù yi bìncìkē.	We'll look into it.

[1] In Niger, the currency is the CFA franc. The word dalā means "five francs" and is the unit used in Hausa, rather than the franc. Hence, dalā sittin is '300 CFA francs' (5 X 60 = 300), and so forth.

[2] rìsītì n.m. 'receipt'

DIALOGUES

A. Kande's mother has sent her to the market to buy corn and some other food-
stuffs for the evening's meal. About two hours after having left, Kande
enters the house. Her mother, who is holding one child and stirring a
pot of soup, accosts her.

Uwargidā:	Kandè, yànzu kikà dāwō? Bàn gayā mikì kì dāwō maza-maza ba?	Kande, is it just now that you have returned? Didn't I tell you to come back in a hurry?
Kànde:	Gā àbîn dà na sayō mikì.	Here's what I bought for you.
Uwargidā:	Mēnē nē wannàn ƙunshī?	What's that package?
Kànde:	Shìnkàfā cè.	It's rice.
Uwargidā:	Bā nā cē kì sayō masàrā ba?	Didn't I say for you to buy corn?
Kànde:	Ai, bābù masàrā à kàsuwā yâu. Kin sạn dà ƙarancin masàrā dà kākā. Don hakà na sayō shìnkāfā.	There isn't any corn at the market now. You know there's a shortage of corn at harvest time. That's why I bought rice.
Uwargidā:	Wannàn bā daidai ba nē. Kin san ùbankì yā fi sôn tuwon masàrā.	That's not good. You know your father prefers corn tuwo.
Kànde:	A ganīnā tuwon shìnkāfā yā fi tuwon masàrā dādī.	In my opinion rice tuwo is better than corn tuwo (rice tuwo exceeds corn tuwo in pleasure).
Uwargidā:	Wātau don hakà kikà ̣sàyi shìnkāfā. Kē dai bā ki dà mammōrā. Nā àikē kì kì sayō masàrā kikà sayō shìnkāfā.	So that's why you bought rice. You are really worthless (you haven't any usefulness). I sent you to buy corn and you bought rice.
Kànde:	Dà in dāwō hannū banzā, nā ga yā kàmātà ̣in sayō makì shìnkāfā. Tô, in kin yi fushī nē, Allāh yà bā kì haƙurī.	Rather than come home (rather than I come back) empty-handed, I saw that I should buy rice. OK, if you get mad, may God give you patience.
Uwargidā:	Tô, kì tattàrà waɗànnân tukwānē kì wankè su. Kumā kì ɗauki ƙanènkì kì yi wāsā dà shī.	All right, gather up these pots and wash them. And take your little brother and play with him.

Vocabulary

banzā n.f.   'nothing, worthlessness'

hannu banzā   'empty-handed'

dà (followed by subjunctive) 'rather than'

dādī n.m.   'physical or spiritual pleasure, pleasure derived from taste or smell'

daidai   'correct, just right'

fushī n.m.   'anger'

ganī n.m. (in this dialogue) 'opinion'

kākā n.f.   'harvest time'

ƙanè n.m.   'younger brother' (ƙânnē pl.)

329

23.1   Intensified Adverbs; Weakened Adjectives

A common process used in Hausa to change the meaning of a word in some way is "reduplication", that is, doubling a word or part of a word. Several types of reduplication will be discussed in this and the follow-ing grammar sections.

a) <u>Adverbs</u> - Adverbs can be completely reduplicated (the whole word is repeated twice) to intensify its meaning. Some examples are

kàɗan	'a little'	kàɗan-kàɗan	'a very little, a tiny bit'
kullum	'always'	kullum-kullum	'unfailingly'
maza	'quickly'	maza-maza	'very quickly'
sànnu	'slowly, carefully'	sànnu-sànnu	'very slowly, carefully'
yànzu	'now'	yànzu-yànzu	'this very minute'

One example of an intensified adverb is found in this unit. This and other examples in sentences are

bàn gayà mikì kì dāwō maza-maza ba?	'didn't I tell you to come back right away?'
yanā̀ tàfiyā̀ sànnu-sànnu	'he's going slowly along'
yànzu-yànzu sukà dāwō	'just this minute they got back'

b) <u>Adjectives</u> - Although reduplication of adverbs intensifies their mean-ing, reduplication of adjectives <u>weakens</u> their meaning. Reduplication of adjectives commonly occurs with adjectives denoting colors and might be said to correspond to "-ish" added to adjectives in English, for example 'blackish'. Reduplicated adjectives <u>can only follow the nouns they modify</u>.

baƙī̀	'black(m)'	baƙi-baƙi ⎱	'blackish, dark blue or green'
baƙā̀	'black(f)'	baƙa-baƙa ⎰	
jā̀	'red'	jā̀-ja-jā̀-ja	'reddish'
gā̀ kàzā baƙa-baƙa		'here's a dark-colored hen'

This type of reduplication can also be used with the same effect of weakening with those nouns which we have been calling "quality nouns".

sanyī̀	'coldness'	sanyi-sanyi	'somewhat cold'
girmā̀	'bigness'	girma-girma	'fairly big'
saurī̀	'speed'	sauri-sauri	'fairly quick'
zāfī̀	'heat'	zāfi-zāfi	'fairly hot'
ruwā̀ yā̀ yi zāfi-zāfi		'the water is fairly hot'

Note that the final vowel of each half of the reduplication is short-ened (except for the first half of <u>jā̀</u> 'red').

23.2   Intensified Verbs and Nouns

Another type of reduplication is the doubling of a single syllable. This type of reduplication is used with many verbs and some nouns for intensification. Most commonly the first syllable is reduplicated and

only this process will be described, though reduplication of the second
syllable follows essentially the same pattern.

Reduplication of the first syllable involves taking the first consonant and vowel (or diphthong ai or au) and the consonant following the
first vowel and doubling them. Thus, in reduplicating kāmā 'catch', we
take kām- and double it, giving kankāmā   To reduplicate tàmbayā 'ask',
we take tam- and double it, giving tàntàmbayā. The consonant at the end
of this doubled syllable will undergo changes depending on what it is
and what the consonant which will follow it is:

t,d,ɗ,s,sh,z,j,c,ts,r,l (that is, all dental and palatal consonants except n) become r.

fìta	'go out'	fìt + fìta	becomes fìrfìta
fādà	'fall down'	fāɗ + fādà	becomes farfàdà
gusà	'move aside'	gus + gusà	becomes gurgùsā

m and n become m before labial consonants (f,b,ɓ,m), ŋ (the sound -ng
in 'sing') before velar consonants (k,ƙ,g), and n before other consonants.

tàmbayā	'ask'	tàm + tàmbayā	becomes tàntàmbayā
kāmā	'catch'	kām + kāmā	becomes kaŋkāmā
			(written kankāmā)
zaunā	'sit down'	zaun + zaunā	becomes zanzàunā

All other consonants become the same as the following consonant. Also,
all the dental, palatal, and velar consonants can optionally become the
same as the following consonant.

shigō	'come in'	shig + shigō	becomes shisshigō
àikā	'send'	àik + àikā	becomes à''aikà

(Remember that all words written with an initial vowel actually begin
with a glottal stop and this glottal stop serves as a consonant in
reduplicatives.)

zàɓā	'choose'	zàɓ + zàɓā	becomes zàzzàɓā
fìta	'go out'	fìt + fìta	becomes either fìrfìta
			or fìffìta
zaunà	'sit down'	zaun + zaunà	becomes either zanzàunā
			or zazzàunā

Note that in the reduplicated syllable, if the original vowel was long,
it becomes short, and if it was a diphthong it becomes -a-.

a) Verbs - Depending on the verb and on the context, reduplicated verbs
   can have the meaning "do the action repeatedly", "do the action to
   several objects of the same kind", or "several people or things do the
   action". One further thing should be noted about the tones of reduplicated verbs: a variable vowel verb which undergoes reduplication remains a variable vowel verb, and a verb which was not does not become
   a variable vowel verb. Thus, for two syllable variable vowel verbs,
   the reduplicated counterpart has the tones low-high-low (since all
   variable vowel verbs begin on a low tone syllable):

333

záɓā	'choose'	becomes	zàzzáɓà
àikā	'send'	becomes	à''aikà

Two syllable verbs with the tone pattern high-low have reduplicated counterparts with the tone pattern high-low-high:

gusà	'move aside'	becomes	gurgùsā
tàrà	'gather'	becomes	tattàrā

All other verbs (monosyllabic, three syllable, and two syllable verbs not covered immediately above) add a reduplicated syllable of the same tone as the original first syllable of the verb:

fìta	'go out'	becomes	fìrfìta

(This is not a variable vowel verb since it is not transitive.)

tàmbayà	'ask'	becomes	tàntàmbayà
gangàrā	'descend'	becomes	gangangàrā

Some examples of reduplicated verbs used in sentences are

kì tattàrà wadànnân tukwānē	'gather up these pots'
yā tàntàmbàyi mutānē	'he (went about) asking people'
kū yârā, kù gurgùsā dàgà nân!	'you kids, get away from here!'
an jèjjèfē shì dà duwâtsū	'he was hailed with stones'

b) <u>Nouns</u> - This type of reduplication is much less commonly found with nouns that with verbs. One group of nouns where reduplicated forms are used is the group of nouns indicating times of day:

sāfe	'morning'	becomes	sassāfe	'very early in the morning'
dare	'night'	becomes	dàddare	'late at night'

yā dāwō gidā dà dàddare	'he came home late at night'

23.3 Imperatives of Three-Syllable Verbs*

a) <u>Variable vowel verbs</u> - When <u>not followed by an object</u> or when followed by a noun object, three-syllable variable vowel verbs have the tone pattern low-low-high and end in <u>-i</u>.

tàmbàyi mutānē!	'ask the people!'
tàmbàyi!	'ask!'

When followed by a <u>pronoun direct object</u>, the pattern is all low with the final vowel short <u>-è</u>.

tàmbàyè ta!	'ask her!'

When followed by an <u>indirect object</u>, the pattern is low-low-high with the ending <u>-ar</u> (which usually becomes <u>-am</u> before the indirect object pronouns).

*There is some dialectal variation. If you find that your informant disagrees with the forms given here, change them accordingly.

334

tàmbàyam mìnì làbārī!　　　'ask about the news for me!'

b) **All other verbs** - When followed by a noun object, verbs other than
-o verbs (20.4) and causative verbs have all low tone. -o verbs
and causative verbs have low-low-high.

àjìyè ƙanènkì!　　　　'put down your little brother!'

kàràntà takàrdā!　　　'read the paper!'

kàkkàwō tukwànē!　　　'bring me (a number of) pots!'

fìrfìtad dà kāyā!　　　'bring the loads out (one by one)!'

In all other cases (when not followed by an object, when followed by
a pronoun object, or when followed by an indirect object) the tone
pattern is low-low-high. Remember, pronoun direct objects have high
tone following all imperatives of verbs with basic high tone.

àjìyē shi!　　　　　　'put him down!'

kàràntā mìnì takàrdā!　　'read me the paper!'

23.4 More on Comparison

In the previous section on comparison (19.4), the way one says
'better than', 'more than', 'does more' was explained. We have not explained how to express the notion expressed in English by a comparative
adjective followed by **than** as in 'John is **bigger than** Bill', 'this is
sweeter than that', etc. This is done very simply by using **fi** 'surpass'
in a sentence of the form 'X surpasses Y (with respect to) quality'.

tuwon shìnkàfā yā fi tuwon
masàrā dādī
'rice **tuwo** tastes better than
corn **tuwo** (surpasses corn **tuwo**
with respect to pleasantness)'

wannàn yā fi wancàn tsādā
'this one is more expensive than
that one'

Àli yā fi Garbà ƙarfī
'Ali is stronger than Garba'

To express the English superlative, the word **saurā** 'remainder' can
be used.

waŋnàn rēdiyō yā fi saurā
tsādā
'this radio is the most expensive'

Kànde tā fi sauran 'yam
mātā kyâu
'Kande is the prettiest girl'

The word **gà** 'with respect to' (see 15.6) can optionally be placed
before the quality noun in such sentences. If the quality noun is to be
put at the beginning of the sentence for emphasis, **gà** must be used.

Kànde tā fi Aishà gà ƙibà
'Kande is fatter than Aisha'

yā fī nì gà gudù
'he runs faster than me'

gà gudù ya fī nì
'he <u>runs</u> faster than me'

23.5 Using the Negative **bà ... ba** with a Whole Sentence

On occasion, **bà ... ba**, which is normally used as a negative with
nē/cē, may be put around a whole sentence instead of the normal negative

335

form of the aspect being used. This type of negative has the meaning 'it's not the case that ... ', or in questions, 'isn't it true that ...?', 'isn't it the case that ...?'.

bà nā cê kì sayō masàrā ba? — 'isn't it so that I told you to buy corn?'

bà yanā̀ zuwā̀ ba — 'it's not the case that he's coming'

If some element is placed at the beginning of a sentence for emphasis, this is the only way such a sentence can be made negative.

bà masàrā̀ kikà sayō ba — 'it wasn't corn that you bought'

bà kullum a kè̀ kwānā̀ à gadō ba — Proverb: "nobody can expect an unbroken run of good luck" (lit: 'it isn't always that one passes the night in a bed' - some nights he may have to sleep on the ground)

23.6 dà Followed by Subjunctive: 'rather than'

The word dà followed by a sentence in the subjunctive aspect may mean 'rather than'.

dà ìn dāwō hannū banzā, nā sayō shìnkāfā — 'rather than come back empty-handed, I bought rice'

sun fi sô sù zaunā à gidansù dà sù zō gidanmù — 'they prefer sitting at home to coming to our house' ('they like better that they sit at their house rather than that they come to our house')

23.7 wannàn, etc. Following the Noun they Modify

In all previous cases we have seen that the demonstratives wannàn, wancàn, etc. preceded the nouns they modified. Less commonly, but with no difference in meaning, they may follow the noun.

kì yankà kuɓèwā waccàn — 'cut up that okra'

GRAMMATICAL DRILLS

Drill 1 - Using the words in parentheses below, construct sentences which have intensified adverbs as shown in the example.

Cue: yanā̀ jîn Tūrancī? (kàɗan)

Student response: Ī, yanā̀ jîn Tūrancī kàɗan-kàɗan

1. sunā̀ tàfiyā̀ masallācī? (kullum)
2. tā dāwō dàgà kàsuwā? (maza-maza)
3. Adèbāyò yā iyà Hausa? (kàɗan)
4. yā kàmātà sù bi wannàn hanyā̀? (sànnu)
5. zā mù kōmō jībi? (jībi)
6. gàra sù zō (yànzu)
7. zā à fìta yâu? (yâu)
8. Ɓarāwô yā shìga ɗākìn? (sànnu)
9. yā̂rā sun kōri awākī? (maza)
10. kin wankè tukwānē? (yànzu)

336

Drill 2 - Answer the questions below affirmatively so that the answer
contains a reduplicated form of the verb used in the question. Noun objects that appear in the questions should be replaced with the appropriate pronoun.

Cue: tā aìkā̀ dà rīgunànmù?
                      aikā (dà) v.intr. 'send (a thing)'

Student response: T, tā a''àikā dà sū

1. kun dāwō dà wurT?   6. yā dàuki kāyā dà yawā̀?
2. tā cē̂ kù zaunà̀?   7. sun nēmā à ōfìs?
3. an fadà̀ mikì?   8. tā tàmbayà̀?
4. an fitad dà shānū?   9. kā sàyā̀?
5. kā dūbà makarantā sōsai?   10. Kànde tā shiryā̀ dà kyâu?

Drill 3 - Change the sentences to imperatives by dropping the yā̀ kàmātà̀
and the first person singular pronoun and changing the tones of the verbs
as necessary. Retain the objects as they are in the cues.

Cue: yā kàmātà̀ ìn ajìyè kāyan nàn

Student response: àjìyè kāyan nàn

1. yā kàmātà̀ ìn dākàtā   6. yā kàmātà̀ ìn rubūtā shi
2. yā kàmātà̀ ìn ƙētàrè kōgT   7. yā kàmātà̀ ìn jarràbā ta
3. yā kàmātà̀ ìn kiyàyè littāfìn 8. yā kàmātà̀ ìn tsallàkà katangā̀
   lissāfT   9. yā kàmātà̀ ìn ajìyē su
4. yā kàmātà̀ ìn bayyànā masà
                                  10. yā kàmātà̀ ìn kyautàtà sàna'àtā̀
4. yā kàmātà̀ ìn karàntā wà yā̂ıā

Drill 4 - Form sentences containing the comparative structure X tā/yā̀/sun
fi Y (quality noun) by answering the question waccē/wànnē/wàdànnē ta/ya/
sukà fi (quality noun).

Cue: waccē ta fi tsàdā̀, hùlar Shēhù kō hùlar Mammàn

Student response: hùlar Shēhù tā fi hùlar Mammàn tsàdā̀

1. wànnē ya fi taurT, nāmàn àkwiyà̀ kō nāmàn tunkìyā̀?   taurT n.m. 'toughness'
2. waccē ta fi kyâu, yārinyàr nân kō yārinyàr cân?
3. wànnē ya fi nauyT, bùhun nàn kō bùhun càn?   nauyT n.m. 'heaviness'
4. wànnē ya fi ƙibà̀, Bàla kō Sulè?   ƙibà̀ n.f. 'fatness'
5. wànè àbinci ya fi dādī, wannàn kō wancàn?
6. wàcè fātà̀ ta fi taushT, wannàn kō wancàn?   fātà̀ n.m. 'hide, skin'
                                                taushT n.m. 'softness'
7. wàcè gwēbà̀ ta fi zāƙT, gwēbàr nân kō gwēbàr cân?   zāƙT n.m. 'sweetness'
8. wànnē ya fi ƙarfT, Īsa kō Àliyù?
9. wàcè rījìyā̀ ta fi zurfT rījìyar ƙauyènmù kō rījìyar gàrinsù?
10. wànnē ya fi saurT, jirgin samà̀ kō jirgin ƙasà̀?

337

Drill 10 - Place the direct object or "prepositional phrase" at the beginning of the sentence for emphasis. Remember that when this is done, the construction bā ... ba around the entire sentence is the only way that the sentence can be negated.

Cue: Kànde bà tà sàyi shìnkāfā ba

Student response: bā shìnkāfā Kànde ta sàyā ba

1. bàn bā sù kyàutā ba
2. bài shìga ta tāgà ba
3. bà zâi gwadà sābon ìngarmā ba
4. bā yā nazàrī
5. bà sù kirāwō dan sàndā ba

6. bā mā kwānā cikin dàkì
7. Mammàn bài àuri bùdurwā ba
8. bà zā à kyautàtà Kanānàn sana'ō'ī ba
9. bài kai gaisuwar iyāyē ba
10. Īsa bā yā kàrātū

Drill 11 - Change the questions by replacing the repeated noun by the appropriate independent possessive form.

Cue: wàccē ta fi tsādā, jàkar AmĪnà kō jàkar HàlĪmà?

Student response: wàccē ta fi tsādā, jàkar AmĪnà kō ta HàlĪmà?

1. wànnē ya fi taurī, wurin gōnar Shēhù kō wurin gōnar Mammàn?
2. wàccē ta fi kyâu, uwar Mammàn kō uwar Shēhù?
3. wànnē ya fi Karfī, dan Abdù kō dan Ùmarù?
4. wàccē ta fi Kibà, yārinyàr Īsa kō yārinyàrkà?
5. wàccē ta fi tsawō, dāminar Lēgàs kō dāminar Jàs?
6. wànnē ya fi dādī, àbincin uwarkì kō àbincīnā?
7. wàccē ta fi àràhā, jàkar Kànde kō jàkar HàlĪmà?
8. wàccē ta fi taushī, fātàr tākalmàn nân kō fātàr jàkar nàn?
9. wànnē ya fi sanyī, daren NĪjēriyà kō daren Rashà?
10. wàccē ta fi tsādā, wuKar Àbūbakàr kō wuKartà?
11. wànnē ya fi dādī, tuwon shìnkāfā kō tuwon masàrā?
12. wànnē ya fi nĪsā, gàrinkù kō gàrinsù?

Drill 12 - Using the cue sentences, form sentences on the pattern in kin yi fushī, Allāh yà bā kì hàKurī.

Cue: an cê minì HàlĪmà tā yi fushī

Student response: in tā yi fushī, Allāh yà bā tà hàKurī

1. an cê minì Mammàn yā yi fushī
2. an cê minì sun yi fushī
3. an cê minì an yi fushī
4. an cê minì kun yi fushī
5. an cê minì mài gidā yā yi fushī

6. an cê minì kà yi fushī
7. an cê minì ma'àikàtā sun yi fushī
8. an cê minì dan sàndā yā yi fushī
9. an cê minì uwargidā tā yi fushī
10. an cê minì an yi fushī

340

Drill 13 - Using the cue sentences below, form sentences on the pattern
kâi, nā àikē kì kì sayō masàrā kikà sayō shìnkāfā.

Cue: Kànde tā dāwō dàgà kàsuwā?

Student response: kâi, nā àikē tà tà sayō masàrā ta sayō
                    shìnkāfā

1. Mammàn dà Sulè sun dāwō dàgà   6. HàdTzà, kin dāwō dàgà kàsuwā?
   kàsuwā?   7. Tsa, kā dāwō dàgà kàsuwā?
2. HàlTmà tā dāwō dàgà kàsuwā?   8. su Audù sun dāwō dàgà kàsuwā?
3. kin dāwō dàgà kàsuwā?   9. Sàlisù dà Shēhù sun dāwō dàgà
4. Bàla yā dāwō dàgà kàsuwā?   kàsuwā?
5. kun dāwō dàgà kàsuwā?   10. Bintà tā dāwō dàgà kàsuwā?

Drill 14A - 14B - Cover up the answers on the right and as each English
sentence is given, give the Hausa translation. Words like 'very',
'right', etc. in 14A, and 'sort of', 'kind of', '-ish', etc. in 14B
indicate that a reduplicated form is called for.

4A 1. I understand Hausa a little bit | inà jîn Hausa kàɗan-kàɗan

   2. this very minute we've come back | yànzu-yànzu mukà dāwō

   3. he's always leaving his book at | kullum-kullum ya kè barìn
      home | lattāfìnsà à gidā

   4. finish the work very quickly | kù gamà aikī maza-maza

   5. he's going very slowly | yanà tàfiyà sànnu-sànnu

   6. here it is very close by | gà shi nân kusa-kusa

4B 1. he has a blackish horse | yanà dà dōkī bakì-bakì

   2. this meat is a little tough | nāmàn nân yanà dà tauri-tauri

   3. bring me that reddish pot | kàwō minì wannàn tukunyā jā-ja-jā-ja

   4. their house is fairly big | gidansù yanà dà girma-girma

   5. I prefer the whitish gown | nā fi sôn rīgā fara-fara

   6. the food is a little hot | àbinci yā yi zāfi-zāfi

Drill 15 - Cover up the answers on the right and as each English sentence
is given, give the Hausa translation. In each sentence, the second clause
begins with gàra 'it would be better that ...'.

1. rather than wait until tomorrow, | dà mù dākàtā har gòbe, gàra mù zō
   we had better come today | yâu

2. rather than send Kande, I had | dà ìn àiki Kànde, gàra ìn tàfi
   better go myself | dà kâinā

3. rather than go out the door, the | dà ɓarāwò yà fìta kòfà, gàra yà
   thief had better jump over the wall | tsallàkà katangā

4. rather than wear the burnous, I | dà ìn sâ àlkyabbà, gàra ìn sâ rīgā
   had better wear the gown |

5. rather than Isa forget their cus- | dà Isa yà màntā dà àlàdàrsù, gàra
   toms, his father had better take | bàbansà yà kai shì makarantar
   him to the Koranic school | Muhàmmàdiyyà

341

6. rather than finish selling the cigarets, he'd better smoke them all	dà yà ƙàrè sai dà tābà, gàra yà shā tà dukà
7. rather than sell this horse, I'd better buy another one	dà ìn sai dà dōkìn nân, gàra ìn sàyi wani
8. rather than lie, he'd better leave the room	dà yà yi ƙaryā, gàra yà bar ɗākì

Drill 16A - 16C - Repeat the initial sentence, then substitute the first cue into the appropriate place in that sentence. As each cue is given, substitute it into the sentence formed from the previous cue so that a new sentence is formed.

16A Initial sentence: tā dāwō

Cues	Student response
1. Kànde	Kànde tā dāwō
2. nā	nā dāwō
3. sayō hatsī	nā sayō hatsī
4. masàrā	nā sayō masàrā
5. shìnkāfā	nā sayō shìnkāfā
6. matà	nā sayō matà shìnkāfā
7. wà uwātā	nā sayō wà uwātā shìnkāfā
8. mikì	nā sayō mikì shìnkāfā
9. yā kàmātà	yā kàmātà ìn sayō mikì shìnkāfā
10. sun cê	sun cê (yā kàmātà) in sayō mikì shìnkāfā

16B Initial sentence: wànnē ya fi?

1. wàccē	wàccē ta fi?
2. tsàdā	wàccē ta fi tsàdā?
3. shìnkāfā tā fi	shìnkāfā ta fi tsàdā
4. tuwon shìnkāfā	tuwon shìnkāfā yā fi tsàdā
5. kyâu	tuwon shìnkāfā yā fi kyâu
6. dāɗī	tuwon shìnkāfā yā fi dāɗī
7. fi tuwon masàrā	tuwon shìnkāfā yā fi tuwon masàrā dāɗī
8. fi tuwon hatsī	tuwon shìnkāfā yā fi tuwon hatsī dāɗī
9. inà tsàmmānī	inà tsàmmānī tuwon shìnkāfā yā fi tuwon hatsī dāɗī
10. à ganīnā	à ganīnā tuwon shìnkāfā yā fi tuwon hatsī dāɗī

16C Initial sentence: Kànde tā dàmi uwargidā   dàmā (i/ē) v.tr. 'annoy'

1. sùrūtùn Kànde	sùrūtùn Kànde yā dàmi uwargidā
2. sùrūtùnkì	sùrūtùnkì yā dàmi uwargidā
3. dàmē nì	sùrūtùnkì yā dàmi nì
4. yā yi yawà	sùrūtùnkì yā yi yawà

5. aikìn nân   aikìn nân yā yi yawā
6. kyâu   aikìn nân yā yi kyâu
7. dācē dà kē   aikìn nân yā dācē dà kē
8. dācē dà yandà a kē   aikìn nân yā dācē dà yandà a kē sô
   sô
9. tuwon nàn   tuwon nàn yā dācē dà yandà a kē sô
10. miyàr nân   miyàr nân tā dācē dà yandà a kē sô
11. future aspect   miyàr nân zā tà dācē dà yandà a kē sô

GUIDED CONVERSATION

A. Discuss the generation gap. Your discussion may be between two members of the older generation discussing the younger generation, between two members of the younger generation, or between one member of each. Areas the discussion might center around are school curricula, dating practices, clothing and hair styles, political opinions, etc.

In the example dialogue, Ali has just asked his father for money for the third time in a week.

Bàba: KudˀT ka kē sô kumā! Mē ya sâ.   You want money again! What for?

Àli: Inā dà bùdurwā.   I have a girl friend.

Bàba: Kai, ɗan shēkarà nē, ka kē   You're a little kid (son of year)
       dà bùdurwā!   (and) you have a girl friend!

Àli: NT, yâu shēkarūnā tarà.   I'm now nine years old.

Bàba: NT, lōkàcîn dà ni kē shēkarà   When I was nine years old, I
       tarà, bàn san wani àbù wai   didn't (even) know what a girl
       bùdurwā ba.   friend was (something called
                                         "girl friend").

Àli: Yànzu lōkàcT yā sākē.   Times have changed.

Bàba: Kū dai yāran zāmànT, kōmē   You kids of today, everything
       nàkù dàban nē.   of yours is different.

Àli: Hakà ne. Màganàrmù mā dàban   That's right. Even our speech
       dà tàkù.   is different from yours.

Bàba: Kū dai, bà kù tàfasà ba,   Well, I think you are trying to
       kun ƙōnē.   get too big for your britches.
                                         (Proverb: "You've burned before
                                         you even started boiling.")

B. Discuss food preparation along the lines illustrated in the example dialogue and using the supplementary vocabulary (as has been the usual practice in Guided Conversation, establish the situation beforehand). An alternative would be to discuss some specific meal which you intended to prepare but which failed or was a great success in some way, for example, the meat burned, no one came, everybody thought it was great, etc.

        girkà v.tr.   'prepare for cooking'

343

dafà	v.tr.	'cook' (general term)	

```
dafā    v.tr.           'cook' (general term)          ┐ All require some
sōyā    v.tr.           'fry something in its own juice'│ sort of pot as op-
tā sōyà àlbasā          'she fried the onions'          │ posed to gasā where
                                                        │ the meat or other
tōyā    v.tr.           'fry in oil'                    │ food is in direct
tā tōya nāmā            'she fried the meat'            ┘ contact with the fire

gasā    v.tr.           'roast, grill'
tā gasa nāmā            'she grilled the meat'

fērē    v.tr.           'peel, strip of skin or hide'
tā fēre dànkalT         'she peeled potatoes'

rēḍè    v.tr.           'pare'
tā rēḍè karàs           'she pared the carrots'

tūṛā    v.tr.           'stir (something thick)'

làntirkì  n.m.          'electricity'

iskā    n.m./f.         'gas'
```

Example conversation: Yahaya, whom we met in Unit VI, has, after 17 units, managed to return from the market. Uwargida puts him to work.

Uwargidā:	Yàhàya, zā mù yi bākT huḍu dà yâmma.	Yahaya, we will have four guests this evening.
Yàhàya:	Tô, mè zân girkà?	All right, what shall I cook?
Uwargidā:	Zā kà yi miyā, kà gasà nāmā, kà dafà dànkalT.[1]	You'll make sauce, roast some meat, and boil some potatoes.
Yàhàya:	Ai sai ìn fārà aikT.	Then I'd better start work.
Uwargidā:	Kà fārà yayyànkà alayyàhō[2] gutsiŋ-gutsin[3] don miyà. Kà zubà tùmātìr dà gishirT.[4]	Start chopping the spinach up fine for the sauce. Add (pour) tomatoes and salt.
Yàhàya:	DànkalT fà?	What about the potatoes?
Uwargidā:	Kà fēṛē shi ̦sòsai, sà'àn nan kà wankè shi.	Peel them well and wash them.
Yàhàya:	Yàyà kumā zân yT dà shT?	What should I do with them then?
Uwargidā:	Kadà kà yi kōmē dà shT sai bākin sun zō.	Don't do anything with them until the guests arrive.

[1] dànkalT n.m. 'potatoes, sweet potatoes'

[2] alayyàhō n.m. 'spinach'

[3] gutsin-gutsin (or gutsun-gutsun) "in fragments"

[4] gishirT n.m. 'salt'

DIALOGUES

A. Probably one of the most colorful festivals that can be seen in the
world today is the <u>Salla</u> that the African Moslems celebrate at the end
of the month-long Ramadan fast. In this dialogue Malam Isa, a native
of Katsina, is entertaining his house guest Malam Sa'idu, who has come
from Bornu Province to experience the <u>Salla</u> in this big city. On the
morning of the <u>Salla</u>, as is customary, various friends drop by to ex-
tend <u>Salla</u> greetings. As the host and the guest are sitting in their
house eating <u>Salla tuwo</u>, Malam Shehu, a friend of Isa, enters.

Shēhù:	Barkà dà Sallà.	Greetings on <u>Salla</u> day.
Īsa:	Barkà kàdai. Wannàn shT nē Mālàm Sà'Tdù dàgà Bàrno. Yā zō̲ don yà yi Kàramar Sallà tàre dà mū.	Greetings to you! This is Malam Sa'idu from Bornu. He has come to celebrate <u>Salla</u> with us.
Shēhù:	Munā farin cikī dà zuwànkà nân. Yàushè ka zō?	We are happy at your coming here. When did you come?
Sà'Tdù:	Jiyà na zō. Nā yi watàn azumT can gàrinmu.	I came yesterday. I spent the month of Ramadan there in our city.
Shēhù:	Yāyā a kàn yį hidimar Kàramar Sallà à Bàrnō?	How do you celebrate <u>Salla</u> in Bornu? (How does one do admini- stration of <u>Salla</u> in Bornu?)
Sà'Tdù:	Mu kàn tàfī masallācin Īdì. Bāyan hakà mu kàņ kōmō gidā mù ci tuwon Sallà. Kumā a kàn tàfī gai dà SarkT.	We go to the Id el Fitr Mosque. After that we return home and eat <u>Salla tuwo</u>. Then we go (one goes) to greet the Emir.
Shēhù:	Hakà mu kàn yi Sallà à Kà- tsiņà. Ammā zā kà gǫ abù- buwā màsu ban shà'awà nân.	That's the way we celebrate <u>Salla</u> at Katsina. But you will see some wonderful things here.
Īsa:	Tō̲ lōkàcin hawan dabā à fàdàr SarkT yā yi.	Well the time for the gathering of the horsemen at the Emir's palace has come.
Shēhù:	Gàskiyarkà. Gāra mù tàshì.	True, we had better be on our way.

Vocabulary

azumT	n.m.	'fasting, the fast of Ramadan'	gāra	'it is best that' (followed by the subjunctive)
Bàrno	n.m.	'Bornu Province' (in northeastern Nigeria, fa- mous for its horses and horsemen)	hidimā n.f.	'serving, administer- ing'
			lōkàcT n.m.	'time, point in time'
dabā	n.f.	'a gathering of horsemen in ho- nor of an impor- tant personage'	Tdī n.m.	'religious festival'
			masallācT n.m. (màsàllàtai pl.)	'mosque'
farin cikT	n.m.	'happiness' (white stomach)	sallà n.f. (sallōlT pl.)	'prayers; festival day, holiday'
			Kàramar Sallà	'the celebration at the end of the fast of Ramadan'

B. Malam Isa and his friends now go to the large open space before the Emir
of Katsina's palace. A large crowd has gathered to await the Emir and
his retinue, who will stop before the palace and receive the greetings
of the provincial chiefs. The latter will charge to within a few feet of
the Emir, rein in suddenly, and raise their lances in salute. Last of all,
the Emir's own bodyguard, resplendent in black costumes covered by chain
mail, will grasp their thick hide shields, canter to the end of the court-
yard, and make the final charge of the day. Amid a tumultuous fanfare
consisting of the beating drums and the firing of 'Dane guns', the Emir
will retire into his palace to receive visitors.

Sà'Tdù:	Kâi, dùbi dawākT!	Say, look at the horses!
Shēhù:	Dūbi irìn adòn dà akà yT musù.	Look at the way they are dressed up (look at the kinds of adorn- ment that have been done to them).
Sà'Tdù:	Inā̀ tsàmmānT wannàn d'imbin jàma'àr̠ dà kàd'e-kàd'ē dà bùshe-bùshe shT nē halāmar zuwàn SarkT.	I think that crowd of people drumming and trumpeting signals (is the sign of) the arrival of the Emir.
Tsa:	Hakà nē. Zâi zō nàn daf dà mū.̠ Sai saurân sù kāwō masà jāhT.	That's right. He'll come here close to us. The rest will then charge and salute him with raised spears (carry to him a raising of spears).
Shēhù:	Kâi, gā 'yan taurT sunā̀ wāsā̀.	Say, there are the 'yan tauri playing.
Sà'Tdù:	Inā̀ màmākT yaddà su kè yîn hakà.	I am astonished at how they do that.
Tsa:	Gā màsu dawākT nân! Sunā̀ jân lìnzāmT à gàban SarkT.	There are the horsemen! They're reining in (pulling the reins) in front of the Emir.
Shēhù:	Mēnē nē ra'àyinkà à kân Sallàr Kàtsinà?	What do you think (what is your opinion on) of Katsina's Salla.
Sà'Tdù:	Gàskiyā, tā yi kyâu.̠ Àmmā dā kā jē̠ kallon Sallā à̠ Bàrnō, dā kā ga abūbuwā̀.	True, it's indeed fine. But if you came and saw the Salla at Bornu, you would see some things.
Shēhù:	Kàmar mē?	Like what?
Sà'Tdù:	Dā kā ga yaddà a kè sâ wà dawākT wàndō.	You would see how they put pants on horses.

Vocabulary

adō n.m.	'adornment'		halāmā̀ n.f. (hàlāmū pl.)	'sign, indication'
bùshe-bùshē n.m.	'blowing (of musi- cal instruments)		jā v.tr.	'pull'
dā̀ ... dā̀	'if it had been that ... then'		jāhT n.m.	'salutes by raising spears'
d'imbT n.m.	'mass, crowd'		kàd'e-kàd'ē n.m.	'beating (of drums)'

346

kallō n.m.	'watching'	
lìnzāmî n.m.	'reins, bridal'	
ra'àyî n.m.	'opinion'	
saurā n.m.	'remainder'	

taurî n.m.	'hardness, toughness' person made invulner-
ɗan taurî	able to knife blades
('yan taurî	
pl.)	through a magic charm and who puʈs on exhi- bitions (wāsā) by drawing a knife across his body without being cut

COMPREHENSION PRACTICE

This comprehension practice is somewhat longer and more difficult than those of the preceding units. It is therefore suggested that the informant read through each of the lettered paragraphs and ask the questions which apply to that paragraph. Then the passage can be reread in its entirety and the procedure previously used for comprehension passages followed.

Hawan Sallā

(A) Anā shagàlin[1] sallā sàu[2] biyu à shèkarà: Sallā K̃àramā dà Sallā Bàbba. K̃àramar Sallā ita cè wâddà a kè yî ìdan an ga watà bāyan azùmin watàn Ràmàdân. Bàbbar Sallā kùwā anā yìntà bāyan kwānā sàbà'in dà yîn K̃àramar Sallā. Irìn abūbuwàn dà kè sâ à gānè kōwàcè irìn sallā a kè yî sū nè: à lōkàcin K̃àramar Sallā sai an yi azùmî na watà gùdā, sā'àn nan à yi sallā. À lōkàcin Bàbbar Sallā bā à yîn azùmî mài tsawō[3] sai dai anā yîn na gàjēren lōkàcî dàgà sāfe har zuwā dāwôwā dàgà Īdì. Kumā dà Bàbbar Sallā, wândà kè dà Īkō[4] yanā yîn layyā[5], wàtō yîn yankā, bāyaıı dāwôwā dàgà Īdì.

(B) Kallon hawan Īdì àbù nè mài ban shà'awā. Shagàlinsà yā bàmbantà[6] dàgà wani wurî zuwā wani wurî. Adon Sallā shî mā ya bàmbantà dàgà wani wurî zuwā wani wurî. À Sakkwato dà Kanò dà Kàtsinà kusan adon mutànensù duk irî ɗaya nè, hakà kumā na dawākinsù. Àmmā à Bàrnō irìn adon mutànensù dàban[7] nè, hakà kumā na dawākinsù. À Bàrnō har a kàn sâ wà dawàkî wandunā kàmar mutànē! À nan, gā bàyanìn yàddà a kè ḥawan K̃àramar Sallā à Kàtsinà.

(C) À rānar K̃àramar Sallā, kōwà ya kàn yi wankā[8], yà ci adō, yà tāsam mà[9] Masallācin Īdì. Ta K̃ofàr Gūgà[10] a kè fìtā zuwā Masallācîn. Ìdan akà gamà sallā, sai à nufō[11] K̃ofàr Sōrō[12]. Tō, à nan nè Hàkìmai[13] dà jàma'àrsù su kè tahôwā bî dà bî[14] gwàrgwadon darajàrsù[15]. Tō, dàgà Masallācin Īdì, ìdan an dāwō, bā à kōmôwā K̃ofàr Sōrō ta cikin K̃ofàr dà akà fìta sā'àd dà zā à tàfi, wàtō K̃ofàr Gūgà.[16] Sai à shìga gàrî ta cikin K̃ofàr Dàgàtansà[17] dà mãsu kàɗe-kàɗē dà bushe-bùshensà, sunà tàfe sunà ta yî. K̃ungìyar[18] Sarkî kùwa, mãsu bàdūjalā[19] nè kè yî musù jà gōrā[20]. Sai 'yan bindigā[21],

347

sai 'yan kwalkwalī^{22}, sai Dōgàrai^{23}, sā'àn nan SarkT. Sarkin Laimà^{24} yanà
rìƙe dà ƙatùwar laimà don SarkT yà sàmi inuwà^{25}.

(D) Ìdan SarkT yā isō bàkin Ƙōfàr Sōrō, sai yà jūyà^{26} yà dùbi yâmma,
Hàkìmai sù yT ta kāwō masà jāhT. À ƙàrshē sai dàkàrun^{27} SarkT sù kāwō
masà jāhT. Sai SarkT yà yT wà jàma'àr tāsà jàwābT^{28}, sā'àn nan yà shìga
fàdàrsà.

<table>
<tr><td>

^{1}shagàli   n.m.   'celebrating'

^{2}sàu   n.m.   'time(s)'
(=French <u>fois</u>)

^{3}tsawō   n.m.   'length'

^{4}īkò   n.m.   'means, authority'

^{5}layyà   n.f.   'sacrifice of
animal during <u>Bàbbar Sallà</u>'

wândà kè dà īkò yanà yîn layyà
'he who has the means makes a
sacrifice (of a ram, a bull, etc.)'

^{6}bàmbantà   v.intr.   'differ, be
different'

^{7}dàban   'different'

^{8}wankà   n.m.   'washing (oneself)'

^{9}tàsam mà ...   'set out for ...'

^{10}Ƙōfàr Gūgà   gate through which
the road from Maradi to Katsina
leads

^{11}nufō   v.intr.   'set out toward'

^{12}Ƙōfàr Sōrō   gate of Katsina
leading to Emir's palace

^{13}hàkìmī   n.m.   'district head'
(hàkìmai pl.)

^{14}bī dà bî   'successively'

^{15}darajà   n.m.   '(social) rank'

^{16}bà à kōmōwà ...;
wàtō Ƙōfàr Gūgà   'one does not re-
turn to the <u>Ƙōfàr
Sōrō</u> (i.e. the
gate to the Emir's palace) through
the gate by way of which one went
out when leaving (to go to the
mosque), that is, the <u>Ƙōfàr Gūgà</u>'

</td><td>

^{17}dagacī   n.m.   'village head'
(dàgàtai pl.)
Ƙōfàr Dagatansà   one of the
gates of Katsina

^{18}ƙungìyà   n.f.   'group (of people),
retinue (of Emir)'

^{19}màsu badùjalà   "drum corps"

^{20}yT muşù jà
gōrà   "leading the way
for them"
(a jà gōrà is what a person who leads
a blind man is called, lit: a "pull-
stick")

^{21}'yan bindigà   "dane-gun bearers"

^{22}'yan kwalkwalī members of the Emir'
body-guard who wear
special helmets (<u>kwalkwalī</u>)

^{23}dōgarī   n.m.   formerly, local po-
(dōgàrai pl.)   liceman, now a mem-
ber of the Emir's
body-guard

^{24}Sarkin Laimà   Emir's umbrella
(<u>laimà</u>) bearer

^{25}inuwà   n.f.   'shade'

^{26}jūyà   v.intr.   'turn around'

^{27}dàkàrē   n.m.   'infantryman'
(dàkàrū pl.)

^{28}jàwābT   n.m.   'speech'

</td></tr>
</table>

<u>Tambayoyi</u>

(A) 1. Sàu nawà a kè shagàlin sallà à Nìjēriyà?

2. Mècē cè Ƙàramar Sallà? Bàbba fà?

348

3. Mề a kề yT à watàn dà kề kàfin Kàramar Sallà?

4. Anã azùmT à Bàbbar Sallà?

5. Mènē nề layyā, kumā wà ya kề yînsà?

(B) 6. Shagàlin ḥawạn Īdì shT nề dàban dàgà wani wurT zuwã wani wurT? Adon sallā fã?

7. À Sakkwato dà Kanồ dà Kàtsinà adon mutānē dàban nề?

8. À Bàrno, adon mutānē ɗaya dà na su Kanồ dà Kàtsinà?

9. Mènē nề a kàn sā̂ wà dawākT à Bàrno?

(C) 10. Mutānē mề su kàn yi kàfin sù tàfi Masallācin Īdì?

11. Yāyā sūnan Kồfàr dà Katsinàwā su kề fìtā zuwã Masallācin Īdì?

12. Yāyā Hàkìmai dà jàma'àrsù su kề tahồwā?

13. A kàn kōmō Kồfàr Gūgà?

14. Fàɗā manà mutānên dà su kề tàfiyā gàban SarkT.

15. Wānē nề ya zō à Kàrshē?

16. Sarkin Laimā, mènē nề aikìnsà?

(D) 17. Ìdan SarkT yā isō bàkin Kồfàr Sōrō, mề zâi yi?

18. Mề Hàkìmai su kề kāwō wà SarkT?

19. Bāyan dàkàrun SarkT sun kāwō masà jāhT, mề SarkT ya yi?

20. Bāyan yā Kàrè jàwābìnsà, ìnā SarkT ya kàn tàfi?

GRAMMAR

24.1 The Habitual Aspect

The only verbal aspect remaining to be studied is the habitual aspect. The meaning of this aspect is that the action is done recurrently or as a habit or custom. As with all other Hausa verbal aspects, context determines whether the time of reference is past, present, or future. We have deferred discussion of the habitual aspect until this late because the continuative aspect can be substituted for it in virtually any sentence. Indeed, some dialects do not even use this aspect, but it is in frequent use in the dialect of Kano, which is the dialect described in this book.

Following is the paradigm of the habitual aspect. It is formed by using the same set of pronouns as for the relative continuative aspect (15.1) except that kàn is used instead of kề. The forms are illustrated with yi 'do'.

na kàn yi	'I usually do'	mu kàn yi	'we usually do'
ka kàn yi	'you(m) usually do'	ku kàn yi	'you usually do'
ki kàn yi	'you(f) usually do'		
ya kàn yi	'he usually does'	su kàn yi	'they usually do'
ta kàn yi	'she usually does'		
a kàn yi	'one usually does'		

yàyā a kàn yi hidimar Kàramar Sallā à Bàrno?	'how is the Small Salla usually celebrated in Bornu?'
mu kàn tàfi masallācin Īdì	'we usually go to the Id el Fitr mosque'
hakà mu kàn yi Sallā à Kàtsinà	'that is the way we go about celebrating our Salla in Katsina'

The negative is formed as for the future and indefinite future aspects: short, low tone bà is placed immediately before the aspect pronoun and a short, high tone ba is placed at the end of the sentence:

| bà a kàn zō ba | 'they don't come' |

This form is rarely used, however, the negative continuative being preferred over it.

24.2 Reduplication Meaning 'doing time after time'

Two types of reduplication (the doubling of a word or part of a word) were described in 23.1 and 23.2. Another type of reduplication changes verbs and action nouns ('singing', 'working', etc.) into action nouns meaning 'constant or repetitive doing of the action'. The entire verb or noun is doubled, the tones on each half of the repluplicant become low-high (low-low-high for three syllable words), and short -e is the final vowel of the first half, long -ē for the second half.

wākā	'singing, song'	wāke-wākē	'repeated singing'
būsà	'blow'	būshe-būshē	'continued blowing'
tàmbayà	'ask'	tàmbàye-tàmbàyē	'repeating asking of questions'

Examples of these forms in use are

munā wāke-wākē à makarantar nàsàriyyà	'we sing songs a lot at the Christian school'
wannàn dìmbin jàma'àr dà kàde-kàdē dà būshe-būshē shī nē hàlāmàr zuwàn SarkI	'that crowd of people who keep beating (drums) and blowing (instruments) is the signal of the arrival of the chief'
mē ya sā ka kē tàmbàye-tàmbàyē hakà?	'why are you asking all these questions?'

24.3 Hypothetical 'if'

In English, the uses of the word 'if' can be divided into two gener-classes*: 1) 'if' expressing some sort of condition which led, leads, or will lead to some conclusion as in 'if it rains, we'll have to go in'; 2) 'if' expressing some hypothetical situation which, if it had been the case, would lead to some conclusion.

Hausa has two different words for these two uses. The first is expressed by the words in or ìdan and was covered in 22.6. The second use is expressed by the word dā.

*'If' can also be used to mean 'whether' in sentences like 'I don't know if he will come'. This 'if' as an introducer of indirect questions was described in 16.3.

350

In dialogue B of this unit, we find

> dā kā jē kallon Sallā à
> Bàrno, dā kā ga abūbuwā

'if you had gone to the Salla at Bornu, you would have seen (some) things'

It is obvious from the context that the person addressed did <u>not</u> go to Bornu, so this is a hypothetical statement.

There is some variation in the way various aspects are used with dā and how <u>dā</u> is used itself. What is probably the most common pattern is given here and the student can note any variation that he may run across. Usually, both clauses of a sentence are preceded by dā and the first clause is in the completive aspect. The second clause may be in the completive as well, or it may be in the indefinite future with or without <u>dā</u> preceding. Further examples are

> dā nā sanī ...

'if I had (only) known ...'
(This is a proverbial expression in Hausa as it is in English.)

> dā an tàmbàyē nì, dā nā yàrda
> dā an tàmbàyē nì, dā nā yàrda
> dā an tàmbàyē nì, nā yàrda

} 'if I had been asked, I'd have agreed' or 'if I were asked, I might agree'

When the clause stating the hypothetical condition is understood, a simple sentence can be introduced by dā to give a conditional meaning. This is the situation in the last line of dialogue B, where the hypothetical condition 'being in Bornu' is understood.

> dā kā ga yaddà a kē sā wà
> dawākī wàndō

'you would see how they put pants on horses'

24.4 Gāra 'it would be best that'

The word gāra 'it would be best that', 'it is best that', 'it is better to' is nearly always followed by a sentence in the subjunctive. As we have seen at other times, in Hausa such words as gāra, yā kàmàtà, dā, etc. are often best translated by using a different verb tense or modal verb in English. Hence, note that the translations of the following sentences are not literal.

> gāra mù tāshì

'we had better be on our way'

> gāra kà yi hakà

'you'd better do this'

Gāra can also be used to complete a sentence using dā + subjunctive 'rather than' seen in 23.6

> dà in dāwō hannū banzā,
> gāra in sàyi wani àbù

'rather than come home empty-handed, it's better that I buy something'

24.5 Uses of the Word sai

One of the most frequently used words in Hausa and one which presents one of the most bewildering range of meanings for the speaker of English is the word <u>sai</u>. Following are some of the most common translations of sai, or ways that sentences containing sai might be translated.

351

a) "only", "except" - These two meanings are linked together since the translation 'except' will be used for negative sentences or affirmative sentences with one of the k͟o͟- forms such as k͟o͟wā͟ or k͟o͟mē͟. The translation 'only' will be used for most other affirmative sentences. Often, sai in affirmative sentences can be translated 'no one but', 'nothing but', 'none but'.

sai nī dà uwargidā dà yârā munā gidā	'only me, the wife, and the children are at home'
làbārī sai àlhērī (in answer to the greeting ìna làbārī?)	'the news is nothing but good'
bâ ni dà kōmē sai jàkin nàn	'I don't have anything but this donkey'
bà mù ci kōmē ba sai shìnkāfā kàɗan	'we didn't eat anything but a little rice'
mun ga kōwā sai Audù	'we saw everyone except Audu'

b) "until" - Sai can be followed either by a time expression like 'three o'clock', 'tomorrow', etc. or by a sentence to mean 'until'. When followed by a sentence, the sentence will be in the completive aspect. Sai dà can also be used to mean 'until' when followed by a sentence (sai dà is not used with simple time expressions) in which case the sentence will be in the relative completive. Sometimes the best translation in English for sai is 'not until'.

bàn dāwō ba sai ƙarfè ukù	'I didn't return until 3:00'
sai gòbe	'see you tomorrow' (until tomorrow)
sai yâu na tàɓà ganinsà	'not until today did I see him' (Note that this sentence might be translated 'only today have I seen him [for the first time]', giving an indication of how the meanings 'only' and 'until' as translations of sai are related)
nā dākàtā matà sai tā zo	'I waited for her until she came'
bā nà fārà,cìnikī sai an buɗè fulōtī	'I don't begin trade until the season is open'
sunà tàfiyà sai dà sukà kai Kanò	'they went until they reached Kano'

In 18.5 we noted that the word har could mean 'until' and that the difference between sai and har meaning 'until' would be explained in the present section.

1A bà sù gan mù ba sai dà sukà kai kàsuwā
1B bà sù gan mù ba har sukà kai kàsuwā } 'they didn't see us until they reached the market'

2A sai gòbe }
2B har gòbe } 'until tomorrow'

352

Though both 1A and 1B may have the same English translation they mean different things: 1A implies that they saw us when they reached the market but not before; 1B doesn't necessarily imply that they ever saw us, that is, during their whole trip to the market they didn't see us. What happened after they reached the market is not covered by this sentence. The difference between <u>sai</u> and <u>har</u> meaning 'until' is, then, that with <u>sai</u>, our interest is centered around what happened or will happen after a certain time, in this case what happened after reaching the market. With <u>har</u> we are concerned with events up to a certain time, but not necessarily after that time, in this case, with the trip to the market but not the events after the arrival at the market.

This makes it easier to understand the difference in meaning between 2A and 2B. Used as a formula when taking leave of a person, 2A implies that tomorrow we will take up where we left off today. On the other hand, 2B suggests that there are some events that will be leading us up to tomorrow and what happens after that time is not of immediate concern. Thus, it would normally be attached to some further context that <u>sai gōbe</u> would not necessarily have to have.

c) "have to", "should", etc.

<u>Followed by completive aspect</u> - When followed by a sentence in the completive aspect, <u>sai</u> can give that sentence the meaning 'have to', 'must'.

sai nā sayō gawàyī	'have to buy charcoal'
wândà duk zā à bā rançên sai yā iya kiyāyè littàttàfan lissāfī	'whoever is going to be given a loan has to be able to take care of the account books'

<u>Followed by the subjunctive aspect</u> - When followed by a sentence in the subjunctive aspect, <u>sai</u> can give that sentence the meaning 'should', 'ought to', 'must', 'have to'. When used with the second person, it may merely have the effect of "softening" an imperative.

sai kà yi ta tàfiyā har kà jē Fùtuwà	'keep going until you get to Funtuwa'
(The English translation uses an imperative, but from context it is obvious that the speaker is not giving a command but is merely giving directions.)	
sai kà mai dà tābàr nân	'you should take those cigarets back'
sai yà dākàtā kàɗan	'he'll have to wait a bit'
in akà yi sātā, sai à kirāwō 'yan sàndā	'if a burglary takes place, the police should be called'

d) "then" (consecutive action)

<u>Followed by relative completive</u> - Sai can be used followed by the <u>relative</u> completive aspect to mean 'then', 'and then', 'when', introducing one of a series of consecutive actions. Sometimes the clause introduced by <u>sai</u> will be preceded by a clause describing the first of consecutive actions. Very frequently such a clause will be introduced by

dà 'when' also followed by relative completive or by other conjunctions such as in 'if/when'. However, context alone may determine that a sentence introduced by sai is one of several consecutive actions, as, for example, in story telling, where it is not uncommon for virtually every new sentence to be introduced by sai. Often, sai will not have to be translated in English.

sai Mammàn ya cè, "kai! kù tsayā!"	'then Mamman said, "hey! stop!"'
zân sàri itàcē, sai mài shī ya zō	'I was about to cut the tree when its owner came along'
dà mukà ji làbārìn, sai mukà zō maza-maza	'when we heard the news, we came very quickly'

Followed by the subjunctive - When followed by a subjunctive, sai can also mean 'then' indicating one of several consecutive actions. As with the relative completive with this meaning, sai may best be left out in English translations. The difference between sai followed by the relative completive and sai followed by the subjunctive is that the completive indicates an action which has already taken place, the subjunctive indicates an action which has not yet taken place or which can potentially take place in the future. As a result, sentences introduced by sai having the meaning 'then' and containing the subjunctive will often be translated with 'will' or 'would'.

dàgà Bicì sai ìn kai gyàdā kusa dà tashàr jirgin ƙasà	'from Bicì I take the peanuts near the railroad station'
in nā ga sàna'àr, sai à bā̂ mài ràncē gwàrgwadō	'when I have seen the business, then its proprietor will be given a proportionate loan'
duk lōkàcîn dà na jē fàdàr Sarkī, sai yà sā̂ baƙar àlkyabbā	'everytime I went to the Emir's palace, he would put on a black burnous'

GRAMMATICAL DRILLS

Drill 1 - Change the sentences below from the continuative aspect to the habitual aspect as shown in the example.

Cue: munā̀ tàfiyā̀ masallācin Ìdì

Student response: mu kàn tàfi masallācin Ìdì

1. kunā̀ tàfiyà kallon hawan dabā̀
2. tanā̀ yī matà adō
3. à Bàrnō anā̀ sā̂ wà dawākī wandunā̀
4. sunā̀ jân lìnzāmī à gàban Sarkī
5. yanā̀ ƙomōwa gidā don cîn tuwon sallā̀

6. inā̀ sā̂ baƙar àlkyabbā
7. munā̀ bayyànā masà dàbāràrmù dàbārā̀ n.f. 'plan'
8. kanā̀ bā dà làbārī
9. anā̀ sanad dà mātā indà zâi zō
10. sunā̀ ajìyè lìttàttàfan lissāfī

Drill 2 - Change the sentences which follow so that they fit the pattern mu kàn kōmō gidā mù ci àbinci.

Cue: zā sù kōmō gidā sù ci àbinci

Student response: su kàn kōmō gidā sù ci àbinci

1. Hàlīmà zā tà jē kàsuwā tà sàyi masàrā
2. ma'àikàtā zā sù tàfi ōfìs sù yi aikìnsù
3. zā mù kōmō gidā mù ci tuwon sallà
4. zân tàfi wurin Sarkī ìn gai dà shī
5. Hàlīmà zā tà dāwō à ƙarfè ukù tà yi wàsā dà ƙanèntà
6. zā kù jē gōnarkù kù cìri cìyàwā?
7. zā sù tattàrà tukwànē sù wankè su
8. zân ɗauki bàrkōnō ìn niƙà
9. zā kì bā nì kubēwā kì kulà miyà
10. zā tà ajìyè ƙanèntà tà tàimàki uwargidā girkī

Drill 3 - Delete the noun(s) or adverb from the cue sentence below and change each verb into its reduplicated form as shown in the example.

Cue: tanā rawā kōyàushē rawā n.f. 'dancing'
Student response: tanā ràye-ràyē ràye-ràyē 'continual dancing'
(w changes to y before e in some words)

1. sunā būsà kōyàushē
   būsà n.f. 'blowing (a trumpet, etc.)'
2. yanā tàfiyà kōyàushē
3. mu kànkaràntà lìttàttàfai irī-irī
4. sunā nōmā kōyàushē à lōkàcin dàminā
5. kinā fasà kwalàbē dà tāsōshī
   tāsà n.m. 'dish'
   (tāsōshī pl.)

6. sunā waƙà kōyàushē
7. munā rubùtà lìttàttàfai dà jàrīdà
8. yanā gyāran mōtàtā kōyàushē
9. anā tàmbayà kōyàushē
10. sunā kallon sallà dà wàsan ƙwallō
    ƙwallō n.m. 'ball'
    ƙwallon ƙafà 'soccer'

Drill 4 - Transform the sentences below so that they fit the dà ... dà pattern as illustrated. Translate so your instructor can check whether you have understood the change in meaning.

Cue: In yā tàimàkē nì, zân gamà aikī.
'If he helps me, I'll finish the work.'
Student response: Dà yā tàimàkē nì, dà nā gamà aikī.
'Had he helped me, I would have finished the work.'

1. In sun dāwō ƙafin ƙarfè ukù, zā mù ci tuwon sallà tàre dà sū.
2. In kā tàmbàyē tà, zā tà nūnā makà fàdàr Sarkī.
3. In kin bā nì kuɗī, zân sayō mikì masàrā.
4. In tā shiryà àbinci, zā sù cī shì.
5. In mun jē fàdàr Sarkī, zā mù ga hawan dabà.
6. In sun ajìyè lìttàttàfan lissàfī, zā sù ƙaru ƙwarai.

355

7. In kā jē kallon sallā̀ à Bàrno, zā kà ga abūbuwā̀.

8. In kin ga 'yan taurᴛ, zā kὶ yi mā̀mākᴛ̄.

9. In màì sàna'ā̀ yā yàrda zâi ajὶyè lὶttàttā̀fan lissāfὶ̄, zā mὺ bā shὶ ràncē̄.

10. In Sarkin Zagᴛ yā gwadà sābon ὶngarmàn, zā à san kō zâi yi gudὺ.

Drill 5 - Change the negative sentences below to affirmative sentences that are introduced by gā̄ra.

      Cue: kadà kὺ k̀ā̄rà yȋn wannàn

      Student response: gā̄ra kὺ k̀ā̄rà yȋn wannàn

1. kadà sὺ tà̀fi fā̄dà̀r Sarkᴛ

2. kadà mὺ tāshὶ

3. kada kὺ tà̀fi Kàṭsinà̀ don kὺ yi K̀àramar Sallā̄ tà̀re dà sū

4. kadà tà̀ jē kallon wā̀san 'yan taurᴛ

5. kadà kὶ yi wà̀k̀e-wà̀k̀ē

6. kadà ὶn yi watàn azùmᴛ̄ à gà̀rinmù

7. kadà kà̀ ajὶyè k̀anènkà̀

8. kadà yà̀ sayō masà̀rā̄

9. kadà kὶ yankà̀ kubḕwā waccàn

10. kadà tà̀ kulà̀ miyà̀

Drill 6 - Change the cue sentences containing gā̄ra to fit the pattern lōkà̀cin cȋn à̀binci yā̄ yi.

      Cue: gā̄ra mὺ ci à̀binci yâu

      Student response: tô, lōkà̀cin cȋn à̀binci yā̄ yi

1. gā̄ra mὺ tà̀fi wurin Sarkᴛ

2. gā̄ra mὺ ci tuwon sallā̀

3. gā̄ra mὺ gai dà̀ Sarkᴛ

4. gā̄ra mὺ tà̀imà̀ki uwarmὺ

5. gā̄ra mὺ yi aikὶn makarantā̄

6. gā̄ra mὺ zὶyà̀rci Audὺ

7. gā̄ra mὺ fā̄rà̀ zuwā̀ makarantar Muhà̀mmà̀diyyā̄

8. gā̄ra mὺ shā giyā̀

9. gā̄ra mὺ sà̀yi gawà̀yᴛ

10. gā̄ra mὺ gyā̄rà̀ mōtā̀

Drill 7 - Put the two cue sentences into a single complex sentence by using in or ὶdan before the first sentence and sai followed by the sub-junctive before the second as illustrated. Translate the resulting complex sentence.

      Cue: Mun jē Bàrno. Mun ga yaddà a kḕ sā̂ wà dawākᴛ wandunā̀.

      Student response: In mun jē Bàrno, sai mὺ ga yaddà a kḕ sā̂ wà dawākᴛ wandunā̀.
                       'When we go to Bornu, we'll see how they put pants on horses.'

1. Kun jē fā̄dà̀r Sarkᴛ. Kun ga hawan dabā̀.

2. Sarkᴛ yā zō daf dà̀ mū. Mā̀su dawākᴛ sun kāwō masà̀ jāhᴛ̄.

3. Kà̀nde tā nik̀à̀ bà̀rkōnō. Tā yankà̀ kubḕwā.

4. Yā̂rā̀ sun zō makarantar à̀llō. Sun kōyō rùbū̄tū̄.

356

5. Bàn ƙàrè sai dà tābàr nan ba. Nā mai dà ita.

6. 'Bàrāwò yā shigō d̀akT. Nā farkā.   farkā v.intr. 'wake up'

7. Kin yi ƙòƙarT. Kin kòyi Hausa.

8. An yi ruwā. HatsT yā yi àlbarkà.

9. Yā sàmi mōtà. Yā tàfi Bauci.

10. Kun tàfi makarantar nàsàriyyà. Kun m̂antā dà àl'àdàrmù.

Drill 8 - Put the two cue sentences into a single complex sentence by
using dà 'when' before the first and sai before the second and changing
both to relative completive. Translate the resultant sentence.

Cue: Mutãnē sun gamà sallā. Sun tāshì kōmāwā gidā.

Student response: Dà mutãnē sukà gamà sallā, sai sukà tāshì
                     kōmāwā gidā.
                     'When the people finished praying, they set out
                     for home.'

1. An yi bùshe-bùshē dà kàde-kàde. SarkT yā zō fāda.

2. 'Bàrāwò yā shigō d̀akT. Yā yi wata ƙārā.

3. Mun gamà cîn àbinci. Uwargidā tā kāwō manà ruwā.

4. Nā ji hakà. Nā yi fushT.

5. Sun gan mù. Sun fitō sù gaishē mù.

6. Dare yā yi. Mutãnē sun fārà wāsā.

7. Mun fad̀à masà làbārT. Yā gōdè masà.

8. 'Bàrāwò yā bazà bàrgō à k̂an katangà. Fàsàs̥sun kwalàbē sun yāgè shi.
                                                   yāgè v.tr. 'tear'

9. JàkT yā hàrbē shì. Yā hàrbē shì.   hàrbā (i/ē) v.tr. 'kick; shoot'

10. Kànde tā kāwō shìnkāfā. Uwargidā tā yi fushT.

Drill 9 - This drill is for practice in using tàre dà '(together) with'
with persons. Cover up the answers on the right and as each English
sentence is given, give the Hausa translation.

1. she has come to prepare food with Halima	tā zō tà shìryà àbìncì tàre dà HàlTmà
2. we have come to store groundnuts with you (pl.)	mun zō mù ajìye gyàd̀a tàre dà kū
3. the bailiff has come to assess the damage with us	muhùtT yā zō yà kimmantà 'Bàrnā tàre dà mū
4. Malam Sa'idu has come to watch the gathering of the horsemen with his friends	Mālàm S̥a'Tdù yā zō yà yi kallon dabà tàre dà abōkansà
5. Halima has come to cut up the okra with her mother	HàlTmà tā zō tà yankà kubēwā tàre dà uwartà
6. Kande has come to play with her little brother	Kànde tā zō tà yi wāsā tàre dà Kànèntà

357

7. the girl has come to grind these peppers together with me	yarinyā tā zō tà nikà bàrkònō tāre dà nī
8. we have come together to greet the Emir	mun zō tāre mù gai dà SarkT
9. they have come together to spend the month of Ramadan in the city	sun zō tāre sù yi watàn azùmT can gàrinsù
10. we have returned together from the Id el Fitr mosque to eat salla tuwo	mun zō tāre dàgà masallācin īdī mù ci tuwon sallā

Drill 10 - Negate the sentences below, which contain the habitual aspect. Remember that even in dialects having the habitual aspect, it is rarely used in the negative, the continuative being substituted.

Cue: mu kàn yi àmfānī dà mânyan mōtōcī
Student response: bā mà àmfānī dà mânyan mōtōcī

1. ta kàn ci tuwon masàrā
2. su kàn kai sù kusa dà jirgin kasà
3. na kàn biyā sù sulè bìyar
4. ku kàn jāwō hankàlin màsu gyàɗā
5. ya kàn gwadà dawākT

6. mu kàn tàfi wurin sallā
7. a kàn tàfi masallācin īdì
8. su kàn jā lìnzāmī gàban sarkT
9. na kàn yi azùmT à gàrinmù
10. su kàn yi kàɗe-kàɗē dà bùshe-bùshē

Drill 11 - Cover up the answers on the right and as each English sentence is given, give the Hausa translation.

1. If you had followed the thief, he would have killed you.	Dà kā bi ɓaràwō, dà yā kashè ka.
2. If I had received my salary, I would have paid you.	Dà nā sàmi àlbāshīnā, dà nā biyā kà.
3. If you hadn't lied, you wouldn't have paid the fine.	Dà bà kà yi karyā ba, dà bà kà biyā tārâr ba.
4. If you hadn't chased off the goats, they would have ruined your millet.	Dà bà kà kòri awākT ba, dà sun ɓātà makà hatsT.
5. If he had helped me, I would have finished my work.	Dà yā tàimàkē nì, dà nâ kàrè aikīnā.
6. If her parents had agreed, I would have married her.	Dà iyàyentà sun yàrda, dà nâ àurē ta.
7. If you(pl) had gone to Bornu, you would have been surprised.	Dà kun jē Bàrno, dà kun yi màmākT.
8. If they had come in the evening, everything would have been re-paired.	Dà sun zō dà yâmma, dà an gyàrà kōmē.
9. If someone had come, I wouldn't have given him anything.	Dà wani yā zō, dà bàn bā shì kōmē ba.

358

10. If we had gone to watch the riding in the salla, we would have seen the district heads.

Dà mun jē ḳạllon hawan sallà, dà mun ga hàkìmai.

Drill 12 - Cover up the answers on the right and as each English sentence is given, give the Hausa translation.

1. we had better be on our way

gāra mù tāshì

2. you'd better do your work

gāra kà yi aikìnkà

3. they had best inform the Emir

gāra sù sanad dà SarkT

4. the child had better come back home

gāra yârā sù kōmō gidā

5. rather than wait here, we'd best be on our way

dà mù dākàtā à nân, gāra mù tāshì

6. rather than follow the thief, I'd better call the police

dà ìn bi ɓarāwō, gāra ìn kirāwō 'yan sàndā

7. rather than go by car, we'd best go by plane

dà mù tàfi dà mōtà, gāra mù tàfi dà jirgT

8. rather than lie, you'd best tell the truth

dà kà yi ḳaryā, gāra kà fàɗi gàskiyā

9. rather than marry a divorcee, you should agree to what your parents said

dà kà àuri bàzawàrā, gāra kà yàrda dà abìn dà iyàyenkà sukà cē

10. rather than go to the slate school, you'd just as well stay at home

dà kà tàfi makarantar àllō, gāra kà zaunā à gidā

Drill 13A - 13D - Cover up the answers on the right and as each English sentence is given, give the Hausa translation.

13A 1. only I saw him

sai nT na gan shì

2. only Mamman can do it

sai Mammàn ya iyā

3. only a little do we want

sai kàɗan mu kè sō

4. only now has the Emir come out

sai yànzu SarkT ya fitō

5. we didn't see anyone except Ali

bà mù ga kōwā ba sai Àli

6. no one knows except me

bā wândà ya sanT sai nT

7. they don't have any other food except yams

bā su dà wani àbinci sai dōyà

8. he won't go to market except on Sunday

bà zâi jē kàsuwā ba sai ran Lahàdì

9. we ate everything except the yams

mun ci kōmē sai dōyà

10. they went everywhere except Daura

sun tàfi kō'ìnā sai Dàurā

13B 1. Kande didn't return from the market until 4:00

Kànde bà tà dāwō dàgà kàsuwā ba sai ḳarfè huɗu

2. I won't see you until tomorrow

bà zân gan kà ba sai gòbe

3. they didn't plant cotton until this year

bà sù shūkà audùgā ba sai bana

359

4. we won't eat until 7:00	bà zū mù ci àbinci ba sai ƙarfè bakwài	
5. not until today have I eaten yams	sai yâu na tabà cîn dōyà	
6. not until yesterday had I seen the Emir	sai jiyà na tabà ganin SarkT	
7. we won't set out until they come	bà zā mù tāshì ba	{ sai dà sukà zō / sai sun zō }
8. Shehu waited until he was called	Shēhù yā dākàtā	{ sai dà akà kirāwō shì / sai an kirāwō shì }
9. they didn't take a drink until they reached Kano	bà sù shā ruwā ba	{ sai dà sukà kai Kanō / sai sun kai Kanō }
10. Isa read until his father came home	Īsa yanà kàrātū	{ sai dà ùbansà ya zō gidā / sai ùbansà yā zō gidā }

13C

1. they have to play again — sai sun sàkè wàsā
2. we have to ask our boss — sai mun tàmbàyi mài gidanmù
3. before a thief leaps the wall, he has to spread a blanket on it — kàfin ɓàrāwò yà tsallàkà katangā, sai yā bazà bàrgō à kâi
4. before we cook the <u>miya</u>, we have to grind the pepper — kàfin mù dafà miyà, sai mun nikà barkònō
5. we ought to greet the Emir — sai mù gai dà SarkT
6. you should return the stolen goods — sai kà mai dà sàtàttun kāyan nàn
7. if you leave the house, you ought to close the door — in kun bar gidā, sai kù rufè ƙofà
8. if they come to town, they should visit us — in sun zō gàrT, sai sù zìyàrcè mù

13D

1. the thief was about to come in when I saw him — ɓàrāwò zâi shigō sai na gan shì
2. we were about to go the the Emir's palace when they came — zā mù tàfi fādàr SarkT sai sukà zō
3. when the trucks arrived, we began to unload the goods — dà mōtōcT sukà zō, sai mukà fàrà saukè kāyā
4. when she heard the noise, she went out to see — dà ta ji ƙārā, sai ta fìta tà ganT
5. when I've taken presents, the betrothal will take place — in nā kai tōshT, sai à yi baiwā
6. when Kande has returned, they will cook the <u>miya</u> — in Kànde tā dāwō, sai sù dafà miyà
7. if they don't hear, they'll tell you — in bà sù ji ba, sai sù fadà makà
8. if I don't like it, I'll put it back — in bā nà sônsà, sai ìn mai dà shT

Drill 14 - Change the continuative aspect pronouns to the habitual or subjunctive aspect as appropriate in the story below.

Kàramar Sallà à Gàrinmù

Ran Kàramar Sallà à gàrinmù munà tāshĩ munà tàfiyà masallācin Tdĩ Bāyan mun yi sallà, munà kōmṑ wā gidā mù ci tuwon sallà. Bāyan hakà, kōwā yanà tàfiyà fādàr SarkT sabō dà kallon hawan dabà. À fādàr SarkT anà ganin mutānē dàban-dàban[1] kàmar 'yan taurT dà māsu kàde-kàde. Māsu dawākT sunà kāwō wà SarkT jāhĩ. Sunà yîn sukùwā[2] sunà jân lìnzāmĩ à gàban SarkT. Dà Kàrshē, SarkT yanà shìgā fādàrsà.

À ran sallà, kōwā yanà yîn adō. Mutānē sunà tàfiyà zìyāràr àbōkansù. Sunà gaishē sù, "Barkà dà Sallà." Àbōkansù kuma sunà amsā[3] musù, "Barkà kàdai." Mânyan mutānē sunà bā dà gōrō kō kudĩ. Kōwā ya kàn cè, "Allàh yà kai mù ta[4] bàdĩ."

[1]dàban-dàban 'of many different kinds' [3]amsā v.tr. 'answer'
[2]sukùwā n.f. 'galloping' [4]ta refers to sallà, that is,
'may God carry us to next year's
(salla); bàdĩ 'next year'

Drill 15A - 15C - Repeat the initial sentence, then substitute the first cue into the appropriate place in that sentence. As each cue is given, substitute it into the sentence formed from the previous cue so that a new sentence is formed.

15A Initial sentence: mun tàfi fādàr SarkT

Cues	Student response
1. masallācT	mun tàfi masallācT
2. masallācin Jumma'à*	mun tàfi masallācin Jumma'à
3. Tdĩ	mun tàfi masallācin Tdĩ
4. continuative aspect	munà tàfiyà masallācin Tdĩ
5. habitual aspect	mu kàn tàfi masallācin Tdĩ
6. kōmō	mu kàn kōmō masallācin Tdĩ
7. gidā	mu kàn kōmō gidā
8. ... mù ci àbinci	mu kàn kōmō gidā mù ci àbinci
9. tuwō	mu kàn kōmō gidā mù ci tuwō
10. tuwon sallà	mu kàn kōmō gidā mù ci tuwon sallà

*The masallācin Jumma'à 'Friday mosque' is the mosque where prayers are held on Friday, the Moslem "sabbath". The masallācin Tdĩ 'Id el Fitr mosque' is a special mosque (a consecrated place for prayer, not necessarily a building) used especially on this Moslem holy day.

15B <u>Initial sentence</u>: an yi Kàramar Sallà

1. hidimar Kàramar   an yi hidimar Kàramar Sallà
   Sallà

2. continuative aspect   anâ hidimar Kàramar Sallà

3. habitual aspect   a kàn yi hidimar Kàramar Sallà

4. bùshe-bùshē dà   a kàn yi bùshe-bùshē da kàɗe-kàɗē
   kàɗe-kàɗē

5. adō   a kàn yi adō

6. à Kàramar Sallà   a kàn yi adō à Kàramar Sallà

7. mutànē   mutànē su kàn yi adō à Kàramar Sallà

8. màsu dawākT   màsu dawākT su kàn yi adō à Kàramar Sallà

9. kàwō jāhT   màsu dawākT su kàn kàwō jāhT à Kàramar Sallà

10. wà Sarki   màsu dawākT su kàn kàwō wà SarkT jāhT à Kàramar
                     Sallà

15C <u>Initial sentence</u>: nē jē Kàtsinà

1. Bàrno   nā jē Bàrno

2. indefinite future   nâ jē Bàrno

3. Màlàm Shēhù   Màlàm Shēhù yâ jē Bàrno

4. ganT   Màlàm Shēhù yâ ganT

5. sallàr Bàrno   Màlàm Shēhù yâ ga sallàr Bàrno

6. yaddà a kè hidimar Màlàm Shēhù yâ ga yaddà a kè hidimar sallà
   sallà

7. à Bàrno   Màlàm Shēhù yâ ga yaddà a kè hidimar sallà
                    à Bàrno

8. yîn adō   Màlàm Shēhù yâ ga yaddà a kè yîn adō à Bàrno

9. wà dawākT   Màlàm Shēhù yâ ga yaddà a kè yT wà dawākT adō
                    à Bàrno

10. sâ wà dawākT   Màlàm Shēhù yâ ga yaddà a kè sâ wà dawākT
    wandunà   wandunà à Bàrno

GUIDED CONVERSATION

1) Discuss the way some holiday is typically celebrated in the United States.
   One student may want to take the role of a Hausa person asking about the
   significance of some holiday and the way it is celebrated, or two or more
   students may wish to compare the way the holidays in question are celebrated in their families. The following holidays are suggestions: the
   Fourth of July (<u>rānar mulkìn kâi</u> 'Independence Day (day of self-govern-
   ment)'), Thanksgiving (<u>rānar bā dà gòdiyà</u>), Christmas (<u>Kirisìmētì</u>),
   Easter (<u>rānar tāshìn kìmāyà</u>), Rosh Hashana and the other High Holy Days,
   Hallowe'en, St. Valentine's Day, Memorial Day (<u>rānar tùnānī</u>), Labor Day
   (<u>rānar ma'àikàtā</u>), a birthday (<u>rānar haihùwā</u>).

Some further vocabulary that might be useful:

hūtū n.m.	'vacation, holiday, day off'	tàlo-tàlō n.m.	'turkey'
jērē n.m.	'parade'	kàbēwà n.f. (kàbèyī pl.)	'pumpkin'
gùzurī n.m.	'picnic (actually, provisions for a trip)	fuskàr bā dà kàmā	'mask, disguise'
dangī n.m. dangīnā sun ziyàrcē nì	'relative' 'my relatives came for a visit'	sōyayyà, n.m. yā̀ gwadā matà sōyayyàrsà	'love' 'he expressed his love for her'
tūtà n.f. (tūtōcī pl.)	'flag'	kātī n.m. wàsan wutā	'card' 'fireworks'

In the following example conversation, Bill, an American student, explains
the meaning of Thanksgiving to Hasan, a Hausa student studying in America.

Bill:	Sànnu Hasàn. Mè zā kà yi Rānar Bā dà Gōdiyā?	Hi Hasan. What are you going to do on Thanksgiving?
Hasàn:	Nā jī munà dà hùtun kwanā biyu. Hùtun mēnē nè?	I heard we have a vacation of two days. What's the holiday for?
Bill:	Wannàn hùtun tunànin sallàr bā dà gōdiyā ta "filgìrìm", wā̀tō mutànên dà sukà sauka dā can à nân Amìrkà.	It's a holiday commemmorating (re-membering) the celebration of giving thanks of the "Pilgrims", that is the people who settled in the olden times in America.
Hasàn:	Mè ku kè yī? Kunà bā dà kyàutā kō wàsā kō mēnē nè?	What do you do? Do you give gifts or play or what?
Bill:	Àbîn dà mu kè yī shī nè dahuwar àbinci irī-irī.	What we do is to cook food of all kinds.
Hasàn:	Kàmar mè?	Like what?
Bill:	Bàbban àbinci shī nè tàlo-tàlō dōmin tàlo-tàlō àbincin filgìrìm na farkō. Sai kà zō kà tayā¹ mu cîn àbinci.	The main dish is turkey because turkey was the food of the original Pilgrims. Come and help us eat (Thanksgiving dinner).
Hasàn:	Tō dà kyàu, nā zō.	Oh good, I'll come.

¹ tayà v.tr. = tàimakà

2) Discuss some special event that has taken place such as a concert, a play,
a sporting event (ball game, track meet, horse or automobile race), cir-
cus, etc. The conversation might either take the form of two or more
students discussing an event that they have attended or a description
of the event by the student(s) who did see the event to the student(s)
who did not. Additional vocabulary might be useful:

makàdī n.m. (makàdā pl.)	'musician'	rawā n.f.	'dancing'
makàdan Tūrāwā	'orchestra'	faifai n.m. (fàyà-fàyā pl.)	'record'
rērà v.tr. tā rèrà wàkà	'sing' 'she sang a song'	wàsā/wàsan kwaikwayō	'play (on stage)'

363

bàk̃T (wad̃andà kè cikin wàsā)	'characters (in a play)'	sukùwar dawākT	'horse race'
(wàsā) mài ban dàriyā	'comedy'	sukùwar mōtōcT	'car race'
(wàsā) mài ban tàusàyT	'tragedy'	fTlin sukùwā	'race course'
k̃wallō n.m.	'ball'	yā ci (sukùwā)	'he won (the race)'
wàsan k̃wallō	'football, soccer'	an cT mù (à sukùwā)	'we lost (the race)'
wàsan k̃wallō na sàndā	'baseball'	zākT n.m. (zākōkT pl.)	'lion'
wàsan gudù	'racing'	dàmisà n.m/f (dāmisōshT pl.)	'leopard'
màsu gudù	'runners'	gTwā n.m/f (gTwàyē pl.)	'elephant'
wàsan tsallē	'jumping; high jump'	ta-bànjamà n.m.	'clown'
wàsan tsallen k̃asā	'broad jump'	gwànin (pl. gwanàyen) bìrkìde-bìrkìde	'acrobat'
wàsan tsallē dà sàndā	'pole vaule'		

Example conversation - two swingers discuss a dance:

Sàlè:	Yàyà rawar jiyà?	How was the dance last night?
Yàk̃ubà:	Kâi! Ai bâ dāmā[1]! Àmmā yawancT[2] dai rawan hai-làif[3] nè.	Wow! It was out of sight! But it was mostly High Life dancing.
Sàlè:	Àkwai makàd̃a kō fàyà-fàyē?	Were there (live) musicians or records?
Yàk̃ubà:	Sai makàd̃a. Sū nè̃ suka sā wàsân armashT.[4]	Nothing but (live) musicians. They're what made the dance extra special.
Sàlè:	Gàskiyarkà! Yàyà rànâr[5] tàkà?	Right you are! How was your date?
Yàk̃ubà:	Kâi! Ai bâ ta dà dāmā! Tanā dà kōmē dà kōmē na màcè.	Wow! She wasn't bad! She had everything a woman should have.
Sàlè:	Tā iyà rawā?	Could she dance?
Yàk̃ubà:	Ai rawā kō mazarT.[6]	She danced like you wouldn't believe (dancing even (like) the king of dancers).

[1] dāmā n.f. 'chance'
bâ dāmā (in this dialogue) 'not bad!, really great!'
[2] yawancT n.m. 'majority'
[3] hai'làif n.m. 'High Life music' (a popular type of music in West Africa)
[4] armashT n.m. 'improvement' (created by adding something a little special)
[5] rānā n.f. (here) ''date''
[6] mazarT n.m. ''the king of dancers''

DRILLS FOR REVIEW

This unit contains drills designed to reinforce the material covered in Units XVIII-XXIV. The student should work through each drill several times until he can respond to the cues quickly without looking at the book. The drills may be used in the language laboratory as well as in class.

Drill 1 - Answer the questions in the indefinite future aspect. Questions where the answer must have a word or phrase to replace a question word have that word or phrase in parentheses following the question. In your answers, replace noun objects by pronouns or drop them entirely as appropriate.

Cue: yàushè zā kù jē gàrī?
                      (bāyan fāɗuwar rānā 'after sunset')

Student response: mwā̂ jē bāyan fāɗuwar rānā

Cue: zā sù gamà aikìn gòbe?

Student response: sā̂ gamà

1. yàushè SarkT zâi fitō? (dà ƙarfè shidà)
2. zā kà ci jarràbā̂wā?
3. ìnā zā mù sàuka? (bārikìn Dàurā)
4. yàushè zā à biyā mù? (jTbi)
5. kanā tsàmmanT zâi cūcē nì?   cūtā (i/ē) v.tr. 'cheat'
6. zā kà àuri bùdurwā kō bàzawàrā? (bùdurwā)
7. kō zā tà kāwō làbārìn HàlTmà?
8. zā kì iyà tsai dà mōtā?
9. ìnā zā à ginà sābon gidā? (à nân)
10. yàushè zā kà gamà nazàrī? (dà ƙarfè gōmà)
11. nā̂ iyà kòyon Hausa cikin shèkarà ɗaya?
12. dōkìnkà zâi ci à sukùwā? sukùwā n.f. 'race'

Drill 2 - Answer the questions in the habitual aspect. Questions where the answer must have a word or phrase to replace the question word have that word or phrase in parentheses following the question. In your answers, replace noun objects by pronouns or drop them entirely as appropriate.

Cue: yàushè kạ kàn farkā? (wajen ƙarfè bakwài)
                   farkā v.intr. 'wake up'

Student response: na kàn farkā wajen ƙarfè bakwài

Cue: su kàn ƙètàrè kōgT à nân?

Student response: T, su kàn ƙètàrē à nân

1. wàcè irìn tābà ka kàn shā? (Mài Zōbè)
2. wā ya kàn yankà rāgō? (mālàm)   rāgō n.m. 'ram'
3. a kàn ga watā à cikin watàn nân?

365

4. yàushè mài gyàdā ya kàn fārà cìnikT? (bāyan an būdè fulōtī)

5. mutānē nawà su kàn shìga jirgin nàn? (mutānē d̂àrT bìyar)

6. ìnā su kàn sàuka à Kàtsinà? (à gidan àbōkinsù)

7. yàyà a kàn fārà yîn tādî à NTjēriyà? (dà gaisuwā) tādî n.m. 'converstio◌

8. wā̂ ya kàn jāwō hankàlin māsu gyàdā? (yā̂rānā)

9. ku kàn gānè àbîn dà ya kè sô?

10. ìnā su kàn yi sukùwar dawākT? (à fTlin nàn)

11. wànè irìn sufùrT ka kàn yi àmfā̂nT dà shT? (mâ̂nyan mōtōcT)

12. à wànè lōkàcT SarkT ya kàn gēwàyà gàrT? (dà yâmma)
    gēwàyā v.tr. 'go around'

Drill 3 - Change the cue sentences below from the continuative aspect to the 'going to' zā̂ ni/zā̂ shi/ etc. forms (18.1) as shown in the example.

Cue: gôbe inā̂ tàfiyà̂ Lēgàs

Student response: gôbe zā̂ ni Lēgàs

1. d̂àlìbai sunā̂ tàfiyà̂ makarantā   6. kanā̂ cân?

2. cikin mākòn gôbe tanā̂ tàfiyà̂ Gwàmbe 7. nā̂ ga yanā̂ tàfiyà̂ kāsuwā

3. an gayā̂ minì tanā̂ zuwā̂ kwâs   8. inā̂ tàfiyà̂ Kanò gôbe
   kwâs n.m. 'course'
                                       9. wànè lōkàcī tanā̂ gidā̂?
4. munā̂ tàfiyà̂ fādàr SarkT
                                       10. sunā̂ tàfiyà̂ fādàr àlk̂àlT sù
5. ìnā ka kè tàfiyà̂?   yi k̂àrā

Drill 4A - 4B - In drills 4A and 4B there are two columns of cues, the one on the left being a set of nouns or pronouns, the one on the right being a set of sentences containing transitive verbs. Take each of the cues on the right in turn and as the set of cues on the left is repeated, put each one into the cue sentence as the object of the verb. That is, for each sentence on the right, put all the cues on the left into it as objects, then move to the next sentence on the right and do the same thing again.

Examples:

            1. SarkT   a. mwā̂ ganT

            2. ita   b. Sallamà yā sanar

Cues (as given by informant)   Student response

a. mwā̂ ganT   mwā̂ ganT

   SarkT   mwā̂ ga SarkT

   ita   mwā̂ gan tà

b. Sallamà yā sanar   Sallamà yā sanar

   SarkT   Sallamà yā sanad dà SarkT

   ita   or   Sallamà yā sanad dà ita
                                   Sallamà yā sanasshē tà

366

4A
1. yârā
2. Kànde
3. minì yārò
4. wà Shēhù dansà
5. shī
6. sū

a. likità yā aunā   likità n.m. 'doctor'
b. kàkā yā shagwàɓā   kàkā n.m. 'grandfather'
c. uwargidā tā àikā   shagwàɓā v.tr. 'spoil, coddle'
d. mālàm zâi tàmbayà
e. wā ya aiko?
f. kù kōmar

4B
1. àlkyabbà
2. lìttàttàfan lissāfī
3. minì kāyā
4. wà dālìbī àllō
5. ita
6. shī

a. ruwā yā ɓātā
b. kì ajìyē
c. wà zâi sāmù?
d. kadà kù barī
e. tà kāwō
f. don mè bà à mayar ba?

Drill 5 - Change the sentences by replacing the demonstratives wannan, etc.,
which precede the noun, by nan/nàn/nàn or can/càn/càn following the noun,
and by changing the possessor to an independent possessive noun or pronoun
depending on whether the cue sentence has a noun or pronoun.

Cue: wannàn gidan SānT nè
Student response: gidan nàn na SānT nè
Cue: wannàn hùlarsà cē
Student response: hùlar nàn tāsà cē

1. wadànnân shānun Bētì nè
2. wànnan ìngarmàn Sarkī nè
3. wancàn ƙauyènmù nè
4. wannàn wākàr Hàusāwā cè
5. wannàn àl'àdàrsù cē
6. wànnan shirìn Ma'aikatar
   Cìnikī dà Sana'ō'T nè

7. wadànnân kāyānā nè
8. wànnan wāsan makarantar nàsàriyyà nē
9. wadànnân mà'àunan gyàdā nè
10. wannàn sàndarsà cē
11. wannàn bàrgon ɓàrāwòn nē
12. waccàn makarantātā cè

Drill 6 - Change sentences of the pattern in yā tàimàkē nì, sai ìn gamà
aikī to fit the pattern dā yā tàimàkē nì, dā nā gamà aikī.

Cue: in tā sayō shìnkāfā, uwartà zā tà yi fushī
Student response: dā tā sayō shìnkāfā, dā uwartà tà yi fushī

1. in mun jē Bàrno, zā mù ga yaddà a kè sà wà dawākT wandunà
2. in sun yàrda dà ajìyè lìttàttàfan lissāfī, zā mù bā sù ràncē
3. in kin yankà kuɓēwā waccàn, miyà zā tà dācē dà yandà a kè sô
4. in an bà shùke-shùkē ruwā, bà zā sù būshē ba
5. in kun saukè dōyà dàgà mânyan mōtōcT, zâi biyā kù
6. in muhùtT yā gayà wà àlƙalT yawàn ɓàrnâr, zâi yi shàrT'à à kân ƙàrâr

367

7. in yằrằnằ sun jāwō hankàlin màsu gyàɗà sù zō rùmfātā, zân sằmi gyàɗà dà yawằ

8. in mun jarràɓà tằllàn Gwalìf dà Fai-Fài, zā mù ƙàrà yawàn kwālin tābằ dà mu kē sayằrwằ

9. in kun tằimàki maƙèrī, zâi gamà gyārā ƙāfin ƙarfè biyu

10. in mun sằ wani àbù wândà zâi yi ƙārā, ɓàrāwō bà zâi shigō ɗàkī ba

Drill 7 - Form questions beginning with don mè? by supplying the logical question to the answers given as cue sentences.

Cue:　　　　　　　sun zō Kanò don sù zìyàrci àbōkansù

Student response:　don mè sukà zō Kanò?

1. tā tàfi Nījēriyà don tà yi aikī

2. ɗàlìbai bā sằ zuwằ makarantā ran Asabàr don bâbu makarantā rân nan

3. Ùmarù yā yi ƙàrar Bètì don shānunsà sun ɓàtà gōnarsà

4. Ma'àikàcin Ma'aikatar Cìnikī dà Sana'ō'Ī yā jē wurin Sarkī don yà bayyànà masà shirìn bā dà ràncē

5. mun bā dà ràncē don mutằnen ƙasâr sù ƙaru

6. Sarkī yā sằ baƙar àlkyabbà don yà gai dà ma'àikàcin

7. tā sayō shìnkāfā don bà tà ga masằrā à ƙàsuwā ba

8. Sarkin Zagī yā gwadà sằɓon ìngarmằ don Sarkī yā cề yà gwadà shi

9. nā bā shì ràncē na jàkā hàmsin don yā yàrda dà ajìyè lìttàttāfan lissāfī

10. sun kai gyàɗà kusa dà tashàr jirgin ƙasà à Kanò don à sayar masà sū

Drill 8 - In this translation drill, there are three parts to each question. One part will use the "basic" form of the verb, one will use an -o verb form of the same verb, and one will use a -u verb form, though not always in that order. Cover the Hausa answers and translate the English cues into Hausa.

1a. who took that bag of peanuts	wằ ya ɗauki wànnan bùhun gyàɗà?
b. this bag of peanuts can't be carried	wannàn bùhun gyàɗà bà yằ ɗaukuwā
c. who carried this bag of peanuts here?	wằ ya ɗaukō wànnan bùhun gyàɗà?
2a. they crossed the river from over there	sun ƙētarō kōgī dàgà cân
b. let's cross the river here	bàri mù ƙètàrè kōgī à nân
c. the river is crossable now	kōgī yanằ ƙètàruwā yànzu
3a. go and ask about the news for me	tàfi kà tambayō minì làbārī
b. Umaru's complaint has been deeply enquired into	ƙārar Ùmarù tā tàmbàyu
c. we asked him the news	mun tàmbàyē shì làbārī
4a. the meat has been well cut	nāmằ yā yànku
b. the butcher cut some meat off for me	mahàucī yā yankō minì nāmằ mahàucī n.m. 'butcher'

368

c. her parents have fixed the bride-price	iyàyentà sun yankà sàdākī̀
5a. let's go into the room	bàri mù shìga d̃ākī̀
b. come into the room	kù shigō d̃ākī̀
c. the room is crowded	d̃ākī̀ yā shìgu
6a. go and buy me some tobacco	tàfi kà sayō minì tābā̀
b. that kind of car can't be bought	wànnan irìn mōtà̄ bā tà̄ sàyuwā
c. I bought these cigarets from the d̃an tebur	nā sàyi tābàr nân wajen d̃an tēbùr
7a. was he shot with a gun?	an hàrbę̄ shì dà bindigā̀? bindigā̀ n.m. 'gun'
b. I was shot with a gun	an harbō nì dà bindigā̀
c. this gun can't be fired by only one man	bindigàn nân bā tà̄ hàrbuwā gà mùtûm d̃aya
8a. the teacher assembled the students in one room	mālàm yā tārà d̃ālìbai cikin d̃ākī̀ d̃aya
b. the children gathered to see the monkey	yâ̄rā sun tàru don sù ga birī̀
c. assemble the students here for me	tà̄rō minì d̃ālìbai
9a. I sent him to buy me some tobacco but he didn't get any	nā àikē shì yà sayō minì tābā̀ àmmā bài sāmō ba
b. an accident took place near our town	wani had̃àrī yā sāmu à kusa dà gàrinmù
c. what's the matter with you?	mḕ ya sàmē kà?
10a. this car can't be repaired	wannàn mōtà̄ bā tà̄ gyàruwā
b. I'll repair the car before 3:00	nâ̄ gyàrà mōtà̄ kàfin k̃arfè̄ ukù
c. can you repair this for me?	kō kā iyà gyàrō minì wannàn?

Drill 9 - Answer the cue questions with a sentence of the pattern <u>an rigā̀ an sanad dà nī̀</u>. Use both long and short forms of the causative verb with those verbs that use either form commonly (the sentences containing verbs with commonly used short forms of the causative are starred).

        Cue: *sunà̄ ciyar masà dà dabbōbī̀?

   Student response: an rigā̀ an ciyar dà sū
           or
             an rigā̀ an cī dà sū

1. *tanà̄ mayar manà dà tābā̀?
2. *yanà̄ tsayar masà dà mōtà̄?
3. kinà̄ sanar wà Bàtūrḕ dà SarkT?
4. kanà̄ zubar matà dà ruwā̀?
5. *yanà̄ fitar mukù dà awākī̀?

6. ma'àikàcī yanà̄ fahimtar wà Bàtūrḕ dà SarkT dàbāràrsà? dàbārā̀ n.f. 'plan' fàhimtà v.intr. 'understand'
7. d̃an sàndā yanà̄ ganar manà dà cājì ōfìs?
8. *anà̄ sayar minì dà àlbasà̄?

369

9. likitā yanā̀ warkar musù dà 'yarsù?
   warkar dà̀ v.caus. 'cure'

10. màì gyàdā̀ yanā̀ tafiyar masà dà
    cìnikinsà?

11. zā kù saukar minì dà bàƙT à
    gidankù?

12. Mālàm ƶâi kōyar mukù dà
    lissāfī?

Drill 10 – Fill in the blanks with the appropriate form of the adjective
shown in parentheses. After you have done this, translate each sentence.

1. (bàḅba) Jiyà àbōkīnā̀ Mạmmàn yā ga ____ mōtōcī cikin ____ gàrī. Ya cè̀
   yanā̀ sôn wata ____ mōtā kàmar wàɗànnan.

2. (jā) Hà̩lTmà̀ tanā̀ sôn ____ tàkàlmī sabō dà tanā̀ dà ____ dūtsèn wuyā̀.
   dūtsèn wuyā̀ n.m. 'necklace (rock of neck)'

3. (baƙT) Sarkī yā sàyi wasu ____ dawākī. Sarkin ZagI yanā̀ hawan wani
   ____ ingarmā.

4. (gàjērē) Mūsā ____ nè̀. Uwargidansà mā ita ____ cè̀. Dukàṇsù ____ nè̀.

5. (sābō) Jị̀yà nā̀ sàyi ____ rīgā dà ____ wàndō. ____ tufàfī sun bā nì
   farin cikī.

6. (ƙàṛamī) Sai kà sā̂ ____ lìttàttàfai à kân ____ tēbùr kusa dà ____
   kujērā.

7. (tsōhō) Yùsufù ____ nè̀. Mātansà mā ____ nè̀. Àmmā 'yarsà bā̀ ____
   ba cè̀.

8. (fạrā) Sālisù yā sà̀yi ____ yādī. ̣Tēlà zâi shiryà masà ____ rīgā.
   Abōkansà sū mā sunà dà ____ rīgunā.

9. (dōgō) Wàcè cè̀ ____ màcèn dà kè̀ kusa dà ____ itàcen càn?

10. (sàtaccē) Kà sā̂ wannàn ____ àgōgo cikin àkwātin dà kè̀ cìke dà ____
    kāyā.

11. (ƙàtō) Yanā̀ dà ____ dōkī dà ____ gōɗìyā. ShT mā ____ mùtûm nè̀.
    gōɗìyā n.f. 'mare'

12. (fạṣsashē) Àkwai ____ kwalàbē dà ____ tukunyā à cikin ɗākī. Wà̀ ya
    fasà su?

Drill 11 – Insert the auxiliary verbs in parentheses into the sentences
below and make whatever other changes may be necessary.

Cue: zân tàmbàyē tà (riƙà̀)

Student response: zân riƙà̀ tàmbayàrtà

1. Īsa yā tàfi makarantar nàsā̀riyyà (dingā̀)

2. màì tābā̀ yā biyà sù (riƙà̀)

3. ma'àikàtā sun ɗàukè sù (iyà̀)

4. maƙèrT yā gyārā̀ shi (sākè̀)

5. nā̀ gan kù (taɓà̀)

6. munā̀ sô mù gan sù (ƙàrà̀)

7. tā ɗìnkà rīgunā̀ (riƙà̀)

8. sun cT shì (dingā̀)

9. mun kōrē sù (iyà̀)

10. an sāmē tà (sākè̀)

Drill 12A – 12B

12A Each of the cues contains a verb with the first syllable reduplicated
    as described in 23.2. Following each cue is a singular noun. Respond
    by substituting the singular noun for the direct object of the verb

370

or the subject of an intransitive verb and change the verb to its un-
reduplicated form. If the cue is a question, answer it by changing
second person to first person if need be. Otherwise, just change the
sentence as directed.

Cue: zā à daddàfà awākin nàn dukà?   (àkwiyà ɗaya kawài)

Student response: zā à dafà àkwiyà ɗaya kawài

1. zā à yanyànkà kàjT dà yawà?   (kàzā ɗaya kawài)
2. kū dukà kun shisshìryā?   (nT kàɗai)
3. kū yārā, kù tsattsàyā!   (kai Audù)
4. ɗālìbai sun rurrubùtà wasTkōkT?   (wàsīkà gùdā)
   wàsīkà   n.f.   'letter' (wasīkòkT pl.)
5. yārā, kù ciccìkà kwalàben nàn!   (kwalabā gùdā)   cikà   v.tr.   'fill'
6. kun kakkàmà kTfàyē dà yawà?   (kTfT ɗaya kawài)
7. dà nạ sā wutà gà rāmT, ɓeràyē gōmà sukà firfịtō   (ɓerā ɗaya)
   rāmT   n.m.   'hole'; ɓerā   n.m.   'rat'   (ɓeràyē pl.)
8. nā kakkaràntà duk wadànnân lìttàttàfai   (ɗaya dàgà cikin lìttàttàfan nàn)
9. kâi!   mū dukà mun gàrgàji!   (nT kàɗai)
10. mài hàrājT yā tàntàmbàyi màsu gyàɗā   (wànnan mài gyàɗā)
11. yāra sun ɓoɓɓóyē cikin itātuwà   (yārō)
12. an ɗaɗɗaukō su sirdT dà lìnzāmT?   (sirdT kawài)
    sirdT   n.m.   'saddle';   lìnzāmT   n.m.   'bridle'

12B Each of the cues contains one of the reduplicated forms described in
24.2. Respond to the cue with the question don mē sukà yi ... with the
action noun from which the reduplicated form is derived in the blank.

Cue: dā sunà yàke-yàkē   yākT   n.m.   'war'
        'in former times they were constantly warring'

Student response: don mē sukà yi yākT?
                  'why did they make war?'

1. gà yārā cân, sunà gùje-gùjē
2. 'yan makarantā sunà wàke-wàkē
3. màsu hàrājT sunà tàmbàye-
   tàmbàyē à nàn
4. jìyà dà dare mutānen gàrT sunà
   ràye-ràyē
5. sun jē kàsuwā sunà kàlle-kàllē

6. àkwai gìne-gìnē dà yawā à ùnguwar
   nàn   ginT   n.m.   'building'
7. à makarantar àllō ɗālìbai sunà
   kàrànce-kàràncē
8. likitōcT sunà yT masà màgàne-màgànē
   likitōcT   n.pl.   'doctors'
9. màkànTkai sunà gyàre-gyàren mōtōcT
10. manōmT sunà nòme-nòmē à watàn nàn

Drill 13 - Form questions on the pattern wā ya tsayad dà sū? by select-
ing the causative verb that corresponds to the verb in the cue sentence
and inserting it into the pattern. Translate each new sentence that you
make.

Cue: sun kōmà

Student response: wā ya kōmad dà sū?   'who returned them?'

371

Cue:	tā tsayā̀
Student response:	wā̀ ya tsayad dà ita? 'who stopped her?'

1. yā shā	6. yā warkḕ	warkḕ v.intr. 'recover from an
2. sun sàuka		illness'
3. tā zaunā̀	7. matàfīyā̀ sun sàuka	
4. yā sanī̀	8. tā hūtā̀	hūtā̀ v.intr. 'rest'
5. sun shìga	9. mōtā̀ tā tsayā̀	
	10. Lawàli yā gàji	

Drill 14 - Translate the following sentences into Hausa.

1. Did anyone leave?	Àkwai wândà ya tàfi?
2. Audu saw no one.	Audù bài ga kōwā ba.
3. Everything has been prepared.	An shiryà kōmē.
4. Did everyone come?	Kōwā yā zō?
5. She didn't see anyone.	Bà tà ga kōwā ba.
6. The worker from the Ministry of Trade and Industry gave each of them a loan of ₦500.	Ma'àikàcin Mà̠aikatar Cìnikī dà Sana'ō'Ī yā bā̀ kōwànnensù ràncen Nairā ɗarī bìyar.
7. We didn't see him anywhere.	Bà mù gan shì kō'ìnā ba.
8. Halima didn't see anything.	Hàlīmà bà tà ga kōmē ba.
9. Will we see you sometime again?	Kō zā mù gan kù wani lōkàcī kumā?
10. Did he see everyone there?	Yā ga kōwā à can?
11. Nothing happened.	Ba àbîn dà ya fàru.
12. She shouldn't tell them anything.	Kadà tà gayā̀ musù kōmē.
13. Everywhere they went they saw her.	Duk indà sukà tàfi, sai sù gan tà.
14. No one left.	Bâ wândà ya tàfi.
15. Did anything happen?	Àkwai àbîn dà ya fàru? or Wani àbù yā fàru?

Drill 15A - 15B

15A Make a complex sentence by introducing the first cue sentence by in or ìdan 'if' and the second by sai followed by a subjunctive pronoun, or if the second clause is negative, by using the negative future. Drop sabō dà from the second sentence. Translate the result.

Cue:	Mutā̀nḕ sun sāmi wànnan tàimakō.
	Sabō dà hakà sun ƙàru ƙwarai.
Student response:	In mutā̀nḕ sun sāmi wànnan tàimakō, sai sù ƙàru ƙwarai.
	'If the people get that aid, they will profit greatly.

372

15B Make a complex sentence by introducing the first cue sentence by dā 'if (it had been that)' and the second by dā followed by the completive aspect, again dropping the sabō dà, Translate the result.

Cue: Mutānē sun sāmi wànnan tàimakō.
Sabō dà hakà sun ƙāru ƙwarai.

Student response: Dā mutānē sun sāmi wànnan tàimakō, dā sun ƙāru ƙwarai.
'If the people had gotten the aid, they would have benefited greatly.'

1. Yā tàimàkē nì. Sabō dà hakà zân gamà gyārā.

2. Mun jē Bàrno. Sabō dà hakà zā mù ga yaddà a kē sā wà dawākt wàndō.

3. Tā sayō shìnkāfā. Sabō dà hakà uwartà zā tà yi fusht.

4. Sun yàrda sù ajìyè lìttàffàfan lissāft. Sabō dà hakà zā mù bā su ràncē.

5. Kin yankà kuɓēwā waccàn. Sabō dà hakà miyà zā tà dācē dà yândà a kē sô.

6. Muhùtt yā gayà masà yawàn ɓarnâr. Sabō dà hakà àlƙalt zâi yi shàrt'à à kân ƙàrar Umarù.

7. Audù yā saukè dōyà dàgà mânyan mōtōct. Sabō dà hakà zā à biyā shì.

8. Yârānā sun jāwō hankàlin māsu gyàɗa sù zō rùmfātā. Sabō dà hakà zân sāmi gyàɗa dà yawà.

9. Yā jarràbà tàllàn Gwallf dà Fai-Fai. Sabō dà hakà zâi ƙūrà yawàn àkwātìn tābà dà ya kē sayârwā.

10. An bā shūke-shūkên ruwā. Sabō dà hakà bà zā sù būshē ba.

11. Mun rufè tāgà. Sabō dà hakà ɓàrâyt bà zā sù iyà shìgā ba.

12. Tsa yā jē makarantar nàsāriyyà. Sabō dà hakà zâi mântà dà àl'àdàrsù.

Drill 16 - Replace the subject noun of each of the cues below by the appro-priate independent possessive marker na/ta, making two complete sentences.

Cue: Mōtàr Shēhù tsōhuwā cē, àmmā mōtàr àbōkinsà sābuwā cē.

Student response: Mōtàr Shēhù tsōhuwā cē. Ta àbōkinsà sābuwā cē.

1. Gàrinmù Kanō nē, àmmā gàrinkù Kàtsìnà nē.

2. Tagùwar Audù baƙā cē, àmmā tagùwar Mammàn farā cē.

3. Gidanmù bàbba nè, àmmā gidansù ƙàramt nē.

4. Ƙasarkù Nìjēriyà cē, àmmā ƙasarmù Amìrkà cē.

5. Àbincin mùtûm tuwō nè, àmmā àbincin àkwiyà cìyāwà nē.

6. Àlƙalàminsà mài tsawō nē, àmmā àlƙalàmīnā gàjērē nè.

7. Ìngarmàn Sarkt baƙt nè, àmmā ìngarmàn Audù jā-ja nè.

8. Yârānā sunà gidā, àmmā yâran Sà'ìdù sunà gōnā.

9. Amaryar Mammàn bùdurwā cē, àmmā amaryar Cirōmà bàzawàrā cē.
amaryā n.m. 'bride'

10. Màtarsà tā iyà dafāwā, àmmā mātātā bà tà iyā̀ ba.

11. Bārikin Birnin KwànnT yanā dà Kàzântā, àmmā bārikìn Bauci bā̂ shi
    dà Kàzântā.   Kàzântā n.f. 'dirt'

12. Dawākin SarkT baKàKē nḕ, àmmā dawākinsù farārē nḕ.

<u>Drill 17</u> - Drop the phrase yā̄ kàmātà and the first person singular sub-
junctive pronoun and make the verb into an imperative.

     Cue: yā̄ kàmātà ìn jarràbà mōtàr nân

     Student responșe: jàrràbà mōtàr nân

     Cue: yā̄ kàmātà ìn fàdā̀

     Student response: fàdī̀

1. yā̄ kàmātà ìn gwadà ìngarmā̄
2. yā̄ kàmātà ìn shigō̄
3. yā̄ kàmātà ìn tàmbàyē tà
4. yā̄ kàmātà ìn shā̄ ruwā̄
5. yā̄ kàmātà ìn kirāwō̄ matàimàkTnā̄
6. yā̄ kàmātà ìn kirāwō̄
7. yā̄ kàmātà ìn tārā̀ su
8. yā̄ kàmātà ìn bT tà
9. yā̄ kàmātà ìn kāwō shì
10. yā̄ kàmātà ìn bazà làbārī̀

11. yā̄ kàmātà ìn kòyi lissā̄fī̀
12. yā̄ kàmātà ìn ci àbinci
13. yā̄ kàmātà ìn biyō̄ sāwun nàn
14. yā̄ kàmātà ìn dàukē shì
15. yā̄ kàmātà ìn bā̄ shì
16. yā̄ kàmātà ìn mai dà tābàr nân
17. yā̄ kàmātà ìn shiryā̀ shi
18. yā̄ kàmātà ìn tàmbayā̀
19. yā̄ kàmātà ìn warkad dà shT
20. yā̄ kàmātà ìn tàimàki ma'àikàtā̄

<u>Drill 18A - 18B</u>

18A Form a comparative construction as illustrated.

     Cue: itàcen nàn yanā̀ dà girmā̄

     Student response: itàcen nàn yā̄ fi wancàn girmā̄

18B Form a superlative construction using <u>saurā̄</u> as illustrated.

     Cue: itàcen nàn yanā̀ dà girmā̄

     Student response: itàcen nàn yā̄ fi saurân girmā̄

1. yā̄rinyàr nân tanā̀ dà kyâu
2. àlKalàmin nàn yanā̀ dà tsawō̄
3. mōtàr nân tanā̀ dà tsàdā
4. duwā̀tsun nàn sunā̀ dà nauyT
5. hanyàr nân tanā̀ dà fādī̀
6. wurin nàn yanā̀ dà taurT

7. yāròn nân yanā̀ dà Kibà
8. rTjìyar nàn tanā̀ dà zurfT
9. ruwan nàn yanā̀ dà zā̄fT
10. tuwon nàn yanā̀ dà dādī̀
11. nāmàn nân yanā̀ dà taushT
12. aikìn nân yanā̀ dà wùyā̀

<u>Drill 19</u> - Each cue will consist of a) a sentence in Hausa containing a
noun modified by a past participle. Following is b) a sentence in English
which in its Hausa translation will contain the "basic" verb from which
the past participle in a) is derived; and c), a sentence in English which
will include the adverbial noun of state (20.3) derived from the verb in b).

The drill may be used either by giving the a) sentence and having the student give the Hausa for both b) and c), or it may be gone through twice, once giving only the b) version following a) given as a cue, and the second time giving only the c) version using a) as a cue. The drill can be done with books closed since the sentences a), b), and c) always follow the same pattern. The translations are given simply because some of the English renderings will be idiomatic.

Cue: a. rùfaffiyar tāgà cē

b. who closed the window?

c. the window is closed

Student response: b. wà ya rufè tāgà?

c. tāgà tanà rùfe

1a. dàfaffiyar dōyà cē
b. who cooked the yam?
c. the yam is cooked

2a. cìkàkkun kwalàbē nè
b. who filled the bottles?
c. the bottles are full

3a. ɗàukàkkun buhunàn gyàɗà nè
b. who took up the bags of peanuts?
c. the bags of peanuts are picked up

4a. hòrarren dōkī nē
hōrā (i/ē) v.tr. 'train'
b. who trained the horse?
c. the horse is broken in

5a. bùɗaɗɗiyar ƙōfà cē
b. who opened the door?
c. the door is open

6a. gàsasshen nāmà nē
gasà v.tr. 'grill, fry'
b. who grilled the meat?
c. the meat is grilled

7a. nòmammen fīlī nè
fīlī n.m. 'open field'
b. who weeded the field?
c. the field is cleared of weeds

8a. rìnànnun tufāfī nē
rinà v.tr. 'dye'
b. who dyed the clothes?
c. the clothes are dyed

9a. ɗìnkakkiyar tagùwā cē
b. who sewed the shirt?
c. the shirt is sewed

10a. rìƙaƙƙen māshī nē
māshī n.m. 'spear'
b. who held the spear?
c. the spear is being held

11a. yànkakken rāgō nè
rāgō n.m. 'ram'
b. who slaughtered the ram?
c. the ram is slaughtered

12a. ɗàurarriyar tunkìyā cē
ɗaurà v.tr. 'tie up'
b. who tied up the sheep?
c. the sheep is tied up

Drill 20 - Answer the questions in complete sentences. Those questions to which you may not know the answer have the answer in parentheses following them.

Cue: jihà nawà à ƙasar Amìrkà? jihà n.f. "state"

Student response: àkwai jihà hàmsin à ƙasar Amìrkà

1. sā'à nawà à cikin kwānā gùdā? sā'à n.f. 'hour'

2. mintī nawà à cikin sā'à gùdā?

3. kwānā nawà à cikin wannàn watà?

4. mākō nawà à cikin shèkarà gùdā?

5. kwānā nawà à cikin shèkarà gùdā?

375

6. shāfī nawà cikin littāfìn nân?

7. mîl nawà dàgà Kanō zuwà Lēgàs? (727)

8. mîl nawà dàgà Lēgàs zuwā Kadūna? (564)

9. à cikin wàcè shèkarā Nījēriyà ta sàmi mulkìn kâi? (1960)
   mulkìn kâi   'independence (government of head)'

10. à cikin wàcè shèkarā Amìrkà ta sàmi mulkìn kâi? (1776)

11. à cikin wàcè shèkarā mu kè?

12. à cikin wàcè shèkarā Usùmānù 'Dan Hōdiyò ya kāwō jìhādī Nījēriyà ta
    arèwa? (1804)   jìhādī n.m. 'religious war (for the purpose of
                                 gaining converts to Islam)'

13. à cikin wàcè shèkarā akà hàifē kà/kì?

14. ƙafā nawà à cikin mîl gudā?

Drill 21A - 21B

21A Using the cues below, form sentences on the initial sentence mun
    tàimàki kânmù by substituting the completive pronouns or verbs as
    illustrated, changing the "-self" constructions as required.

          Cue: sun
          Student response: sun tàimàki kânsù
          Cue: zàrgā   (i/ē) v.tr. 'blame'
          Student response: sun zàrgi kânsù

Initial sentence: mun tàimàki kânmù

1. sun   3. nā   5. zàrgā   7. mun   9. kun
2. kun   4. kin   6. kā   8. hadā   10. sun
                              v.tr. 'join together'

21B Follow the instructions for 21A. Your cues for this part of the
    drill will be the independent pronouns.

Initial sentence: nī dà kâinā na ƙàrà fāɗin gōnātā

1. sū   3. kū   5. fìta dàgà gàrī   7. nī   9. shī
2. kai   4. mū   6. ita   8. bā nā sôntà   10. mū

Drill 22A - 22D - Repeat the initial sentence, then substitute the first
cue into the appropriate place in that sentence. As each cue is given,
substitute it into the sentence formed from the previous cue so that a
new sentence is formed.

22A Initial sentence: yā zō makarantā

Cues   Student response
1. Īsa   Īsa yā zō makarantā
2. ɗan Abūbakàr   ɗan Abūbakàr yā zō makarantā
3. fārà   ɗan Abūbakàr yā fārà zuwā makarantā
4. dingà   ɗan Abūbakàr yā dingà zuwā makarantā
5. future aspect   ɗan Abūbakàr zâi dingà zuwā makarantā

376

6. subjunctive aspect   ɗan Àbūbakàr yà dingà zuwā̀ makarantā

7. sai   sai ɗan Àbūbakàr yà dingà zuwā̀ makarantā

8. nàsāriyyà̀   sai ɗan Àbūbakàr yà dingà zuwā̀ makarantar nàsāriyyà̀

9. don yà kōyi TūrancT   sai ɗan Àbūbakàr yà dingà zuwā̀ makarantar nàsāriyyà̀ don yà kōyi TūrancT

10. sāmi ilìmin zāmànT   sai ɗan Àbūbakàr yà dingà zuwā̀ makarantar nàsāriyyā̀ don yà sāmi ilìmin zāmànT

22B Initial sentence: zâi zìyàrcē mù

1. Mālàm Sà'Tdù   Mālàm Sà'Tdù zâi zìyàrcē mù

2. yâu nē̄   yâu nè̄ Mālàm Sà'Tdù zâi zìyàrcē mù

3. inā̀ tsàmmānT   inā̀ tsàmmānT (yâu nē̄) Mālàm Sà'Tdù zâi zìyàrcē mù

4. zâi gan mù   inā̀ tsàmmānT (yâu nē̄) Mālàm Sà'Tdù zâi gan mù

5. sallā̀   inā̀ tsàmmānT (yâu nē̄) Mālàm Sà'Tdù zâi ga sallā̀

6. sallàr nan   inā̀ tsàmmānT (yâu nē̄) Mālàm Sà'Tdù zâi ga sallàr nan

7. ta Kàtsinà   inā̀ tsàmmānT (yâu nē̄) Mālàm Sà'Tdù zâi ga sallàr nan ta Kàtsinà

8. completive aspect (relative)   inā̀ tsàmmānT (yâu nē̄) Mālàm Sà'Tdù ya ga sallàr nan ta Kàtsinà

9. negative completive   inā̀ tsàmmānT (yâu nē̄) Mālàm Sà'Tdù bài ga sallàr nan ta Kàtsinà ba

10. LaƊā̀   inā̀ tsàmmānT Mālàm Sà'Tdù bài tabà ganin sallàr nan ta Kàtsinà ba

22C Initial sentence: yā mai dà tābā̀

1. ɗan tēbùr   ɗan tēbùr yā mai dà tābā̀

2. 'yan tēbùr   'yan tēbùr sun mai dà tābā̀

3. sai dà   'yan tēbùr sun sai dà tābā̀

4. continuative aspect   'yan tēbùr sunā̀ sai dà tābā̀

5. har kwālin tābā̀ nawà   har kwālin tābā̀ nawà 'yan tēbùr su kḕ sayârwā

6. kàmar   kàmar kwālin tābā̀ nawà 'yan tēbùr su kḕ sayârwā

7. ɗàrT bìyar   kàmar kwālin tābā̀ ɗàrT bìyar 'yan tēbùr su kḕ sayârwā

8. mètan   kàmar kwālin tābā̀ mètan 'yan tēbùr su kḕ sayârwā

9. sai   sai kwālin tābā̀ mètan 'yan tēbùr su kḕ sayârwā

10. à watā̀   sai kwālin tābā̀ mètan 'yan tēbùr su kḕ sayârwā à watā̀

22D <u>Initial sentence:</u> nã̂ gayà̰ masà̀

1. nĪ dà kâinā   nĪ dà kâinā nã̂ gayà̰ masà̀
2. sū dà kânsù   sū dà kânsù sã̂ gayà̰ masà̀
3. wà mài gidā   sū dà kânsù sã̂ gayà̰ wà mài gidā
4. habitual aspect   sū dà kânsù su kàn gayà̰ wà mài gidā
5. completive aspect   sū dà kânsù sukà gayà̰ wà mài gidā
6. sanad dà   sū dà kânsù sukà sanad dà mài gidā
7. kirāwō   sū dà kânsù sukà kirāwō mài gidā
8. iyà̰   sū dà kânsù sukà iyà̰ kirāwō mài gidā
9. rˌigā   sū dà kânsù sukà rigā sukà kirāwō mài gidā
10. kirāwō 'yan sàndā   sū dà kânsù sukà rigā sukà kirāwō 'yan sàndā

378